D0745917

WITHDRAWN
UTSA LIBRARIES

THE OTHER WELFARE

THE OTHER WELFARE

Supplemental Security Income
and U.S. Social Policy

**Edward D. Berkowitz
and Larry DeWitt**

CORNELL UNIVERSITY PRESS   ITHACA AND LONDON

Copyright © 2013 by Cornell University

All rights reserved. Except for brief quotations in a review, this book, or parts thereof, must not be reproduced in any form without permission in writing from the publisher. For information, address Cornell University Press, Sage House, 512 East State Street, Ithaca, New York 14850.

First published 2013 by Cornell University Press
Printed in the United States of America

Library of Congress Cataloging-in-Publication Data

Berkowitz, Edward D.
    The other welfare : supplemental security income and U.S. social policy / Edward D. Berkowitz and Larry DeWitt.
        p. cm.
    Includes bibliographical references and index.
    ISBN 978-0-8014-5173-7 (cloth : alk. paper)
    1. Supplemental security income program—United States—History.
2. Public welfare—United States—History.   3. United States—Social policy.
I. DeWitt, Larry, 1949–   II. Title.
    HD7125.B474 2013
    368.38'2—dc22   2012033633

Cornell University Press strives to use environmentally responsible suppliers and materials to the fullest extent possible in the publishing of its books. Such materials include vegetable-based, low-VOC inks and acid-free papers that are recycled, to-tally chlorine-free, or partly composed of nonwood fibers. For further information, visit our website at www.cornellpress.cornell.edu.

Cloth printing   10 9 8 7 6 5 4 3 2 1

Library
University of Texas
at San Antonio

Dedicated to the Social Security Administration and its employees, who have created some of the greatest social policy monuments of our time, often under adverse conditions.

Contents

Preface

This book reflects a collaboration between an academic and a public historian. Since collaboration on a historical monograph is relatively rare, it might help orient the reader to explain this one. Ed Berkowitz is an academic historian. His attraction to the Supplemental Security Income (SSI) program stems from the ways the program intersects with much of his previous work. In particular, he has written about disability policy, Social Security, and the seventies—all things that inform this book. He has also had experience in the realm of welfare reform, both writing about the topic and, briefly, working on the topic in Washington settings.[1]

Larry DeWitt is a public historian. Although trained in the history and philosophy of science, he has spent almost all of his adult life working for the Social Security Administration. As a fieldworker in Los Angeles and Phoenix, he has actually served on the front lines of the SSI program, taking applications and determining benefits. Called to central headquarters, he has observed the executive leadership of the agency at close range. His main project has involved his work as the agency's chief historian, creating an in-house Social Security archive, curating a Social Security museum, and establishing a large and widely used website on Social Security's history.

Larry's position as chief historian has enabled us to utilize the many archival files and agency publications that are part of the historical collections in the Social Security Administration's history office. These records complement research into two other types of primary sources. One is the formal record created by Congress through such things as committee reports, hearings, and floor debates, as well as all of the supporting reports by committee staffs, the General Accounting Office, and the other agencies under Congressional control. The other is the account left behind by newspapers and other periodicals that report on national politics and local affairs. The book makes extensive use of the *New York Times*, the *Washington Post*, and the *Los Angeles Times*, all neatly collected in easy to search digital editions.[2]

What emerges from the sources is a historical narrative that chronicles the development of the Supplemental Security Income program from its creation in 1972 into the twenty-first century. Even though the book was written in Baltimore, it is an inside the Beltway endeavor, one that reflects the action from the top down rather than social history that describes events from the bottom up.

The book looks at political struggles that have often taken place inside the Ways and Means Committee and the Social Security Administration. The agents of change tend to be subcommittee chairmen, federal judges, television producers, or Social Security Commissioners rather than, say, welfare rights activists.[3] In this sense, the book represents an exercise in what might be described as formal policy history. We nonetheless hope that the reader's eyes will not glaze over, since, as we try to show, all of these political and bureaucratic decisions have important human consequences.

In this collaboration, therefore, we have sought to create a book that is in touch with the sources, that reflects the bureaucratic realities of running a large and complex program, and that succeeds, at least in places, in getting beyond the details of one program to observe larger historical patterns.

Like any book, this one has benefited from the support, help, and advice from many other collaborators. Our list of debts begins at home, and we would like to thank our wives—Emily Frank and Gabriela DeWitt—for tolerating weekend meetings and other distractions. At Cornell University Press, Michael McGandy has supported this project from its very beginnings. At George Washington University, Michael Weeks, the patron saint of the history department, has, as always, been both thoughtful and helpful, as have colleagues Bill Becker, Leo Ribuffo, Richard Stott, Cynthia Harrison, Kimberly Morgan, Kathy Newcomer, and Marcy Norton. The University also provided direct financial support that made publication of this volume possible.

At the Social Security Administration, Richard Gabryszewski and Eric DeLisle of the history office provided aid and support. Tamber's Restaurant in Baltimore catered the collaboration. Finally, many friends and colleagues inside and outside of academia, including Chris Howard, Chris Foreman, Pamela Larson, Virginia Reno, Eric Kingson, Kim McQuaid, Daniel Beland, Jennifer Erkulwater, Molly Michelmore, Felicia Kornbluh, Jennifer Bertolet, Martha Derthick, Allen Jensen, Brian Balogh, Gareth Davies, and Christina Dempsey Chronister, have come to our aid. Although Robert Ball and Monroe Berkowitz died before the appearance of this book, their insights and example remained with us as we wrote it. We are grateful to each of these individuals and institutions.

THE OTHER WELFARE

Introduction

In 1972 Congress, with the active support of the Nixon administration, created a new welfare program to replace three older programs. The older welfare programs depended on federal grants to the states, and much of the policy action in terms of benefit levels and administrative rules took place on the state level. Known as Supplemental Security Income (SSI), the new program relied upon federal administration to provide, in the official language of the House Committee on Ways and Means, "monthly cash payments in accordance with uniform, nationwide eligibility requirements to needy aged, blind, and disabled persons."[1]

SSI created nationwide benefit standards for welfare in what insiders called the adult welfare categories. This audacious effort at welfare reform marked the high tide of the expansive welfare state of the postwar and Great Society eras. The Social Security Administration (SSA), which ran the SSI program for the entire nation, maintained the same basic benefit rate everywhere in the United States. A person who sought aid from SSI filed an application in a Social Security office, rather than in an office of the local or state welfare agency. Those aged, blind, or disabled people who qualified received U.S. government checks every month and were free of much of the oversight and supervision that social workers exercised over other welfare recipients.

What happened after 1972? Did the audacious effort at welfare reform succeed? Between then and now, the program developed in three unexpected ways. Over time, it became a disability program, rather than a program that primarily served the elderly. Expected to erase the stigma from the receipt of government benefits in the manner of Social Security, it instead drew the criticism from politicians who accused SSI recipients of corrupting children and exploiting the nation's immigration laws for personal gain. Created with the hope of making the federal government the primary provider of cash welfare benefits, it nonetheless contained wide variations among the states.

The basic argument of this book is that, contrary to the predictions of policymakers in 1972 and the historians who subsequently wrote about the program, SSI failed to meet its initial objectives. Instead it became a typical federal welfare program of the last quarter of the twentieth century. Two quotations set the tone of the book. The first comes from Senator Russell Long, an enthusiastic SSI supporter, who told his Senate colleagues in 1972 when SSI was under discussion, "One of the most ambitious things in this measure is the proposal of the Finance Committee for a program that would provide $3.1 billion additional income for the aged, blind, and disabled." "We would not call it a welfare program in the future," he said, because "the benefits this would provide would be so far beyond that which is being provided . . . that we think this should not be regarded as a welfare program hereafter."[2] The second quotation comes from Jay Eisen, a California lawyer charged with investigating the program after its implementation: "You remember those early missiles, the ones that got two or three feet off the pad and crashed? That was SSI."[3]

Like the space program, SSI eventually got off the ground. It then followed an unexpected trajectory. The first part of this book deals with the creation and implementation of the SSI program. The second part concerns the effect of the disability crisis on the program and the problems of running a disability program for children. The third part tells the story of SSI's role in the 1996 welfare reform. The conclusion briefly examines the aftermath of the 1996 law and considers the policy lessons of SSI's history.

The Old System—Aid to the Elderly, Blind, and Permanently and Totally Disabled

SSI started large and became larger. When the program went into operation in 1974, it already served nearly four million people, most of whom had been beneficiaries of the adult category welfare programs for the elderly, blind, and disabled that SSI replaced. Elderly recipients provided the preponderance of the initial SSI beneficiaries. Growth continued after 1974, even though those years marked what historians have called a turn to the right in American politics that made the climate less hospitable for liberal social programs and for welfare programs in particular. In December 2010, for example, SSI served some 9.1 million recipients, who received benefits worth about $48.1 billion. A substantial change had occurred in the nature of the SSI caseload as well. In 2010, the number of disabled people outnumbered the elderly people on the rolls by a factor of more than four to one.[4]

SSI replaced a welfare system created by the 1935 Social Security Act that reflected a New Deal revision of Progressive Era public policies. In this founding legislation for the modern welfare state, the federal government made grants to the states for programs in aid of indigent dependent children, the elderly, and the blind. The specific categories chosen in 1935 reflected previously established state programs that shifted welfare provision away from institutional care of the poorhouse variety and toward cash payments for special classes of needy individuals. The aid to the blind category, unlike the other two, owed its existence to serendipitous events that took place in Congress.

Beginning in the Progressive Era and continuing through the twenties, states established programs to aid needy dependent children in the form of widows' pension laws. The modern Aid to Families with Dependent Children (AFDC) program (later the Temporary Aid to Needy Families law) developed from these state programs.[5] States also adopted old age pension laws, and these became the basis for the aid to the elderly category in the Social Security Act.[6] By 1934, some twenty-eight states operated old age pension laws that, more often than not, provided meager benefits. Even Massachusetts, a wealthy state known for high social welfare benefits, paid an average of only $25 a month, with local governments having to come up with two-thirds of the cost. But that figure compared favorably with Mississippi, which had no old age pension program at all.[7] The Social Security Act of 1935 added federal funds to defray some of the costs and increase the benefit levels of these programs, created incentives for all states to start such programs, and induced the states to run welfare programs that operated everywhere in that state, rather than in particular counties.

The committee of cabinet-level officials that wrote the 1935 Social Security Act, assisted by a large staff recruited specifically for that purpose, decided against establishing a welfare category for the blind in the omnibus social welfare law that launched the modern welfare, Social Security, and unemployment insurance programs.[8] It did not seem sensible to single out the blind for special treatment when other people with disabilities, such as the deaf and people with mobility impairments, suffered equal if not greater hardship. That view prevailed throughout the lengthy consideration of the legislation by the House Ways and Means Committee. The Senate Finance Committee, however, invited representatives of private organizations who worked with the blind to testify. Robert B. Irwin, the Executive Director of the American Foundation for the Blind, appeared in this capacity and offered legislative language that would have extended aid to the elderly to blind individuals who were fifty years of age or older.[9] S. Merwin Sinclair, President of Executives of State Commissions and State Agencies for the Blind, argued that "the handicap of blindness on top of the handicap of age in a great majority of cases makes it a practical impossibility for even an employable blind person of 50 years or older to secure employment."[10]

The Senate Finance Committee proved receptive to these pleas. When Senator Pat Harrison (D-Mississippi) presented the bill to his colleagues on the Senate floor, he mentioned that his committee had added pensions for the blind to the bill already passed by the House.[11] The blind would have their own welfare category in which pensions could be paid to any needy blind person. That meant that the Senate even went beyond the request of the agencies representing the blind, which had hoped for a program that began at age fifty. Harrison hinted at the reasons for this largesse when he told his colleagues that he did not "know when any committee was ever moved more than was the Senate Finance Committee when several old gentlemen, who were totally blind, were led into the committee room by their dogs and presented their case for aid to the blind in this country." Harrison pointed to the low employment rate among the blind— only an estimated 15 percent had jobs and very few were self-supporting—as a reason for "encouraging and financially assisting" state pensions for the blind.[12]

The federal government tried to supervise the new state welfare programs created by the Social Security Act, so that, for example, local officials did not link the receipt of benefits to a beneficiary's political party. Congress did its best, however, to tie the hands of the federal administrators in establishing national benefit standards. Even after 1935, therefore, states remained the primary players in the public assistance field, and variations in benefit levels in different regions of an individual state persisted.[13] Even though New York had to offer welfare benefits in the designated categories in every county, the benefit levels in New York City were higher than the benefit level in the rural upstate town of Malone. The benefits in Malone, in turn, were higher than those paid anywhere in Mississippi.

The 1950 amendments to the Social Security Act added a new and final category to the list of federally aided state welfare programs. The new category owed its existence to a political fight that showed how the politics of welfare could not be separated from the politics of Social Security in the postwar era. The fight concerned whether to add disability insurance to the Social Security program. As matters stood in 1950, the Social Security program paid benefits to the elderly, their dependents, and their survivors. Advocates of an expanded Social Security program wanted the program also to provide benefits to people who had to drop out of the labor force, short of the normal retirement age, because of a physical or mental disability that prevented them from working. The House supported disability insurance, and the Senate opposed it. As a fallback position, Congress agreed to a new public assistance program for the permanently and totally disabled as part of a large legislative package that made up the 1950 Social Security amendments.[14]

The distinctions in this debate, which might look on the surface to be quite technical and arcane, actually mattered. Social Security Disability Insurance (SSDI) would have functioned as a benefit payable as a matter of right to people who met the definition of disabled. Provided they were covered by the Social Security program, they would not have to prove they were poor in order to qualify. If they received benefits, they would take the form of a monthly check issued by the United States Treasury. Aid to the Permanently and Totally Disabled (APTD), the choice of legislators in 1950, functioned as a welfare program. That meant beneficiaries needed to pass a means test—prove they were poor and not merely physically or mentally impaired—to qualify for benefits. Successful applicants would receive checks from state or local welfare departments and in all probability need to check in periodically with local caseworkers or social workers.

The 1950 creation of APTD—the last of the building blocks for SSI—illustrated how legislators layered new programs on top of old ones without concern for the pile of programs—often with contradictory or overlapping missions—that remained in place. In this case, few if any people questioned whether the new Aid to the Permanently and Totally Disabled category should in effect supersede the old Aid to the Blind program, since presumably the blind were also disabled. Instead, in a pattern that was typical of American political development, Congress created Aid to the Blind in a casual manner in 1935 and left it in place as newer programs, such as Aid to the Permanently and Totally Disabled, came along.

In this way, the American social welfare system often amounted to a historical catalog of categorical programs representing different approaches to solving the problems of social policy. Supplemental Security Income was unique because it replaced the older aid to the elderly, aid to the blind, and aid to the permanently and totally disabled welfare programs. It substituted one federal program for many state and local programs, and SSI moved welfare for the aged, blind, and disabled from the state and local levels to the federal level of government, with the basic rules the same across the nation.

SSI, therefore, provides a test case of modern welfare reform. Its proponents sold it as both a simplification and an improvement over existing welfare programs. If these proponents had a model of a successful social welfare program in mind, it was Social Security, which appeared to operate more efficiently than other social welfare programs and to engender far less political controversy. SSI would be like Social Security. It would be run by the same agency, and it would operate at the national level. Welfare beneficiaries would be treated with the same dignity as Social Security beneficiaries. Indeed, many SSI recipients would also be getting Social Security. The new program would provide the elderly and the disabled with a modest, but nonetheless significant, supplement to their Social Security benefits that would ensure that they did not live in poverty.

Despite this grand ambition, SSI has not provoked much comment from historians and political scientists in part because historians misunderstand the events that led to SSI's creation. SSI was part of a great bundle of programs and reform proposals that Congress considered between 1969 and 1972. The one that has received the most attention is President Nixon's proposed reform of the Aid to Dependent Children program, known as the Family Assistance Plan (FAP). This plan would have created a new, federally administered welfare category for poor families with children. Instead of limiting welfare to single mothers and their children, it would have extended welfare to two-parent families with children, even if one of the parents was working. The program failed to pass for fear that it would be costly, add many people to the nation's welfare rolls, and not provide sufficient incentives for people to enter or remain in the labor force.[15]

If the Family Assistance Plan failed, however, other key proposals in the same legislative package succeeded. In particular, Congress created SSI, raised Social Security benefits significantly, and added a feature to Social Security that assured that benefit levels would increase with the cost of living. Nixon's social welfare proposals of this period were not legislative failures. On the contrary, they resulted by 1972 in a major expansion of the welfare state. We should remember not just the failure of FAP but the great success of Social Security and SSI.

Unimpressed by these accomplishments, some historians argue that the social welfare politics of the period between 1969 and 1972 reinforced old gender and racial patterns. The adult welfare categories and Social Security fared well, and the Aid to Dependent Children program fared badly. Linda Gordon, a leading feminist scholar of welfare and modern social policy, writes that, "In 1974 OAA {Old Age Assistance} and Aid to the Blind and Disabled were folded into the social insurance system under the Supplemental Security Income program. This left *only* AFDC as a maligned 'welfare' program."[16] In other words, Congress rewarded the elderly and the disabled but punished single mothers, a disproportionate number of whom were black. That replicated a long-standing pattern, according to another recent scholar, in which benefits were "more generous to the elderly and infirm than to able-bodied adults." And "able-bodied adult recipients were much more likely to be nonwhite," so that SSI reinforced an enduring pattern of discrimination "against poor, Black families." SSI, the program that went disproportionately to whites, represented a comparatively good deal. Its beneficiaries received "the same federal funding, federal administration, and automatic cost of living adjustments afforded recipients" of Social Security.[17]

These accounts of SSI mistake the wish for the deed. In an effort to show that programs for women and racial minorities were shortchanged in the Nixon era, historians paint too sharp a contrast between AFDC—the old program for mothers with dependent children—and SSI—the new program for the elderly, blind, and disabled. In particular, SSI was never folded into the social insurance system. It started and remained a means-tested welfare program.

In SSI individuals receive benefits according to what the program defines as their "countable income." The more countable income they have, the less they receive in SSI benefits. Individuals who have resources in excess of $2,000 do not qualify for the program at all.[18] These conditions do not apply to Social Security, since Social Security contains no means test.[19] Furthermore, Social Security benefits include features not found in SSI. For example, a person covered by Social Security can elect to retire and begin receiving monthly benefits at age sixty-two, but elderly SSI recipients do not have a similar option. A married Social Security recipient can receive a benefit for his spouse and his dependents in ways that have no clear analogue in SSI. Social Security, a social insurance program, remains a much better deal than SSI, a welfare program.

If SSI has not been folded into Social Security, as historians claim and its creators hoped, what did happen to it from the era of its creation in the early seventies to the present day? This book pursues that historical question, mindful of how the American welfare state after 1972 differs from the ones that preceded it. Political scientists have enriched our understanding of the recent American welfare state by demonstrating that it is not just small and underdeveloped compared to more "advanced" welfare states in other countries. In this spirit political scientists have brought attention to America's "hidden," misunderstood, submerged, and "delegated" welfare state. America, it seems, carries out its social policy in unique ways, using such methods, models, and techniques as tax expenditures, federalism, and giving responsibility for administering important social policies to private, rather than public, entities.[20] SSI functions as a more visible part of the welfare state than, say, the features in the tax code that support private health plans. It nonetheless shares some hidden or misunderstood features with other social programs.

SSI's history shows that, because of the way the contest over President Nixon's social welfare proposals was framed, a radical welfare program appeared conservative. Considered in isolation, SSI would have engendered considerable political controversy. As part of a package that also included the Family Assistance Plan, SSI looked to be a prudent expansion of America's welfare state. In this manner, it was not unlike the 1935 Social Security program—a sharp departure from past precedent that nonetheless gained political respectability in the context of the radical policy proposals that were current at the time.[21]

SSI covered the adult welfare categories. FAP, the proposed replacement for AFDC, would have gone to less respectable single mothers, a disproportionate number of whom were African Americans. (Its proponents failed to sell the notion that its real beneficiaries would be the working, deserving poor and that a program that rewarded work and "intact" families would replace a stigmatized welfare program.) Because of that political positioning, conservatives with influence over the policy process such as Senate Finance Committee chairman and Louisiana Senator Russell Long supported SSI and opposed FAP. As always, the historical context mattered.

The Social Security Administration received responsibility for running SSI because of its reputation for competence and its proven record as an agency that served large numbers of people efficiently. It tried to apply the most advanced public administration procedures, as they were understood in 1972, to the new program. That meant an emphasis on mechanized operations and, in particular, on the computer as a tool for collecting data, determining benefits, and sending out checks to the right people in the right amounts.

Contrary to the hopes of the Social Security Administration, the new program got off to a bad start in 1974. Created at the end of the long run of postwar prosperity, the program opened for business in the stagflation era of the seventies.[22] It therefore faced a form of future shock. The bad economy helped fuel a rise in applications for benefits and put pressure on both state and federal budgets. Inflation, a particular feature of the bad economy, led to rising benefit levels, because SSI, in a special feature added to the program after 1972, linked the consumer price index and the benefit level.

The flawed implementation of SSI stripped away some of the Social Security Administration's previous reputation for competence. In a declining economy, people's situations necessitated frequent adjustments in benefit levels because SSI was a welfare program that reflected a person's shifting income and resources. Frequent adjustments strained the capacity of the SSA computers. Checks went out to the wrong people in the wrong amounts or failed to go out to the right people in the right amounts.

Unplanned Policy Shifts

After the start-up glitches, SSI entered another phase of its history that featured a shift in the program's identity from one intended primarily for the elderly to one that served mainly people with disabilities. The fact that SSI emerged as a disability program created its own complications. Disability, whether in Social Security or welfare programs, was a difficult concept to define and hence to control. Disability was a much less secure and stable benefit category than old age. Differing from notions of old age, sickness, or functional limitation, it involved a subjective judgment about whether someone was capable of working.[23] Adding to the complications, the SSI program contained the unique feature of paying benefits to children who were disabled. If disability meant an inability to work, what, exactly, did it mean for a newborn, a toddler, or an adolescent to be disabled?

SSI inherited institutional structures from existing programs, and in particular the Social Security Disability Insurance program. Without giving the matter a great deal of thought in 1972, Congress allowed the SSA to process SSI disability claims using the same administrative and bureaucratic apparatus that already applied to Social Security Disability Insurance. The states, not the federal government, ran the disability determination offices. The states decided whether a person was disabled, according to a law passed by Congress and regulations formulated by the Social Security Administration. This feature added the problem of variation by state to a public administration task that was inherently difficult.[24]

Uncertainty about whether the people on the SSI rolls were "really" disabled meant that the program faced skeptical critics who worried that the disability category could be easily manipulated by applicants. Doubts about whether the applicants truly deserved the benefits undercut political support for the program. Therefore, SSI encountered problems merely because it was a disability program, something that its creators, who thought they were creating a program for the elderly, failed to foresee.

SSI became embroiled in controversies surrounding disability policy in the seventies, eighties, and nineties. The 1980 legislation attempted to create incentives for disabled SSI recipients to leave the rolls and enter the labor force. The Reagan administration's implementation of these 1980 amendments produced a firestorm of protest that deserving people were being cut from the rolls. Congress reacted by passing new legislation in 1984 that made it easier for people already on the disability rolls to remain there. The courts responded in 1991 with a major decision that loosened the requirements for disabled children to get SSI. In 1996 Congress overturned the 1991 Supreme Court decision through legislation.

The Policymaking System for SSI

Martha Derthick's 1979 classic, *Policymaking for Social Security*, provides a model for this book. In the manner of Derthick, we want to describe policy-making for Supplemental Security Income. Writing from the Brookings Institution for an audience of policymakers, political scientists, and political historians, Derthick analyzed how a small group of program executives and Congressional insiders made policy for Social Security.[25] She devoted chapters to the program executives at the Social Security Administration and the political figures in the White House, Congress, and the Department of Health, Education, and Welfare. All of these figures remained important in SSI but with some significant differences in what intellectual historian Daniel Rogers has called "the age of fracture."[26] In particular, program executives, who enjoyed considerable autonomy over the development of the Social Security program before the seventies, exercised much less control over SSI. Some of this control went to the President and other executive branch officials who determined policy and made initial decisions about spending levels. Some went to Congress, with its expanded system of subcommittees and the increased turnover in the leadership produced by transitions from one political party to the other. Wilbur Mills and Robert Ball, the legendary leader of the Ways and Means Committee and the long-serving and widely respected head of the Social Security Administration, respectively, had few counterparts in the policymaking system that applied to SSI.

Derthick rounded out her list of policy influences with the conservatives who opposed the expansion of Social Security, expert critics who framed the intellectual debate over Social Security, and public opinion. Conservatives and expert critics played a larger role in SSI than in Social Security. The conservative critique of the program led to major program modifications that accompanied welfare reform in 1996. In that year SSI faced the same sorts of criticisms and many of the same legislative outcomes as the supposedly unique AFDC program. Intellectuals helped shape this critique in significant ways. By way of contrast, the intellectual commentary on Social Security came mainly from program executives and program insiders close to the executives.

Concerned with Social Security, Derthick omitted policy actors and forces that were crucial to the development of SSI.[27] The federal courts, for example, played an active role in the history of SSI. One could easily omit the AFL-CIO from a history of SSI, but it would be impossible to exclude the federal courts.

Derthick, in her 1979 book, did not think to mention the media. If Social Security policy before 1979 consisted largely of inside maneuvers by bureaucrats and Congressional committees, SSI policy after 1972 repeatedly responded to what Commissioner Michael Astrue called "sound bite and anecdote."[28] These bites and anecdotes came from the newspapers, television stations, and other members of the modern media. Flexible in its choice of subjects, the media spread stories about children who were coached to act crazy in order to receive benefits, immigrants who exploited the generosity of Americans, and substance abusers who fed their habits with SSI dollars. The media did more than report on current events. It also produced stories in ways that influenced popular opinion. In the days of Social Security's great expansion, the media often played the role of cheerleader, putting the press releases from the Social Security Administration into print. In the post-Watergate days of SSI's growth, the media strived to uncover the story behind the story. That often meant exposing the inadequacies of government programs or injustices done to the people on the programs' rolls.

The Stigma of Welfare

So the late twentieth-century policymaking system for SSI differed from the system that produced the great expansion of Social Security from 1950 to 1972. Furthermore, SSI beneficiaries did not become the prototypical Americans who contributed to and benefited from the Social Security program. Instead, each of the major categories of program recipients developed a politically sensitive connection to perceived welfare cheats and other unsavory characters whose presence undermined the public's support for SSI.

The disabled category in SSI harbored the substance abusers. Substance abusers presented the public with many of the same quandaries as did the appearance of a drunk who was panhandling on the street. Although the person asking for money was in obvious need, some worried that their spare change would go toward more alcohol. Benevolence in this case only made the problem, which many people saw as self-inflicted, worse. The media played its part through stories such as the one about the Denver liquor store owner who received SSI payments on behalf of people with drinking problems and used the money to run up a large tab.[29] In response, Congress eventually passed two major laws that made it hard for someone to qualify for SSI on the basis of substance abuse alone and cut back the benefits that substance abusers received. The first law came from a Democratic Congress and the second from a Republican Congress.

The old age category in SSI also ended up creating a group of recipients who were considered undeserving and against whom Congress felt the need to take punitive actions. Casual decisions made at one point in time produced large consequences at other points in time. Allowing noncitizens to be eligible for SSI benefits reflected the spirit of the times as well as historical serendipity. When

SSI was under consideration, no federal law barred the states from denying welfare benefits to noncitizens. The states did what they wished. The state of Arizona precluded lawfully admitted aliens from participating in any of its adult category programs, unless the alien had lived in Arizona for fifteen years. Then in June 1971, just when Congress was considering SSI, the Supreme Court struck down the Arizona law. The decision received special mention in a Senate Finance Committee report. Legal aliens became eligible for SSI. Congress, preoccupied by what seemed to be larger and more consequential policy issues, said little about including legal aliens.[30]

In time, paying welfare benefits to noncitizens became controversial. Reinforced by traditional attitudes about "deserving" and "undeserving" welfare recipients, the cohort of noncitizens on SSI proved to be an especially vulnerable group. The notion developed that some people came to this country to take advantage of its generous social welfare programs (an interesting rebuke to those who complained about America's undeveloped welfare state). At a time when the immigration rate was rising and, inevitably, leading to social tensions, stories circulated about immigrants who brought their parents to this country and, instead of taking care of them, helped them get on SSI. As with many stories about welfare abusers, the evidence to support these claims was thin. Aliens made up about 10 percent of the SSI population, and their numbers peaked at 12 percent. They became visible, however, because so many of them were concentrated in the old age category.

Beyond these particulars, the hope here is that history illuminates public policy and that the history of SSI helps improve our understanding of America's welfare state. A steady state program description might lead someone to conclude that social policy is either incomprehensible or nonsensical. Why, for example, have a national program in which disability determination is handled by the individual states? Why make special provisions for the blind when the law does not provide such special accommodations for, say, the hearing impaired? Why emphasize the inability to work as a measure of disability at a time when advocates for disability rights emphasize the capabilities of people with disabilities and insist that it is often the physical design of the workplace, rather than the inherent capacities of people with disabilities, that keeps disabled people from jobs? Why administer aid to dependent children at the state and local levels and aid to disabled children at the federal level? These perfectly reasonable questions can best be answered not through elaborate social science exercises in hypothesis testing but, rather, through the simple device of chronicling the process of change over time.

The resulting narrative demonstrates how a logical sequence of events can produce outcomes that might appear irrational at any particular time. Academics in such esoteric subfields as American Political Development and historical sociology already know these things, as work on such subjects as path dependency and policy feedbacks demonstrates.[31] Here, then, is a case study in the political development of one program in the welfare state that we hope will trouble, as the academics like to say, the conventional wisdom and add a solid account of an important program that deserves a close historical treatment.

CREATING A NEW WELFARE PROGRAM

The Politics of Welfare and Social Security
Reform in the Nixon Administration

By putting welfare reform on the policy agenda in 1969, President Richard Nixon started the process that led to the passage of Supplemental Security Income (SSI) in 1972. Richard Nixon, a Republican, presided over a major expansion of the welfare state that, although it did not include the Family Assistance Plan (FAP) that he unveiled in 1969, did include the creation of a major new welfare program. SSI, as the program became known, marked a major change in the way that American welfare programs were administered and financed. The emergence of this program becomes clearer when it gets put into the context of the Congressional and social welfare politics of the time. In particular, the Senate used SSI as a bargaining chip in the negotiations with the House that led to the lower house abandoning its support of FAP. SSI became the conservative alternative to FAP, one that fit neatly into the major expansions of Social Security that were another key feature of social welfare politics in the period. Understanding the emergence of SSI, therefore, requires attention to actions in the White House, the Senate, the House of Representatives, and the federal bureaucracy concerned with Social Security and welfare.

Toward the Family Assistance Plan

It began with President Richard Nixon, who had campaigned for the presidency in 1968 by, among other things, criticizing the Great Society's social programs and the welfare programs embedded in that policy. Nixon disapproved of the mix of services and income supports, administered at all levels of government, which characterized Lyndon Johnson's social policy. As President he sought something that might plausibly be termed a Republican or, better yet, a Nixon alternative to the existing system.

That alternative turned out to be the Family Assistance Plan. Under the tutelage of adviser Daniel Patrick Moynihan and against the advice of other close advisers such as economist Arthur Burns, Nixon proposed what people at the time called a negative income tax. The key ideas were an income guarantee—an amount of money that every American family with children would receive—and a low tax or takeaway rate on welfare benefits. In other words, a hypothetical welfare recipient would not have his or her benefits reduced by a dollar for every dollar earned. That feature provided, at least in theory, an incentive to work because working increased a welfare recipient's total income at the same time that the income guarantee provided protection for those unable to work.

A June 1969 memo from Moynihan to Nixon described the administration's potential welfare reform proposals as "the first major change in social welfare policy since the Elizabethan Poor Laws." He said that, by moving fast, the President could "*dominate and direct this social transformation. . . .* The end result—if you wish it to be—will be *your* change." He offered the President the prospect of "a genuinely new, unmistakably Nixon, unmistakably needed program, which would attract the attention of the world, far less the United States" (emphasis in original).[1]

The Family Assistance Plan

On August 8, 1969, President Richard Nixon unveiled the Family Assistance Plan to the nation on television. The proposal involved offering welfare to all poor families with children, including intact families with a working parent. In other words, Nixon and his advisers wanted to extend welfare beyond the original four categories and provide it to the working poor who had children. The Nixon proposal, in a breathtaking break from precedent, called for federal, rather than state, administration of the new welfare category and for the abolition of the old Aid to Families with Dependent Children (AFDC) program.

In his televised address to the nation, Nixon termed the existing welfare system a "colossal failure" that "breaks up homes," "penalizes work," "robs recipients of dignity," and "grows." He noted that in the past eight years some eight million people had been added to the welfare rolls. The failure of welfare confronted the President with a problem that required a drastic solution. In the spirit of making a bold break with the past, he proposed a basic federal guarantee for a family of four with no outside income of $1,600 a year.[2] As with Presidents Hoover and Johnson before him, he hoped for nothing less than the abolition of poverty, something once thought impossible but more likely to imagine in an era in which the nation had sent a man to the moon.[3]

In October 1969 the House Ways and Means Committee took up the measure in eighteen days of hearings. The fact that the Committee acted so promptly was a good sign. On measures that Committee Chairman Wilbur Mills (D-Arkansas) firmly opposed, he could be deliberate to the point of obstruction, and he controlled the Committee's agenda, which in turn controlled the agenda of the House of Representatives. In the Kennedy era, for example, he had stalled for the entire length of that administration in his deliberations over Medicare.[4] Welfare reform struck him as an urgent problem, and he believed that the administration's proposal merited serious consideration.

Ways and Means did not, however, look at the Family Assistance Plan in a vacuum. Instead, in a move that had great significance for the eventual passage of SSI, the Committee took up Social Security, Medicare, and the other welfare titles at the same time it examined FAP. Aware of how the Committee operated, the Nixon administration accompanied FAP with proposals to liberalize Social Security and make changes to the other welfare categories. In particular, the President suggested that benefit increases in Social Security, instead of being legislated by each Congress on an ad hoc basis, should be automatically adjusted to the inflation rate. When the cost of living rose, Social Security benefits should also rise.[5] The President also made it clear that, under his proposals, the adult categories would be continued—in other words, he did not intend to alter the entire welfare system—but with raised benefits that would be paid for mostly by the federal government. If the Aid to Dependent Children program was to be radically reformed, the adult welfare categories were to be liberalized.

Secretary of Health, Education, and Welfare, Robert Finch, a close associate of the President's with ties that went back to Nixon's California days, presented the details in his October 1969 testimony before the Ways and Means Committee. The aged, blind, and disabled would receive a minimum of $90 a month per person, and while states would continue to administer the programs, national minimum benefit standards, national eligibility standards, and uniform administrative procedures would govern the program. In other words, the administration wanted both to liberalize benefit levels and strengthen program administration, using the federal government and its monetary payments as a force to ensure uniformity. States could supplement the benefits they paid, and they even had the option of turning over the administration of the program to the federal government. "In this way," said Finch, "we should be able to move toward a single administrative mechanism for transfer payments, taking advantage of all the economies of scale which such an automated and national administered system can have."[6]

For the states, a key detail of the adult welfare proposal centered on how much the federal government would contribute. The administration proposed that the federal government would pay the first $50, half of the next $15, and, should the state wish to go further, a quarter of the remaining amount. In those states that had low welfare payments, the beneficiaries would see direct increases in their benefits. In those states with payment levels higher than the contemplated federal standard, the beneficiaries would not necessarily see an increase in their benefits. But the proposal held advantages for the high-paying states as well. In effect, the state could save money by substituting federal dollars for state dollars in the first portion of its welfare payment (as opposed to matching federal dollars with state money under the old system). The Department of Health, Education, and Welfare (HEW) estimated that establishing a federal minimum of $65 financed in this manner would save the states some $400 million. The reform of the adult welfare categories therefore offered fiscal relief to the states and promised raised benefits in many of the states.[7]

From the beginning of the long debate over SSI, it became clear that making changes in the adult welfare categories would be easier than the radical reform of AFDC. Simply put, the adult welfare categories presented policymakers with fewer problems than did AFDC. Secretary Finch noted that, "neither work incentives nor family stability incentives"—prominent features of the discussion about reforming AFDC—were the answers to what he described as the "dependency" of the people in the adult welfare categories. "In the last analysis," he said, "it must be our obligation to move toward an adequate income level for the aged, blind, and disabled," since the way that the nation treated its deserving poor constituted "one of the measurements of a just and humane civilization." Few of the members of the Ways and Means Committee, however conflicted they might have been over the Family Assistance Plan, disagreed with that sentiment.[8]

In June 1969 some two million elderly people received welfare benefits, which was an increase of only 17,000 from the previous year. About 10 percent of the elderly were on welfare, although, as with the rest of the state systems, the percentages varied greatly from state to state. For example, 2.7 percent of Connecticut's elderly but 40.7 percent of Louisiana's elderly received benefits. Part of the reason for the disparity was that in more industrialized and prosperous states, such as Connecticut, more of the elderly received Social Security benefits. Nationally, more than half of old age assistance beneficiaries also received Social Security benefits, a fact that suggested that the problem was a diminishing one that would eventually be handled through more generous Social Security benefits.

The aid to the blind rolls, limited by the small number of poor blind people in the country, and the aid to permanently and totally disabled category also exhibited a reassuring trend toward stability. Some 80,000 blind people received welfare benefits. By way of contrast, 6.6 million people were on the AFDC rolls, and the trend line was rising (see Figure 1-1).[9]

The number of permanently and totally disabled was rising at a rate of more than 10 percent a year, but the numbers were still relatively modest—755,000 people in June 1969. Indeed, the relatively low numbers prompted the administration to raise its proposal for a minimum benefit from $65 to $90 a month. Such a minimum benefit would raise benefits in thirteen of the lowest paying states, such as Mississippi, which paid less than $40 a month, and still make it possible for New Hampshire to pay more than $116 a month.[10]

It seemed a simple matter to reform the adult welfare categories, and the political payoff promised to be generous. The Family Assistance Plan, by contrast, involved radical surgery on the nation's welfare system. Noting the contrast, the *Portland Oregonian* editorialized at the time that Nixon's proposals "would not disturb adult aid to the aged, blind and disabled—except to increase minimum benefits."[11]

Despite this reassurance and the general goodwill that accompanied the proposal to reform the adult welfare categories, disturbing the status quo inevitably drew complaints from people who felt their favored position in the old system threatened or people who wanted the reforms to go further. The representative of the National Federation of the Blind worried that change might work to the disadvantage of the blind by lumping them together with the elderly and others with disabilities. He noted that two-thirds of the states made "separate and special provision for their blind citizens who require help in meeting their basic needs." The "problems and needs of the blind," he argued, were different from other groups requiring aid.[12] On the expansive end of the spectrum, Norman Lourie, an influential spokesman for the National Association of Social Workers, suggested that the adult welfare categories should simply be folded into the Social Security program. In other words, everyone on the public assistance rolls who was elderly, blind, or disabled should be taken off those rolls and signed up for Social Security, with its more generous, less stigmatized, and more uniform benefits.[13] The director of Cleveland's welfare department made a similar suggestion to "transfer all aged, blind, and disabled assistance to the Social Security Administration," as a sort of test case for the federalization of the other welfare programs.[14]

To the surprise of many, Wilbur Mills and the Ways and Means Committee decided to back the Family Assistance Plan, which created the real possibility that the measure might make it through the House and ultimately become law.

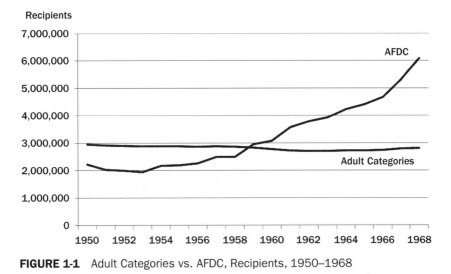

FIGURE 1-1   Adult Categories vs. AFDC, Recipients, 1950–1968

Since, even if FAP passed, it would be a lengthy process, Mills decided that certain politically important matters needed to be expedited. At the end of 1969, with FAP and the indexing of Social Security benefits to the rate of inflation still pending, Mills collaborated with his Republican colleague John Byrnes (R-Wisconsin) on a 15 percent increase in Social Security benefits. The Senate passed a similar benefit increase that it attached to a Tax Reform Act. As a result, 1969 ended with a 15 percent benefit increase in Social Security (in a year when the inflation rate was 6 percent) and the likelihood of serious consideration of FAP and other welfare matters in the second Congressional session, which would begin in 1970. The 15 percent Social Security increase illustrated the confusing simultaneity of events in this period. Following just one legislative proposal, such as indexing Social Security benefits or FAP, risked missing other significant developments in social welfare policy.[15]

Political Action in 1970

By the spring of 1970, Mills and his committee had a measure, which they called the Family Assistance Act of 1970, ready to report to Congress. As expected, they included the reform proposals for adult assistance in the bill and provided some of the details that had been lacking in previous proposals. The Committee announced that the bill would "substantially improve the effectiveness of the adult assistance programs." Despite the reservations expressed by organizations representing the interests of the blind, the bill would combine the three adult categories into one program with uniform requirements "for such eligibility factors as the level and type of resources allowed and the degree of disability or blindness." The Committee chose to set the minimum benefit at $110, which was higher than the amount recommended by the administration. It also made the formula of federal grants simpler than the Nixon administration had originally proposed, although on paper the formula looked quite formidable. Under the Committee's plans, the federal government would pay 90 percent of the first $65 of average payments to adult assistance recipients and 25 percent of the remainder (up to a limit that the Committee would allow the Secretary of HEW to set). Furthermore, the Committee's bill permitted the states to enter into agreements with the federal government so that the federal government administered the combined adult program, with administrative costs to be paid by the federal government.

The Committee encouraged the states to administer the program for adults in a liberal manner. For example, the states would not be allowed to set a qualifying age above sixty-five for its elderly welfare recipients, nor could the states exclude an alien who had lived in the country legally for at least five years from receiving aid. States would also not be allowed to set stringent residence requirements nor impose the responsibility of supporting an adult welfare recipient on a relative other than a spouse. It amounted to a comprehensive reform proposal of the adult welfare categories within an even more ambitious reform plan for the working poor.[16]

Mills followed the customary practice of explaining the bill to his colleagues at the start of the House debate that began on April 15, 1970. He reported that the adult welfare categories had not "presented any serious problems to the Ways and Means Committee or to the Congress." The numbers in these categories were declining and would continue to decline "as more and more of our people become eligible for social security benefits." He painted a stark contrast between the adult programs and AFDC. "If you want an example of an open-ended proposition where we are completely helpless to put any restraints, controls, or limitations on it or to make an improvement on it," he pointed his colleagues toward AFDC, an expensive program that "encourages family breakup." It therefore struck Mills as reasonable to experiment with the Family Assistance Plan and to provide the elderly, blind, and disabled with a minimum of $110 so that "these unfortunates . . . have enough to live on." "I think," he concluded, "that the adult public assistance recipients—the old, the halt, and the blind—are most deserving of any additional help we can give them."[17]

Although the bill passed the House—a major milestone in the history of the American welfare state—it ran into considerable problems when it reached the

Senate and Chairman Russell Long's Committee on Finance. Two problems related to Congressional and social welfare politics prevented the passage of major welfare reform legislation in 1970, despite considerable effort in both the House and the Senate.

The first problem was that Wilbur Mills objected to the indexing of Social Security benefits to the rate of inflation, even though his colleagues in the House and the Senate appeared to favor the measure. Because of his feelings, he used his discretionary powers not to go to conference with the Senate at the end of the year. That put an end to legislative discussions on a comprehensive Social Security, Medicare, and welfare bill for the year.

The second problem was that Russell Long opposed the Family Assistance Plan. As a consequence, FAP failed in the Senate, and because the Senate and the House did not go to conference, Long's opposition effectively killed the plan for the year and the Congressional session. If one highlighted FAP, it appeared to be an unproductive year, yet Congress made substantial progress on the reform of the adult welfare categories. Both the Senate and the House approved major changes in the adult categories but never got the chance to meet in conference to resolve their relatively minor differences.

Both Russell Long and Republican Senator John Williams (Delaware), also a Finance Committee member, objected strenuously to FAP. Long did not agree with Representative Mills that it was the answer to the welfare mess. Where Mills chose to see the work incentive features of the negative income tax and the family preserving feature of allowing intact, working families to receive welfare, Long thought that FAP would do little more than subsidize the same old welfare mothers to remain on welfare in an era where welfare recipients enjoyed procedural rights that made it difficult to compel them to work or throw them off the rolls. Senator Williams, for his part, realized that the way that FAP interacted with the other already established programs created substantial inequities. Welfare included more than a cash benefit. It also came bundled with such things as Medicaid, food stamps, and subsidized housing. Losing one often meant losing all, a situation that made it costly for someone to leave the welfare rolls and complicated the problem of creating a welfare program with work incentives. Williams asked the Department of Health, Education, and Welfare to prepare a series of charts that demonstrated the inequities of FAP. These charts showed that under the President's plan a welfare mother in Chicago who made $720 a year ended up with $6,128 in the form of cash, public housing, food stamps, and medical care. A mother in similar circumstances who earned $5,560 received a total of $6,109.[18] (Williams was not trying to improve FAP by highlighting its inequities so much as trying to use these inequities as an argument to prevent its passage.)

If FAP divided conservative southern Democrats like Mills and Long, it also split northern liberal Democrats for reasons that had consequences for the history of SSI. The year the Senate first considered FAP was also the year that the Supreme Court ruled in the case of *Goldberg v. Kelly* that welfare beneficiaries had the right to an evidentiary hearing before their benefits could be terminated.[19] This decision marked the culmination of a series of cases that protected the rights of people on welfare. In Oakland, California, for example, a woman was thrown off the AFDC rolls after authorities raided her house and discovered a man was living there. She appealed the decision to the courts. This action helped launch the Alameda County Welfare Rights Organization and led to a judicial decision that government raids on the homes of welfare beneficiaries violated the Fourth Amendment's protection against illegal search and seizure.

These developments created new sorts of legal entitlements to welfare that would prove important to the history of SSI. Furthermore, the people involved in the legal battle over welfare in California ended up playing significant roles in the creation of SSI. For example, Tom Joe, a blind person with training in economics who worked for California State Representative Philip Burton, played a part in the Oakland case.[20] Later, at the time of FAP and SSI, Joe joined John Veneman, another California legislator, in Nixon's department of HEW, where Veneman served as Under Secretary and Joe worked with him on welfare reform. Burton, a Democrat, went on to win election to Congress from a San Francisco district. He became a major power in the House of Representatives at just about the time when FAP reached the Senate Finance Committee.[21]

Consideration of FAP in 1970 produced an unusual political dynamic. The presumably liberal members of the National Welfare Rights Organization (NWRO), a group that lobbied for the legal protection of welfare rights and the expansion of welfare benefits, and the presumably conservative Louisiana Senator both opposed FAP. The welfare mothers in the NWRO came from states like New York and Illinois that already paid higher welfare benefits than those promised by FAP. Like the blind, they knew how to work the existing system to maximum advantage and resisted fundamental reform.[22] Long, by way of contrast, opposed FAP because he felt it offered the welfare mothers too much. If the welfare mothers thought FAP would not expand the system enough, Long believed it would expand it too much. This peculiar dynamic helped defeat FAP in the Senate, even though the liberals in Richard Nixon's Department of Health, Education, and Welfare, who now included newly appointed HEW Secretary Elliot Richardson, pushed hard for the measure to no avail. "I must emphasize that FAP is the highest priority in the department," Richardson told the head of the Social Security Administration in August 1970.[23]

Even though the Senate turned down the Family Assistance Plan in 1970, it pursued all of the other items in the comprehensive legislative package, including adult assistance, with at least as much vigor as the House. The Senate version of adult assistance reform retained the original elderly, blind, and disabled welfare categories as separate programs but included a $130 national minimum for individuals and $200 for a couple.[24] Just as the House outbid the administration on the benefit level for welfare recipients in the adult categories, so the Senate, which despite the personal predilections of Russell Long and other southern Senators was the more liberal body, outbid the House.

Political Action in 1971 and the Origins of Supplemental Security Income

The 1970 defeat of FAP and the tabling of welfare reform in the adult welfare categories might well have ended the discussion of welfare reform in the Nixon era. Instead, the new Congress that convened in 1971, still under Democratic control and still under the influence of Wilbur Mills and Russell Long, decided to take up the matter again. In part that decision reflected the continuing interest of Mills in FAP and the fact that important issues related to Social Security—in particular whether Congress would accept the Nixon proposal to index benefit levels in Social Security to the rate of inflation—remained unresolved. And if Mills moved on FAP, then Russell Long would need to counter.

As always, Congress thought of welfare reform and changes in Social Security as part of one big legislative package. In 1971, as opposed to 1970, significant movement occurred on one part of that large package. In a major about-face, Mills decided to endorse the notion of indexing Social Security benefits to the rate of inflation. In a characteristic manner, he moved from opposing the measure to taking charge of its legislative enactment. That meant at least one of the major players changed his position on one of the major items in 1971, creating a new political dynamic.

As a result, the window for changes in the adult welfare categories remained open in 1971. Indeed, the winter and spring of 1971 turned out to be crucial in the development of SSI. Key players in the process included Nixon's welfare reformers in the Department of Health, Education, and Welfare such as Under Secretary Veneman and staff member Tom Joe, legislative leaders Wilbur Mills and Russell Long, and the executives of the Social Security Administration and in particular Social Security Commissioner Robert Ball. Democrats Mills and Long relied heavily on Robert Ball as a tutor, just as Republican Veneman depended on Ball to design and implement the program.

Robert Ball and the Social Security Administration

Robert Ball, who enjoyed a reputation as an exceptionally intelligent and well organized administrator, brought considerable expertise to the task. He began at Social Security as a field representative in 1939. With only minor interruptions, he worked himself up through the ranks to become, in effect, the program's chief operating officer and legislative tactician in the fifties, and, beginning in 1962 and continuing through the Kennedy, Johnson, and the first term of the Nixon administrations, the presidentially appointed Commissioner of Social Security. Among his many accomplishments, he led his agency through the successful 1965 and 1966 implementation of the Medicare program, a task that was considered among the most difficult domestic policy undertakings in the nation's history. Although unknown to the general public, he earned a reputation among Washington social welfare policy insiders for making government, so often cumbersome and inefficient, work effectively.[25]

As Robert Ball recalled the matter, the idea for Supplemental Security Income came from Veneman and Tom Joe, who were anxious to include the adult measures as a complement to the Family Assistance Plan. The fact that Joe was himself blind made him particularly sensitive to the existence of the adult categories. "Veneman and Joe called me in," said Robert Ball, "and said, 'This is what we want to do and SSA ought to administer it—what do you think?' "[26]

What Veneman and Joe wanted to do was to have the federal government take over the adult assistance programs and administer them with uniform rules on a national basis. It was an audacious suggestion. As a general rule, states parted with programs that employed a significant number of people and awarded benefits to voters only very reluctantly. The history of Social Security and welfare was littered with failed attempts by federal authorities to assume control of programs that were run at the state level by state employees.[27] For a Republican administration to make the suggestion appeared remarkable. It can only be understood in the context of the even more unusual proposal for the federal government to institute and run FAP. Russell Long, in particular, sought a constructive alternative to FAP and settled on SSI, although he needed considerable convincing that the federal government, rather than the states, should administer it. The decision to propose the federalization of the adult welfare categories also took place in the context of the frequent increases in Social Security benefits that marked the era. With Social Security increasing so rapidly, it appeared that Social Security, rather than welfare, would carry an increasing amount of the load in the adult categories.

Because of its reputation for possessing esoteric expertise not duplicated elsewhere in the government and for performing its duties in a competent manner, the SSA operated with relative autonomy. Over the years this autonomous agency had developed an ambivalent attitude toward welfare. When the Social Security Act was passed, Congress assigned a wide range of responsibilities for administering the various parts of the Act to the newly created Social Security Board (later the Social Security Administration). Welfare and the social insurance programs were new federal entities, and Congress put the Social Security Board in charge of them. Although the Bureau of Public Assistance, staffed by dedicated social workers, remained a key part of the SSA, the SSA put the needs of the social insurance program above those of the welfare program. Despite some grumbling that the SSA did not give welfare the attention it deserved, the welfare programs stayed in the Social Security Administration, at least until Robert Ball became commissioner in 1962.[28]

Ball's background was in social insurance, and he could see that welfare, with its controversies over illegitimate children and its rising benefit rolls, promised to be a very divisive program in the sixties. It appeared prudent to let the social workers and others concerned with welfare, and in particular with AFDC, out of the SSA and give them their own agency in HEW. As a consequence, welfare left the SSA and settled into HEW's new Welfare Administration. A social worker who was influential in professional circles and who administered the welfare program in the state of North Carolina (Ellen Winston) headed the Welfare Administration. This moment coincided with Ball's settling in period as Commissioner. A separate welfare agency also emphasized the importance that the Kennedy administration placed on its version of rehabilitation-oriented welfare reform. These contingencies suggested a natural division of labor: the SSA would concentrate on income maintenance, and other parts of HEW would focus on rehabilitation.

By 1971, when discussions over the adult assistance plan heated up, it was as though the social workers had never been part of the SSA.[29] Even though the agency would eventually agree to administer the SSI program, the SSA still kept its distance from welfare programs. The Nixon administration had tried and failed to interest the SSA in running FAP. Soon after the February 1970 breakthrough when it became clear that Wilbur Mills would support FAP, it also became clear that the SSA would not be the lead agency in administering the program. Ball told his superiors in HEW that its implementing FAP would be as difficult as putting a man on the moon.[30]

On the adult assistance titles, though, Robert Ball felt he could not demur in the same manner. He volunteered to help out with Nixon's reform of the adult welfare categories because he felt he had little real choice and with the thought that taking over the adult welfare categories just might help his agency. "Although I think it is desirable to have a separate organization administer the Family Assistance Plan, I don't see how one could defend such a separate organization for the adult categories," he told a former Social Security Commissioner who remained in touch with the political situation. He noted that most of those on old age assistance, some 60 percent, were already Social Security beneficiaries. He thought that figure would soon rise to 80 percent and that people newly eligible for old age assistance "just have to come primarily from among social security beneficiaries, since over 90% of all the aged are eligible for social security now." Not as much of an overlap between public assistance and social insurance existed in the disability categories, but Ball realized that "we are the only national agency with the organization and experience to make disability determinations."

If Ball had no use for FAP and believed welfare to be an inferior form of social protection to social insurance, he nonetheless saw advantages for his agency in the plans to reform the adult welfare categories. Universal coverage under Social Security remained a long-term goal, relegating welfare "to what I hope will in the long run be people who are in and out of coverage under the social security system." Ball felt confident that the "long-range result of a Federalized (welfare) program administered by the Social Security Administration will be to give an impetus to still further improvements in contributory social insurance."[31]

In March and April 1971, the SSA, reconciled to being the lead agency on the project, conducted an inner bureaucratic discussion about what to recommend to the Nixon administration and the Ways and Means Committee on the adult assistance programs. Robert Ball coordinated the discussion and served as the chief point man to Congressman Mills, Secretary Richardson, and other high-level HEW officials. He relied heavily on agency veterans who had participated in the other great Social Security efforts, such as the design and implementation of disability insurance in the fifties and of Medicare in the sixties, which had energized an agency largely devoted to the repetition of routine tasks.

For specifications about the new adult assistance program, he turned to Ida C. Merriam, the tough-minded Assistant Commissioner for Research and Statistics who was fiercely devoted to Ball. Merriam had a degree from the Brookings Institution, when it functioned as a graduate education center as well as a think tank, and prided herself on her ability to work under pressure. Others in the loop included Jack Futterman, who headed the Office of Administration and had served for many years as Ball's assistant, and Arthur Hess, who, like Ball, had worked himself up from a field office to a position of authority as the second in command of the agency. Hess had earned a reputation as the man who had ironed out the details of disability insurance and Medicare and headed their successful launch. Each of these individuals, along with others who ran the SSA's data processing and field operations, possessed years of administrative experience.

On March 1, 1971, Ida Merriam sent a memorandum to Robert Ball with specifications for a federal assistance program for the adult categories that she hoped would lay the basis for cost estimates. The cost estimates were of course politically sensitive and would have to be carefully vetted by the Department and by the SSA's own Office of the Chief Actuary. They also involved a level of speculation about the future course of social policy. What, for example, should planners assume about benefit levels in the future—would they be automatically increased in the same way that Mills now proposed to do for Social Security beneficiaries?

Merriam's specifications served the helpful purpose of focusing the SSA on the important questions that the new adult assistance program raised. In general, what sorts of income and financial assets should be included in the determination of whether a person was poor? Merriam argued that bonds, stocks, and saving accounts that yielded an income of more than $1,500 a year should disqualify a person but that the value of person's home could be disregarded. Should benefit levels be the same everywhere or should they vary by area of the country or by the cost of living in a given locale? Did some groups, such as the blind, need more than other groups, such as the elderly? What would happen to people in institutions, whose needs were already taken care of by a public program, or to people who lived with a nonrelative who provided them with room and board? Merriam, like most of her colleagues, wanted as much uniformity as possible, with states responsible for any special supplementation, so as to make the program as easy as possible to administer.

The disability side of the program raised its own sorts of questions and in particular just how should disability be defined. Merriam assumed that the definition of disability for the new program would be similar to the definition already used in the Social Security Disability Insurance (SSDI) program, which centered on the inability to work because of a physical or mental impairment.[32] If such a definition were adopted, the new program could build on the administrative capacity of the established SSDI program.

Most of these questions raised issues that would ultimately be decided in Congress. The SSA therefore engaged in highly contingent work in which planners made assumptions and the parts of the agency with contacts to the political decision makers became both the servants of the politicians and advocates of the decisions that the bureaucracy had already made. If the agency waited until final Congressional action to begin planning, it knew from experience that it might be too late to implement the program effectively and in that case Congress would lay the blame on the bureaucracy for failing to follow Congressional instructions.

The work that Ida Merriam and others did circulated among a group of some dozen people at the SSA, including officials in the Office of the Commissioner, the Office of Administration, the Office of the Chief Actuary, the Bureau of District Office Operations, the Bureau of Retirement and Survivors Insurance, the Bureau of Data Processing, and the Bureau of Health Insurance. Among the members of this group, the opinion of Robert Ball mattered most. He scrutinized all memos that would ultimately go to the Department or the Ways and Means Committee with special care, dictating comments that a team of secretaries, who often worked in shifts around the clock, transcribed. Always, Ball tried to keep the strategic interests of his agency in mind. He noted, for example, that Congress was considering changes in the disability insurance program that might "reduce the number of assistance recipients and put more on the social security rolls." He suggested that the agency might work up a list of changes in Social Security to submit with the welfare reform plans, "so as to minimize the impact of supplementary assistance."[33]

The SSA tried to anticipate the needs of the politicians who legislated social policy so as to move policy in the direction that it favored. In the Nixon administration, however, the agency needed to tread softly. The SSA, for example, traditionally encouraged all people who were eligible to participate in its programs, but Ball did not know if such a view would fly in the Nixon administration. He said, "We take so completely for granted that we'll search every nook or cranny for a possible eligible that it never occurs to us that some people [might not take that] view." Ball believed that once the program got going the agency would go all out to find beneficiaries, "but it may not be something that everybody is willing to accept at this point."[34]

Robert Ball did as much as he could to influence members and his superiors in the executive branch without appearing to overstep his authority. Where he disagreed with the administration, he introduced what he called "some element of doubt" into the discussion. He also made sure that neither Congress nor the administration got the idea that administering an adult assistance program would be easy. On the one hand, he wanted to communicate the message that the SSA could handle the job of taking over the state welfare programs for the aged, blind, and disabled. On the other hand, he wanted his masters in the Department and in Congress to know that it would be a difficult job that would require more resources and lots of new employees for his agency. He told Futterman to stress the "tremendous initial impact" that such a program would have and that it would "require quite a lot of people and all that stuff." He thought it bad strategy to characterize "it in the beginning as not an overly difficult task." "I don't think we have to persuade anyone that we're the right organization. I don't see that's a problem. The problem is to get them to see that it's not a simple matter of just taking over a going load, which is what I think is in Mills' mind now."[35]

The agency's preferred approach might be a more cautious one than Congress would take. For example, SSA officials suggested that their agency might tackle the problem of old age assistance first and then wait for a year before taking over the state programs for the blind and disabled. It might also be easier if the agency started with people already on the state rolls before enrolling new people in the program, all as part of a "phased" effort rather than a "frantic one."[36]

At the same time the SSA tried to influence the contents of the program and manage expectations, it needed to come up with a basic approach on how to run the new program. Should it, for example, create a new bureau to handle the new program? Whatever bureaucratic structure that the agency decided upon, it had to create a coherent system design for the new program, including operations for building a file for an applicant to the new program, reaching a decision on an applicant's eligibility, and assuring that the successful applicant received a check in a timely manner. The initial bias was to work with a minimum of paper and create a system in which all essential data "would be in the computer."[37]

Action in the Ways and Means Committee

As the bureaucrats discussed these and other matters, the Committee on Ways and Means met in executive session in the spring of 1971. When it came time for final decisions on important matters, Mills preferred to work in confidential executive sessions, a setting removed from the obligatory political pieties and grandstanding that often characterized public hearings. The Social Security Administration and, in particular, Robert Ball were important participants in these executive sessions, acting often as a surrogate staff to the Committee. Even though a new Congress and a new Ways and Means Committee met in 1971, Wilbur Mills regarded the public hearings he had already held in 1970 to be sufficient for the new round of welfare reform.[38]

On May 26, Wilbur Mills reported out the Social Security Amendments of 1971 to the House. Although the bill covered many subjects, the Ways and Means Committee emphasized welfare reform in its report. AFDC took pride of place. The Committee noted its concern over the ten million people on the AFDC program and "the exploding number of broken families which are becoming increasingly dependent on welfare for all their needs." "There are some areas of cities," the Committee noted to its horror, "where it is rare to find even one family which is not on welfare." Because of the gravity of the problem and the ineffectual nature of previous solutions, the Committee once again endorsed the Family Assistance Plan.[39]

Unlike the bill in the previous session, however, the 1971 proposal contained the new version of the adult assistance plan that had been developed by the Nixon administration and the Social Security Administration. No longer would the state programs for adult welfare recipients be left in place. Instead they would be replaced by "one combined adult assistance program which would be federally administered by the Social Security Administration and would have nationally uniform requirements for such eligibility factors as the types of resources allowed and the degree of disability or blindness." Each beneficiary would receive enough assistance to bring his or her monthly income up to $130 in 1973, $140 in 1974, and at least $150 after 1974. States could supplement these amounts at their discretion, and the federal government would administer these supplements without charge to the states for the costs of administration.[40]

The shift from an option for federal administration of the adult categories to a mandated federal program was a major milestone. To justify this shift, HEW and the SSA emphasized the presumed efficiency and effectiveness of federal administration as the stated purpose for federalizing the adult categories. After all, the state programs suffered from an astonishing lack of uniformity. There were over 1,350 different governmental units—a combination of state, county, and local agencies—administering the adult categories, each with widely differing rules and procedures.[41] Payment levels varied by over 300 percent between the states.[42] The need, then, was to make the system more coherent and its administration more efficient, as HEW Secretary Richardson explained in testimony before the Senate Finance Committee: "Consistent with President Nixon's New Federalism, the division of responsibility in H.R. 1 assigns functions to the level of government which can best perform them."[43]

Explaining its recommendation to create a new adult assistance program, the Committee on Ways and Means noted that the adult categories were characterized by "smaller numbers of people, smaller budgets, and more nearly static beneficiary rolls," qualities that made them "more susceptible to rapid and efficient reform than the family programs." Most people in these categories would continue to rely on supplemental assistance to maintain their incomes, but some of these people might receive very small Social Security benefits. The Committee concluded that, "Contributory social insurance . . . must be complemented by an effective assistance program" (it would supposedly benefit some 6.2 million people in its first years).[44]

Ways and Means went out of its way to indicate that it wanted the SSA to administer the new adult assistance program. It reported that in considering the legislation the Committee "became convinced that successful administration of the proposed plan could be achieved by utilizing the administrative structure of the Social Security Administration." The SSA, with its 50,000 employees, 850 local offices, and 3,500 contact points with the public, was a large organization that operated from coast to coast and offered much in the way of administrative expertise. The Committee sweetened the pot for the SSA by suggesting that the agency would receive even more employees to run the new program.[45] The Committee wanted the new program to benefit from the SSA's administrative capacity but also admonished the SSA to maintain "the unique identity" of its social insurance and welfare programs by requiring separate applications and issuing separate checks.[46] So the new program was to be a little like Social Security but not too much like Social Security.

A similar subtle distinction applied to the Committee's decision to federalize the adult welfare categories. The Committee sought uniform benefits across the nation but realized "a complete uniformity of assistance levels throughout the nation is not presently attainable nor even necessarily desirable." States that paid lower benefits than the new federal level would probably be content to accept the higher benefits from the federal government. States that already paid higher benefits might want to supplement those benefits. In the permissive spirit of welfare policy, the Committee noted its desire to leave "each State, completely free either to provide no supplementation of Federal assistance payments or to supplement those payments to whatever extent it finds appropriate in view of the needs and resources of its citizens."[47] The Committee realized that the old system of state administration provided more opportunities to meet "special needs" than would the new federal system. Caseworkers at the state and local levels could, for example, talk with an applicant, see if he required special assistance for housekeeping, and add something to his grant for that purpose. Ways and Means wanted such discretionary payments to remain at the state level and not be part of the new federal program.[48]

In other words, there would be a uniform national benefit, but in fact benefits would not be the same across the nation because some states, but not others, would supplement the basic benefit and some states, but not others, would continue to run special needs programs, the contents of which would be different from state to state and even from place to place within a state. The realities of the federal system trumped the goal of national uniformity even at a time when the desire to have the federal government take over the welfare system was at its height, just as the realities of a social welfare system already splintered between social insurance and public assistance reduced the potential for administrative efficiencies in a newly federalized system.

Disability: Hidden Continuity, Sleeper Provisions, and the Unworthy Poor

Aid to the disabled represented a prime area for achieving administrative efficiencies. The Committee recommended that the definitions of disability and blindness in the new proposed welfare program be the same as those in the existing Social Security Disability Insurance program. These definitions, in the opinion of the Committee, "provide reasonable, objective, and fair tests of disability which are appropriate for the proposed program." It made this statement mindful of the fact that the disability rolls were rising, that the disability part of Social Security led to far more disputes and legal hearings than did the rest of the Social Security program, and that the tough definition of disability—"the inability to engage in any substantial gainful activity by reason of a medically determinable physical or mental impairment which can be expected to result in death or has lasted, or is expected to last for not less than 12 months"—had proved very difficult to enforce and engendered many Congressional complaints.[49]

It nonetheless recommended keeping the old disability definition in the new program. The definition of disability and the process of disability determination had been contentious matters ever since they had first arisen in the late thirties. In 1952, as part of the intricate bargaining that preceded the passage of substantive disability insurance legislation in 1954 and 1956, Congress had agreed to a system in which the states—acting under contract to the federal government—rather than the federal government made the initial disability decisions. Such a system, it was thought, brought the process closer to the community and created more possibilities for a person with a disability to be rehabilitated (the same political dynamic that had led to the creation of Aid to the Permanently and Totally Disabled in 1950).[50] Once the decision about the disability determination process was made, it simply got reified in subsequent legislative programs without a great deal of critical thought. No one wanted to reopen the controversy.[51] If Congress passed welfare reform in 1971, it would extend the life of a political compromise that reflected the historical contingencies of 1952.

Of course, legislators saw things differently in 1971 than they would later in the decade. In 1971 Aid to the Elderly remained the single largest adult welfare category, and policymakers thought of the new adult category welfare program as benefiting the elderly more than people with disabilities. A major rise in the disability rolls lay just ahead, but it was not yet on the legislative radar at a time when the welfare "mess" consumed so much time and effort.

Although the new bill preserved much of the past in its administrative detail, it also contained sleeper provisions. Legislators hoped to slip these through in a moment when the window for change was clearly open and when Congress was overwhelmed with other parts of the complex and controversial legislation. The usual place to make these sorts of changes was on the floor of the Senate, because the House voted for Social Security legislation under a closed rule that did not permit too many changes and the Senate traditionally permitted amendments during the floor debate. The Ways and Means Committee felt the weight of legislating for the House. Wilbur Mills and John Byrnes, the chairman and ranking member, regarded themselves as stewards of public programs who had to resist appeals for costly extensions of programs. For all of their caution, however, sometimes a cause caught their eye, and they deemed it worthy enough for inclusion in one of their bills. In the case of the 1971 legislation, one such cause was disabled children.

In the adult welfare categories, most beneficiaries were, by definition, adults. Blind children, who were relatively small in number, but not permanently and totally disabled children, had the right to assistance under the existing rules. Children in low income households tended to receive benefits from AFDC, rather than from one of the other categories. The 1971 House bill proposed a major change in this practice that might be thought of as a major change in a minor part of the bill—hence its relative invisibility. The Committee noted that disabled children who lived in low income households were "among the most disadvantaged of all Americans and that they are deserving of special assistance in order to help them become self-supporting members of our society." Since the needs of disabled children were "often greater than those of nondisabled children," Ways and Means wrote benefits for disabled children into its new program in the adult welfare categories.

That seemingly innocuous and reasonable-sounding provision added to the problems related to the definition of disability. The definition of disability, the one that policymakers so glibly extended from one generation of laws to another, focused on the inability to work. Children, particularly children with disabilities, did not work in the conventional sense of holding down a full-time job outside of the home. The Committee nonetheless took a stab at a definition. A child under eighteen would be "considered disabled under the bill if he suffers from any medically determinable physical or mental impairment of comparable severity." In other words, the child would get benefits if his or her impairment was comparable to one that in an adult would be expected to result in death or last no less than a year. Yet so much of the adult definition centered on such things as the inability to do one's previous work or engage in any "substantial work which exists in the national economy," regardless of whether there were vacancies in such work. All of that seemed irrelevant to children. At a minimum the definition would pose a major challenge for the state disability determination offices—the ones thought up back in 1952—to handle.[52]

Since Ways and Means had not held public hearings in 1971, the demand for childhood disability benefits did not come from a group pleading its case in an open session of Congress. In 1935 blind people with Seeing Eye dogs had marched into the hearing room, captured the hearts of the Senators, and gotten Aid to the Blind written into the Social Security Act. In the 1971 case of benefits to disabled children, someone close to the legislative process, with a special interest in the subject, must have slipped the provision into the bill. It was not likely to have been Robert Ball. He wanted to make the legislation easier to administer, not harder. It could have been one of the Committee members or a staff member to such a member, but the culture of Ways and Means discouraged this sort of addition to an already much extended bill. The likely responsible party was HEW staffer Tom Joe, who understood better than most the needs of disabled children, and who enjoyed privileged access to the Committee's deliberations through HEW Under Secretary John Veneman. Joe later claimed credit for the provision, although he made his claim much after the fact. A leading scholar on this matter reports, "Tom Joe was the one who during congressional debate in 1971 had slipped into the legislation the clause that made children eligible for SSI." Joe said that he deliberately made the phrase vague and did not want people to discover it.[53] Few did, at least not until it exploded as a major policy issue some fifteen years later.

The Ways and Means Committee knew that it would also have to confront other issues related to disability. Certain categories of disability blurred the distinction between the worthy and the unworthy poor. If a drug addict or an alcoholic applied for benefits, for example, he or she might well be unable to engage in substantial gainful activity and hence disabled in the legal sense of the term. At the same time, Congress did not want to reward such people for their bad behavior, any more than it wanted to bestow benefits on the mothers of illegitimate children. The solution was to highlight drug and alcohol addiction as a treatable medical problem. The addicts would only be allowed to receive benefits if they underwent "appropriate, available treatment in an approved facility."[54]

When Mills presented the plan to the House of Representatives in June 1971, few of the Congressmen queried him on the problems related to the disabled. Mills made it seem simple. Deciding if someone was incapacitated was "a medical question. The individual will be sent to a doctor to examine him, who will determine if he has such incapacity." Mills implied that a doctor could look at someone and decide if he was able to work, when in fact the history of the disability insurance program argued that the decision was complex and led to many disagreements. He reported that the Social Security Administration would need "relatively little additional personnel to run the new program," even though his Committee's own report implied otherwise.[55]

Few Congressmen wanted to know the details of the proposal for the adult welfare categories. They accepted, in the words of Judge Smith, a crusty Congressman from Virginia who was as conservative on social policy questions as anyone in the House, "the basic merits of any legislation designed to assist our senior citizens, the disabled, the blind, the infirm."[56] "We can take care of the poor, the aged, and the disabled, yes, I think the Government very definitely has a mission in that respect," added Representative Omar Burleson of Texas. Representative Mitchell (D-North Carolina) argued that separating the blind and disabled "from the rest of the welfare morass is certainly a great step forward toward more extensive welfare reform."[57] Although the entire bill passed, support for the Family Assistance Plan was grudging and support for the adult welfare plan was enthusiastic. By rule, the Congressmen had to accept or reject an entire package, not just individual parts of it, and they decided to accept it.

Action in the Senate in 1971

Once again, the Senate needed to take up the measure and come up with its own proposal. The Senate was on record as opposing the Family Assistance Plan, favoring the continued administration of the adult categories by the states, and of limiting aid to the disabled to people eighteen years of age or older.[58] It considered these matters and a host of others in eighteen long days of hearings that started in the summer of 1971 and went into the winter of 1972. Unlike in the House, which had not held public hearings in 1971, Russell Long promised a "thorough evaluation of the welfare features of H.R. 1."[59] At this point he regarded the changes in adult welfare categories as political cover for rejecting FAP. "To keep them from coming back with something that was going to make the whole nation into a welfare state, I felt the way to spike their guns on that would be take all the money they estimated on this family program and apply that to the aged," Long later said.[60]

The canny Long had already taken care of an important piece of business by putting through an increase in Social Security benefits earlier in the 1971 session. That action severed, at least for the moment, the popular cause of raising Social Security benefits from the FAP proposal, at a time when FAP needed all of the political camouflage it could muster. Long included the 10 percent increase in a debt ceiling bill. Mills, who still had not worked out the details of FAP, the adult welfare categories, and indexing Social Security benefits to the rate of inflation at the time when this proposal appeared, went along with Long's maneuver. The Social Security increase passed the House with only three dissenting votes.[61]

When the Senate hearings began in the summer of 1971, Elliot Richardson, the new Secretary of HEW and the lead witness for the administration, backed the already passed House bill with enthusiasm. His statement reinforced President Nixon's earlier endorsement of the House bill as "an important landmark in the history of both social security and public welfare reform" and a "momentous step."[62] Long encouraged Richardson to discuss the details of the adult assistance proposal. "Now, Mr. Secretary," he said, "I have been desirous of increasing the payments for the aged people in this country. We know there is not much abuse in it. If these old people qualify in the first instance they are not going to have much income thereafter." When Richardson responded by citing the payment levels in the new legislation, Long replied, "Well I applaud that. I would like to see it higher, especially for the couple, but I believe that that is a good provision."[63]

Later in the hearings Long reasserted his view that he was "in favor of providing a comfortable income level to those who are disabled, those who are unable to work, those who are aged, for little children, if you can't make parents do their duty. But this thing of providing a program where parents are able to victimize their children and live on the public with a comfortable guaranteed annual wage for not working could destroy the nation, in my judgment."[64] Even the extremely conservative general counsel of the Liberty Lobby agreed with Long "that certainly the sick, the handicapped, and the aged should be provided for—anyone who is incapable of work."[65]

The issue was not whether the federal government would pay for the adult welfare categories but whether the federal government or the states would administer the program. Long and the representative of some conservative organizations, such as the National Federation of Independent Businesses and the State Chambers of Commerce, favored keeping administration at the state level.[66] Spokesmen for social work organizations and most state governors preferred that the federal government take over the programs and free the financially pressed states of the administrative responsibility of running them. The debate in the Senate Finance Committee even included a preview of the 1980 presidential election, with California Governor Ronald Reagan testifying in favor of state administration and Georgia Governor Jimmy Carter arguing in favor of federal administration.

The spokesman for the Catholic Charities, who had long supported the liberalization of public assistance and Social Security, presented an eloquent brief explaining the arguments in favor of federalization. The needs of the needy aged, blind, and disabled were "relatively stable, readily identifiable, and likely to continue." The causes of their indigence were "easily recognized and understood by others and therefore their need is more readily accepted." To assure equality of treatment and equitable determination of eligibility, "This rightly should be a Federal program. . . . The administration of it by the Social Security Administration should provide the same efficiency as marks the operation of the OASDI [Old Age, Survivors, and Disability Insurance] program."[67]

Senator Long let such statements pass uncontested and reserved his closest cross examination for the Governors, including Carter and Reagan, who testified on federalizing the adult welfare categories. Long regarded the Governors as natural allies in the fight to keep administration and the locus of political power and government employment at the state level. He stressed that, whatever happened, "we are going to provide more benefits for the deserving cases; we are going to do that for the aged, disabled, blind, children," and that those benefits "are going to be paid for entirely by Federal revenues." The issue for Long was "just who is going to do the paperwork." He noted that unemployment compensation was run at the state level and people were very happy "with the amount of State discretion that is left in the program and State administration appeals to the people in those States and it appeals to a majority in the Congress." He wondered, therefore, why a similar arrangement should not prevail in public assistance, with the governors appointing the welfare administrators in their states. Was it really necessary, he asked the state governors who testified before him, to have a federal takeover?

In a typical reply, the Governor of Rhode Island argued that social services should remain with the states but that it would be better to have eligibility determined and payments made at the national level, although he would follow the Senate's wisdom on the matter. Long pressed the Governor on the matter. He thought that retaining state responsibility would make officials more accountable than "if you have one simply enormous thing administered by one man at the top with a lot of people in there that neither you nor I can do anything about." He forced the Governor to admit that "you would get a lot better accountability if we retained some State responsibility in this matter."[68]

State governors worried far more about their finances than they did about losing control over the employees who ran the welfare programs. The Governor of Ohio noted that it mattered "very little whether the employees . . . are in the Federal employ or in the employ of the State of Ohio."[69] Governor Richard Oglivie of Illinois testified that the present system was threatening his state "with financial chaos." Illinois state officials determined that their appropriation of $1 billion for welfare would fall some $107 million short of paying for the program. In

1969 the state had passed an income tax, never a popular political measure, and only three years later found itself in a "financial straitjacket," because welfare absorbed some 84 percent of the state's increase in revenue for fiscal 1972. In calendar year 1971, more than 200,000 people joined the welfare rolls in Illinois, causing monthly disbursements to rise from $68 to $91 million and crippling the state's capacity to provide other essential services. Not surprisingly, the Governor welcomed nearly any measure that kept welfare away from him. He wanted to take the aged, blind, and disabled "out of public aid" and put them "under social security."[70]

Not all of the Governor's colleagues agreed. Although 1972 marked the peak of what might be called the federal reformation of welfare programs, a counter-revolution had already begun. The battle was joined most sharply in the state of California. Tom Joe and John Veneman, who both came from California state government, led the Nixon administration's drive to federalize the adult welfare categories. Governor Ronald Reagan, also a California state official, disagreed with their views, and he went to Washington to announce his differences.

Reagan faced an uphill battle. Governor Jimmy Carter of Georgia seemed to express the views of a bipartisan consensus when he told Long's committee that "income maintenance programs should be federally funded and federally administered. Economic need is influenced by forces beyond the control of local and state officials and the response to it must be national in scope. . . . I am in accord with plans to transfer to federal administration the present assistance programs for the aged, blind, disabled."[71] Governor Reagan countered that, "Federalization of the payments programs will mean the creation of a greatly enlarged federal bureaucracy, inherently less able to meet the needs of the people than the current State/Federal partnership. . . . In addition to creating a massive federal bureaucracy, HR 1 forces states like California, that have attempted to administer equitable welfare programs, to turn their programs and their money over to the federal government." Long agreed with Reagan far more than he did with Carter.[72]

Legislating Supplemental Security Income in 1972

Just as Wilbur Mills capitulated on the question of indexing Social Security benefits to the rate of inflation, so Russell Long gave way on the question of federalizing the adult public assistance categories. Both matters worked themselves out in the summer and fall of 1972. Long worried that the lengthy Senate consideration of the comprehensive bill put such important matters as a Social Security benefit increase at risk, and he, as well as everyone else, realized that as the presidential election grew closer, neither party wanted to take political chances, such as by enacting the Family Assistance Plan. The Senate, where presidential candidates still came from in the early seventies, contained many members with the presidential nomination, rather than the details of social welfare legislation, on their minds.

Senator Long acquiesced in a legislative maneuver that involved Frank Church (D-Idaho), an ambitious member of the Senate with recognized expertise in foreign policy who wanted to establish his domestic policy credentials and who would run for the Democratic presidential nomination in 1976. The success of the maneuver, which concerned a 20 percent raise in Social Security benefits and indexing Social Security benefits to the rate of inflation, allowed Long to postpone final consideration of welfare legislation until just before the 1972 election.

Robert Ball, anxious to get the indexed benefits, and Wilbur Mills, anxious to get higher Social Security benefits because he, too, entertained presidential or at least vice presidential ambitions, persuaded Church (D-Idaho), the Chairman of the Senate Aging Committee, to introduce the 20 percent benefit increase as an amendment to a bill providing for the extension of the public debt limitation. Church's bill also included indexing future Social Security benefits to the rate of inflation. The debt limit legislation passed, and President Nixon, now deep into the 1972 campaign, signed it on July 1, 1972.[73]

With a Social Security benefit increase off the table for the legislative session, Congress still needed to complete its work on the comprehensive H.R. 1 bill that the House had passed in 1971. In the summer of 1972, the Finance Committee still held to its position in favor of state, rather than federal, administration of the adult welfare categories and against providing public assistance to disabled children (other than the blind). In the official language of the Committee, it would continue state administration of the programs in aid of the aged, blind, and disabled but "would set a federal minimum" for these individuals.[74]

By the fall, with the election only weeks away, Long's Committee changed its mind on the adult assistance parts of the bill. It reported a bill to the Senate that "would replace the present State programs of aid to the aged, blind, and disabled with a new wholly Federal program of supplemental security income."[75] Not only had the Committee reversed its decision on state administration but it also gave the adult public assistance program a new name: Supplemental Security Income. Supposedly the new title came from Under Secretary John Veneman. The Committee offered few explanations for changing its position on state administration, noting only that "in the course of the deliberations leading up to the committee's decision to recommend the new federally administered program, it became convinced that by utilizing the administrative structure of the

Social Security Administration excessive expansion of the Federal bureaucracy could be avoided."[76] Someone, such as Robert Ball, must have changed Russell Long's mind. Maybe Long thought that agreeing to federalize the adult categories provided him with more protection against the Family Assistance Plan, which he continued to oppose.

The Senate did insist on one important difference from the House bill. It opposed disability benefits for children under eighteen, and the Finance Committee engaged its House counterpart directly on the measure. The Ways and Means Committee argued that, "Making it possible for disabled children to get benefits under this program, if it is to their advantage, rather than under the programs for families with children, would be appropriate because their needs are often greater than those of nondisabled children."[77] The Finance Committee disputed the House analysis, stating on the contrary that: "The House justified its inclusion of disabled children under age 18 under aid to the disabled . . . on the grounds that their needs are often greater than those of nondisabled children. The needs of disabled children, however, are generally greater only in the area of health care expenses. In all but the two States that do not have Medicaid programs, children now eligible for cash assistance are covered under existing State medical assistance programs. Disabled children's needs for food, clothing, and shelter are usually no greater than the needs of nondisabled children."[78]

The Senate did not consider the bill until September 28, 1972, with the impending election now a major distraction. When Long presented the comprehensive bill, he gave the changes in adult assistance a particularly favorable twist. "It is our view—and I am satisfied that this is the view of the average man on the street—that we should provide adequately for people who are aged. We do not have any real argument about that. The committee decision was overwhelmingly that we should provide a very generous level of benefits to the aged, disabled, and the blind. . . . Those are expensive programs, but they do tremendous amounts for people, and in that area there is no argument worthy of the name, because I am satisfied that the Senate and the House of Representatives also will be willing to go along with a proposal that provides that people who have done the best they could with what they had to work with would be assured of a level of income which would more or less lift them out of poverty."[79] Senator Bennett, the ranking Republican on the Finance Committee, added that the Committee had "tried to be very generous" to the aged, blind, and disabled and "to raise their income in such a way they would be free as far as possible from any stigma of being dependent on welfare."[80]

At this point in the process, the Senators were not in the mood to debate the fine points of public policy. Few wanted to consider the problems of deciding if someone was disabled or the advantages of federal versus state administration. Most Senators wanted to go home and campaign in their districts. The Nixon administration also appeared content to stick with the hand it had been dealt. The President could argue that he had tried and failed to pass the Family Assistance Plan and that might be more attractive for him than the Democratic Congress actually passing FAP. Either way he could campaign on his more responsible position on the welfare "mess" than Senator McGovern's position (McGovern was proposing a guaranteed annual income for *every* American family in the form of a demogrant). The President expressed his general attitude in a conversation with Elliot Richardson in the middle of September. "The sooner this Congress is out of town the better off we will be," he said.[81]

Long made it even easier for the Senate to oppose FAP by giving it a special opportunity to vote on the adult assistance title in the bill. He said that the Senators might like to record themselves on this title. He noted some Senators would want to vote for the whole bill and others might want to oppose it. "One of the most ambitious things in this measure is the proposal of the Finance Committee for a program that would provide $3.1 billion additional income for the aged, blind and disabled," he said. "We would not call it a welfare program in the future," he added, "The benefits this would provide would be so far beyond that which is being provided . . . that we think this should not be regarded as a welfare program hereafter. . . . It is for that reason that we refer to it as supplemental security income for the aged, blind, and disabled."[82] Long offered his colleagues the pleasant prospect of expanding welfare benefits without even voting for a welfare bill. Accepting the offer, the Senate voted 75 to 0 in favor of the adult title. The larger bill passed the Senate by a smaller margin.

The Senate and the House rushed to hold a conference committee to resolve their differences over H.R. 1. In general, the committee followed the House on the adult assistance titles and the Senate on the Family Assistance Plan (no FAP in other words), and both bodies consented to the result. On the issue of disabled children, the House version of the 1972 legislation included disabled children in SSI and the Senate version did not. The Senate receded to the House position in conference, without comment or reported debate.

The final measure specified that full monthly benefits in the adult assistance categories would be $130 for an individual and $195 for a couple. Any income the person might have would be offset against the SSI payment amount. Thus if an individual had $100 in other income his SSI payment would only be $30. If someone had income above $130, he would not be eligible for SSI. A person receiving Medicaid in a hospital and nursing home would be eligible to receive $25 a month if he had no other income. Individuals with more than $1,500 and couples with more than \$2,250 in resources would not be eligible for benefits, although a home, a car, and a life insurance policy would not be counted as resources.[83]

The measure used the Social Security definition of disability, included disability benefits for children under eighteen, and contained the comparable severity standard for defining childhood disability.[84] The President signed the measure, which had consumed two Congressional sessions and taken up nearly all of his first term, into law at the end of October. He called it "landmark legislation that will end many old inequities and will provide a new uniform system of well-earned benefits for older Americans, the blind, and the disabled. . . ." A few days later Nixon would win the election in a landslide that also returned a Democratic Congress to Washington.[85]

Conclusion

Although Congress had dealt with benefit increases in Social Security in separate legislation, the scope of the new law was nonetheless impressive. It represented a clearing of the reform agenda that had been building up in the sixties and early seventies. For example, it specified for the first time that Social Security benefits for widows and widowers would be 100 percent of basic benefits (rather than a reduced percentage), overturning a decision originally made in 1939. It expanded Medicare into new areas, the first such expansion of that program by creating Medicare coverage for Social Security Disability Insurance Beneficiaries and for persons with End Stage Renal Disease. All of that and more were in addition to the Supplemental Security Income program.

Few people realized it at the time, but the 1972 legislation marked the very apex of the American welfare state. Indexing Social Security benefits to the rate of inflation meant that the program would expand throughout the inflationary seventies, without Congress having to do anything about it. The nation would never pass national health insurance as envisioned in 1972 or the Family Assistance Plan. The 1972 extensions of Medicare and Supplemental Security Income were about as far as the country would go in the direction of a welfare state run by the federal government.

In the legislative process, SSI had become a conservative substitute for FAP that masked the radical change that the new program represented. For the first time, the federal government agreed to step in and run welfare programs previously run by the states, creating the possibility of national benefit standards for the aged, blind, and disabled. Wilbur Mills and Russell Long reassured their colleagues that federalizing the adult categories was the right thing to do and the popular thing to do, even though Long was a very late convert to the cause. The Senate voted for the change in the adult welfare categories unanimously, implying that it was without controversy, despite differences in the Senate and House versions of the bill and the issues that had already arisen in the Senate hearings.

Only a few Congressmen saw the significance of the new program. Philip Burton—the California liberal who claimed credit for being the first person to urge a national minimum for adults as part of the Nixon welfare reform—told his colleagues that "when the history of this particular legislation is written—it will be noted that this new—supplementary security income—particularly with a federally administered program to maintain income for our aged, blind and disabled, with a federally stated minimum, will prove to be the one most remarkable achievement that this particular conference committee report contains."[86]

A YEAR IN TRANSITION

Why Planning for the New Program
Became Difficult

If the Social Security Administration (SSA) had learned any lesson between 1935 and 1972, it was that the process of implementation mattered. New programs, like Supplemental Security Income (SSI), could not be launched without extensive preparation. Part of the drill involved encouraging SSA employees that the task ahead of them was important and persuading them that it would end in success. Social Security Commissioner Robert Ball kicked off the process at the end of 1972 when he gave his employees one of his patented pep talks.[1]

Ball believed that his agency performed better when it was faced with a challenge and that implementing the new program and converting some 3.3 million blind, disabled, and aged people from state to federal benefits would be "the greatest challenge in the history of the organization."[2] At the same time, SSI offered compensating advantages to welfare recipients and to the SSA. Implemented properly, SSI would help destigmatize the receipt of government benefits. Through the way that the agency intended to run the SSI program, the SSA would show that welfare clients could be treated with dignity, so that, as Ball put it, "it is expected that there will be much less stigma, if any, attached to the receipt of Supplemental Security Income." SSI would be welfare done right, a straightforward income maintenance operation without any of the dubious services that the states and local governments were delivering so ineffectively. SSI would be a poster child for a new automated style of welfare that relied on using the latest computer technology to get checks out to people.[3]

The expansion of Social Security between 1969 and 1972 and the robust shape of the economy made the difficult task of implementing SSI somewhat easier. The 1972 Social Security legislation, with the 20 percent benefit increase, indexing future benefits to the rate of inflation, and raising the wage base on which workers and their employers paid Social Security taxes, marked a major expansion of Social Security. More elderly people on Social Security would mean fewer elderly people who would need SSI. Higher Social Security benefits meant lower SSI benefits. A special Social Security benefit increase, from $84.50 to $170 for some 150,000 people who had worked for thirty years or more at low-paying jobs, would also ease some of the pressure on SSI.[4]

The robust state of the economy would also help. A strong economy might, at least in part, lessen the demand for SSI and other welfare benefits. Just weeks after Robert Ball spoke to his employees, the financial and business editor of the *New York Times* filed a story with the lead that touted an economic boon "that may prove to be unrivaled in scope, power and influence" when compared to previous economic expansions.[5] A few days later the paper reported that the personal income of American families and individuals had risen by $74.4 billion in 1972, "a figure much larger than the entire national income of most countries in the world." Higher wages and an increase in the number of people at work helped account for an 8.6 percent increase in personal income over the previous year.[6]

Despite these advantages, SSI never realized its initial promise because of political, economic, and administrative factors that materialized in 1973, even before the program began formal operations. After President Nixon won a resounding victory in the 1972 election, he made major changes in the executive branch that deprived the SSA and the Department of Health, Education, and Welfare (HEW) of the leadership team that had engineered the 1972 amendments. Although these 1972 elections did little to disturb the Congressional leadership, perennial Ways and Means Chairman Wilbur Mills experienced personal problems that meant he could not play the same active role in SSI's implementation as he had in its passage. Contrary to expectations, the economy deteriorated, and an era of high inflation and high unemployment—just the sort of conditions that might force people to apply for welfare—began. Worsening economic conditions forced Congress to adjust the SSI program even before it went into operation, complicating the already difficult administrative tasks.

In addition, a piece of legislation with the simple premise that benefit levels should be the same across the nation became quite complex to administer. None of the states wanted to spend more money under SSI than under the old program. Neither Congress nor the states wanted individual recipients to receive less money under SSI than under the old program. Most states wanted their beneficiaries to retain special benefits particular to that state, such as heating allowances or rent supplements. Assuring these results required a great deal of technical tinkering that added to the program's complexity. Where the regime in place in 1972 might have resisted pleas for special statewide features in the SSI program, the new regime proved more receptive to those pleas. As a result, the program acquired significant differences from state to state that added to the complications of implementing SSI. The turnover of leadership in the SSA meant that the federal administrators trying to solve these problems had less experience and, in all likelihood, less competence than the administrators they had replaced.

Each of these things changed the outlook for the success of the SSI program. The year 1973 became one of transition from the optimism of the sixties to the pessimism of the seventies. Born in the sixties, SSI came of age in the seventies.

Changes at the Top

Nixon's victory in the 1972 election meant changes in his cabinet and in the subcabinet agencies. The President announced that Elliot Richardson would leave his post as Secretary of HEW at the end of January 1973. His successor would be Caspar Weinberger. The two had much in common. Both had served as Attorney General of their respective states; both were graduates of Harvard Law School and members of the Republican Party. Yet there were key differences best expressed by the notion that they came from different wings of the Republican Party. If Richardson, a former Massachusetts state official, represented the eastern liberal wing of the Republican Party, Weinberger came from the western, conservative wing of the party. Such distinctions were never hard and fast. Still, Weinberger's politics came as much from conservative Ronald Reagan, whom Weinberger had served as Director of Finance, as from liberal Republicans, such as former California Governor and Supreme Court Justice Earl Warren. In 1970 Weinberger had arrived in Washington—part of a wave of California officials who would populate the upper reaches of the federal government in the Nixon and Ford eras—and served as Chairman of the Federal Trade Commission and as Deputy Director and Director of the Office of Management and Budget.[7]

In the history of American social welfare policy, the identity of the Secretary of HEW had not made too much of a difference. At this point in the Department's development, however, the replacement of a liberal by a conservative regime at HEW did matter. It was a sensitive time, with the Department about to implement the SSI program. Richardson looked with favor on Robert Ball and the SSA. Weinberger held no special brief for Ball or the SSI program.

Robert Ball used to argue that the successful launch of Medicare was due to the fact that his superiors in the Department of HEW, many of whom were his former colleagues at the SSA, did not meddle in the operation. The launch of SSI would not take place under such favorable circumstances. The Department would want to know how the SSA went about the sensitive matters of taking over the state welfare rolls and negotiating with the states on how the new program was to be administered.

Then, almost as soon as Richardson left, Robert Ball lost his job as Commissioner of Social Security. President Nixon wanted more control over the sub-cabinet agencies in his second term. He had been forced to keep Ball on during his first term, not only by Richardson's insistence, but also by the general bipartisan respect Ball enjoyed on Capitol Hill. With his final election behind him, Nixon felt free to move against Democratic holdovers like Ball. Richardson passed along word to Ball that he would not be retained by Weinberger. On January 5, 1973, the White House confirmed that Ball would resign as Commissioner.[8] March 30 would be his last day in office, although he had packed up his things long before that. In the interim, Arthur Hess, Ball's Deputy, would be the Acting Commissioner.

Although the SSA operated with a sense of bureaucratic routine that depended on no single individual, Ball was in fact a charismatic leader who not only inspired the rank and file at the agency but also kept the expansive tendencies of his subordinates on one another's territories in check. He also had the best Congressional contacts and best relationship with Congressional leaders of anyone in the agency. His departure at a critical time—he had wanted to stay on through the implementation of SSI—hurt the agency.

It almost amounted to a case of bait and switch. Congress had passed SSI in close consultation with the SSA. Now the main Congressional contact at the SSA was leaving and taking his conceptual plans for SSI with him. It was further proof that SSI was passed in one era and implemented in another. Throughout Washington the architects of the liberal social policies of Nixon's first term were in retreat.[9]

Accommodating the New Program

Robert Ball did his best to get SSI started, but by the beginning of 1973 his agency was already behind. The long delay in Congressional consideration of H.R. 1 had hindered planning efforts. Because of the crush of preparing for Congressional hearings, Ball had left his Deputy, Arthur Hess, in charge of the planning process for what would become Supplemental Security Income. In the absence of firm executive direction, officials in the various SSA bureaus argued over the design of the program.[10]

In a February 1973 message to his employees, Ball called implementing SSI "our greatest task." He realized that completing the task depended on the capabilities of computer technology and in particular on the creation of a computerized Supplemental Security Income Record. This record would be stored in the SSA's main computers, but officials in local offices would be able to use the modern Advanced Records System to query the record and receive a response in thirty seconds or less. Some 450 district offices would be connected to an even newer communications network that would be able to handle 13 million characters of data per day. An SSI System Planning and Development Work Group worked to put the finishing touches on these systems.[11]

In the best management style, the SSA set up long-term and short-term goals and established deadlines for achieving them. For example, all of the data from state and local case records would be put into the federal system by November 1973 for initial payments in January 1974. The master computerized SSI program record would be in place by April 1973 and the new telecommunications system—the one that could handle the 13 million characters—would be ready by November. As technical personnel worked toward these goals, other agency officials pursued political negotiations with the states, with the hope of reaching final decisions by July on two key matters posed by the 1972 SSI legislation. The law permitted the states the right to pay adult welfare recipients in their particular state a higher benefit than the federal benefit specified. This practice was known as state supplementation. A second decision that states needed to make was whether they wanted to administer this supplementation themselves or to entrust the federal government with administering it.[12]

In the midst of this complex planning and Robert Ball's preparations for leaving the agency, the SSA adjusted its internal organization to accommodate the new SSI program. In November 1972 Ball told his Division Heads that the planning office in charge of the adult welfare categories would be made into a permanent program bureau. He emphasized the importance of the "identification and visibility of the new program." Therefore, the Bureau of Supplemental Security Income for the Aged, Blind, and Disabled would join the Bureau of Retirement and Survivors Insurance, the Bureau of Disability Insurance, and the Bureau of Health Insurance as a basic component of the organization.[13]

A new bureau required a new bureaucrat. Ball chose Sumner G. Whittier to head the SSI program. Whittier was a Massachusetts Republican who, like Elliot Richardson, had had experience in the Eisenhower cabinet and in the Massachusetts government. He had served in the state legislature and as the state's Lieutenant Governor from 1953 to 1957. He ran for Governor of Massachusetts on the Republican ticket in 1956 and lost. President Eisenhower then appointed him as the Director of insurance programs at the Veterans Administration (VA), and he became that agency's administrator in 1957. When John F. Kennedy, another Massachusetts politician whose victory over Henry Cabot Lodge for a Senate seat in 1952 had set in motion the events that led to Whittier's loss in the gubernatorial race, became President, Whittier left the VA and went to work for Michigan Blue Shield and later the national office of Easter Seals.[14] He came to the SSA with experience in state government and in social programs but very much as an outsider who operated at a disadvantage in his dealings with the old Social Security hands. And Robert Ball and Elliot Richardson, who had acquiesced in the decision to hire him, would soon be gone, leaving him to fend for himself in an increasingly hostile atmosphere. He was the wrong kind of Republican as far as the Department was concerned and the wrong kind of bureaucrat as far as the SSA was concerned.

Whittier had the delicate task of folding the Bureau of Supplemental Security Income into the SSA's other operating units. For the crucial data processing operation, he would have to depend on the Bureau of Data Processing. This Bureau would design the SSI program computer system and give it the ability to maintain central SSI records, the operating capability to compute SSI payments, and the capacity to instruct the Treasury to issue a check. For disability determinations, he would have to rely on the Bureau of Disability Insurance, which was given almost complete control over that operation. For the interactions between local SSA officials and SSI clients, he would have to put his program in the hands of the Bureau of District Office Operations.

Despite the reliance on computers and high speed phone lines and the other accoutrements of modern technology, local Social Security offices would stand at the very heart of the operation. In order for the system to work, a lot depended on the interviews between local Social Security officials and clients seeking SSI benefits. Before a District Office could key in all the information and send it to the master computer at supersonic speed, a local official needed to gather sensitive data about, for example, a person's financial assets.[15]

These local officials would have more discretion over SSI benefits than they did over traditional Social Security benefits. In the Social Security program, local officials labored under many layers of review. For example, higher-grade employees in the Payment Centers could document the work of the local field office employees as deficient and return it to the local office for further development. Traditionally, no benefits could be authorized in the Social Security program without a second review in a regional payment center. By 1974 the regional Payment Centers handled about a quarter of the new claims and did much of the post-entitlement work on existing accounts. The new SSI program broke this established mold. The agency did not create payment centers for the new program. Instead, claims representatives in local offices received full authority to award claims and to conduct all other business related to the program.

Regulatory Decisions

Administering a welfare program demanded that the SSA make regulatory decisions about matters that simply did not come up under Social Security. The official ideology of the SSA discouraged flat, one-size-fits-all benefits. Retirement benefits varied by the average wage a person had earned during his working lifetime, by his marital status, and by whether or not the federal government considered him disabled. SSI retained some but not all of these distinctions. Couples, for example, received higher benefits than single individuals. Like the established Social Security program, the new SSI program also discouraged flat, one-size-fits-all benefits, but where Social Security emphasized wages, SSI focused on a person's financial resources. In the Social Security program, a person could own the Hope Diamond or the Dallas Cowboys, and those facts would be irrelevant to his Social Security benefits. Social Security paid benefits to the rich and poor alike, without regard to their financial resources. The SSI program imposed a means test on its beneficiaries. For example, an elderly person with no ready cash who owned the Hope Diamond would be expected to sell it, and the proceeds might well disqualify him for SSI benefits.

Under the elaborate rules for SSI, a person had six months to dispose of his nonliquid assets, if those assets were worth more than the $1,500 ($2,250 for a couple) he was allowed to keep. If a person refused to dispose of his resources, he would not be eligible for SSI benefits. If such a person was already receiving benefits, then those benefits would be taken away from him, and he would be expected to pay back the government.[16]

The details of these and other matters needed to be worked out and written down in the form of regulations governing the new SSI program. The value of a home presented a particularly sensitive issue. A person who lived in the Breakers Mansion in Newport, Rhode Island, received his Social Security benefits with no further questions asked. Giving welfare benefits to a person living in a mansion raised the question of why a person with such a valuable asset should be asking the government for money. Congress left the sensitive aspects of the problem to the executive branch. A person's home would not be counted against his asset limit if the home were of "reasonable value," since the Committee wanted "to avoid disincentives to home ownership." Still, the Committee declined to set a reasonable value for a home, preferring to leave that decision to the Secretary of HEW.

States followed many different practices in their approaches to the problem. Thirty-three states and the District of Columbia did not specify a maximum dollar amount for a house. Other states set allowable values that the homes of welfare beneficiaries could not exceed, but they ranged by a factor of ten between Alabama ($2,500) and Hawaii ($25,000). Idaho state authorities ruled that a home "must not substantially exceed the market value of modest homes in the community."

One purpose of SSI was to eliminate such extreme variances in state practices, even though everyone realized that housing costs were much higher on the island of Manhattan than in Manhattan, Kansas. Still, people realized that owning an expensive home raised questions. If someone could afford to maintain an expensive home, that suggested that the person's income and resources were beyond the program's limits. So the SSA set a liberal maximum level for a house at $35,000, a high amount considering that half of the elderly welfare beneficiaries with houses owned homes worth $10,000 or less and only 9 percent of such beneficiaries owned homes valued at more than $25,000. At the same time, the SSA recommended that there be "development tolerances." Couples with a home valued at $30,000 or more, with no mortgage to pay, would be singled out for further investigation to see if they were hiding assets from the government.[17]

That agency decision did not suit the Department of HEW, which circulated the SSA recommendation to its own senior staff. In the era of Caspar Weinberger, this staff included Robert Carleson, the man widely credited with putting Governor Reagan's welfare program in place in California. Nor was Carleson the only one in the Department to recommend caution on SSI. James B. Cardwell, the Comptroller and Assistant Secretary of the Department, who would be named the new Commissioner of Social Security in the fall of 1973, said that the $35,000 limit on houses presented a political problem. "While our intentions are good," he advised Secretary Weinberger, "and we're only trying to treat the aged, blind, and disabled population equitably and reasonably, the only fact that's going to hit the public eye is that we're allowing welfare recipients to own $35,000 houses. I have serious doubts that we can tolerate a $35,000 upper limit." The Secretary approved the idea of further investigation of people with homes at the upper edge of the range but knocked the permissible level of a house in the continental United States down to $25,000.[18]

Many of these initial decisions rested as much on political perception as on social science. For that reason, the SSA spent time considering the appropriate color for an SSI benefit check. Social Security checks were standard issue government green, and the question was whether SSI checks should also be green. If someone got a government check of a different color, officials worried, it "would single out the recipient as someone on 'welfare' and have a demeaning effect." Congress intended that the SSI administrative process would provide "dignity and self-respect" for the individual. Banks were used to cashing Social Security checks—one of the rituals of American life was the parade of elderly people to banks and savings and loans at the beginning of each month to deposit their Social Security checks—and officials wondered if the banks would be comfortable with the new checks. In the end, officials in the Treasury and at the SSA decided that the administrative value of having two different checks for Social Security and SSI, each with a distinctive color, outweighed any advantages of keeping the SSI check green. Plans proceeded on that basis. SSI beneficiaries would get checks in the mail, but they would be gold, not green.[19]

Outreach

At the same time federal officials considered these delicate questions, they also grappled with the politically sensitive problem of outreach. The question concerned how aggressively the government should seek potential beneficiaries for the program. The SSA had a long tradition of going all out to bring people and their benefits together and to encourage people to sign up for all available programs.[20] In the limited time Ball had left, he took steps to find people who might be eligible for SSI. He was particularly interested in letting people on the Social Security rolls with low benefits know about the new program.

His reasons went to the heart of the Social Security ideology. It was a program that related benefits to average or accrued wages, a relationship that many insiders believed to be key to the program's popularity and political longevity. One earned Social Security benefits over a lifetime of employment. Certain aspects of the program, legislated by Congress over the years, worked against this principle, such as the notion that there should be a minimum Social Security benefit, regardless of one's earnings record. The higher the minimum, the more it undermined the relationship between wages and benefits, yet raising the minimum had political appeal for Congressmen anxious to help their poorer constituents.[21]

Passage of SSI changed the terms of the equation. The new program might provide a de facto minimum for Social Security benefits without undermining the relationship between wages and benefits. In the process, it might undercut some of the support to raise the Social Security minimum benefit and as a consequence strengthen the Social Security program (an interesting reversal from the early days of the program when high welfare benefits posed a threat to the survival of the Social Security program). Ball therefore felt it important to contact Social Security beneficiaries and tell them about SSI. He singled out the seven million Social Security beneficiaries with a benefit of less than $150 a month for an individual or $215 for a couple who were not already receiving Old Age Assistance from the states. He had his agency prepare a pamphlet that explained the new program and asked recipients to send back a postcard to Social Security on which they listed basic information that might help determine their eligibility for SSI. The pamphlet explained that the new program was "different from social security. We don't know if you'll be eligible for these supplemental security income payments, but if you have little or no income besides your social security you may be."

Ball sold the outreach measure to his superiors as a way of cutting down on the "very large number of inquiries and interviews" that his agency expected to receive. In the usual prolix style that he used when he was trying to persuade people who did not necessarily share his views, Ball said that the strategy might "result in slightly higher beneficiary rolls at a sooner point than would be the case if one were to rely entirely on general publicity; but I'm not sure of this at all, and in any event, I think it would be true only for the very short run."[22]

The Introduction of a Complicated System of State Supplementation

In the old age insurance program, Social Security officials had the luxury of establishing a new program. In the welfare programs, the states had gotten there first and laid down the basic rules. These rules reflected differences in social provision from state to state and from place to place within a state, not to mention distinctions among types of welfare recipients in a particular state. With the SSI program, Congress hoped to introduce a leveling uniformity that would do away with many of these differences.

Two problems complicated this approach. In the first place, states resisted the change, despite the financial advantages it brought them. In the second place, the change to SSI meant that some beneficiaries might actually be worse off under the new program, a result that neither Congress nor the state governments wanted. Congress engineered the program so that it yielded financial benefits to all states in the form of reduced costs. Each state received a windfall from the new federal SSI benefits. Although Congress also wanted to ensure that every beneficiary gained from the program, it proved difficult to guarantee that result. Because of the many forms that state benefits took and because of the wide differences in benefit levels among states, it turned out that some beneficiaries in as many as thirty-eight states might actually receive less under SSI than under the old state programs. Congress hoped that the states would step in and pay special state benefits—the process known as state supplementation—that would assure that the new law made no beneficiary worse off under SSI than before.

Federal policymakers assumed that high benefit states, such as New York, would opt to pay state supplements in order to maintain the pre-SSI benefit levels. Even with the costs of these supplementary benefits, New York and other high benefit states would still save money in their adult welfare categories as a result of SSI. SSI, after all, gave the states more federal money for each beneficiary than they had received from the old federal-state Aid to the Elderly, Aid to the Blind, and Aid to the Disabled programs. To make sure that the states did the right thing and in aid of system-wide efficiency, Congress sweetened the deal by allowing the federal government to administer the state supplements at no cost to the states.

It did not force this arrangement on the states. They could elect to pay the optional state supplements and, if they chose to supplement, they had the option of administering the supplements themselves at their own expense or having the federal government administer the supplements for free. In theory, electing to supplement and to have the federal government administer the supplement freed a state of additional responsibilities, except to reimburse the federal government for the state money it dispersed to the state's residents. To underscore the unity of federal and state interests, the SSI program would issue one check to each recipient that included the basic federal benefit and the optional state benefit. Only states that administered the supplements themselves would send a separate state check to the recipients.[23]

Always conflict averse in the matter of federal-state relations, Congress took an additional step to make SSI palatable to the states. It issued a guarantee that no state would be in a worse financial condition under SSI than under the old programs, even if the state opted to pay state supplements. Something called a "hold harmless" provision put a cap on state liability for state expenditures under SSI. The conceptual idea involved figuring out how much a state had spent on Aid to the Elderly, Aid to the Blind, and Aid to the Disabled in calendar year 1972. If it turned out that the state spent more than that amount on its state supplements under SSI, then the federal government assumed responsibility for the excess. So if, for example, the state of Minnesota's costs for the adult welfare categories came to $1 million in 1972 and if it spent $2 million on state supplements to SSI in 1974, then the federal government would pay Minnesota $1 million.

This rule had two immediate consequences. In the first place, states had an incentive to make their measured calendar year 1972 expenses be as low as possible. The higher the 1972 expenses, the more costs that the state would have to assume. That in turn heightened the financial stakes in the negotiations between state and federal auditors as they tried to estimate those expenses. In the second place, once the state spent more than the amount of its 1972 expenses on state supplements, the states had an incentive to pay supplements that were as high as possible, since the federal government would pick up the tab. In the case of the hypothetical example from Minnesota, should the state expend $100 million on state supplements, then in theory the state would pay $1 million and the federal government would pay $99 million for those state supplements. In addition, the federal government was on the hook for the cost of the basic benefit that each beneficiary in Minnesota received just as it was in Mississippi or any other state. The state of Minnesota was unlikely to pay benefits that made welfare recipients better off than taxpayers. That suggested a practical limit on the state supplements, yet the possibility for high and potentially uncontrollable federal expenditures still existed.

To protect the interests of the federal treasury, the SSI law contained yet another complex feature known as the "adjusted payment level" (APL) which functioned as a cap on federal payments to the states. The adjusted payment level was a measure of the average benefit the state paid to someone in the adult category in January 1972 who had no other income. In a sense, it measured the limits of the state's generosity in January 1972. The provision meant that a high benefit state could not raise its benefits at federal expense beyond the average benefit level it had previously paid. By way of contrast, a low benefit state might have its benefit level raised because the federal minimum SSI payment exceeded the old state payment level.

Once again, the creation of a new statistical construct changed the incentives involved in the federal-state relationship. The states wanted their hold harmless level that defined their financial responsibility kept low, but they wanted their adjusted payment level that set the federal financial responsibility to be as high as possible. It made for a confusing and counterintuitive arrangement, not to mention one that was fraught with conflict as people tried to determine the proper amounts of the two levels.

Despite its complexity, the new system produced a coherent approach to the matter of state supplementation. The hold harmless level set the lower limit and the adjusted payment level determined the upper limit of federal financial liability. Payments that fell into this zone became known as "protected state payments." If a state wanted to supplement its residents above the adjusted payment level, it would have to pay the extra amount itself. So, as illustrated by Figure 2-1, the federal government paid benefits up to the SSI payment level, states paid the benefits up to the hold harmless level, the federal government paid the benefits up to the adjusted payment level, and states paid benefits beyond that.

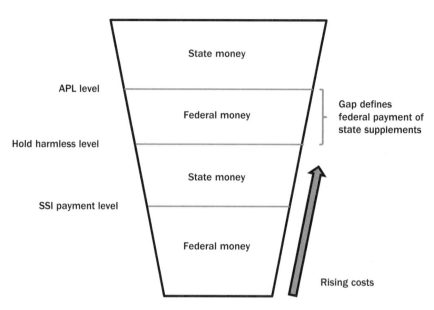

FIGURE 2-1   Federal vs. State Responsibility for Supplemental Payments

Source: Authors' summary.

The system of state supplementation meant that SSI, the new law that sup-posedly made social benefits uniform from state to state, actually held different consequences for different states. A high benefit state, such as New York, might make it to the top of the chart; a low benefit state, such as Mississippi, might only reach the SSI payment level. In a high benefit state, SSI functioned as a federal minimum payment and as an aid to payments above that. In a low benefit state, SSI became a new sort of federal payment program that replaced the old state system. Only in the low benefit state did the program transform welfare in the manner that the creators of SSI envisioned. SSI was a radical welfare reform in Mississippi and only an incremental reform in New York City.

Congressional Reconsideration—Round One

By the summer of 1973, it became clear to policymakers that SSI implementa-tion faced a number of problems. It seemed that every action to simplify the welfare system brought a political reaction. For example, although SSI benefits were intended to replace Food Stamps for the elderly, disabled, and the blind on welfare, Food Stamps had their own legislator defenders who were reluctant to see their program downgraded.[24]

In April 1973 the National Council of State Public Welfare Administrators voted for a one-year delay in the implementation of SSI, with continued state administration in the meantime, even though the National Council favored complete federal financing of both administrative costs and aid payments. The vote divided state and local social welfare administrators. David Swoap, head of the California program and soon to be called to Washington for a top position at HEW, supported the delay. Ellis P. Murphy, the Los Angeles County Welfare Director, warned against attempts by state welfare administrators "to scuttle the first fundamental welfare reform since 1935" for what he described as "purely political" reasons. Governors did not want to give up welfare checks that went out with their signatures.[25]

As political maneuvering took place on the state and local levels, Congress reconsidered some details of the program in late June 1973. The catalysts for action were two serious problems that had already become evident. The first involved the runaway inflation that was just starting to manifest itself. The Consumer Price Index in May 1973 was 5.5 percent higher than in May 1972. At the time the SSI payment levels were set in 1972, they reached roughly the median level of the existing state assistance programs. By the summer of 1973, the contemplated SSI standard fell below the prevailing state levels in one or more categories in thirty-eight of the fifty states. Inflation and state benefit increases between the summer of 1972 and the summer of 1973 accounted for the change. Moreover, if the value of Food Stamps received under the old state programs but slated to be eliminated in SSI was factored in, the SSI payment levels were actually below the corresponding state levels in one or more programs in forty-four states and below all the state programs in forty-one states.[26]

The other problem concerned the optional state supplements. Congress assumed that all the states that were paying higher assistance rates than the SSI payment level would elect to provide optional state supplements. After all, they had already taken action to assist their residents at these levels, and SSI relieved them of the vast bulk of their welfare costs in the adult categories. When Congress examined the situation in June 1973, however, it discovered that many high benefit states had no intention of providing optional state supplements, or if they did, the benefits would still fall below their old payment levels. A study from the period estimated that in the twenty-five highest benefit states, up to 70 percent of converted beneficiaries would in fact suffer a reduction of income due to SSI.[27]

Responding to the first problem about the adequacy of the SSI payment level, the Finance Committee decided to attach an SSI benefit increase to a veto-proof bill extending the debt ceiling. That meant that even before the program went into effect, SSI benefits would rise by $10 a month for individuals and by $15 a month for couples. The Senate Finance Committee took the opportunity of making this revision to suggest other changes in the program, all in a liberalizing direction. A couple with an elderly husband and a younger wife not yet sixty-five would receive an added "essential person" grant.

Responding to the second problem involving the state supplements, Congress added another feature to SSI policy. It ruled that no individual who had been on the state rolls in December 1973 would receive a lower benefit when SSI started in January 1974. States with higher benefit rates for a particular person in a particular situation needed to offer what program administrators called "mandatory state supplements" at the state's expense. The law used June 1973 benefit levels as benchmarks and in that manner created another statistic that would need to be estimated and agreed to between the state and federal governments. As a result of these June 1973 proposals, the SSI program, which was intended to simplify social welfare provision and which had not yet even gone into effect, contained hold harmless levels that protected the states, adjusted payment levels that protected the federal government, and "mandatory state supplements" that protected individual welfare recipients.

Because members of Congress believed that their obligations to protect their constituents and home states against harm outweighed their commitment to a new, more uniform social welfare program, the June 1973 changes in the SSI law met with little or no Congressional opposition. Senator Russell Long cited his concern for the poor "who have been victimized the most by inflation."[28] According to his Committee, the "unanticipated steep rise in the cost of living" and the realization that SSI would create "unintended consequences in payment to current assistance recipients" motivated the changes.[29] Congress, anxious to get out of town for the Fourth of July recess, moved quickly on the measure. Senator Abraham Ribicoff set the tone when he called SSI "a brilliant concept of our chairman (Long) to take the aged, blind and infirm out of poverty and outside of welfare."[30]

Although the changes to SSI passed easily, Congress still needed to make some political concessions to the Nixon administration. In particular, it had to accommodate the executive branch's concerns over the federal budget. For that reason, the conference committee chose July 1974, rather than January 1974, as the date of the benefit increase, so as to limit the impact on spending for fiscal year 1974.[31] Long told his colleagues that he considered "this delay very unfortunate but we were unable to prevail."[32]

The change or correction in the law came in July 1973, just when the SSA was starting to take applications for the new SSI program. It marked another complication in the implementation process, since benefit levels would need to be adjusted to the new levels, new questions about "essential persons" would need to be asked, and new procedures for the mandatory state supplementation would need to be established. Moreover, within months of the program's start, payment levels would have to be adjusted, with the potential for additional beneficiaries to qualify under the higher income thresholds. The changes made it more difficult to disseminate accurate information about the program at a crucial time in the implementation period. The *Chicago Defender*, which reached a minority audience that was a prime target of SSI, reported at the beginning of July 1973 that the new program would provide at least $130 a month for one person and $195 a month for a couple. It failed to mention the new legislation that would raise benefits to higher levels in July 1974.[33]

The Promise of Technology

Meanwhile, the work on the nuts and bolts of implementation continued at the SSA. Along with the shift to a new business model—with SSI caseloads being handled exclusively in field offices—the SSA decided it was vital to build a new computer system for the program. The agency argued that SSI, paid to those in dire financial need, required a quicker turnaround than the typical four-month Social Security claims process. Also, SSA officials believed that to try and fold the unique SSI requirements into the existing Social Security computer system made little sense. Although many SSI beneficiaries would also receive Social Security or what the agency called Title II benefits, only about 5 percent of Social Security beneficiaries were expected to qualify for SSI. Furthermore, SSI involved coordination with the states for the state supplements, requiring the creation of a new system of state data exchanges. Finally, officials noted that the information required for a Social Security claim (earnings history, age, etc.) tended to be information already contained in the SSA's wage databases. By way of contrast, the information needed for SSI (income, resources, and living arrangements) had to be provided by the claimant and then entered into some automated database. For all these reasons, the SSA embarked on a major computer modernization effort as part of the SSI implementation.[34]

On August 14, 1973, the anniversary of President Roosevelt's signing of the Social Security Act, Acting Commissioner Hess sent out a bulletin to his agency. He reported on the progress made in implementing SSI in a way that he hoped would sustain the morale of his employees. "Despite the size and complexity of this enterprise," he wrote, "I am confident that SSA is successfully meeting what is perhaps its greatest challenge." As proof of the SSA's ability to stay on top of the job, Hess reported that the process of converting current recipients from the state to federal rolls was "well along," and the agency fully expected that some

3.3 million people would receive their checks in January. He noted that the conversion, which involved working with multiple state and local agencies, was ahead of schedule, despite the fact that the states still needed to make key decisions about supplementing their benefits.[35] He pointed with pride to an agreement between the SSA and the General Services Administration, which allowed the SSA to acquire its own high speed telecommunications network. The name of the new network—the Social Security Administration Data Acquisition and Response System (SSADARS)—underscored its high-tech nature.

Hess and his colleagues hoped that the new network would mark a significant improvement over the old SSA telecommunications system. The existing system, although sufficient for the Social Security program and its leisurely processing times, depended on outdated teletype technology, with long strings of perforated yellow tape used to transmit information between the Baltimore computer center and local field offices. At peak performance, the system sent about 100 words a minute over the network. Replies, at the same rate, came back hours or days later. The new SSADARS system, designed to accommodate the needs of the SSI program, transmitted at 1,200 words a minute. It handled about 10,000 "queries," or requests for information, each day from the field offices. For the first time, the field offices would have direct access to the master computer databases in Baltimore. To complement this fast communication system, the SSA installed a new IBM System 370 Model 165, with three times the power of its predecessor, to handle the SSI workload. Hess noted that the computer was "the single most important tool" at the agency's disposal in meeting the January 1974 deadline.[36]

Despite the optimistic talk of top-level officials like Hess, people inside the SSA knew that the development of the new computer system was not going to be easy. Midway through the fourteen-month implementation project, Bill Hana, the director of the SSA's computer operations, told his colleagues that he needed three more years to develop the system. In the haste to launch the new program on time, no one wanted to hear his warnings.[37]

Congressional Reconsideration—Round Two

During the final leg of the SSI implementation, another complication arose. Congress contemplated another round of Social Security and SSI benefit increases, which would be the second of the year. The Senate was considering a 7 percent increase, the House an 11 percent increase, in Social Security benefits. On November 7, 1973, the House Ways and Means Committee recommended that SSI recipients receive an increase of $10 a month for individuals and $15 a month for couples in January and a further increase of $6 for individuals and $9 for couples in July.[38]

The great inflation of the seventies had unhinged the policy environment. The House Ways and Means Committee, hardly given to panic, reported that just since the enactment of Social Security legislation in July 1973 that the cost-of-living index had "risen more rapidly than at any time since the post-World War II period." In just three months, the index had risen at a seasonally adjusted annual rate of 10.3 percent, and the food component of the index had risen at a rate of 28.8 percent.[39] Something needed to be done. When the new SSI program began in January 1974, beneficiaries needed to receive higher benefits than they had been promised in the October 1972 and July 1973 legislation.

SSI, it seemed, was passed in the era of postwar prosperity and implemented in a new era of high inflation. As expectations changed, Congress made hasty efforts to adjust the program. All of the fancy hardware would need to be adjusted at a time when the bureaucracy was distracted by many difficult tasks. It put a further stress on an already very complicated and difficult process.

Although SSA officials knew that another SSI benefit increase would put considerable strain on the agency, they felt they had no choice but to acquiesce to the wishes of Congress. The House Ways and Means Committee reported on November 9, 1973, with less than two months until SSI went live, that it wanted to raise the basic SSI benefit for people with no outside income or resources from $130 to $140 for an individual and from $195 to $ 210 on January 1. It amounted to moving up the increase, previously scheduled to go into effect at the beginning of July 1974, to January 1974, with still further changes to take place in July.

The Committee reported that the SSA testified that this change was "administratively feasible."[40] This acquiescence to what the agency knew would be an extremely difficult task reflected the change in leadership in the SSA and Congress. Robert Ball was no longer testifying before Wilbur Mills. Instead, new Social Security Commissioner Cardwell, his feet barely on the ground, and his Deputy, Arthur Hess, appeared before Al Ullman (D-Oregon), who was filling in for an ailing Mills. At that point, nearly the entire cast of characters associated with SSI had changed, including Ball, Elliot Richardson, and Wilbur Mills.

The second SSI law in 1973 engendered more controversy than the first in large part because of a dispute between the high benefit states and lower benefit states. Representative Martha Griffiths (D-Michigan) objected to a provision inserted in the House bill that permitted high benefit states—already at their Adjusted Payment Levels—to pay increased SSI benefits at no additional cost to the state. These states wanted to "pass along" the November increases in the form of higher payments, which could only be accomplished by increasing the state supplements. These states therefore wanted an ad-hoc increase in their APL levels so that the federal government would bear the cost of these increased state supplemental payments.[41]

The chief beneficiaries of this provision, which would cost the federal government $175 million, were California and New York.[42] Not surprisingly, representatives from those states wanted to keep that money in the bill. Bella Abzug, the outspoken Congresswoman from New York, argued, "We are not talking about giving people thousands of dollars but of allowing people an extra $10 per month. It is simple justice."[43] Representative James Corman of California added that the provision was "the only way we can get the $10 increase to these very needy people."[44] On November 15 the Griffiths amendment, despite the eloquence of Abzug, Corman, and others in the New York and California delegations, passed by a vote of 246 to 163.[45]

The House moved quickly, which was critical with the beginning of the program so close at hand. On November 15 it approved the legislation and its two-step rise in both Social Security and SSI benefits.[46] The Senate moved more slowly and added some three dozen amendments to the bill it passed on November 30. These amendments necessitated a conference.[47] It took until December 20, with Congress anxious to adjourn for the year, to work out the details of the bill.

The final version contained some eight provisions related to SSI. The most important was the benefit increase. The legislation also contained a benefit increase for "essential persons" who had been grandfathered into the law earlier in 1973. In most states, beneficiaries would still be allowed to receive Food Stamps, contrary to the provisions in the original 1972 law. Congress also tinkered with the rules that applied to people grandfathered onto the SSI rolls. For example, one already on the state rolls would be allowed as much in resources (assets) under SSI as one was allowed in the old state assistance plan.[48] The most important rule concerned disability benefits under SSI. In particular, for a person to receive SSI benefits because of a disability, that person needed to have been on the state rolls in July 1973 and not added after that in an attempt to take advantage of the more lax state standards.[49]

The situation arose because members of Congress had received reports that New York was manipulating its welfare rolls. Local officials there realized that it was more advantageous for a woman to be on the SSI rolls than on the Aid to Families with Dependent Children (AFDC) rolls, since SSI benefits were much cheaper to the state and higher to the beneficiary than AFDC benefits. As a consequence, the state rushed to transfer women with disabilities from AFDC to SSI in the hope that they might be grandfathered into the new program. The Senate reacted adversely to this maneuver and took steps to stop it in the late-year legislation. Paul G. Simmons, the Deputy State Commissioner of Social Services for Governor Nelson Rockefeller, complained that it was "pretty late" for Congress to be changing the rules, but to no avail.[50] Congress decided that people added after July would have to meet the strict federal disability standards and more importantly for administrators would have to be examined by federal officials to determine if they met the federal disability standard in the SSI law. But it was too late to prevent these latecomers from being part of the conversion, so the SSA was ordered to review their cases no later than the first three months of 1974 and to determine whether they qualified under the federal rules—a completely new and unplanned workload for the agency.

In a further example of policy changes rippling through complex programs with unintended consequences, this provision led to further problems because the federal government could not examine all of the affected people before the March 31, 1974, deadline. That meant that these people would have to be dropped from the SSI rolls and then, perhaps, reinstated later. This would result in additional legislative fixes in 1974.

President Nixon, feeling the effects of the Watergate crisis and preoccupied by the energy crisis, did not sign the 1973 legislation until January 3, 1974—three days *after* the start of the program. Despite his problems with Watergate and the energy crisis, Nixon applauded the new legislation. He remarked, "Protection against inflation for the aged, blind, and disabled is another very major consequence of this new law" for "especially deserving people."[51]

The 1973 changes further complicated an already complex system of state-federal relationships and further undermined the uniformity and simplicity that were the supposed hallmarks of the new SSI program. The experience with two large states—New York and California—illustrates just how far the realities of SSI fell from its ideals.

The Experience in the States—New York

In 1973 the Social Security Administration needed to keep one eye on Congress and the other eye on the states. Each state had to make basic decisions on whether it wanted to pay supplementary benefits and, if so, whether it wanted the state or the federal government to administer those benefits. Each state had to work with the SSA on transferring people from the old state and local rolls to the federal rolls. In a state like New York, these decisions involved lots of people and lots of money.

On August 15, 1973, Governor Nelson Rockefeller, eventually to become Vice President under Gerald Ford, wrote the Department of HEW that New York had opted to contract with the SSA to pay optional and required state supplements. In October Rockefeller announced that the state had decided on what form the optional state supplements would take in New York. The Governor also let HEW know that his state intended to contract with the SSA for federal determination of eligibility for Medicaid for people eligible for SSI, which was yet another option left to the states by the SSI law. The Governor carefully reserved the right to renegotiate the contract for supplemental benefits at the end of six months or by providing 120 days' notice to the federal government.[52]

Rockefeller's letter listed no fewer than ten payment levels for the optional state supplements. Individuals living alone would receive a state supplemental benefit of $76.85, but individuals living with others would get $24.15. The state proposed to pay couples living alone and couples living with others at the respective rates of $99.93 and $50.93. The state then specified three levels of congregate care. The first included family care in a private family home, such as private homes licensed by the state to provide for persons who did not require hospitalization but who were unable to function independently in their homes. The second applied to residential care for the mentally disabled, such as halfway houses, hostels, private proprietary or nonprofit homes for adults that provided protection and care in a supervised environment for people who did not require medical or nursing care but did require the "personalized services of attendants to assure their safety and comfort," and state-approved community residential facilities for the mentally disabled. The third category consisted of residential facilities for the mentally retarded.

The state's plan for its optional supplementation also allowed for geographic variations. It proposed that people in family care who lived in New York City receive $150 and those living in the rest of the state get $95. It suggested that people in residential facilities for the mentally retarded be paid at three different rates, depending on whether they lived in New York City ($509), in the suburban areas around New York City ($485), or in the rest of the state ($170).[53]

In this manner, the state of New York opted to maintain the distinctions of the old welfare system in the new welfare program. The levels of what the state called "congregate care" reflected existing arrangements for the mentally ill and the mentally retarded. Although the SSI law contemplated a uniform rate for the blind, disabled, and the elderly, New York wanted to discriminate within the disabled category to maintain special arrangements for people with mental disabilities. The SSI law contained a basic rate for the entire country. The New York supplement to that law proposed three geographical regions in that state alone. That decision replicated existing geographical divisions in the state. The state dispensed welfare benefits at the local, rather than the state, level and asked the localities to make contributions to those payments. In the new supplemental payments, the local contributions would continue. It seemed appropriate, therefore, that upstate counties did not have to pay as much for the state supplements as did the counties that comprised New York City. State supplements became, in effect, memorials to the old state-federal welfare program.

The SSA received the communication from the state of New York by the middle of October 1973 and had to negotiate any proposed changes and enter into a contractual arrangement with the state in time for the January 1, 1974, start of the program. The schedule left very little time for the federal government to make changes in the New York optional state supplements and very little time to effect the technical adjustments to the system that would ensure that SSI beneficiaries received the right payments in the right amounts by the beginning of January.

Officials in the Bureau of Supplemental Security Income did look at the New York proposal, although they made few changes. The lawyers offered only marginal comments, such as the suggestion that the word "hostel" was archaic and required further elaboration.[54] Those responsible for designing the systems that would be used to pay the benefits gave the proposal closer scrutiny. Renny Di-Pentima, the Social Security official who did a great deal of work with the SSI computer systems, asked pointed questions in an effort to clarify the terms in the proposal. "Which living arrangement applies," he asked, "if the applicant/recipient lives independently, in a rooming house (with or without food service), or hotel and the facility is not listed by the State as a congregate care facility, level I, II, or III?"[55] Other aspects of the New York plan, such as the requirement that a person live in the state for at least a year in order to qualify for state supplements, another throwback to an older welfare tradition, elicited no comments at all from the SSA. Instead, the SSA welcomed the fact that the proposal contained no additional income disregards that would apply to the state supplements but not the basic federal benefits, no liens on a person's house, nor additional provisions that obligated relatives to make contributions to the beneficiary.[56]

On November 13, 1973, the Regional Commissioner of the Social Security Administration and the New York State Commissioner of Social Services signed a twenty-two page agreement that also included eleven pages of supplementary material. The agreement delineated the respective responsibilities of the federal government and the state. It made it clear that the federal government would make eligibility determinations and benefit payments for the state supplementary program. The state had the obligation of providing the SSA with the names and addresses of blind, disabled, and elderly residents who were on the state rolls in December 1973. The agreement went into considerable detail about the audit procedure that would be used to verify the relative financial responsibility of the state and the federal government. It made sure that the state got reimbursed for any expenses it incurred in the SSI program. It contained explicit language about the federal government's liability for erroneous payments. If the state could identify cases where the federal government had made errors, then the federal government would take financial responsibility for those errors. If the federal government could show that the errors came from "erroneous initial payment data" that it had received from the state, then the state would bear the financial responsibility. The agreement also set a provisional level of $160,487,000, subject to audit and subsequent adjustments, as the state's payments for calendar year 1972. This figure in turn set the cap on the state's liability. As for the state's adjusted payment, which measured the federal government's liability for the state supplements, the agreement set the figure at $199.66 for an eligible individual and $304.49 for an eligible couple. These figures, like the ones for the state's 1972 expenditures, were subject to audit and subsequent adjustments.[57]

Although much of the contract language was legal boilerplate, it contained many details that applied only to the state of New York that had been worked out quickly between the state and the federal government. The hurried process put more pressure on the federal government, which faced an inflexible January 1, 1974, deadline, than on the state government. It also necessitated using estimated or provisional figures that would produce disagreements between Albany and Washington almost as soon as the program began.

Even with the agreement in place, the state of New York still felt the need to make provisions for emergency payments. These payments covered contingencies that the state traditionally handled in its welfare programs but were not explicitly included in SSI. The SSI program relied on uniform cash payments. The state of New York wanted to assure the availability of grants, with expenses split between the state and local social service departments, for such things as the replacement of clothing or furniture lost in a fire or other disaster, the repair of heating equipment, and the purchase of clothes and furniture after a person was discharged from a mental hospital. In other words, the old relationship between the client and the caseworker would not vanish under SSI. Faced with an emergency, a client could still go to the local welfare office and, even if on SSI, could still receive assistance for particular purposes.[58]

The Experience in the States—California

California presented the SSA with even more problems than did New York.[59] At the end of September 1973, the Sacramento legislature remained at work on appropriate legislation for SSI supplemental payments. John Burton, the member of the California Assembly whose brother had exerted influence over the 1972 legislation from his seat in the federal Congress, asked the SSA Regional Commissioner in San Francisco to testify on SSI before a committee of the California legislature. Burton referred to the critical situation posed by the need to settle legal questions before the January 1, 1974, implementation date. He raised questions about the federal government's reluctance to administer a state supplemental program that provided "an unlimited exemption" for an applicant's home and that permitted other resource exclusions in excess of the federal limits.[60]

The working plan for the federally administered optional state supplemental payments in California contained no geographic variations but included three living arrangements, a one-year residency requirement, and an additional income disregard to cover the expenses of an ineligible spouse of an SSI recipient. The three living arrangements involved people who lived in a nonmedical room and board facility, people who lived in the household of another, and independent living for people who lived on their own. The state-proposed payment levels involved two different payment levels for people in the first living category, five different payment levels for people in the second living category, and six different payment levels for people in the third living category. The state also wanted to differentiate the payments according to whether a person was aged, blind, or disabled. For example, an aged individual living independently, with no outside resources, would receive a state supplement of $221, but a blind individual in a similar situation would receive $237. A couple in which one person was aged and the other blind who lived independently would be entitled to a supplement of $413. If, however, one member of the couple was blind but the other disabled in some other way, then the state supplement would be reduced to $394.[61]

California state officials signed an agreement with the federal government on December 5, 1973. It contained income exclusions that were not listed in the 1972 law, such as funds for readers to the blind attending a public school or university in the state of California. It set nine different adjusted payment levels, such as one for an aged eligible individual and another for an aged individual and that individual's eligible blind spouse. It included not three but four living arrangements. Unlike the proposed plan, the final agreement added a category for an independent living arrangement without cooking facilities. For example, an aged individual in an independent living arrangement without countable income or resources would receive a state supplement of $235 a month. If the aged individual lived in a place without cooking facilities, then the state supplement would be increased to $260.[62]

Where New York emphasized the need for different payment levels in different geographic areas, the California plan offered advantages to different groups of welfare recipients. In particular, it reflected the special privileges that the blind had acquired in the state—the result of a well-organized movement on behalf of the blind that sought both welfare benefits and other state benefits in aid of independent living.[63] Although these sorts of special privileges were antithetical to the spirit of the federal SSI law, they survived in the state supplementation programs.

Signing an agreement with the state of California did not end the matter of that state's supplemental payments. A lawyer from the San Francisco Neighborhood Legal Assistance Foundation objected to the fact that the agreement did not include a $25 supplement for "the personal and incidental needs of a person receiving care in a medical facility under the Medi-Cal Act," even though the state had provided for such payments in the recently passed Burton-Muscone-Bagley Income Security Act for Aged, Blind, and Disabled Californians. The lawyer argued that a proposed federal regulation barring the federal government from administering such a state supplement was "fatally defective." The lawyer petitioned HEW Secretary Caspar Weinberger, a fellow Californian and San Franciscan, to allow the federal government to administer the state supplement with the $25 payment to people in Medicaid institutions. He wrote on behalf of a coalition that included disability rights activist Ed Roberts, head of the Disabled and Blind Action Committee of California, and the Reverend Ed Peet, the California Legislative Counsel for Older Americans.

The incident illustrated the crosscurrents that affected California politics. The state was home to Governor Ronald Reagan, who entertained thoughts of running for President in 1976 and who had opposed federal control over the adult welfare categories. It also provided a home base for many of the leaders of the disability rights movements who helped get a key disability rights law enacted in 1973 and who would spearhead demonstrations in 1977 to force the federal government to implement the 1973 law.[64]

Although the matter of the state supplement to Californians who lived in Medicaid-funded institutions remained unresolved at the end of 1973, the state and the federal government did manage to execute a modification to the agreement that they signed on December 17, 1973. It required the federal government to indicate either in a separate notice or on the face of SSI checks the fact that "State funds are part of the payment." In this way, the state of California managed to have the federal government administer the state supplement program and save the state government from having to pay those administrative costs while, at the same time, making sure that the recipients of the checks knew that not all of the money in the check came from the federal government. The tradition of allowing the states to take credit for welfare payments remained alive in the state of California.[65]

Trouble related to the California agreement lay just ahead. A federal audit of data used to compute the state's adjusted payment level, completed in early 1974, revealed apparent inaccuracies in the levels used in the agreement signed in December 1973. The estimated levels governed state supplementary payments made between the beginning of January and the end of June 1974. The auditors recommended that revisions be made that would reduce the adjusted payment levels by amounts that varied from $6.28 for the elderly to $1.65 for the blind. These small sums, applied to California's 1974 SSI caseload, produced large consequences. If the recommendations of the auditors were followed, they would save the federal government some $2.5 million per month in California. The dispute created significant friction over what might be called data diplomacy between the state and the federal government from the very beginning of the SSI program.[66]

New York and California, the two largest states situated across the country from one another, did not establish models for other states to follow in their optional state supplements. Each state tackled the problem according to its existing welfare practices. New Jersey, just across the Hudson River from New York City, included five types of living arrangements in its state supplement program. New Jersey honored such distinctions as those living in licensed boarding care, those living alone, those living with an ineligible spouse, those living with one or two other persons, and those living with three or more others. The supplement for individuals living in licensed boarding care was more than twice the supplement of someone living with three or more people.[67]

All in all, the SSI program about to go into operation featured a complicated mix of state supplement configurations. Some states had only mandatory supplements, some only optional ones, and some had both. Texas, a large and consequential state, had neither mandatory nor optional supplements.[68] Some states selected federal administration of the supplements, and others decided to administer the supplements themselves (see Table 2-1).

The Final Push

As the states and the federal government clambered to make final preparations for SSI, local officials began to take an active interest in the new program. No one in New York was certain of how many people, beyond the ones already on the state rolls, would apply for the new program. New York City launched a drive on November 19 to search for more than 200,000 people over the age of sixty-five who might be eligible for SSI; 74,000 people already received aid to the elderly. Mayor John Lindsay awarded a contract to the Community Council of Greater New York to conduct the search. The Council planned to hire a team of eighty people to go canvassing from door to door in such neighborhoods as the Lower East Side, Washington Heights, South Bronx, Coney Island, and the

TABLE 2-1   SSI and State Supplementation, by Category, January 1974

	FEDERAL ADMINISTRATION	STATE ADMINISTRATION
Mandatory and Optional	California, D.C., Hawaii, Iowa, Massachusetts, Michigan, Nevada, New Jersey, New York, Pennsylvania, Rhode Island, Washington, Wisconsin	Alabama, Alaska, Arizona (optional only), Colorado, Connecticut, Idaho, Kentucky, Missouri, Nebraska, New Hampshire, North Carolina, Oklahoma, Oregon, Vermont
Mandatory Only	Arkansas, Delaware, Florida, Georgia, Illinois, Indiana, Kansas, Louisiana, Maine, Maryland, Minnesota, Montana, Ohio, South Carolina, South Dakota, Tennessee, Utah, Wyoming	Mississippi, New Mexico, North Dakota, Virginia, West Virginia

Source: James C. Callison, "Early Experience Under the Supplemental Security Income Program," *Social Security Bulletin* 37, no. 6 (June 1974): 3–11, Table 1.

Rockaways. "We know that many elderly have lived in desperate poverty rather than apply for old age assistance," Lindsay said, adding, "The stigma of applying for welfare should be greatly reduced by the transfer of income assistance to the Social Security Administration."[69]

Even if the stigma were reduced, wrenching changes lay ahead. Under the old program for the elderly, blind, and disabled administered by the city, with federal and state funds, some 20,300 people received special welfare rent checks, made out to them and their landlords. The checks meant that the landlords could be assured of receiving rent money from some of their poorest tenants. The ones who received the special rent checks had histories of not paying their rent or were not considered competent to manage their own affairs. SSI would give these same recipients one check and expect that they would use the proceeds to pay their rents and meet other needs. Landlords naturally worried that this new practice would make it less likely for them to collect rent from their tenants. Jules Sugarman, the city's Human Resources Administrator, urged the landlords to be patient and advised the courts to "look carefully at any eviction proceedings."[70]

Meanwhile in California officials conjectured that as many as 650,000 elderly, disabled, and blind people could be added to the 500,000 already on the rolls. Although welfare rights lawyers accused SSA officials of distributing misleading information about the program and of cutting back on outreach efforts, SSA officials claimed they were "working like mad" on the problem. The director of the SSA's Central Los Angeles office said that he and his agency had met with many groups, including the Red Cross, welfare rights organizations, and senior citizen groups, to spread the word about SSI. "The great unknown is the aged," said

Ralph Abascal, a lawyer with the San Francisco Neighborhood Legal Assistance Foundation. "Everyone knows that a large number of aged have never applied for a variety of reasons, mainly the stigma of welfare and a lack of full awareness of the benefits available."[71]

Lowering Expectations

The Social Security Administration, for its part, did what it could to lower expectations about the new program. Arthur Hess admitted that the original estimate of six million people on SSI had been overstated. He confessed that the government had planned to start searching for eligible elderly, blind, and disabled people in February 1973 but decided to wait. "We could have sold it earlier," Hess said, "It was just that we didn't feel we were prepared to handle the large number of inquiries and potential claims then."[72]

The people in local Social Security offices already felt overburdened. The head of the agency's Bureau of District Office Operations told his local managers that the implementation process had not gone smoothly. The "overall state of readiness to handle the unprecedented and totally new program responsibilities is not quite as adequate as we would like it to be," he said. Preparations had not gone according to schedule, and a great deal still needed to be done. Not all of the state cases had been added to the SSI rolls, in part because of the overwhelming volume of data received from the 1,350 state and local jurisdictions and in part because some of that data was incomplete or contained inaccuracies. In many cases, the SSA would have to move ahead with incomplete data and that was bound to lead to problems. Nor were all of the pieces of sophisticated computer equipment that were supposed to aid the implementation process ready. It was unclear, for example, whether the SSADARS system would be operational by January 1 and how long it would take for all of its "sophisticated facets" to come online.

The Bureau Chief still felt that his agency could bring the implementation off and that gold-colored checks would be going out by the millions in January. There would, however, be glitches. Not everyone would receive a check with the correct amount, and not everyone entitled to a check would actually receive one. The agency would have to muddle through in part by setting priorities and settling for less than perfection. Not all problems could be corrected in a timely manner. Some form of triage would be needed. People with no resources demanded priority over people with resources whose SSI check would be small.[73]

Conclusion

All in all, 1973 turned out not to be an ideal year to implement the Supplemental Security Income program. For one thing, the personnel involved in the process changed from the program's passage to its implementation. The absence of Robert Ball hindered the SSA's performance, if only because he would have been better able to communicate with Congress about emerging problems. The change in command in the Department of HEW meant that the heads of the Department were much less sympathetic to SSI than were their predecessors. The new leadership team at HEW bent over backward to accommodate the states. The House Ways and Means Committee operated for much of the time without the services of its longtime leader. For another thing, objective conditions changed. The energy crisis and the deteriorating economy put pressure on social programs just when time and resources were needed to attend to setting up a complex program. Congress, spurred by the high inflation rate, felt it necessary to pass two major laws related to SSI, even though the program had not yet gone into effect and changes in law complicated the implementation process.

Each of these things complicated the implementation process at a major point of change for America's welfare state from the euphoria of the Great Society to the sober reality of the seventies. It remained to be seen what would happen when the program went live in January 1974.

LAUNCHING THE PROGRAM

Why the Program Began Badly

When Disneyland opened to the public on July 10, 1955, many things went wrong with the rides and other attractions, but no one seemed to mind. Disneyland became a conspicuous success in 1950s America—the perfect blend of high tech and nostalgia. When Supplemental Security Income (SSI) began operations on January 1, 1974, the program also experienced many glitches. In the case of SSI, unlike that of Disneyland, the public reacted to these glitches by proclaiming the program a failure. It seemed to mark the leading edge of a series of failed government ventures that became emblematic of the seventies, just as Disneyland came to represent the great successes of the fifties. The press reinforced the negative perception in the public mind by running a series of articles that reported on SSI's failures. The clear nature of this reporting in 1974 contrasted with the cautious, jargon-ridden bureaucratic memos and Congressional staff reports that had attended the program in 1973.

Just about everything that could go wrong with SSI did. Soon after the program started in January, the Social Security Administration (SSA) began to receive reports about problems. Because the law differed from place to place, the problems varied from state to state. In Florida, for example, 3,300 cases involving Cuban refugees were not paid in January and February. In Pennsylvania the problem was overpayments, and in Oregon and Washington the problem involved payments to households containing an "essential person" as defined by the July 1973 law. The things that went wrong tended to overshadow the basic facts that some 3,560,000 SSI checks went out in the first week of 1974 and 95 to 98 percent of the beneficiaries received their checks promptly.[1]

The 1974 launch of SSI marked a strong contrast with the start of Medicare in 1966. Many people commented on the excellent performance of the SSA in implementing that new program. In October 1966 President Johnson made a special trip to Baltimore to commend the SSA on its good work.[2] Nothing similar happened with SSI. Instead SSA Commissioner James Cardwell reported on problems. Some people who had been on the state welfare rolls did not receive a federal check, and some people who received a check did not get the right amount. "It's still a brand new program. . . . And, for one reason or another, some people won't get their checks," Cardwell said.[3]

Medicare, started in the warmth of July, appeared to symbolize what the federal government could do right. SSI, implemented in the bitter winter of the Watergate scandal and the oil crisis, showed how the government could get ensnarled in red tape and create, rather than solve, problems. Medicare proceeded in an orderly manner. In SSI, the crush of new clients paralyzed the operations of the SSA. The reception rooms of Social Security offices across the country overflowed with disgruntled SSI clients. The SSA had to hire a hundred security guards to deal with the chaos. Medicare helped the elderly, the quintessential worthy group. SSI offered welfare benefits, a much less desirable commodity than medical care, to, among others, forty to fifty thousand drug addicts and alcoholics.[4]

The SSA brought in old administrative hand Jack Futterman, one of Ball's chief lieutenants who had retired at about the same time as Ball, to report on SSI's implementation. Reading the press reports, Futterman observed that SSI was "of no high interest to the media, except to the extent that it may furnish dramatic stories of failures of the Federal bureaucracy."[5] These failures became the things that lingered in the public mind at a time of more general societal failure. The executive branch of the government, which had once performed astounding feats of social engineering, such as launching the Medicare program, could not make the SSI program run efficiently.

Chaos in New York

New York and California, America's media capitals, set the tone for press coverage of the SSI program. In New York City, 1974 began with concerns that local banks would not cash SSI checks. The banks worried that they would lose money if they cashed checks that had been forged or otherwise improperly presented to them.[6] As things turned out, getting banks to cash checks proved to be the least of SSI's problems in New York City.

A week into the new program, the *New York Times* ran a story that read like a dispatch from a battle zone. The paper reported on the thousands of poor people—some of whom were drug addicts—who jammed the city's twenty-three Social Security offices. It described the resulting scenes as "chaos," with large crowds shivering in the cold or waiting in reception areas or drafty corridors for hours, "only to be told to return another day, as complaints mushroomed over missing or misdirected checks or other matters." Some of the clients refused to leave the office when asked to do so, and the employees began to fear for their safety. At the busiest Social Security office in the country, located on Broadway between 51st and 52nd Streets in the heart of midtown, employees refused to open the doors until the security detail had been increased from the usual two security guards to twelve private guards, two city policemen, and two U.S. marshals. In the South Bronx office, employees decided to lock the doors at 11:30 in the morning. By that time they had already admitted 450 people, triple the normal daily capacity and enough to keep the office fully occupied for the day. One of the people waiting in the midtown office, a drug addict, complained that he had not received his check and worried about being evicted from his single-room occupancy apartment. "I'm not angry," he said, "but it's a hassle waiting all day." He described the scene as "wild." "You could have a riot here."[7]

The next day the paper painted a picture of elderly and disabled people subjected to callous treatment at the hands of federal bureaucrats. In the below-freezing weather, SSI applicants waited "in lines that stretched as much as a block outside many of the 23 local Social Security Administration offices and wound through corridors and up staircases." For the most part, it was a good-natured crowd, but the people on line complained of the SSA's lack of preparation for the new program. It was a slap in the face to the SSA's stellar reputation. "It's been a complete change of atmosphere" from the SSA's "well-established program," said Norman Berger, the Assistant District Manager at the South Bronx office.

It jarred SSA employees when an elderly man collapsed on the sidewalk in front of the midtown office or when "a large woman who walks with a cane" was turned away from the local welfare office and referred to the Social Security office and then sat in the reception room with two hundred other people waiting for her name to be called. The woman worried about eviction. Her landlord "keeps knocking on my door," she said. The transition to the new program clearly confused this woman and other clients.[8]

In remedying these situations, the SSA faced the bureaucratic constraints of the federal government. For example, a missing check could not simply be replaced by a local Social Security official canceling it and writing another. Instead, Treasury Department protocol for replacing a missing check needed to be followed, and that involved an investigation that could take six to eight days. For the thousands of people without a check, the delay constituted a real hardship. Patchwork remedies, such as the city issuing an emergency check, required more bureaucratic routines to be followed, more visits to government offices, and more delays.[9]

In New York the local Social Security officials did their best to improvise. Officials took the unorthodox step of chartering buses, with heat and toilets, to park outside of eight of the city's Social Security offices. The buses served as overflow waiting rooms, a clean well-lighted place for SSI clients. One elderly woman reported that she had waited outside of a Social Security office for four hours in order to report that she had not received her check. Like many of her counterparts, she had to come back to the Social Security office the next day, but this time she got to wait in the bus. "I really don't mind very much now that I can sit in the warm bus," she said.[10]

Despite the high volume of criticism in New York and elsewhere, SSI did bring about some changes in the nation's social provision. There was, for example, the case of Gerte Tuckler, a seventy-year-old woman who lived on the Upper West Side of Manhattan. She stood four feet six inches tall and had a compressed spine that made it difficult for her to walk and gave her respiratory problems. The elevator in her building was broken, which made it a trial for her to leave her sixth-floor apartment. She was nonetheless too proud and self-reliant to apply for welfare. "You have to go through a means test," she said, "And I just couldn't go through that." She, like many of her elderly counterparts, regarded welfare as beneath her dignity. SSI, because of its association with Social Security, was free of that taint.[11] Mrs. Etta Postmander, who worked in the Mayor's Bronx Office for the Aged, said that many elderly individuals "won't go near welfare. Welfare's a dirty word. But when Supplemental Security Income came in, it was covered by its tie with Social Security, and that they'll take."[12]

These attitudes helped account in part for the fact that in the first half of 1974 the SSI rolls expanded by 60,000 beneficiaries in New York City. The new program had begun with 180,000 cases transferred from the state rolls and reached 220,000 in July (20,000 had been terminated, mostly because of death). These statistics indicated that the program had worked as intended. Still, it did not operate with the efficiency for which its founders had hoped. In the first three months of 1974, for example, some 7,697 people joined the rolls of the city's home relief program. Many of these people were waiting for SSI benefits and were part of the program's dissatisfied clientele.[13]

Dissatisfaction appeared to be the main emotion surrounding the program during its first months in New York City. The *New York Times* wrote editorials criticizing the new program. When the program began in January, the paper's editorial page noted that the program had turned thousands of aged, disabled, and blind people "into human shuttlecocks," forced to stand outside for hours in the bitter cold and driving snow.[14] In October, the paper noted that SSI, a "brave experiment in guaranteeing a basic minimum income for the needy aged, blind, and disabled" had brought "increased hardship and despair—instead of the promised dignity—to hundreds of thousands in New York and other states." The long lines that remained outside of federal and local offices stemmed from "bureaucratic unpreparedness."[15] At the beginning of 1975, the *New York Times* editorial page described SSI as "a nightmare . . . that condemned the needy to long delays in certification and check issuance." Even more importantly, the program paid benefits that were too low to meet basic needs in the face of a 12 percent increase in living costs. The *Times* hoped that Congress would revise SSI to take into account regional differences in living costs.[16]

The Reaction in New York Builds

Grievances about SSI soon reached the Governor and the legislature in Albany. In the spring of 1974, for example, the Community Service Society of New York and the Community Council of Greater New York reported on hundreds of people who came to them for help after being turned away by the state Department of Social Service and the federal Social Security Administration. They asked the state legislature in Albany for immediate aid for people whose federal checks had been delayed. They requested special funds that would allow SSI beneficiaries to replace lost possessions after a burglary and meet other unexpected contingencies. They asked that SSI beneficiaries be allowed to receive state checks if, because of a bureaucratic snafu, their SSI checks were for less than the amount to which they were entitled.[17]

In New York City, the rising cost of rent forced SSI beneficiaries to move from bad to worse apartments. Under the old system, these people received a special rent supplement from the state. Under the new system, their SSI check was supposed to cover all of their expenses, including food and housing. Among other unintended consequences, it meant that people had more money in their rooms, putting them at greater risk of theft. A city specialist in single-room occupancy said, "Some even carry their money with them into the bathroom." It also meant they had less money for rent. As a result, many moved from what the *Times* described as "small and often squalid quarters in single-room occupancy hotels into smaller and even more squalid quarters in rooming houses."

The single-room occupancy hotels, mostly old apartment houses converted to single-room facilities, had a clientele of welfare recipients, former drug addicts, and former patients in the state mental health hospitals. With the end of the system of separate rent checks, these facilities grew wary of accepting SSI beneficiaries for fear that they would not have enough money to pay the rent. The Hotel Aberdeen on West 32nd Street, for example, charged $180 a month rent, and SSI recipients, who received perhaps $206 a month, could not afford the rent. The Hotel Aberdeen, in common with other facilities of its type, stopped taking SSI beneficiaries. That forced welfare beneficiaries to move to illegal boardinghouses in Brighton Beach and Queens and, in extreme cases, to sleep on the streets or in subway stations.[18]

Part of the problem was that SSI had the misfortune to start at a time of acute economic hardship. The fact that rents were rising in Manhattan had nothing to do with SSI. It did, however, make it more difficult for SSI beneficiaries to make ends meet. A delayed, lost, or reduced check created real hardship. The state and local governments, which had expected that SSI would provide a respite from welfare problems, had to step in with emergency assistance. Governor Wilson announced plans to spend $1.4 million on such aid, including money for possessions lost to burglary or vandalism, and special home relief for people waiting while the federal government determined their eligibility for SSI.[19]

New York State legislators resented the fact that they had to dip into their own coffers to tide over a program that was supposed to save them money. The State Assembly's Committee on Social Services issued a report in the summer of 1974 that criticized SSI for being such a bad deal for New York. According to the report, many New York State residents were actually worse off under the program. It forced them to deal with "the frequently insensitive attitudes of two bureaucracies." In the opinion of the Committee, the program should be scrapped and replaced with a "flexible framework of Federal benefit levels related to interstate variations in the cost of living."[20] In other words, New York was not getting its fair share from the program and wanted more.

Not surprisingly, Social Security employees in New York reacted adversely to their SSI experiences. Commissioner Cardwell visited Social Security offices in Manhattan in January and February and had what he described as a "shocking experience." The Social Security employees were upset: "They didn't like this program, they did not like what they had to do, they did not like the attitude of the beneficiaries, they didn't like the way they were being treated by the local public assistance office and they were up in arms." SSI not only proved to be an unpleasant program to work with, but it also caused the service given to the traditional Social Security clients to decline. It lowered the morale of the entire agency.[21]

The Situation in California

Similar problems occurred in California as in New York. There too there were delays and other bottlenecks at the start of the program. By the middle of January 1974, the number of delayed or missing checks in California topped thirty thousand. According to the regional Social Security commissioner in San Francisco, the problem caught the agency "by surprise. We never expected this problem." In Los Angeles, where 200,000 people were enrolled in the program, police were called to a Social Security office to remove a distraught person who had not received his check. People who tried to phone Social Security to report a missing check found the phone lines jammed. Wanda Sawyer, a Culver City resident whose respiratory problems made it difficult for her to go outside, tried for eight days to reach Social Security by phone. "I got past the recordings only once but they said they were terribly swamped and hung up," she said. SSA officials told Paul Nicholson that his SSI check was missing because of "computer foul-ups" which would be corrected in a few days. Despite this assurance, his check failed to arrive, and his landlord threatened to evict him. Clayton Davis said he was out of food: "I don't have a dime and I can't work. What am I going to do?"[22]

In California, as in New York, the glitches in the SSI system persisted for much of 1974. The case of seventy-four-year-old "Mrs. E. S." illustrated some of the problems in Los Angeles County. When the SSI program began in January, she did not receive a check. For the next seven months, she developed a routine. She waited for her check to arrive, and when it did not, she walked four blocks and took the bus to the district Social Security office. After she had spent an hour or so in the office, her caseworker gave her an order for a loan from Los Angeles County. After another four days, she took two buses to get to the County offices and waited for half a day in that office and received her "emergency" check. A Social Security official explained that each month Social Security workers thought they were putting her data into the computer but somehow the information never got there. "I have no idea why," the manager of the Social Security office in Hollywood said.[23]

Similar problems arose in nearby Orange County. One woman received an SSI check, but she broke her knee and went into a convalescent home. There her Medi-Cal helped pay for her room and board and, by law, the amount of her SSI check was reduced. When she received a full SSI check by mistake, she sent it back and then could not get reinstated after she left the convalescent home. That required her daughter to drive sixty miles from her San Fernando Valley home to the Garden Grove Social Security office each month. The daughter found the Social Security employees "sweet" but harried. Each time they promised her that a check for her mother would arrive the next month, each month between May and September it failed to arrive, and each month the daughter made another sixty-mile trip to the Social Security office.

The Social Security officials said they were swamped with work that came from transferring some seventeen thousand aged, blind, and disabled welfare cases from the hand-kept records of the Orange County welfare rolls to the SSA computers. The fragile process produced many errors. Some people got more money than they were entitled to receive, and some got none at all. Checks went out to the wrong addresses and to people who had died. If someone's living arrangement changed, necessitating that the benefits be recomputed, the computer refused to accept the change. Checks that were returned caused the computer to think that the beneficiary had died and to terminate the account. The failures meant that Orange County had to authorize emergency loans at a cost of some $339,000 to the County. In Anaheim, Social Security officials reported 130 complaints in the first week of January. Although the SSA managed to reduce this number, it still recorded 47 complaints in the first week of August.[24]

By the end of the year, the atmosphere in a Social Security office in south central Los Angeles resembled that in a local welfare office. Welfare did not appear to be improved by its association with Social Security; rather, the process seemed to be operating the other way around. Thirty-eight staff members worked in the Broadway-Vernon office, about half of whom interviewed clients. The number was up from twenty-four at the beginning of the year, with the new hires almost entirely devoted to SSI. "We're suffering," said Jim Hodgson, the Assistant Director of the Huntington Park district office. "We know a lot of people have lost confidence in our goodwill. We've always prided ourselves that at least we always responded immediately to critical situations. We haven't been able to do as well this year."

Long lines and long waits characterized the Broadway-Vernon Social Security Office in Los Angeles. Almost all of the clientele was black. When the sixty-seventh client of the day arrived in the office at 9:30 on a December morning, all of the chairs in the waiting room were occupied, and fifteen people were standing. As the day dragged on, the air, saturated with cigarette smoke, became stifling. One woman in the office on routine Social Security business of replacing a lost Social Security card soon gave up and left. Another woman became so frustrated by her interview with a Social Security employee that she began to cry. "I got so mad in there I almost passed out," she said. "This is my third time here for the same thing," another SSI applicant told a newspaper reporter. "They keep telling me I got the wrong forms or not enough copies."[25]

Patchwork Legislation

In the face of continuing problems in New York, California, and elsewhere, the Social Security Administration received increasing criticism in Congress. Congresswoman Elizabeth Holtzman (D-New York), who represented a district in Brooklyn, requested that the Treasury Department, headed by George Shultz, change its regulations so that SSI beneficiaries could get emergency payments when their checks did not arrive on time.[26] By the end of January 1974, Commissioner Cardwell found it necessary to send what he called a progress report to the members of the House of Representatives. He tried to sound positive. The agency certified some three million payments that totaled $345 million. Cardwell felt compelled to add, however, that the agency had identified some 200,000 problems. For example, 100,000 people did not receive their checks. He nonetheless pointed out that the vast majority of SSI recipients were getting their checks "properly and on time."[27]

Such information provided little to cheer the Congressmen who were hearing from angry constituents. Promises of progress and bringing things under control were undermined at the beginning of each month, as reports surfaced of continuing problems with SSI. In January 1974, some thirty thousand Southern Californians did not receive their checks on time. In February, between ten and twelve thousand people in Northern California did not get their checks because of what the agency described as computer problems. The performance in February was better than the performance in January but not good enough to make the problems go away.[28] Even though James Cardwell claimed that most of the "problems" in January had been corrected, the problems continued.[29]

Congress hesitated to make major changes in SSI or other social programs in 1974. The Democrats, in the majority in Congress, hoped to use the disarray in the Nixon White House, which persisted until Nixon's resignation in August, to improve the party's performance in the 1974 Congressional elections and give the party a leg up for the 1976 presidential election. The Democrats delayed such things as a discussion of national health insurance in the hope that they could do better in 1975 than in 1974. Hence, legislation on SSI and Social Security tended to be of a remedial nature, correcting what were perceived as urgent problems.

Disability legislation served as a case in point. It was technical in nature and did not lead to partisan political debate. In the legislation passed at the very end of 1973, the Senate had inserted a provision that people added to the state disability rolls after July 1973 and then grandfathered on to the SSI rolls be reexamined by the federal government to see if they met the stringent federal disability standards for SSI. It gave the states a three-month grace period before the provision became effective. In the middle of March 1974, the Social Security Administration informed the state of New York that some forty thousand disabled people would be dropped from the rolls at the end of the month.[30]

In response, Congress passed a new law, which the President signed, extending the period until the end of 1974 in which people admitted to the state disability rolls after July could remain on the SSI rolls. At the same time, though, Congress made it clear that if a person were examined by federal authorities (in reality, state authorities acting under contract to the federal government) and found not to be disabled under the federal rules, then that person could be dropped from the SSI rolls.[31]

Even this minor bit of legislation produced some carping in Congress, not about the legislation itself but rather about the SSI program. Dan Rostenkowski (D-Illinois), an emerging power on the House Ways and Means Committee and a future Committee Chairman, noted that the disability problem was "indicative of the myriad of problems that have arisen as a result of the enactment of the supplemental security income—SSI—legislation." Bella Abzug (D-New York) characteristically spoke with less restraint. "I have watched the painfully slow, if not dangerously inept, administration of the SSI program," she said, "Thousands of my constituents—the elderly, the blind, and disabled poor who are least able to bear the hardship resulting from bureaucratic snafus—have suffered needlessly at the hands of this merciless program."[32]

Constituents complained to Congress but also took advantage of the divided nature of American government and brought legal actions in courts. In October 1974, for example, a district court judge in Baltimore ruled that no one could be removed from the SSI rolls without receiving a hearing. It was an application of the procedural rights for welfare clients being applied to SSI. It made it more difficult for the SSA to take people off the rolls once they had, for whatever reason, gotten on them.[33] To cite another example among many, Judge W. Arthur Garrity in Boston ruled on May 14, 1975, that the SSA in Cambridge, Massachusetts, needed to process SSI claims within forty-five days. "We talk about property rights," said the Judge, "but no property right is equal to the right to get food to keep body and soul together, and the right to money to keep a roof over your head. A right of this nature is the most fundamental right."[34]

The closest thing to a major Congressional reform of SSI that occurred in the program's first year concerned cost of living adjustments. Social Security beneficiaries were set to receive automatic cost of living adjustments to their checks at the beginning of July 1975. The law carried no comparable provision for SSI. Instead, SSI benefit increases needed to be legislated by Congress, and a failure to do so meant that the benefit levels would remain steady. In the severely inflationary economy, static benefit levels amounted to falling benefit levels. Furthermore, for dual beneficiaries, the ones receiving a green Social Security check and a gold SSI check, a rise in the Social Security benefit could mean a compensating reduction in the SSI benefit. It seemed logical therefore to implement automatic cost of living adjustments in the SSI program that would work in tandem with the Social Security benefit increases. At the end of May 1974, the Nixon administration advocated such a move.[35]

Congress proved amenable to the measure. Senator Walter Mondale (D-Minnesota) led the effort in the Senate to enact an automatic cost of living adjustment in SSI. Senator Long noted that the measure was supported by the administration and backed by his Committee. In arguing for the amendment, Mondale made an important point about the American welfare state. It was possible that a Social Security benefit increase might increase someone's assets enough so as to make him ineligible for SSI. That fit the general notion that Social Security should predominate over SSI. If a person lost his SSI benefits, however, he also lost his entitlement to Medicaid, since getting one thing, SSI, also brought the other, Medicaid. For many people, Medicaid provided benefits not available through Medicare (the health insurance program that came with Social Security), such as benefits related to long-term care. In the future, Medicaid would become the single most important benefit for many people receiving SSI, illustrating how the lack of a general health insurance program created the need for many backdoor links between social benefits and health insurance. By simultaneously raising Social Security and SSI benefits, that problem could be alleviated, at least in part.[36]

The cost of living adjustment for SSI proved to be one of the last pieces of legislation that President Nixon signed into law. He approved the measure on August 7, only a few days before his resignation. The measure provided that benefit increases in Social Security and Supplemental Security Income would move in tandem, with SSI increased by the same percentage as Social Security and with the increased benefits payable in the same month. Income limitations that cut people off from SSI would also be indexed to the rate of inflation.[37]

When Gerald Ford took over from Nixon, SSI did not constitute a priority for a President who needed to get up to speed on foreign and domestic issues and who had to respond to the problem of inflation. One of his early initiatives was to hold conferences on inflation in which he reached out to experts for their ideas on how to deal with rising prices. SSI came up only tangentially at these conferences. Dr. Louis Gerrard, the Director of West Virginia's program for the aged, noted, for example, that people living on Social Security and SSI had little money left after meeting the rising costs of housing, food, fuel, and medical care. "We're talking about a generation that is very religious," he said, "Over and over we find people who have stopped going to church because they're embarrassed because they can't give a donation."[38]

Patchwork legislation continued, but none of these measures changed the climate of opinion about SSI. One provision provided, for example, that the SSA could reimburse the states for the general assistance loans they made to people who were waiting for their SSI applications to be processed.[39] Neither political party moved to engage the many complaints about SSI in a more comprehensive way.

Congress Examines the Program

Instead, Congress continued to investigate the program, even as horror stories continued to appear in the local media. In San Pedro, south of Los Angeles, people still shuttled between the Social Security and county and local offices to receive their SSI payments, their interim emergency payments, and the cards that entitled them to Medicaid. Some fifteen months after the start of the program, as many as six hundred aged, blind, and disabled people in the San Pedro area were not receiving their SSI checks. The local state assemblyman put two interns to work on a permanent basis trying to sort out the problems. As many as thirty people with complaints about SSI visited the San Pedro Social Security office on a daily basis. In the District of Columbia, mentally ill patients leaving St Elizabeth's Hospital waited for long periods for their SSI checks to arrive. On Long Island, elderly citizens told the local Congressman that their SSI checks did not enable them to make ends meet. Mary Scalice of Deer Park said that after she paid all her bills she was left with one dollar until her next check arrived. Another elderly SSI recipient on Long Island subsisted on oatmeal because she could not afford better.[40]

Democrats in Congress, invigorated by salutary results in the 1974 elections in which the party picked up forty-six seats in the House and four in the Senate, tried to highlight the insensitivity of the foundering Ford administration. The Senate Special Committee on Aging called in Commissioner Cardwell and interrogated him at length about such things as a report that delayed SSI checks had driven two recipients to suicide. Cardwell admitted that the program had "gone the wrong way." Senator Edward Kennedy (D-Massachusetts) brought up the example of Mrs. Maude Morse of Saugus, Massachusetts. The eighty-six-year-old woman received the wrong payment for three months, no payment for the next four months, a retroactive check to cover the missing four months, and no check the following month. "This is no way to be treated by the federal government," said Kennedy.[41] The earlier enthusiasm for the program of Kennedy and his colleagues appeared to be forgotten.

The House Ways and Means Committee conducted more formal and lengthier hearings on SSI in the new style of the post-Watergate Congress. At the beginning of 1975, Mills was deposed as Committee Chairman as part of the more general revolt among the so-called Watergate freshmen against the seniority system and the heavy concentration of power in the Committee. One result was that the Committee, which had always made its crucial decisions as a committee of the whole, established permanent subcommittees.[42] Several of these subcommittees pursued the subject of SSI in the summer of 1975.

The process began in the new Subcommittee on Public Assistance, headed by Richard Fulton (D-Tennessee), the sixth-ranking Democrat on the full committee but the subcommittee Chair. Once again, Cardwell testified. It was a feature of the modern Congress that when things went wrong federal officials had to appear before committee after committee because of the general diffusion of power that had taken place. In his testimony, Cardwell noted that he had appointed an SSI Study Group to look into the SSI program, a sure sign of bureaucratic backpedaling.

The Congressmen attacked Cardwell from all directions. They worried about the thousands of people who had not received checks and about the low benefit levels in the program but also about people who had received overpayments. State and local officials filled the hearing record with case studies of people in need. There was, for example, the lady on Long Island who could manage for three weeks only and after that lived on glasses of milk. At the same time, some states were withholding payments from the SSA because of alleged overpayments in the state supplement program (funded by the state government but administered by the federal government). The Congressmen criticized Social Security for not managing the welfare rolls well and not promptly terminating people who were ineligible. Cardwell could only fall back on the complexity of the program and the policy process. For someone terminated from the rolls, for example, he pointed out that the courts required the SSA to offer the person an additional written notice that afforded the opportunity for a face-to-face hearing with an SSA official. He expressed frustration that SSI represented about 12 percent of the SSA caseload but consumed some 70 percent of the agency's manpower.[43]

Two months later, SSI Bureau Chief Sumner Whittier and Commissioner Cardwell appeared before the House Ways and Means Subcommittee on Oversight, chaired by the eleventh-ranking Democrat on the full committee. Whittier had to explain the complexities of the benefit increases that Congress had legislated in 1973. He noted that a person who received a check for $130 early in January 1974 might receive a check for $150 early in February. The reason was that the January check did not include the benefit increase legislated in December 1973. The February check contained the benefit increase for January and the new regular benefit of $140. Hence, the person would get a check for $140 in

March. "Now, sir, I ask you," said Whittier, "if you are a beneficiary receiving that check with those absolutely mandated-by-law changes, try to comprehend and understand."[44]

Cardwell testified on how the SSI program had "degraded the quality of our service." He said that SSA employees had a special *esprit*, based on their pride in their mission and satisfaction with their work. The work was "so neat and clean" because employees were helping grateful people "obtain an earned right." These same employees observed "the tensions and the difficulties and the animosities . . . that surrounded the administration of public assistance programs at the state level." SSI required that the SSA administer one of those programs. "They were now being asked to deal with clients who in some cases were hostile. They saw their own reputations being downgraded." It all seemed to confirm the conventional SSA wisdom that programs for poor people made poor programs. The agency's productivity suffered, and its morale declined.[45]

The Politics of Benefit Increases

In the midst of this somber reckoning with SSI, the agency prepared to enter the new world of automatic benefit increases. This feature of the programs, legislated in July 1972 for Social Security and August 1974 for SSI, allowed Congress to set benefit levels if it so desired. If Congress failed to act, then increases, based on the consumer price index, took effect automatically, with the first increases showing up in benefit checks on July 1, 1975. At this point not only was the SSI program under siege but the Social Security program, so often applauded in Congress and other centers of power, also faced criticism. A long-range imbalance in the Social Security trust fund had developed, the result of inflation, unemployment, rising disability rates, and lower than expected birthrates. The President sought to link disciplining the Social Security program with the fight against inflation by proposing that the benefit increases be limited to 5 percent. Congress, not predisposed to do the President a favor and with the option of having an 8 percent increase by doing nothing and letting the automatic benefit increases take effect, declined the President's invitation. The era of automatic benefit increases began on schedule in July 1975.[46]

For most SSI recipients, the benefit increases kicked in with the Social Security benefit increases. For some SSI recipients living in high benefit states such as New York and California, the situation was more complicated. Secretary Weinberger, in announcing the benefit hike, noted that people who lived in states that paid state supplements would receive the benefit increase only if their state decided to pass that increase along to recipients. Alternatively, the state had the option of using the increase to defer some of its costs for the state supplements. The matter of the "pass through" went back to the debate over SSI benefit rates in 1973 and to Martha Griffiths's campaign to block the federal government from paying for benefit increases in states that supplemented SSI benefits above the federal levels.[47]

In 1975, therefore, a new debate over SSI began in many of the states across the nation. This one concerned whether the state should appropriate new money for SSI to compensate for inflation and to reflect the automatic benefit increases that would take effect in July. The debate came at a time when local and state governments were strapped for funds in the face of the worst recession of the postwar era. In New York City, for example, officials feared that the city government might be forced into bankruptcy. The city already spent $1 billion of its own funds to help pay some of the costs for its one million welfare beneficiaries.[48]

The state of New York, facing lower tax revenues because of the widespread unemployment and higher costs because of New York City's financial difficulties, did not feel it could afford to pass the benefit increases in SSI to the program's beneficiaries. That decision meant that some 392,159 SSI beneficiaries in New York (240,000 in New York City) would receive the same SSI payment in July 1975 as they had in June. Stephen Berger, Acting Commissioner of Social Services, called the cost of living increase in SSI "illusory," since it would cost $30 million that the state, facing a deficit "of hundreds of millions of dollars," simply did not have at its disposal. Jean Janover, Chairman-elect of the Citizens' Committee on Aging of the Community Council of Greater New York, vowed to bring up the matter when she testified before the House Ways and Means Committee.[49]

In Albany, New York, state legislators held their longest session since 1911, not adjourning until the middle of July. SSI became a contentious political item. Governor Hugh Carey, a Democrat from the city, wanted to appropriate funds that would allow all SSI beneficiaries to receive an 8 percent increase. The lower house granted the Governor's request, but the upper house held up the measure and insisted it be coupled with a provision that would penalize New York City for having so many ineligible people on its welfare rolls. Eventually the upper house relented, and the bill with the 8 percent increase reached the Governor. It would cost an estimated $16 million. The episode demonstrated how SSI, primarily a federal program, became enmeshed in state politics.[50]

The Overpayment Problem

At the federal level, the Ford administration made an effort to assert its presence in the SSI debate by announcing a review of welfare programs in the summer of

1975. The President asked John Veneman, the former Department of Health, Education, and Welfare (HEW) Under Secretary and now counselor to Vice President and former New York Governor Nelson Rockefeller, to lead the effort. It marked the continuation of the campaign to simplify the welfare system by unifying the eligibility rules across programs and by substituting cash for services wherever possible. Caspar Weinberger, who had recently left his position at HEW, wanted to eliminate Food Stamps, AFDC, and SSI and replace them with cash grants based on income. The fact that he put SSI on the list was a measure of its unpopularity.[51]

Some believed that SSI payments were too low, and others countered that people were getting payments that they did not deserve, driving up costs at a time when the federal deficit was soaring. Even before the welfare program review could begin, a new SSI crisis developed that marked yet another adverse event in the long rollout of the program. The Social Security Administration announced in August 1975 that SSI had overpaid its clients $403,798,830.74 in its first year and a half. The agency also implied that the figure was preliminary and could go as high as $1 billion. The errors might be even more costly if one considered the people who received Medicaid benefits but were not in fact entitled to them.

Social Security took refuge behind the law of large numbers. The overpayments only amounted to about 3 percent of the total payments in the program, and they were balanced by $35 million in underpayments. Commissioner Cardwell said that the program was "over the hump" and that the major errors had been cleaned up. He added, in language that was very uncharacteristic of his agency, "Erroneous payments are a fundamental part of any benefit payment system."

The *Washington Star*, the city's afternoon paper that was fast losing revenue to the *Washington Post* of Woodward and Bernstein fame, took the lead in exposing SSI's problems. The paper reported that the cascading series of errors in SSI produced what it described as "severe morale problems" at the SSA. Jay Eisen, a California lawyer helping that state's legislature investigate the program, compared launching SSI with the start of the nation's space program. "You remember those early missiles, the ones that got two or three feet off the pad and crashed? That was SSI," he said.[52]

The exposure of the overpayment problem in the national press exacerbated other problems in SSI. States refused to pay their share of the supplemental payments on the theory that they were being charged for overpayments made by the SSA. More than half of the nation's fifty states withheld money totaling $206 million from the SSA. Deborah Davis, a Pennsylvania official who directed the conversion of the state welfare rolls to the SSI program, said that many of the program's problems could be traced to SSA incompetence. The SSA received accurate figures from the state, but key punch operators working for the SSA entered the wrong numbers into the computer. Someone listed as receiving $60 a month from the state of Pennsylvania would be entered into the system as receiving $600. That in turn generated an overpayment, which led to more errors in an effort to correct the overpayment.

State officials charged that the SSA did not understand the fluid nature of the welfare system and the need to monitor the caseload on a consistent basis. In the California state programs that had preceded SSI, some twelve thousand cases had entered the system each month, but some nine thousand were terminated each month. California officials charged that the SSA failed to take people off the rolls in a timely manner. The only people removed from the rolls were those who had died or those who had come forward to say they were ineligible. As a result, the SSA spent too much of the state's money on the SSI program. The state in turn refused to pay some $80.4 million to the federal government. In New York the situation was similar. The state owed some $81.6 million to the SSA. The state declined to pay up because, as the head of the Department of Social Services said, "Their numbers change as fast as the numbers on the tote board just before the window closes at the race track." He thought that the federal government probably owed the state money rather than the other way around. His counterpart in California told the House Ways and Means Committee, "A well-managed bureaucracy could handle this program. But we do not have a bureaucracy. We have an adhocracy, a whirling collection of ad hoc staffs, teams and projects trying to straighten out ad hoc problems."[53]

State accusations of bad management on the part of the federal government mirrored the allegations that the federal government had once made against the states. Before 1972 the federal role in welfare was to see that the states spent the money they received from Washington wisely. The view from the nation's capitol was that state bureaucrats lacked the professional expertise of their federal counterparts and took haphazard actions that resulted in a patchwork of state and local programs. Now state welfare workers condemned their former overseers in the federal government for similarly slapdash practices. These incidents marked a major moment of reconsideration in America's welfare state, away from the logic of creating nationally uniform, federally administered programs and back toward the use of state discretion to match social policy to local conditions.

The overpayment problem once again invited the participation of the courts. Legal service advocates who helped poor people negotiate the legal system counseled that people cut off from the rolls should get a lawyer. "I used to think people did just as well representing themselves before the Social Security Appeals Board," said Adele Blong of the Center on Social Welfare Policy and Law in New York City. "But now I see that unless they have professional help they might not get what the law promises."[54]

If legal representation at hearings helped rectify individual cases, legal service lawyers found that a better way to achieve mass results was to bring a class action suit against the federal government. One such case involved a group of SSI recipients from California, including Catherine Cardinale of Santa Cruz. In January 1974 she received an SSI check for $195. She told the local Social Security office that it was probably more than the law entitled her to get, but the local SSA officials said that if she received it it must be for the proper amount. Her checks continued for the same amount in February and March. In April her check fell to $98.80, and Social Security officials told her that the reduced amount was to recoup the overpayments she had gotten in the first three months of the year. She sued the federal government and became part of the class action suit that reached the federal courts. The government argued that the errors resulted from "clerical or mechanical error" and thus did not require the agency to notify the recipient in advance and give her a chance to appeal. U.S. District Court Chief Judge William B. Jones disagreed. He ruled in August 1975 that the government could not stop SSI payments or reduce payments without giving the beneficiary prior written notice and "some opportunity to contest a determination," no matter if the overpayment was the result of human or machine error. The Judge ordered HEW to send notices to all 4.5 million SSI recipients informing them of their procedural rights in order to prevent what he called a "grievous loss."[55]

As the courts worried about people being cut off from benefits, President Ford objected to the high costs of the overpayments and the mismanagement that such payments implied. When he read newspaper accounts of the $403,798,830.74 in overpayments, he ordered Office of Management and Budget Director James T. Lynn to make sure it did not happen again. He asked Lynn to conduct a new review of the program, working in tandem with the Department of HEW and the SSA.[56]

Ironically, at the same time that the President was trying to clamp down on overpayments, other political officials were calling attention to the thousands of people who were eligible for the program but had not claimed their benefits. A freeholder in Hackensack, New Jersey, announced that payments were awaiting the blind and disabled, if they would only apply for them. The Red Cross in that state launched a campaign to tell people about the new program. In Washington, D.C., officials estimated that some six thousand people—not on the District's welfare rolls in 1973 and hence not grandfathered into the new program—qualified for SSI payments, but only about twelve hundred of those people had applied. An Illinois State Senator noted that there were thousands of people eligible for SSI who had not claimed it.[57]

The Balance Sheet

In 1975 it was difficult to balance the pluses and minuses of the SSI program. As one could read in the popular press, much had gone wrong with the SSI implementation. Some of the problems stemmed from the complexity of the law, with its mind-numbing combination of a basic federal benefit, optional state supplements, mandatory state supplements, benefit raises legislated in 1973, automatic benefit increases created in 1974, and hold harmless provisions. Even if one put aside the unpredictable way in which these features interacted with one another, each feature created its own administrative problems. The system of state supplementation, for example, threatened to replicate all the inefficiencies and complications of the system that SSI replaced. Every state with a supplement wanted payment levels that varied by conditions that differed from state to state. As a practical matter, these variations had to be translated into policy and procedure for SSA field employees, and each state supplementation program required a different computer program.[58]

Adding to these basic problems, the SSA's traditional organizational structures did not blend well with the innovative administrative procedures and new technology demanded by SSI. The SSI program, designed to be an integrated whole, had to accommodate a fragmented bureaucratic structure. As one insider noted: "The new SSI Bureau Director, Sumner G. Whittier, and his deputy, Paul Cotton, found themselves responsible and accountable for implementing the program, but controlled virtually none of the resources needed to do so."[59]

As political scientist Martha Derthick has noted, SSI put great stress on the SSA. Taking on an entirely new program meant that the SSA had to hire more staff and open new offices. Between 1972 and 1977, staffing levels increased by 53 percent, and the number of field offices expanded from 926 to 1,318.[60]

This large cadre of new, inexperienced personnel found itself hard-pressed to cope with the demands of SSI. Veteran employees also faced new challenges as they now had to master SSI policy and procedures as well as those in the traditional Social Security program. This double demand created such a strain that the SSA eventually required its Claims Representatives to specialize in either Social Security or SSI.

Everyone conceded that successful implementation of SSI depended on the new computer systems that stood at the heart of the new program's operating system. Nearly all of the problems that arose in the implementation process affected the design and performance of these systems and created major difficulties when the program went into operation. Legislated in 1972, implemented in 1973, and launched in 1974, the SSI program incorporated improvements in computer technology that had arisen since the implementation of retirement and survivors benefits in 1940, disability benefits in 1957, and Medicare benefits in 1966. With the experience in the use of computer technology gained from these previous programs, the SSA felt it could administer the adult welfare categories more efficiently and effectively than the states.

Problems with the new computer system, the new telecommunications network, and the system of automated data exchanges with the states arose almost immediately. The conversion of the three million existing state beneficiaries from the old state to the new federal rolls presented the first difficulties. The 1,350 state and local agencies involved in administering the old system used a bewildering array of technologies to maintain their records. They ranged from old handwritten ledgers, to typed sheets of paper, to primitive computer tapes, to more modern computer disks whose formats were often incompatible with the federal system. To get the information from one system to the other necessitated a great deal of data entry through manual keying—someone looking at a paper record and typing the information into the federal computers. As in any such process, many errors occurred.

Indeed, at the end of the process the states managed to transfer upward of 200,000 people onto the SSI rolls without even giving the federal government the underlying data on their entitlement, including such basic data as their living arrangement or payment amount and other income. To cope with these cases, the SSA adopted a policy of filling the missing data gaps with whatever assumptions were most advantageous to the beneficiary.[61] These assumptions would subsequently have to be checked and corrected, and in the meantime both overpayments and underpayments occurred.

Along with this generic conversion problem, the SSA faced another difficulty. Some states turned over their state records to the SSA early in the fourteen-month conversion period. This seemingly helpful act created unanticipated problems. If a state turned over its records in, say, May 1973, there was a high likelihood that some of the recipients' circumstances would change between then and January 1974. Such changes often meant that the January 1974 check was issued in the wrong amount for such people. Worse yet, the states lobbied HEW to adopt a policy of allowing them to transfer cases to the SSI rolls without reviewing them to make sure that everyone being transferred was still an eligible state recipient— passing off the inevitable errors onto the feds.

While some states created unanticipated problems by turning over their records early, others produced similar results by delaying their state supplement plans until the very end of the implementation period. New York did not even offer its proposal until October 1973, and the state and federal authorities completed their negotiations November 13. California did not sign its contract with the federal government until December 5, 1973. Privately, SSA officials suspected that these states, and others, were intentionally dragging their feet, hoping to use the resulting time-pressure to force concessions from the federal government.

Last-minute legislative changes aggravated the problems. Every change in the law, even the most minor ones, required the SSA to rewrite hundreds, if not thousands, of lines of computer code. When Congress decided in July 1973 to change the program by adding mandatory state supplements and payments for "essential persons," this decision forced the SSA to rewrite forty of the eighty computer programs it had been developing for the system. Debugging changes in computer code consumed a great deal of time, especially with seventies-era software tools.

When SSI began on January 1, 1974, the telecommunications network had never been tested or debugged, nor was it even fully installed. The computer software to handle changes to recipient records was not finished, and the State Data Exchange system had not yet been tried. The agency had never performed pilot tests on the process of taking an SSI claim in a field office and transmitting information back and forth between Baltimore and the field in real time. As Derthick observed, the launch of SSI in January 1974 "was the trial run for a brand-new computer system, and it was a trial for which the SSA was not ready."[62]

Although a lack of readiness was evident in many areas, some areas stand out. The SSA began taking new claims for SSI benefits in July 1973, but the programmers did not have time to build any management information capabilities into the new system, so keeping track of pending cases was done manually. Worse yet, the system was programmed to accept new claims but had no capability to edit and correct mistakes made in inputting data into the system, so cases with errors were kicked out of the system. Cases rejected by the automated system often were put at the bottom of the stack and deferred in order to process new business. In May 1974 the agency discovered through a manual audit that of the one million new claims taken between July 1973 and January 1974, only 300,000 or so had been processed. The rest were, as Derthick reported, "piled up in all available storage spaces, while the field office staff struggled with the day-to-day interviewing work load, much of which stemmed from these unprocessed and unprocessible claims."[63]

Because the new SSI system was not fully integrated with the existing Title II system, employees had no immediate way to verify the accuracy of Social Security numbers or quickly assign new ones. The staff began assigning "dummy numbers," especially in conversion cases where the payment was being held up because of some error in the state data. Because 475,000 dummy numbers were assigned in this way, some beneficiaries received two SSI checks every month, one for their actual Social Security number (SSN) and one for their dummy number. One SSA employee working in California reported that he conducted a redetermination on a recipient in the summer of 1977 and discovered that the computer system had been issuing the man two SSI checks every month since January 1974.[64]

The SSA estimated that the new telecommunications network might have to handle as many as ten thousand queries per day. During the first few days of the program, the daily query rate ranged between fifty and sixty thousand. By the end of that first week the network crashed and simply stopped working. The SSA applied emergency patches to the system, allowing the telecom network to come back up, but only by "spooling" data to offline storage. In the language of the program managers, the system no longer supported real-time inquiries. While the system was down, inquiries and claims traffic backed up in the local offices; as soon as the computer system was restored, this flood of backlogged transactions would crash it again. In desperation, SSA officials ordered employees in field offices to avoid multiple inquiries for status on pending cases. As a result, the SSA often sent claimants home without any information, asking them to come back again the next day when the computer might give them some answers. In many cases, answers took a long time to arrive.[65]

This combination of poor policy planning, last-minute legislative meddling, and overreliance on not-yet-ready computer systems caused the SSA to stumble badly at the start of the SSI program. One employee observed, "SSA had a record of just taking on challenge after challenge after challenge and meeting it. . . . SSI put an enormous chink in our armor. It was the first time we were knocked back on the ropes."[66]

Despite these problems, the SSA managed to transform the state rolls into federal rolls. In the first week of 1974, the federal government issued checks to more than three million new SSI recipients, a real administrative accomplishment.[67] To be precise, in January 1974 the SSI program paid 2,955,959 individuals more than $260,159,000 in federal SSI or federally administered state supplements (another 259,763 received state supplements only). The federal SSI payments averaged $88.01, although this figure obscured some significant differences by beneficiary category. The average SSI payment for aged beneficiaries was $74.54; for the disabled it was $105.04, and for the blind $106.05.[68] For the first time in American history, the federal government had assumed responsibility for the basic income support of the nation's impoverished aged, blind, and disabled.

Nearly every state benefited financially from the introduction of the SSI program. For example, the average state cost for an aged beneficiary in Louisiana in October 1973 was $73.47; under SSI, the cost to the state declined to $20.43. New York's average cost for an aged beneficiary went from $108.32 to $74.75.[69] The program also represented a good financial deal for the beneficiaries who lived in those states. In twenty-six states, the average federal payment was higher than the old state payment for the aged and the blind; and in twenty-nine states, the new federal payment exceeded the old state payment for the disabled. When one included the state supplements, the average SSI beneficiary received more in January 1974 than in the previous month in all of the thirty-one states in which the federal government administered the state supplement.[70]

Conclusion

The launch of the SSI program tarnished the SSA's reputation. In August 1975 President Ford singled out the SSI program for remedial attention. At about the same time the *Washington Post* offered a scathing review of the program. It head-lined the piece, "The SSI Fiasco." The *Post* argued that the SSA had oversold the potential of computers to administer social programs, exhibiting "a euphoric ten-dency" to believe "that a computer can do anything." What SSI demonstrated was the computer's capacity "to make mistakes—particularly when it is programmed by people who are none too clear about the rules, which change from time to time." Even as the President worked to cut the cost of social welfare programs, SSA computers "were hard at work writing incorrect and overstated checks." Indeed, the failure of SSI jeopardized the expansion of the American welfare state. Unless the administration fixed SSI, "it will lose the public confidence and support that are crucial to further progress." Programs of the complexity of SSI should be started "only after extensive and careful preliminary testing on a small scale." Be-fore there could be an expansion of the national welfare system, the SSA needed "to show Americans that it is competent to make the system work."[71]

It fell to Arthur Hess, now the Acting Deputy Commissioner at the SSA, to re-spond to this attack. He admitted that there had been severe problems, but that the SSI program did not deserve to be called a fiasco. He again fell back on the law of large numbers. "The fact remains," he wrote, that the program "is putting $400 million a month (almost all of it through correct payments) into the hands of 4.2 million of our very neediest aged, blind, and disabled people." Those figures amounted to one million more people and $200 million more than under the old federal-state system. The agency could not claim perfection, but Hess, like Com-missioner Cardwell, felt that the problems had been identified and that the agency had turned the corner. Future improvements lay in making the system simpler and not encouraging the state-by-state variations that contributed to the system's complexity.[72]

If SSI was supposed to be the poster child for a new automated style of federal social welfare, it failed its initial test. The machines did not operate as advertised, perhaps because of the inherent limitations of the machines but also because of the interaction between humans and machines that reinforced the truism learned by generations of mathematics students: garbage in, garbage out. The errors displeased conservatives, who regarded them as exemplifying how the overambitious reach of the federal government led to waste and corruption. The same errors disturbed liberals, who worried that people in need were not receiving enough government help. Federal officials in the SSA lamented their inability to make the system run smoothly. State welfare officials regretted that federal mistakes caused people to fall back on the states at a time of severe fiscal stringency. Furthermore, federal overpayments led the federal government to overbill the state governments for supplemental payments, leading to friction between the federal government and the states in a program that was supposed to improve federal-state relations. Judges, for their part, saw SSI as undercutting the procedural rights of welfare beneficiaries. The President regarded SSI as a costly program that would make his administration look bad and further complicate the welfare mess. Congressmen heard about SSI almost exclusively as a problem in a context that required their offices to intervene to correct bureaucratic problems.

The solution of 1972 had become the problem of 1975. A program created in an era of optimism about the federal government's administrative capacity and about the future growth of the economy debuted in January 1974 at a time of major domestic disruption. A program intended to federalize welfare maintained the imprint of the federal-state system. SSI did not appear to be the model for future welfare reform but, rather, another in a series of failed programs that required a substantial overhaul. Just about everything that could go wrong with SSI did, and unlike Disneyland the program never really recovered from its troubled debut.

THE EMERGENCE OF A DISABILITY PROGRAM

How the Program's Fundamental Identity Changed

In what had become something of a ritual, Social Security officials appeared before a House Ways and Means Subcommittee in the fall of 1976 to talk about the Supplemental Security Income (SSI) program. The Regional Commissioner for New York testified about how his agency had issued leaflets in Yiddish, Spanish, Chinese, Russian, Polish, Italian, German, Greek, and French informing the public about the program. He also touted the television ads advertising the program. One featured boxing champion Muhammad Ali and aired on all six New York stations. Another starred Felix Millan, the All Star second baseman for the New York Mets, who spoke in Spanish. The Regional Commissioner claimed that these various appeals had resulted in more people finding out about the program and signing up for it.[1]

Commissioner James Cardwell gave an upbeat assessment of the program in his subcommittee testimony. "Significant progress has been made and is continuing to be made," he said. The program had achieved its "full operating status," with reduced backlogs, a quicker claims-taking process, and improved computer systems. "I also believe," he added, "we are bringing under control, slowly but surely, the problem of inaccurate payment rates." The Social Security Administration (SSA) had, in effect, tamed SSI with the result that workloads were leveling off and the growth of the caseload was slowing down.[2]

One could plausibly argue that the problems that afflicted SSI in 1974 and 1975 reflected the considerable difficulties of starting up the program. The processes involved in moving beneficiaries from the old state and local system to the new federal system invited errors. It took time to bring the process under control, but the conversion of the records was a one-time event that occurred only at the start of the program. Once beyond this momentous task, the program operated more efficiently.

At the same time, first impressions meant a great deal, and SSI made a bad first impression. It failed to become a model for the conduct of American social policy. In this regard, it stood in stark contrast to the older and more established Social Security program. Social Security had provided a template for the expansion of the American welfare state. Once the old age and survivors insurance program was successfully implemented, it became the model for disability insurance and health insurance. Policymakers realized that they could expand the American welfare state by portraying new programs as incremental expansions of Social Security.[3] Few people regarded SSI as a similar building block.

By 1976 policymakers had gained enough perspective on SSI to draw lessons from its difficult period of implementation. The Supplemental Security Income Study Group, appointed by the commissioner in 1975 and composed of experts in public administration, concluded that programs administered at the federal level could not be totally responsive to individual needs. It decided that needs-based programs were complex and that complexity created difficulties in administering such programs.[4] The group recommended that the objectives of such programs be limited, and it observed that new programs cost money and should not be sold to Congress on the basis of their ability to save money.[5]

When policymakers examined the data from the first years of SSI, they made an even more fundamental discovery. As Commissioner Cardwell told the Ways and Means Subcommittee in 1976, "Within the caseload of almost 4.3 million recipients there has been a shift where almost as many disabled people as aged people now receive SSI benefits."[6]

The trend was unmistakable and for the most part unanticipated. When the program started in 1974, most people gained eligibility through old age. The discussion about the program centered on serving the aged population. The initial estimates of the program's growth posited that by the end of 1975 there would be almost two aged beneficiaries for every disabled beneficiary.[7] The prediction was that by June 1975 there would be 3.8 million aged and 1.8 million people with disabilities served by the program. Experts expected the number of people with disabilities on SSI would grow but that the number of aged people on SSI would grow even more. The disability number turned out to be accurate, but the predicted number of aged people was seriously off.

Far fewer aged people joined the SSI rolls than predicted, perhaps because of the Social Security benefit increases legislated by Congress in 1973 and anticipation of the cost of living increase that would show up in the July 1975 Social Security checks. In the SSI program's first four and a half years, the number of aged people on the rolls remained relatively stable, but the number of disabled people increased by some 68 percent. Hence when the program began in January 1974 the disabled accounted for 40 percent of the caseload, but in June 1978 they made up 51 percent of the caseload. In the future the disparities between the two groups would only grow wider.

From the beginning, the program picked up more applications from people applying on the basis of disability than on the basis of old age. In 1974, for example, about 60 percent of all applications for SSI were made on the basis of disability or blindness. By 1978 four out of five applications came from people who claimed to be disabled, and two out of three people were admitted to the rolls on the basis of disability.

The composition of the caseload held important public policy consequences. For one thing, disability benefits were more costly than old age benefits. Although the rules for both groups were essentially the same, people with disabilities tended to be poorer and to have fewer resources at their disposal than elderly people. Far fewer of the disabled received Social Security benefits than did the elderly, for example, because fewer people with disabilities, including children, had work histories. As a result, people with disabilities tended to receive higher SSI benefits than did elderly people on SSI. By definition, people with disabilities were younger than elderly beneficiaries. That meant that, barring recovery or entering the labor force, they would receive benefits over a longer period of time and generate greater costs than did the elderly. It also cost more for the SSA to process a disability claim than an old age claim, since the disability claims process involved assembling more evidence, a far greater chance of appeal, and the frequent use of expensive medical expertise. Once on the program rolls, both groups received entitlement to Medicaid, but many of the elderly also had access to Medicare, which paid many of their expenses for acute medical care, and many of the people with disabilities had impairments that led to frequent encounters with the health care system.

The fact that benefit levels varied by states, when one factored in the state supplements, further complicated the situation. The prevalence of disabled beneficiaries tended to be greater in the high benefit than in the low benefit states. As a rule, the high benefit states had both larger general populations and higher SSI caseloads than the low benefit states, helping to account for the emerging majority of disabled beneficiaries on the SSI rolls. A snapshot of the SSI caseload in June 1978 revealed that the New York caseload contained 226,388 people with disabilities, 3,970 blind people, and 151,657 aged people. In Alabama, by way of contrast, the aged outnumbered the disabled by some 35,473 people.[8]

These disparities added to the diversity of a supposedly uniform system. Not only did benefit levels differ by state but so did the very nature of the caseload.

Some states ran an old age program. Others operated a disability program, with the general trend of the entire SSI system moving toward a disability program.

The trend toward becoming a disability program had important implications for the future of the program. No longer could it be viewed, as its name implied, as supplemental Social Security, benign payments to elderly citizens who had worked all their lives but could not make ends meet on Social Security alone. It now became swept up in a different policy conversation that concerned the growth of disability benefits more generally. Policymakers had originally discussed SSI in the context of welfare reform. Now it became part of what might be described as disability reform.

The disability reform discussion of the seventies culminated in major legislation in 1980. Throughout this discussion in Congress and in other centers of power, people focused not on SSI alone but rather on all disability programs, and in particular on Social Security Disability Insurance (SSDI). Hence the Senate Finance Committee staff reported in April 1977 that "the phenomenon of persistent growth in disability as a basis for benefits is not unique to SSI." It pointed to the similar rise in the Social Security disability rolls. At the end of 1972, at just about the time Congress was legislating SSI, the Social Security disability rolls contained 3.1 million disability insurance beneficiaries. By the end of 1974, SSI's first year of operation, the number of disability insurance beneficiaries had grown to 3.7 million, and it reached 4.6 million in October 1976. The simultaneous emergence of SSI as a disability program made the problem seem that much more ominous. During fiscal year 1973, for example, a total of $6.7 billion went to recipients of Aid to the Permanently and Totally Disabled and disabled Social Security beneficiaries. Policymakers expected this figure (now composed of the new SSI program and the SSDI program) to reach $12.5 billion in fiscal year 1976.[9]

Such statistics led to a search for the reasons that the disability rolls had grown and to fashioning legislative remedies to end the rise. The growth of the disability rolls was counterintuitive in the same sense as was the rise of the Aid to Families with Dependent Children (AFDC) welfare rolls in the sixties. The AFDC rolls rose during a time of economic prosperity. The disability rolls increased at a time when people were living longer and, at least on the surface, healthier lives. Why, then, should the incidence of disability be increasing? One possible explanation centered on the trade-off between morbidity and mortality. As people lived longer lives, they faced the increased risk of suffering the infirmities of old age. A rise in life expectancy did not therefore signal a decrease in disability. Yet such general trends did not account for declines in labor force participation among working age men. Between 1969 and 1978, for example, the number of men between the ages of forty-five and sixty-four who reported themselves unable to work increased from 72 per thousand to 101 per thousand. Economists pointed to other factors as a cause, such as a decline in job opportunities for older workers. During the seventies, the labor force experienced not only the shock of the economic downturns with their accompanying unemployment but also a major effort to accommodate younger workers in the baby boom cohort and female workers of all ages. The newer, fresher, younger, and less expensive workers might have shouldered the older workers aside. These older workers sought escapes from the labor force in the form of disability benefits, which offered the replacement of a significant part of their wages.[10]

If such an explanation were true, it explained only part of the puzzle. How, after all, did the older workers get past the disability certification process and enter the rolls? This aspect of the problem led policymakers to examine the disability determination process more closely. They discovered a complex system that was overburdened with the tasks of handling increased SSDI claims and, after July 1973, with SSI claims as well. In 1974, for example, 1,396,500 people applied for SSI on the basis of disability or blindness, 1.2 million people filed applications for disability insurance, and a half a million people applied to the black lung program, which was yet another disability program that Congress directed the SSA to administer. The increased caseloads overwhelmed state disability determination offices. In the words of the Senate Finance Committee, the states responded by "speeding up the processing of the cases," and the SSA reacted by reviewing fewer state decisions. The result was "a decline in the quality of decisions which were made." By decline in quality, the Committee meant that too many people who did not meet the stringent standards of the law were nonetheless finding their way on the rolls.[11]

The work that the state disability determination offices did on both SSI and SSDI claims represented only the first stage of a multifaceted process. If a person was denied at the state level, he could pursue his case through various levels of appeal. The denied applicant could ask for a reconsideration and if still denied could take his case in front of an Administrative Law Judge (ALJ). These judges reversed many of the states' decisions. Nor did that exhaust the avenues of appeal. A person denied by an administrative law judge could take his case to the Appeals Council of the Social Security Administration and, if still not satisfied, to a federal district court. More than one out of every five people admitted to the disability rolls employed the appeals process to get there.[12]

The existence of such a large and sprawling system motivated Congress to search for the missing link. Perhaps some states were not as tough with disability applicants as they should be. Perhaps ALJs should be encouraged to follow the law more closely. The general feeling was that the disability programs were, as the Senate Finance Committee staff put it, "in a general state of disarray." Studies made by the General Accounting Office (GAO) showed that the same case sent to ten different state agencies produced a "significant lack of agreement" among the states. Disability appeared to be a subjective benefit category that fluctuated with changes in the bureaucratic and economic climates.[13]

Disability in the Press

Congress kept a window on the world by monitoring the coverage of social issues in the popular press. In a Congressional environment that was thick with oversight subcommittees, newspapers—fresh from their Watergate triumphs and not yet threatened by cable television or the Internet—often provided the spark for the committee investigations that produced dramatic hearings and, in a curious sort of media feedback, big headlines.

In the seventies, newspapers and magazines tended to spread the impression that the disability programs were out of control. A cover story about the Department of Health, Education, and Welfare (HEW) that *Time* ran in June 1978 directed the reader's attention to disability insurance, an "innocuous-sounding program" that cost $1.5 billion in 1965, $13 billion in 1978, and with costs predicted to reach $25 billion in 1985. The number of people receiving disability payments had tripled in thirteen years to a level greater than the population of Virginia or Norway. *Time* asserted that the people on the disability rolls were not necessarily disabled. Instead, "the definition of disability has been stretched to the point where it can cover a case of nerves, a lingering depression, even chronic headaches." The program offered few incentives for claimants to go to work. Instead, disability claims swamped HEW, creating a backlog of 133,860 cases.

Never a publication to shy away from editorial judgments, *Time* quoted Joseph Califano, President Carter's HEW Secretary, to the effect that society's attitude toward work was changing, and accepting public benefits no longer bore its former stigma. It concluded that "disability insurance has lost sight of its original purpose. Instead of helping to put people back on their feet, it is encouraging them to remain prostrate, permanent wards of society." In short, the disability insurance program contributed to welfare dependency and sapped people's will to work. Although the magazine did not make the connection, it took little imagination to see that SSI, a true welfare program far more dominated by disability than was the Social Security program, might also lead to dependency.[14]

The *New York Times* reported the story in more restrained terms. It portrayed the rise in disability benefits as a mystery. "What we don't know dominates what we know for sure," said the Assistant Secretary for Planning and Evaluation in President Ford's Department of HEW. Another bureaucrat who worked in the same office called it "a sleuthing problem." The *Times* mustered some convincing figures to demonstrate the rise in disability payments and the public sector's increasing role in making those payments. It pointed out that medical science had rendered such disorders as tuberculosis less disabling, yet the Civil Service reported that the rate at which federal employees took disability retirements had tripled in twenty years, citing mental disorders, cirrhosis of the liver, and loss of hearing as the causes of the disabilities. Similarly, the paper reported that in 1965 fewer than half a million people applied to the SSA for disability benefits, but that the figure had risen to 1.2 million in 1974. In 1965, 4.8 of 1,000 persons paying into the Social Security trust funds received disability benefits; by 1974 the number had reached 6.2. "It's hard to believe that the incidence of disability is actually rising that fast," the Assistant Secretary said.[15]

Although much of the ensuing discussion focused on SSDI, rather than on SSI, the facts that the two programs shared a common definition of disability and used the same disability determination process meant that reforming one program inevitably involved changing the other program. The Congressional debate over disability programs that took place between 1975 and 1980 featured proposals to lower the replacement rate (the percentage of a person's previous wages that Social Security replaced) in SSDI and to tighten the disability determination process. The replacement rate discussion, which concerned things like the benefit computation formula and the payment of family benefits in SSDI, had no analogues in SSI. The reform of the disability determination process had as great, if not greater, potential effect on SSI as it did on SSDI.

Mental Disability and Deinstitutionalization

As policymakers pursued disability reform by trying to tame the rise in the disability rolls, they tended to miss important differences between the work-related SSDI and the welfare-oriented SSI program. Both programs served people with disabilities, yet the caseloads differed in important ways. The older workers on SSDI had disabilities caused by diseases of the circulatory system, such as heart disease (28.3 percent of the new awards in 1979) and diseases and impairment of the musculoskeletal system such as a bad back (17.3 percent of the new awards in 1979). Mental disorders, which included psychiatric illnesses and mental retardation, accounted for only 11.3 percent of the new awards in 1979. The SSI caseload had a different profile: 17.5 percent of the new SSI awards for 1977 went to people with diseases of the circulatory system and 9.8 percent to people with diseases of the musculoskeletal system and connective tissue. In SSI, unlike in SSDI, the largest single category of new awards in 1977 was for people with mental disorders. More than one applicant in three who entered the SSI rolls in 1977 did so because of a mental disorder. Within that category, mental retardation accounted for over half of the new beneficiaries. Although there were overlaps in the caseloads of the two programs—older heart disease patients with no resources other than Social Security might qualify for both programs—SSI served people with mental disabilities far more than did SSDI.[16]

SSI tapped into a new group—those with chronic mental illness and mentally retarded people—who had not as a rule been served by the disability insurance program. When SSDI started operations in 1957, many of these people spent their lives in and out of custodial institutions that held them for long periods of time. Depending on the onset of their illness (and in the case of the mentally retarded, often from birth), the members of this group did not have the opportunity to develop a steady attachment to the labor force. That disqualified them from receiving disability insurance, except as a dependent of someone who did. The advent of SSI in 1974 coincided with a period of time in which the states released many people from mental hospitals and residential "schools" and other institutions for the mentally retarded in the hope that these people would be better off in the community, with a modicum of independence, than they had been in the institutions. Their disability status and their lack of resources meant that they qualified for SSI.

Not created with the mentally ill or the mentally retarded in mind, SSI ended up as the primary means of supporting their lives in the community. The origins of the deinstitutionalization movement had little or nothing to do with SSI. The movement stemmed from a series of interrelated developments in the law, the psychiatry profession, and public finance. In a sense, it was a civil rights movement. Just as victories in court striking down the constitutionality of separate but equal schools and other public institutions helped fuel the black civil rights movement, so a series of court rulings paved the way for what might be called the abandonment of state mental hospitals. In trendsetting cases, the federal courts defined a right to treatment in the least restrictive environment and accepted the right of mental health patients to use the courts to challenge admissions to a mental health institution. These legal developments coincided with trends in the psychiatry profession to bring about what President Kennedy described as a "bold new approach" to mental health. The new approach depended on the use of therapeutic drugs to treat the overt symptoms of mental illness and on the desire "for most of the mentally ill to be successfully and quickly treated in their own communities and returned to a useful place in society." The institutional manifestation of this new form of treatment was the community mental health center. The federal government facilitated these centers, dedicated to prevention and treatment rather than custodial care, through construction grants and staffing grants legislated in 1963 and 1965, respectively.[17]

President Kennedy and his sister Eunice Shriver also focused public attention on the mentally retarded. Traditionally, the advocates for this group felt that they had been forced to take second place to the far more visible and influential champions of mental health. Pressed by his sister Eunice and motivated by his family's experience with his sister Rosemary, who had been lobotomized in an effort to calm her violent behavior, Kennedy kept mental retardation on a par with mental health. The same 1963 law that helped establish community mental health centers also authorized funds for the construction of mental retardation research centers and mental retardation treatment centers. In that same year, Congress also passed the "Maternal and Child Health and Mental Retardation Planning Amendments." These legislative developments, in tandem with rights-based court decisions, helped ensure that there would be a deinstitutionalization movement among the mentally retarded and that many of them would eventually be placed in community homes and educated in public school systems.[18]

Public finance also played a role in the deinstitutionalization movement. The passage of Medicaid in 1965 led to a process in which the states moved many elderly residents from state mental health hospitals to nursing homes. Because of the way the Medicaid program was structured, the move saved the states' money. As a result, the population in the mental hospitals became both younger and less likely to remain in the hospital for extended periods of time. Between 1970 and 1975, the number of patients housed in state mental health institutions dropped by 11 percent a year, compared with a decline of less than 2 percent between 1955 and 1965. This development came just at the time when SSI, with its federal reimbursement of welfare costs, was being created and implemented. States learned how to use the new program to facilitate the transition of mentally ill patients from the hospital to the community. The program helped sustain a movement that was already under way. Between 1970 and 1986, for example, the number of inpatient beds in state and county mental hospitals declined from 413,000 to 119,000, and the average length of stay dropped to twenty-eight days.[19]

During the sixties, the AFDC welfare rolls expanded, in part because of the great migration of southern blacks to northern cities. During the seventies, the SSI rolls filled up with mentally ill people migrating from the state hospitals to the community. These trends had adverse effects on the public images of both welfare programs. AFDC, begun in the Progressive Era and expanded in the New Deal as the community's way of allowing widowed mothers to remain in the home and take care of their children, became associated with blacks, rather than just whites, and with single mothers who had never married, rather than respectable widows. SSI, envisioned as a program for the elderly who were members in good standing of the deserving poor, started to serve a group of people with mental disabilities. These were people, in the words of *Time* magazine, "with a case of nerves, a lingering depression, even chronic headaches." Like the unwed mothers on AFDC, they were less respectable than their predecessors on the rolls.

The Face of Deinstitutionalization

The chronically mentally ill and the mentally retarded presented an odd and sometime disturbing face to the community that endeared few of them to the established residents in their neighborhoods. SSI recipients became not just benign fellow citizens in need of aid but also disturbed, menacing, and even malevolent individuals who were shunned by their neighbors. Their very presence in a neighborhood tended to lower the property values. To cite a specific example, Gerald Kerrigan lived on Manhattan's Upper West Side in 1978. He exhibited odd behavior patterns, such as insisting that his trousers, which he acquired from the Salvation Army or Goodwill, had silver rather than gold zippers. He often stopped on Broadway to look down and examine his zipper to make sure that it was silver. He lived in a 7 by 11 foot room in the Continental Hotel on West 95th Street. The hotel, a place of frequent petty crime and other nuisances, housed 192 people, 92 of whom were former patients in mental health hospitals. A social worker, whose salary was paid for by the city of New York, offered counseling to the Continental Hotel residents. When Kerrigan received his $238.65 SSI check each month, he turned it over to the social worker who took money out to pay the rent, settled the bill that Kerrigan had run up at a local restaurant, and gave him $2.50 a day for spending money.[20]

Gerald Kerrigan fared better than a former patient with the case name of Edward M. After his release from the Rockland State Hospital in Orange County, the police found him wandering the streets and took him to the Men's Shelter on the Bowery in Manhattan. Soon afterward a bus pulled up to the shelter, and a man approached Edward offering him work in South Carolina. Like an impressed seaman in eighteenth-century England, Edward headed off to South Carolina. At first the experience there doing agricultural work agreed with him, but then he stopped taking his medicine and began experiencing hallucinations. He entered a South Carolina State Hospital before he was sent back to the Men's Shelter in the Bowery. The workers there helped him apply for SSI in the hope that he could rent a room in a single-occupancy hotel. He still faced a wait for his benefits and in the interim lived on $2 a week in the shelter, enough for him to buy a couple of packs of cheap tobacco.[21]

Although there were exceptions, places like the Continental Hotel, where Gerald Kerrigan lived, were squalid, crime-ridden places. The people who ran these sorts of residences claimed that the poor service they provided stemmed from the fact that SSI payments were so low. Irwin Steinhouser, who owned the Far Rockaway Manor Home for Adults, charged that, "The State of New York has demonstrated a callous disregard for the elderly, fragile, and former mental patients who live in adult homes." He proposed that the SSI payments of $386.70 to people in the homes be increased to $690. In this way, he linked the problems of the deinstitutionalization movement with shortcomings in SSI, to the detriment of SSI's reputation as an efficient and compassionate social program.[22]

Congress quickly made the conditions in boardinghouses and other facilities containing SSI beneficiaries the focus of investigations that brought more bad publicity to the program. A New Jersey Congressman convened a hearing in Atlantic City to examine the conditions of boardinghouses for seniors in the once swank but now deteriorating ocean resort. Representative William J. Hughes opened the hearing of the House Committee of Aging by pointing out that most residents in these houses subsisted on their SSI checks. He said that the residents turned their entire checks over to the proprietors in return for room and board. He complained that the rooms were not clean and "the boarding house diet is so meager that residents are forced to panhandle on the streets in an effort to obtain money for food." In this way the Congressman implied that there was a connection between the SSI program and the forces that were bringing about the decline of Atlantic City and America's other urban centers.[23]

The City Council of New York held similar hearings that exposed the fact that many of the nine thousand city residents who lived in "adult homes" received bad food and lived under substandard conditions. A sixty-year-old man who lived in one of the city's adult residential care facilities testified that the food he received was "not fit for a dog to eat" and said that the residents received unnecessary physical exams so that the doctors could augment their reimbursements from Medicaid and Medicare.[24] Another investigation exposed the conditions of former mental patients living in private homes in Queens with no supervision or proper food. According to a state Senator from the area, these people were being "shanghaied, hijacked into these homes" and then being "blatantly ripped off." A Federal Housing Administration inspector visited the homes and found faulty plumbing and cockroach infestation. The situation was so bad that in one of the homes a police detective discovered a badly decomposed corpse; none of the six other residents had noticed. On a trip to one of the homes, a journalist saw residents who lived without heat in the winter and amid rotting food and stopped-up plumbing all of the time.[25]

The government, it seemed, had reached the limits of its ability to do good.[26] Seventeen thousand of the twenty-four thousand people who lived in the five hundred adult-care homes in the state of New York in 1978 received SSI checks: the program subsidized and sustained the adult-care home business. People in the business engaged in predatory practices. Many residents turned over their SSI checks to their landlords, who learned to set the cost of care equal to the amount of the benefits.[27] SSI, it seemed, allowed the unscrupulous to prey on the weak.

That perception stimulated states to regulate the settings in which SSI recipients lived more aggressively. In New Jersey, for example, the state sent out inspectors to boardinghouses to protect residents from "vicious practices." The state also wanted to guard against "inappropriate discharges" from mental hospitals or schemes in which any time a board housing landlord had a vacancy he called the state mental institutions and received a new tenant. It sought to end illegal practices such as those practiced by the proprietor of Joseph's Rest Home in Linden, New Jersey. Proprietor Julius Kube registered thirty-one boarders in his licensed sheltered care facility but placed fifteen of them in unlicensed homes he ran in nearby Elizabeth. All thirty-one of the residents qualified for $308 a month SSI checks, even though those in the unlicensed homes were supposed to receive smaller checks. When state inspectors came around to check on a client registered as living at Joseph's Rest Home but actually living elsewhere, Mr. Kube would send for the client and serve the inspectors coffee until the resident arrived.[28]

It came as no surprise that few people wanted the deinstitutionalized mentally ill or mentally retarded to live in their neighborhoods. Every time the state proposed opening a community home for the mentally retarded on Long Island, for example, it met with vehement opposition from local property owners. The state faced a court order to empty the Willowbrook State School on Staten Island and needed to place the former residents somewhere.[29] The people living in the affected communities sometimes reacted to the idea of having mentally retarded people housed in their towns in overwrought ways. In Greenlawn in Suffolk County arsonists burned one planned residence to the ground. In Smithtown the local board voted 4 to 1 to oppose a suggested site in their community. One council member said that the site would not be good for the retarded residents because they would be "picked on" by local children. The Not in My Back Yard sentiment prevailed in many similar communities.[30]

Illegal Aliens and Other Local Concerns

Of course, not everyone's backyard looked the same. In California, for example, the features of SSI that led to controversy were the exclusion of illegal aliens from receiving SSI benefits and the effects of inflation on the asset test that governed SSI payments in the state.

One California case concerned Mercedes Cardenas Paz, a seventy-five-year-old widow from Guatemala, who had come to the United States in the early fifties. She found work in Los Angeles as a live-in baby sitter for Spanish-speaking families. Then her health deteriorated, and she could no longer work. Members of her Roman Catholic parish allowed her to live in a tool shed at the rear of their house, an arrangement she found agreeable. She met her other needs through the charity of fellow parishioners and neighbors, but a friend convinced her to apply for SSI. Ms. Paz qualified for benefits, except for the fact that she was an illegal alien. No one had told her how to change her immigration status, and she worried that the U.S. immigration authorities would deport her. The law on this matter was quite clear. The SSI statute restricted benefits to those who were "lawfully admitted for permanent residence" or "permanently residing under color of law." Paz was neither of these things.

Community workers pressured the SSA to make an exception for elderly illegal aliens on humanitarian grounds. Although sympathetic to the plight of Mercedes Paz and others like her, the SSA replied that it had to uphold the law. It did what it could. For example, it did not discontinue payments to illegal aliens who had somehow slipped past the authorities and gotten on the SSI rolls until those beneficiaries exhausted all of their legal appeals. To do more required a change in the law.[31]

Outside of Ms. Paz's neighborhood on the south side of Los Angeles and other places in which many longtime residents who had never bothered to clarify their immigration status lived, such a measure stood little chance of Congressional passage. The momentum was swinging the other way, as many influential policymakers questioned the wisdom of providing SSI benefits to *legal* immigrants. The nation was just beginning to feel the effects of the 1965 immigration law that would in time change the face of America. In a time of recession, such as the mid-seventies, people saw immigrants as threats to their jobs. That bred resentment against people who came to America, agreed not to become a public charge, and then collected SSI and other welfare benefits.

In 1975 the GAO reported that large expenditures of government money went to immigrants and their families within five years after their entry into the United States. Congress began to consider a measure that restricted public assistance for newly arrived immigrants. Liberal Republican Senator Charles H. Percy

(Illinois) pointed to a "gaping loophole in the law" in which aliens "who have never contributed significantly to the American economy" became eligible for SSI and other benefits after living in the country for only thirty days. Percy proposed that the sponsors of legal aliens, not the government, become responsible for the welfare of aliens during their first years in the country and that Congress establish a residence requirement of from three to five years for SSI eligibility.[32]

The presence of immigrants on the SSI rolls, like the association between the program and the chronically mentally ill, stigmatized the program. Controversies over whether immigrants legally admitted for permanent residence should be allowed to receive SSI became a continuing feature of SSI politics.[33] The issue became a flash point in welfare reform through the Clinton administration.[34]

Economic uncertainty, which contributed to the tension over aliens receiving welfare benefits, destabilized the SSI rolls in California and elsewhere. Inflation increased the monetary value of houses in California and led to an increase in the tax accessed market value of the houses. As a result, property taxes increased at a time of declining real income, fueling resentment that would lead to the 1978 passage of the famous Proposition 13, which put a cap on property taxes in California. The advocates of Proposition 13 mobilized middle-class California voters in support of the measure, but the rising market value of homes affected less well-off Californians as well. In the San Fernando Valley, for example, thousands of SSI recipients stood to lose their benefits because the assessed value of their homes had risen above the $25,000 limit. Such people were being penalized for the inflation from which the program was supposed to protect them. They appealed to California authorities to assure that their SSI benefits be continued. The state authorities geared up for a major deluge of applicants to the Department of Public Social Services' Excess Home Value Program and pleaded with the state Congressional delegation and federal authorities for legislative relief that did not cost the state money.[35]

The Program as Out of Control

Even as SSI faced the adverse consequences of the deinstitutionalization movement, the new immigration, and stagflation, administrative problems that had plagued the program from the beginning, such as the overpayment of benefits, persisted. Just when administrators began to feel confident that the problem had been solved, they would be reminded of the overpayments again by way of an audit or a statistical report. Nagging reminders of poor past performance put a drag on the program's present performance.

At the beginning of 1976, for example, came word of $547 million worth of overpayments in the program's first two years. Commissioner Caldwell promised that computer controls that the agency had put in place meant that "significant improvement" lay ahead. He noted that the error rate had dropped slightly, from 24.8 percent to 24.4 percent between the second half of 1974 and the first half of 1975. At the same time, he admitted that the recovery of the overpayments "is expected to be limited."[36] No sooner had policymakers absorbed these figures when an independent audit showed $197 million in overpayments during the program's *first six months of operation* in 1974. According to the audit, the state of Delaware had errors in 89 percent of the payments made in that state. New York, with an 87 percent error rate, was just behind. That percentage amounted to $30.2 million misspent in New York, with $18.5 million attributed to state officials and $11.7 million blamed on the federal Social Security agency. An HEW audit soon confirmed those figures.[37]

In April 1976, Commissioner Cardwell noted that figures just in for the error rate between July and December 1975 meant that error rates still exceeded 23 percent. He expressed disappointment in the figures. In November 1976, the GAO weighed in with its estimate that the program had made over $1 billion in overpayments in its first two years. It seemed that the agency's past performance got worse and worse, creating more and more doubts about its present performance.[38]

A popular metaphor of the time compared government to something that was not only ineffective, as in its handling of the deinstitutionalized mentally ill and immigrants, but also out of control. It was the seventies version of a recurrent complaint in American history that government did not serve the best interests of the people. In the seventies, people charged that the government expanded in an uncontrollable manner, costing more and more money and doing a less and less effective job. And SSI served as a primary exhibit of an out of control government program.

When the *Washington Post* set rising reporter Haynes Johnson to work on a series about the bureaucracy, he chose to highlight the problems of the SSA in general and of SSI in particular. The three-part series ran under lurid headlines, such as one that mentioned "the bureaucratic jungle." Coming at the beginning of the Carter's administration third month in office, the series played to the public's interest in taking stock of the government at a time of political transition. The articles painted a picture of an agency in crisis that occurred, according to Johnson, "when its work force was changing, when public attitudes about government were becoming more cynical and yet when greater demands were still being placed on government agencies." As the SSI program demonstrated, the SSA handled those demands badly. It failed to get the checks out in time, and the program became "an unmitigated disaster."[39]

In a sidebar on the second day of the series, the paper included comments by Commissioner James Cardwell. He said that what was happening to his agency was the "result of very complex developments" such as Watergate and "the general public disillusionment with and cynicism toward government in general." Cardwell pointed out that it was hard for his agency to hire competent workers, both because of the stumbling blocks that the union and the civil service put in the agency's way and because of failing urban school systems that no longer produced qualified workers.[40]

Meanwhile, his agency relied on computers, "banks of machines in gray casings," to do much of its work. Unlike the poorly trained workers, the computers were part of an impersonal and faceless government "that never stops, that continues moving on its own momentum . . . no matter who sits in the White House or occupies the Cabinet officer's chair." These computers, in short, were part of a government that was not amenable to control. "I think managers most everywhere today do not have full control over computers," Cardwell told Johnson. As viewers of the 1968 film *2001: A Space Odyssey* knew, technicians could not always get the computer to do what the managers wanted it to do. Depending on a technology that the agency could not really control led to the "traumatic experience" with the SSI program, in which "computers were spewing out erroneous information resulting in massive over- and under-payments."[41]

Haynes Johnson let Robert Bynum, the SSA Associate Commissioner for Program Operations, sum up the lessons of the SSI experience. Bynum advised that the President and Congress should be "very, very careful about enacting new programs" and should not do so without taking a careful look at the existing programs and being willing to eliminate some of them. "If this President and this Congress don't somehow get a grasp on how to do that over the next four years," Bynum said, "then we are truly going to reach a chaotic kind of situation in this country."[42] In other words, unless America changed its approach to government, failed programs like SSI would litter its future.

Congress, unwilling to face this sort of existential critique, tweaked the SSI program but did not alter it in any fundamental way. In the summer of 1976, for example, the Ways and Means Committee approved legislation that continued the SSA's authority to reimburse the states for the interim payments they made from their general assistance programs to people who were waiting to go on the SSI rolls. It also extended a provision that allowed SSI recipients to be eligible to buy Food Stamps. The Senate agreed to the provisions, and President Ford, in the middle of a presidential campaign with Governor Jimmy Carter, signed them into law.[43]

The Carter Administration and Welfare Reform

When the Carter administration arrived in 1977, it wanted to move beyond these sorts of minor tweaks to the law and effect more fundamental change in the nation's provision of welfare and medical care. Unlike earlier Democratic administrations, Carter's appointees were wary about asking the SSA to take on new responsibilities.[44] The SSI experience had lowered the agency's reputation. "When we got there," said Hale Champion, a former California government official who served as Under Secretary in Carter's HEW, "Social Security was really rocky. . . . I think it was an organization that was over the hill." Stanford Ross, Carter's appointee as Commissioner of Social Security, agreed with this assessment. When the Washington lawyer and former Johnson White House staffer and Department of the Treasury chief counsel took over at the SSA in 1978, the "elderly" nature of the agency stunned him.[45]

In one of his first actions, newly appointed HEW Secretary Joseph Califano, another Washington lawyer who had been a prominent domestic policy staffer in the Johnson White House, led a departmental reorganization. He announced the creation of a new HEW agency devoted to health care that he called the Health Care Financing Administration (HCFA), which brought the Medicare and Medicaid programs together for the first time. As a practical matter, the establishment of the HCFA meant that the SSA lost its responsibilities for running Medicare, a program that it had created, implemented, and run for over a decade. In general, the old program-centered bureaus, such as the Bureau of Retirement and Survivors Insurance, lost power in the Carter era.[46]

Although SSI survived the initial rounds of reorganization in the Carter era largely intact, the Carter administration nonetheless left a major imprint on SSI. A new type of SSI program, one that featured disabled beneficiaries and contained enhanced work incentives, emerged from a long legislative process that culminated in the passage of disability legislation in 1980. Welfare reform served as the starting-off point in this process of change.

Welfare reform, which was on the Carter administration agenda from the very beginning, inevitably involved SSI. Officials in the Office of the Assistant Secretary for Planning and Evaluation in HEW and in the Department of Labor regarded SSI as one of the problems of the old welfare system that needed to be addressed in the reform discussions. The initial plans were ambitious in scope. Despite the pleas of veteran welfare reformers such as Richard Nathan from the Nixon administration not "to institute a brand new system . . . and build on the programs we have," the Carter administration moved in a different direction. The President proposed to simplify what a reporter described as "the maze-like income-assistance program" by consolidating AFDC, SSI, and Food

Stamps into a single program. The idea that animated the administration was to separate the employables, people expected to work, from the unemployables, people excused from the labor force. The former group was to receive the guarantee of a job and the latter group was to get a guaranteed annual income. The idea failed to capture enough Congressional interest for passage, and the notion of a guaranteed annual income fell from the nation's policy agenda, surviving only in programs from an older era such as SSI and in indirect schemes such as the Earned Income Tax Credit.[47]

Although the Carter welfare reform initiative was a legislative failure, it nonetheless exerted an influence over other social welfare laws of the period. In this regard it resembled Nixon's Family Assistance Plan: a grand failure but the impetus for major changes in the welfare system, such as SSI. In particular, the President's Better Jobs and Income Act, first announced in August 1977, suggested some changes in SSI in the hope of strengthening work incentives for the program's disabled beneficiaries.

To understand these changes, it helps to remember that SSI, like all social programs, was a hybrid that combined features of a 1972 era welfare program and a disability program. As a by-product of the Family Assistance Plan, it contained provisions that were intended to encourage work among welfare beneficiaries by not reducing benefits for every dollar a person on the rolls earned. In determining eligibility for SSI and the amount of a person's SSI benefits, program administrators disregarded the first $65 of monthly earnings and half of the remaining earnings. To illustrate the resulting arithmetic, an SSI beneficiary earning $105 a month would only have his SSI benefit reduced by $20. As a disability program, SSI paid benefits to people who were "unable to engage in substantial gainful employment." Hence a program for people who were by definition unemployable nonetheless had provisions that mitigated the penalties for those on its rolls who worked. As a disability program also, SSI operated under many of the same rules as SSDI. One rule that applied to both SSDI and SSI dealt with what program insiders called the substantial gainful activity (SGA) test. If a person earned more than a level of money set by the Secretary of HEW—$230 a month in 1988—that person was not considered disabled and therefore was ineligible to enter or remain on the SSI rolls.

Carter's welfare reformers wanted to strengthen the links between work and welfare. They suggested two program changes in SSI. The first involved changing the rules so that a person could earn more money without being cut from the rolls. The technical means of accomplishing this change was to modify the SGA test so that a person maintained his eligibility for SSI until "his or her countable earnings reach the level allowed under the basic Federal benefit schedule." As a practical matter, the proposal meant that if the basic federal SSI benefit was, say,

$300, then a person earning $400 a month could remain on the rolls. This change marked a departure for the program. No longer would SSI confine its benefits to the deserving poor who were excused from the labor force or, if working, made very small amounts of money. Now it could serve people with disabilities, such as the newly deinstitutionalized mentally ill, who might want to hold a regular but low paying job.

The Carter welfare reformers intended the second change to make it easier for someone on the SSI rolls to experiment with working. The program already contained a nine-month trial work period during which a person who tried to work and failed to hold a job over the period of nine months could go back on the rolls. The trial work period resembled the training wheels on a child's bicycle, a temporary aid on the way to learning how to ride a bike. After nine months, however, the training wheels came off, and a person who fell out of the labor force needed to go through the time-consuming process of reapplying for benefits. Under the President's welfare proposal, a person would be considered "presumptively disabled" for five years. In other words, if a person had to go back on the rolls after four and a half years on the labor force, he could do so without any delay.[48]

Although the Carter welfare reform program failed to pass Congress, the Ways and Means Committee picked up the ideas for reforming SSI on its own. It framed legislation that paralleled the earlier welfare reform legislation on "presumptive disability"—the five-year period in which a person could reclaim benefits—and on changing the SGA level.

In support of the presumptive disability proposal, the Committee cited cases of harmful delay in the SSI program. The Westside Center for Independent Living of Los Angeles, a new type of organization that encouraged the independence of people with disabilities and supported their lives out in the community rather than in hospitals or similar institutions, provided the Committee with the case of Mr. X. Diagnosed with multiple sclerosis, Mr. X received SSI. He nonetheless went to work and earned some $600 a month for a year and then was terminated from SSI. When his condition worsened, he applied again for SSI but had to wait six months because of the length of the time it took for the disability determination system to process his application. During that period, he also did not receive housing assistance or the Medicaid benefits that would have paid for attendant care. His health grew worse and foreclosed the chance that he would ever reenter the labor force. The Committee believed that "many disabled individuals receiving SSI benefits would like to work." Uncertain about their ability to maintain a regular job and afraid of losing both their jobs and their benefits, they did not take available jobs. The House proposal sought an end to that sort of debilitating uncertainty.[49] In a similar spirit, the Senate Finance Committee noted that it heard "persuasive testimony to the effect that the prospect of having to undergo a waiting period, which in some cases may be prolonged, is a significant deterrent to individuals who wish to attempt reentry into employment but are unsure of their success."[50]

The House also tackled the notion of changing the Substantial Gainful Activity rules under SSI. In particular, the House voted to increase the SGA level so that a person remained eligible for SSI up to the point where his earnings, minus the income disregards in the law, equaled the level of the SSI benefit. At the same time, the House decided to make income disregards more generous than in the existing law. The law already allowed a person to disregard the first $65 of his earnings and 50 percent of his remaining earnings. The House now added "work related expenses" to the list. A person with a disability might, for example, require special equipment in order to hold a job. The cost of that equipment could be excluded in determining his "countable" earnings. Should a person need attendant care—often a substantial expense, since it meant hiring help on a continuing basis—then that cost could be excluded as well.

An SSI recipient from Minneapolis testified that what disturbed him about SSI was the assumption that "if you are disabled, you are not capable of working. In my mind this is saying that because my legs or arms don't function, my brains aren't functioning either." SSI defined disability as not being able to work. The man from Minneapolis wanted to change the definition so that disability referred to a person with particular impairments and functional limitations who nonetheless had the right to a job. This new orientation pointed away from the old charitable concept of disability toward a new civil rights-based concept. It was the logical outcome of court rulings that delineated the rights of people in mental hospitals and of other people with handicaps such as mental retardation.

"The concept of employing the disabled recipient is a good one," noted a witness from the Center for Independent Living in Berkeley, California, perhaps the most famous of such centers and the home of many leaders of the disability rights movement. It would bring "social involvement and respectability" to the SSI beneficiary and "reduced dependency on public dollars" to the taxpayer. It therefore made sense for a person to work and to receive welfare benefits at the same time.[51]

Although the House passed both of the SSI reforms that the Ways and Means Committee proposed in 1978, the measures failed to clear the Senate and become law. There were at least two reasons. First, some people worried about changing the rules for SSI but not SSDI.[52] Second, the Carter administration, preoccupied by welfare and Social Security reform, wanted more time to fashion its own disability proposals.

When the Senate Finance Committee considered SSI legislation in 1978, it heard from people with disabilities who supported the measure, but it also received testimony from the Carter administration recommending delay. Handicapped "consumers," such as Hale Zukas, affiliated with the Berkeley Independent Living Center, urged the Senate to adopt the measures. Zukas noted that he received $188 a month in SSI, $548 in attendant care, and $70 in wheelchair maintenance from Medicaid for a total of some $800 a month. At those rates, if he took a job that paid less than $15,000 a year, he would lose money, and even if he found such a job he would have to decide if it was secure enough for him "to forego the lifetime security of my present benefits."[53] Don Wortman, the acting Social Security Commissioner in the period after Cardwell left and before Ross arrived, argued that the proposed legislation would change the basic meaning of disability and open the SSI program to people capable of self-support in spite of their impairment. Such people were not, as he put it, totally disabled "in the traditional sense." The way that the various income disregards worked, it was possible that people making more than $10,000 would still qualify for SSI, something that gave the Carter administration "serious reservations."[54]

Congress might well have passed SSI reform in 1978. By waiting until 1979, it inadvertently embroiled SSI in a larger debate over Social Security reform, and a generalized debate over the disability rolls.

Among the policy issues inherent in both the SSI and SSDI programs was a sense that the disability rolls were growing too large and too costly. When the SSDI program was enacted in 1956, actuaries projected that by 1980 the program would cost 0.43 percent of payroll. The actual cost that year was more than three times the original estimate. The costs of the disability portion of the SSI program almost doubled between 1974 and 1980 (from $2.7 billion to $5.2 billion).[55] The rising costs hinted at another problem: perhaps the costs were so high because many people who were no longer disabled were lingering on the rolls.

This suspicion received support from studies of the disability rolls undertaken in the late seventies, in just the period when Congress was considering disability legislation. In April 1978 the GAO reported on a study of SSI disability cases. It sampled the cases of 402 individuals who had been put on the SSI rolls in 1973 to determine if they were in fact disabled. It discovered that 62 percent of the case files did not contain sufficient evidence to establish the existence of a disability. The GAO then selected 175 more cases and asked the SSA to obtain current medical evidence to assess their eligibility. The SSA discovered that 10 percent were not disabled.[56] In response to this GAO study, the SSA conducted a sample study of its own of the SSDI population. Of a sample of 3,154 SSDI beneficiaries, it found that 567 (18 percent) were not disabled.[57]

As a result of these studies, by 1979 policymakers believed that perhaps as many as 850,000 of the 5.7 million disability beneficiaries of the two programs were not currently disabled, at a cost of billions of dollars in unnecessary expenditures.

Beyond this concern over costs and ineligible people on the rolls, widespread dissatisfaction with the disability determination process also motived legislative discussions in the late seventies. The time it took to decide a hearing case was a particular point of irritation. In fiscal year 1977 it took 215 days for an applicant initially turned down by the SSA to get a decision on his appeal at a hearing.[58] Policymakers also worried about the apparent lack of uniformity in the disability decision-making process. In fiscal year 1977, the ALJs reversed about half the decisions made by the state disability determination offices.[59] This suggested to policymakers that the two levels of the administrative process were somehow "playing by different rules."

The press played up the problem. In a series of stories in October 1978, the *Kansas City Star* reported that the allowance rates among the judges in the region ranged from a low of 36 percent to a high of 72 percent. In the downtown St. Louis office, one judge allowed 84 percent of his cases and another allowed barely 35 percent.

Internal agency policies may have explained part of the problem. Prior to 1975 the SSA's Appeals Council reviewed a sample of ALJ allowances. Starting in 1975 these reviews were suspended in response to the pressure of rising workloads. The Appeals Council would then only see an ALJ decision if it was a denial of benefits and the claimant appealed the decision. If the ALJ had allowed the case, it would not be reviewed. The potential for perverse incentives concerned policymakers.

In addition to these issues related to costs and potential abuses, policy issues also produced concern. For example, a complaint of pain was not factored into a disability decision unless there were "objective findings" to support the subjective complaint. Another issue involved "non-severe" impairments. If a person's impairment(s) was judged to be non-severe, the claim was summarily denied, without consideration of vocational or other factors. Some argued that consideration of vocational and educational factors might "tip the scales" in the claimant's favor in close cases.

SSI thus became caught in a policy whiplash that resulted in all of these problems affecting it just as much as they affected SSDI. So a host of both administrative and policy problems afflicted the disability determination process in the late seventies, suggesting that legislative action was likely.

The 1980 Legislation

The 1979 legislative proposals endorsed by the Carter administration involved relatively uncontroversial matters regarding SSI, some far more contested changes to SSDI, and a set of general disability reforms that affected both programs.

The SSDI controversy stemmed from a sharp break between the Carter administration and Social Security advocates such as Robert Ball that occurred at the end of 1978. The administration sought to change the SSDI benefit formula so as to reduce the percentage of a person's wage that disability benefits replaced, lower program costs, and slow the growth of the benefit rolls. Ball and his allies, who included former AFL-CIO Social Security expert Nelson Cruikshank and Johnson's former Secretary of HEW Wilbur Cohen, objected strenuously to these changes.[60] As a result of these developments, the relatively uncontroversial matter of putting work incentives into the SSI program—already agreed to by the Ways and Means Committee, the full House, and the Senate Finance Committee— became part of a contentious political discussion in 1979 and 1980.

In pushing the administration's disability reforms, Carter appointees tried to make common cause with the Social Security Subcommittee of the House Ways and Means Committee. The subcommittee had already worked on and approved changes in the benefit structure of disability insurance, although these changes had not made it past the subcommittee. When Joseph Califano unveiled the administration's disability proposals before the Social Security Subcommittee on February 22, 1979, therefore, he hoped for a sympathetic reaction.

Califano invoked the familiar image of a program that was out of control. He noted that that from 1965 to 1975 the number of people receiving disability insurance almost doubled and costs increased fivefold. If the Carter administration did not put on the brakes, the cost of the program would rise to $33 billion by 1990. Something needed to be done so that disability benefits did not get completely out of hand. At the same time, the Carter administration also sought to modify both the SSI and the SSDI programs so that those with the desire could, in the words of one disability rights advocate, "walk off" the rolls. Califano said that "beneficiaries who can go to work should be encouraged to do so."[61]

The Ways and Means Committee processed the Carter disability proposals through its subcommittee structure. That meant that Representative Jake Pickle of Texas fashioned a bill to modify SSDI through the Social Security Subcommittee that he headed. At the same time, Representative Corman of California worked on an SSI bill through his Public Assistance Subcommittee. As a result of this process, the House passed not one but two disability bills. The procedure spared the SSI measure from the vituperative criticism that the SSDI bill received from a vocal minority of liberal Congressmen. Wilbur Cohen, Robert Ball, and their allies mobilized this opposition through a hastily constructed organization they called Save Our Security. Hence Pickle's bill met with an unfriendly reception from Claude Pepper, who saw himself as the elderly's advocate in Congress, and other like-minded members. Corman's SSI measure engendered none of that controversy.

Corman's SSI bill built on the work that the Carter welfare reformers and his own subcommittee had already done. It included the ideas of raising the substantial gainful activity level, providing a trial work period, and allowing former recipients to go back on the rolls without delay. Under the terms of the bill, a worker's countable earnings would be reduced in three ways: an initial $65 deduction, followed by a deduction to cover impairment-related work expenses, and then reducing the remainder by 50 percent. Only if this reduced amount exceeded the SSI benefit level would a person be removed from the rolls for earning more than the substantial gainful activity amount. Even then a worker removed from the rolls would keep his disability status, including his right to Medicaid, for a two-year trial work period. And if the worker passed through the trial work period and lost his disability status, he would remain "presumptively disabled" and hence eligible for quick reinstatement for the next four years. The Committee hoped in this manner to make it worthwhile for SSI beneficiaries to work and to remove some of the risk that going to work entailed for an SSI beneficiary.

Corman's bill contained other features from the incremental SSI reform agenda that had developed over the years. In particular, it tried to specify the legal rights of SSI applicants in a manner consistent with the rulings of the courts. Rather than just informing someone that he had been denied benefits, the HEW Secretary would be required to explain the decision. The decision notice had to contain a citation of the pertinent law and regulations, a summary of the evidence, and the reasons for the decision. The bill also authorized the government to conduct demonstration projects that held the promise of improving the administration of the program.[62]

When the House took up the SSI bill early in June 1979, it passed the measure with no real debate. Representative Corman explained how the bill worked, and Representative Barber Conable, the ranking Republican on Ways and Means from upstate New York, announced his support of the bill. Congressman Stark captured the measure's appeal by saying that it would help severely disabled individuals who wanted to work without, at the same time, giving "anybody a free ride." The measure carried by a vote of 374 to 3.[63]

Operating in a different manner, the Senate combined Corman's SSI bill and Pickle's SSDI bill into one piece of legislation. The Senate bill therefore contained its version of the controversial Carter administration cuts in disability insurance benefits, such as changing the formula used to calculate disability benefits. The Senate Finance Committee reworked the details but retained the basic notions of raising the SGA for SSI beneficiaries who went to work and providing a trial work period.

Since the Senate, unlike the House, was working simultaneously on SSI and SSDI, it also proposed reforms that would apply to both programs. In particular, the Finance Committee bill included a standardized SGA test that applied to both SSDI and SSI. People in both programs could deduct their impairment-related work expenses and other costs such as attendant care and medical equipment from their countable earnings. The Senate, in other words, proposed to raise the amount of money someone receiving SSDI or SSI could earn without being removed from the rolls. The innovation was to create rules that applied to both programs.

The Finance Committee did attend to one important detail that applied uniquely to SSI. Its bill would restrict SSI benefits to legally registered aliens who had resided in the country for three years. In this manner it attempted to close what legislators perceived as a loophole in which recently arrived immigrants were able to get on the rolls. Senator Charles Percy (R-Illinois) argued on the Senate floor that newly arrived immigrants to America were ripping off the system and that the program's loopholes needed to be closed. In the five states with the highest immigration rates, about 37,500 newly arrived aliens (some of whom were refugees granted special status) received almost $72 million in SSI benefits. Percy wanted to make a sponsor's affidavit, signed when a lawful alien was admitted to the country, a legally enforceable contract. Percy's amendment, which occasioned the most comments related to SSI of any item in the bill, eventually passed unanimously.[64]

If restricting benefits to immigrants was a popular cause, so too was the administrative reform of the disability programs to address the issues that had been exposed in the late seventies. The Senate Finance Committee and the House Social Security Subcommittee attempted to make rules and create incentives that would reduce the disparities in disability decisions from one state to another, such as requiring the HEW Secretary to issue binding regulations on the state disability determination agencies and granting the authority for the federal government to assume control of the disability determination function in states that processed cases too slowly or made too many "incorrect" decisions. Senator Bellmon (D-Oklahoma) sponsored an amendment that required the SSA to conduct a review of ALJs' decisions to make sure they were not allowing too many cases. This seemingly minor provision later proved to be politically explosive. The legislation also mandated the federal government to review more of the decisions from the states before they were announced to the applicant.

In response to the issue of malingerers swelling the disability rolls, the Senate ordered that SSI and SSDI beneficiaries be reexamined every three years to make sure that they were still disabled. This single provision would prove to be the most consequential in the bill, even though at the time it seemed an incidental detail in a complicated bill. In fact, this would spark the greatest period of controversy in the history of the disability program.[65]

In addition to Percy's discussion of how immigrants abused SSI, the Senate floor debate on disability featured a lively speech from Senator Edward Kennedy (D-Massachusetts) on the dangers of cutting back on Social Security benefits. He called the measure "watershed legislation"—which was not intended as a compliment. Senator Robert Dole (R-Kansas) chose to counter Kennedy's criticism by pointing to the positive features of the legislation. He emphasized "the work incentive features of the bill." The legislation showed, according to Dole, that "Society is finally beginning to realize that there are options to a life of confinement for disabled individuals and that with a little imagination and creative thought handicapped persons can lead active lives and find employment suitable to their skills."[66]

Although the process was long and drawn out, President Carter, in the midst of a presidential campaign that featured a challenge from Senator Kennedy, who used the Social Security issue against him, signed the measure into law on June 9, 1980. The law contained features that had been developed in the Carter welfare reform, Social Security financing, and disability policy discussions.

The final version allowed SSI and SSDI beneficiaries to deduct "extraordinary impairment-related work expenses" from their earnings for the purpose of determining whether they were engaging in SGA. The law provided a two-year trial work period in which a person would be reentitled to benefits if the work attempt was not successful. It authorized a three-year experiment to allow SSI recipients who earned more than the SGA to keep their cash benefits and Medicaid up to the point where their countable income (the amount after all the allowable deductions) reduced their SSI cash benefits to zero. The law featured various measures to improve program administration, such as reviewing the status of a disabled individual, with a nonpermanent disability, at least once every three years, and a review of more ALJ decisions. In the future a denial notice would have to be expressed in "understandable language" and include a discussion of the specific evidence and reason for the denial.

The legislative process marked a moment when the window for change in the eight-year-old SSI program was open. As a result the legislation included some features that applied peculiarly to SSI. One such provision applied to children on SSI. The regulations regarding the portion of parents' income "deemed" to the child applied to children up until age eighteen. The program made an exception for students between the ages of eighteen and twenty. For such children, the rules concerning a parents' income extended until the child reached twenty. The new law ended this anomaly and provided that all deeming of income and resources from parent to child would end when the child reached age eighteen.[67]

Conclusion

In the first two years of the SSI program, policymakers tended to dwell on the administrative problems that led to overpayments, underpayments, missing checks, backlogs of applications, and jammed Social Security offices and phone lines. After this shakedown experience, policymakers began to concentrate on the SSI program that had emerged. They discovered that the caseload was dominated by people with disabilities, not the elderly people they had expected. As a disability program, SSI became an integral component of the deinstitutionalization movement by providing income support to people released from mental hospitals and mental retardation facilities. This development changed the perception of the SSI caseload. As a disability program, SSI also became enmeshed in a policy discussion about the growth of disability benefits at the same time that it figured in the welfare reform plans of the Carter administration. The focus on disability benefits motivated policymakers to concentrate on the disability aspects of SSI, rather than on the entire program.

The 1980 legislation was the sum of all of these changes. The SSI program remained substantially the same. It did not, as the Carter administration proposed, get folded into a larger income maintenance program. The fundamental definitions of disability and blindness stayed the same, as did the basic procedures for disability determination. Congress modified the program nonetheless. The new SSI program featured more federal oversight in the disability determination process—a partial response to the chaos of SSI's implementation in 1974 and 1975 and to the concern about lack of uniformity in the process.

The new SSI program differentiated between the elderly and the disabled on its rolls. For the elderly, it continued to be a retirement supplement. For people with disabilities, however, it offered the possibility of working and either leaving the rolls or remaining on the rolls with Medicaid benefits and reduced cash benefits. The idea that animated the major changes in the 1980 legislation was that people who qualified as disabled could nonetheless enter the labor force.

Getting people with disabilities to walk off the rolls fit a common pattern. It was a humane measure that reduced expenditures, not unlike the deinstitutionalization movement. It provided balance to Social Security legislation that could otherwise be perceived as part of a campaign to cut Social Security benefits. It meshed with the common perception that work was better than welfare.

Like all such ideas that expressed a future hope, it remained largely untested. Congress took the word of the people with disabilities—usually politically savvy and highly motivated people who saw themselves as a member of a minority group that was discriminated against in the labor force and victimized by the design of public policy—who testified before it. These activists wanted to redesign the built environment and reconfigure the labor market to accommodate people with disabilities. The reconfiguration of the labor market involved changing the income support system for people with disabilities so as not to exclude people earning money from also receiving benefits. Chief among these benefits were the cash payments of SSI and the Medicaid coverage that often accompanied such benefits. Just as Congress responded to the needs of the blind in 1935, so it made provision for a new generation of handicapped citizens in 1980.

In 1972 Congress created a law that produced unintended consequences upon its implementation. In 1980 it modified that law in part to remedy the adverse effects of the 1972 law. The dynamic process continued. The 1980 law would also produce unintended consequences that would lead to further changes.

THE CONTINUING DISABILITY REVIEWS

How the Politics of Controversy Hindered the Program

Just as the passage of Supplemental Security Income (SSI) tended to put an end to discussions of comprehensive welfare reform in 1972, so the 1980 disability law should have cleared the agenda. The rise in the disability rolls, which motivated the 1980 law, receded as a topic of political debate. Responsibility for the management and oversight of SSI fell back on the bureaucrats in the Social Security Administration (SSA) and the subcommittee staffs in Congress. People at the higher levels of policymaking could focus on the many other problems that demanded their attention. This peaceful scenario lasted for less than a year. By the spring of 1981, a new crisis involving disability policy and SSI arose. Problems in the disability program commanded the attention of the mass media, Congress, the courts, and the President alike for the rest of President Reagan's first term in office.

The Safety Net

A thumbnail sketch of the SSI program in 1981 revealed that the program, now nine years old, had some four million people on its rolls. The benefits cost about $8.6 billion, one-quarter of which was paid by the states. About half of SSI beneficiaries also received Social Security benefits. Most of the people on the rolls lived in their own households, and the typical beneficiary was disabled rather than elderly. Although the matter had attracted little attention, the rolls of the so-called adult welfare program included some 230,000 disabled children.

Critics often accused the U.S. social welfare system of skewing its benefits toward the middle class, rather than the truly needy. In reality, women and minorities consumed a disproportionate amount of the benefits, as one might expect in a program with a needs test. Twenty-seven percent of SSI beneficiaries were black, which was more than double the percentage in the national population. Two-thirds of all SSI beneficiaries were women, including more than three-quarters of the elderly people on the rolls. Old age benefits in both Social Security and SSI went disproportionately to women, in part because their life expectancies exceeded those of men.[1]

Despite the recent flurry of attention over people on the disability rolls who did not belong there, the program appeared to be doing its job. In the expression that became popular when Ronald Reagan took office in 1981, SSI functioned as part of the nation's "safety net," catching people who fell into poverty. It did other complex things as well, such as providing income support to the chronically mentally ill who could not gain a hold on the labor force. The program nonetheless attracted attention, at a time when the nation faced larger than expected budget deficits, simply because it was one of the two biggest federal cash welfare programs. Furthermore, its benefits were indexed to the rate of inflation, and it operated as an entitlement program with benefits available to all who met the eligibility criteria. Those features drove up the program's cost at a time of high unemployment, high inflation, and high interest rates.[2]

In nominal terms, the cost of federally administered SSI benefits rose from $5 billion in 1974 to $7.7 billion in 1980.[3] During this period, federal SSI payments increased 53 percent, and federally administered state supplements increased 46 percent. The federal share of the cost increases went from $3.8 billion to $5.8 billion. So the direct budget costs to the federal government for the SSI program had grown by $2 billion over a seven-year period. These were the fiscal circumstances of the program as the Reagan administration contemplated the mandated Continuing Disability Investigation (CDI) process.[4]

The Reagan Administration's Initial Actions

The Reagan administration arrived in 1981, after an election that knocked out many of the Democrats' post-Watergate gains and allowed the Republicans to capture the Senate for the first time since 1953. Even before taking office, Reagan's officials conducted a well-publicized discussion of ways to cut the federal government's expenditures. In mid-February the new administration released a blueprint for the federal budget with the title "America's New Beginning: A Program for Economic Recovery." The section on Social Security included proposed reductions in the disability program, a major part of which would come from investigating people on the disability rolls as mandated under the 1980 law and removing those who were found ineligible.[5]

Carter's people had estimated a net savings of $10 million in the first four years of the reviews. The Reagan administration, relying in part on a new GAO study about the size of the nondisabled population on the disability rolls, claimed a projected savings of more than $1.4 billion in the first four years and a total of $3.4 billion over six years.[6]

In order to achieve the larger savings, the administration decided to accelerate the reviews. The original schedule called for the reviews to begin in January 1982 and be completed within three years, but the administration began the reviews in March 1981. Truncating the implementation phase of the law caused problems for the bureaucratic planners and contributed to some bad policy decisions. A 1985 internal SSA briefing paper concluded that the decision to accelerate the reviews was "costly" because of "mistakes made early on which can be attributed to insufficient lead-time" and "negative PR."[7]

As for SSI, it fared well in the initial phases of the 1981 budget-cutting discussions. In February, White House Press Secretary James Brady, who in a few weeks would become a household name after the attack on Reagan's life, announced that seven programs would be exempt from Reagan's proposed spending cuts. SSI made the list. It joined the basic Social Security retirement program, compensation for disabled veterans, the school lunch program, Medicare, Head Start, and the summer youth jobs program as "untouchable" programs. The list nicely captured some of the federal government's most politically appealing programs. Brady said that the exemptions would make good on Ronald Reagan's promise to preserve benefits to "the truly needy."[8]

The list contained some noteworthy omissions. For example, although the administration promised to protect Social Security's basic retirement benefits, it made no pledge to preserve other features of Social Security, such as the minimum benefit and student benefits and, most importantly for SSI, disability insurance. Nor did the list include Aid to Families with Dependent Children (AFDC), Food Stamps, or Medicaid, each of which affected SSI beneficiaries. So technically the list spared SSI, but in fact it left open the possibility of cutting important features of the program.[9]

One program at risk was Medicaid, which provided health insurance for many SSI recipients. The administration suggested that excessive benefit provisions made Medicaid "a very poorly managed program" that failed "to provide cost-effective services to those most in need." The Reagan administration wanted to gain Congressional approval to enact cuts that would force the states, which ran the program on a day-to-day basis, to reduce fraud and mismanagement.[10]

In general, the Reagan administration hoped to reduce domestic federal expenditures by preserving programs that served the truly needy, eliminating frivolous programs, reducing fraud and waste in all programs, and ending the mismanagement of federal programs. Although the administration's "New Beginning" report and its FY 1982 budget plan suggested only modest changes in Social Security, Office of Management and Budget Director David Stockman was secretly at work on a more far-reaching set of Social Security initiatives. Department of Health, Education, and Welfare (HEW) Secretary Richard Schweiker's May 12, 1981, press conference to release the new proposals took much of Washington by surprise. The most controversial of the new proposals involved an immediate 38 percent reduction in the value of early retirement benefits (those taken before age sixty-five). The disability proposals included eliminating all consideration of educational and vocational factors in disability determinations.

When news of this package of proposals reached Capitol Hill, it provoked an immediate response. In a stinging rebuke to the President, the Senate voted 96 to 0 in a "sense of the Senate" resolution to reject the administration's proposal on early retirement benefits. This huge misstep meant that Reagan lost control of the policy agenda. Congress never formally considered the administration's Social Security and disability plan, and the President withdrew it in September. The President continued to believe, however, that there was "widespread abuse" of the disability system, "which should not be allowed to continue."[11] In this atmosphere, the CDIs that had been authorized by the 1980 disability legislation survived as major tools to realize savings in the disability programs.

Early Policy Decisions

At this point, the administration made critical policy decisions that produced unintended consequences. The first decision involved what program insiders called "folder reviews." To file most claims, beneficiaries went to a Social Security office for a face-to-face interview with a federal official. The SSA, concerned about the massive amount of work this standard procedure would entail, decided to do the CDIs as "folder reviews." The Disability Determination Services (DDS) examiner would simply review the case file and decide whether the evidence indicated the person was disabled. A beneficiary might not know about the review until she received a notice that her benefits were being terminated.

The second procedural issue concerned whether the reviews would depend on old evidence in the case folder or seek new evidence on which to base the decision. The state DDS administrators lobbied the SSA against any new requirement to review old evidence, arguing that it would be time-consuming, costly, and in many cases impossible because the evidence was no longer available. The SSA decided that the CDIs would be based only on new medical evidence. Most beneficiaries would receive a consultative examination in which a doctor would briefly examine them. In this manner, the procedure allowed the government's medical officer to overrule the beneficiary's own doctor.

The third substantive policy issue centered on the question of whether a person's condition had to show medical improvement before her benefits could be terminated. Some argued that, if a person was properly put on the rolls in 1974 and her condition had not changed, then no obvious reason existed to terminate her benefits. Instead of making this presumption, the agency decided on de novo reviews that were based on a wholly new assessment of the person's current condition. To do otherwise, according to the SSA, meant that someone filing a new claim might be found ineligible, while someone on the rolls with exactly the same condition continued to receive benefits because her condition had not improved.[12]

Still another issue involved the assessment of multiple impairments. To receive a disability benefit or to remain on the rolls, a person needed to have a severe impairment. That meant an applicant who suffered from a combination of multiple nonsevere impairments could not receive benefits. Anyone without a severe impairment would be removed from the rolls in the CDI process.[13]

Rather than selecting cases randomly for review, the SSA targeted the initial reviews on those beneficiaries who were most likely to have recovered from their disabilities. The administration also directed the SSA to focus the initial rounds of reviews more on the Social Security Disability Insurance (SSDI) program than on the SSI program, because the resultant cost savings would be higher.[14] These two decisions, perfectly defensible as administrative protocols, became public relations disasters. Because of the targeting, the initial cessation rate was much higher than policymakers expected, and more people with mental impairments would be in the first round of reviews, as they were more likely to have disabilities from which recovery was possible. The disproportionate number of persons with mental impairments in the early reviews created a perception that an especially vulnerable population had been singled out for unfair treatment.

For someone cut from the rolls, the consequences were severe. The DDS identified a point in time when a person was no longer disabled and then demanded that a terminated beneficiary pay back any benefits he had received since he was no longer officially disabled. A person who had been on the rolls for years might owe the federal government a considerable sum of money.

The Disability Reviews Begin

Reagan administration officials made the decision to accelerate the reviews in the transition period between the Carter and Reagan presidencies. As one SSA official described the situation, the new Reagan administration, like the Carter administration before it, had a "mind set" of "curbing the disability program." Reagan's transition team knew about a study that used Washington state data to show that many of the people on the SSI caseload did not belong there and had gone on the rolls during the chaotic SSI start-up period in 1973 and 1974. Anxious to make cost reductions in the federal budget, Reagan officials showed more interest in SSDI than SSI as the disability benefits under SSDI tended to be higher than under SSI, and so finding a nondisabled person on the SSDI rolls promised more "bang for the buck." As the SSA official put it, "If there were problems in SSI there was going to be problems in DI of like magnitude. . . . And we were off to the races."[15]

The bureaucrats at the SSA were worried about accelerating the reviews, but the Reagan administration, which generally distrusted the career bureaucrats in the federal agencies, rejected their advice. The transition team froze Acting SSA Commissioner Herbert R. Doggette Jr. out of its meetings. Doggette reported: "I was not consulted regarding the CDI policy."[16] Rhoda Davis, the career SSA executive in charge of the disability program, presented the agency's formal implementation plan at a briefing for HEW and transition officials in the Commissioner's conference room on the ninth floor of Social Security's headquarters in Baltimore. At the end of her presentation, she warned the new administration against undertaking the accelerated reviews. When they asked her why not, she replied, "Because the DDSs can't do it. . . . And you're going to have the same problem you had in the mid-seventies in terms of drowning in caseload." She worried in particular that the state disability determination offices did not have sufficient staff to handle the significantly higher workload that the Reagan administration contemplated. No one listened to her.[17]

The Reagan plan involved accelerating the pace and increasing the volume of disability reviews. After the accelerated reviews began in March 1981, the workloads of the state disability determination offices exploded (Figure 5-1).[18] In a typical year, the SSA processed around 147,000 CDIs. This figure rose to 160,000 in 1980, to 257,000 in 1981, and eventually it reached more than half a million.[19]

The rate at which the DDS found beneficiaries ineligible responded to legislative developments and to what policy insiders called the "adjudicative climate" For example, the cessation rate, which averaged about 22 percent in fiscal years 1975 and 1976, rose in 1977 as policymakers articulated concerns about the growth of the disability rolls. In 1978 the General Accounting Office (GAO) is-

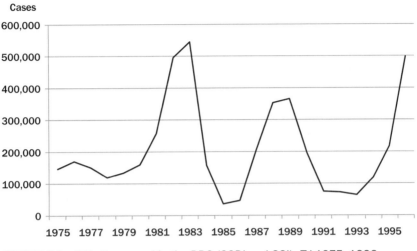

FIGURE 5-1   CDIs Processed in the DDS (SSDI and SSI), FY 1975–1996

sued a report that alleged that large numbers of ineligibles were receiving benefits, and the cessation rate rose to 46 percent. It stayed at that level until 1984, when the policy winds would shift dramatically again (Figure 5-2).[20]

Although Reagan administration officials apparently expected the disability reviews to be stealth operations that left no footprint on the public landscape, "horror stories" about people unjustly removed from the rolls soon began to appear. Because of the early policy decision to make the CDIs a folder review without any face-to-face contact, the state disability determination offices inevitably terminated the benefits of some people who were still clearly disabled. Picking up these cases, the media reinforced an impression of the administration as heartless and the bureaucracy as incompetent and made it difficult for the government to defend its policies credibly.

At the end of September 1981, the *New York Times* ran a front page piece about New Yorkers who were losing their benefits. Some 1,300 New Yorkers, or 38 percent of the first group examined, received notices that they were to lose their benefits. This high termination rate of nearly 40 percent was an ominous sign. Conditioned by the GAO and SSA studies, Congress and the public had expected a termination rate of 20 percent; a rate nearly twice this high suggested that the government was undertaking a wholesale "purge" of the disability rolls.[21]

Congress soon began to ask questions about the reviews. In a routine hearing on the Social Security appeals process, for example, Representative J. J. "Jake" Pickle (D-Texas), who as much as anyone was associated with the 1980 law and wanted it to succeed, asked an SSA official testifying before him in late October 1981 about the reviews. He noted that the administration claimed some $200

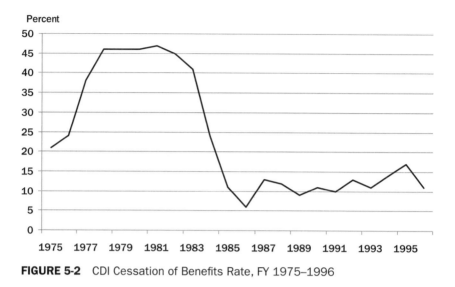

FIGURE 5-2   CDI Cessation of Benefits Rate, FY 1975–1996

million in savings from the continuing disability reviews but wondered about the number of people who would appeal the decisions to remove them from the rolls and how successful they would be in having their benefits restored. As it turned out, the administration expected a 60 percent reversal rate, raising doubt about just how effective the review process would be in reducing costs.[22]

Intermezzo

Before the disability reviews erupted into a major controversy, the Reagan administration pursued other projects related to SSI. In particular, the administration wanted to follow up its successful tax cuts of 1981 with measures to shift responsibilities away from the federal government and toward the states. One idea that surfaced in the 1982 State of the Union address involved SSI. The administration proposed to take over all payments for Medicaid and SSI and to shift all AFDC payments to the states. That idea, like nearly all of the President's substantive domestic policy proposals, failed to take hold. Instead, Congress remained fixated on the process of people being removed from the disability rolls.[23]

In March 1982, officials in Reagan's White House openly floated another idea that had perhaps been implicit in their 1981 financing proposals. These changes would require eligible SSI applicants to have a disability that was expected to last twenty-four months instead of twelve and to base disability more on medical and less on vocational factors. In the context of the disability reviews, these proposals only increased the suspicion of the administration's goodwill. Some charged that the proposals were particularly inappropriate for SSI, which only a year before the administration had exempted from budget cuts. They questioned whether the real purpose of the proposals was to serve as a stalking horse for changes in the larger and more expensive SSDI program.[24]

A proposal that fared better concerned overpayments in the SSI program. One problem that dogged the SSI program from its beginning was the difficulty of getting accurate information about a beneficiary's assets. The Reagan administration, eager as always to root out waste in social welfare programs, confronted the problem by requiring SSI recipients to make Internal Revenue Service (IRS) information on outside income, such as bank accounts, available to the SSA. The SSA wanted access to any form 1099 filed with the IRS on behalf of any SSI beneficiaries to discover unreported interest income. In this way it hoped to recover some $140 million per year in SSI overpayments.[25] The agency asked SSI recipients to sign consent forms that allowed government officials to look at information in their tax files; failure to grant consent could result in a cessation of benefits.

The matter ended up, as so many aspects of social policy did, in the courts. A legal aid group asked a federal judge to prevent the SSA from cutting off SSI benefits to people who refused to let the agency see their tax records. Bruce M. Fried, a lawyer who worked for the National Senior Citizens Law Center, told reporters that SSI recipients had "expressed fear and uncertainty" that their benefits would be cut off. The ongoing continuing disability reviews lent credence to these fears. The judge issued a temporary restraining order against the SSA. Then, in July 1982, he lifted the order and ruled in the SSA's favor. Judge Gerhard Gesell said that the practice of obtaining the information about the SSI beneficiaries did not violate the privacy provisions found in such legislation as the 1976 Tax Reform Act.

The SSA hoped that the decision would improve the administration of the SSI program. No longer would SSA field officers have to call up neighborhood banks to get financial information about an SSI applicant. "This new program is a way to get that same information automatically," said Deputy SSA Commissioner Paul Simmons. It marked a victory for the sort of automated systems that were supposed to have made SSI an exemplary program but had fallen into disrepute in the wake of the implementation and continuing disability review scandals.[26]

The Congress Becomes Concerned

If many Reagan proposals seemed fanciful, the disability reviews remained a reality for nearly all of the President's first term and generated intense battles in Congress and the courts. Congressional leaders in the House emphasized the issue of the disability reviews because it made good politics to do so and because constituents and local government officials kept the Congressmen supplied with horror stories.

The administration tried to defend its efforts by reminding Congress that when the SSI program began in 1974, the states rushed to transfer people from the old Aid to the Permanently and Totally Disabled rolls to the new SSI rolls. "There is no question in my mind," said Commissioner John Svahn, "that back several years ago there was a lax administration of the disability program and that there was a considerable amount of dumping, if you will, by some large States when the Federal Government took over the SSI program." Representative Barber Conable, the upstate New York Republican, criticized Svahn for removing people without sufficient investigation of their condition. Svahn agreed that making decisions "on very slim evidence" was a problem, but reminded the Congressmen that there were many people on the rolls who just did not belong there.[27]

In this spirit Senator Donald Riegle of Michigan (D) testified before the Ways and Means Social Security Subcommittee in March 1982. He questioned the validity of a procedure in which some 69 percent of those thrown off the rolls and who appealed the decisions had their benefits reinstated. He wondered if it was necessary for these people to suffer financial hardship and emotional insecurity during the appeals process. All of his regional offices were flooded with requests from people who wanted his help with the continuing disability reviews. State officials who worked in Michigan's Disability Determination Offices also approached the Senator to express their discomfort about making terminations that they felt were wrong. These things were happening at a time when Michigan faced an unemployment rate of 16 percent, raising the odds against people terminated from the rolls ever finding another job.[28]

Case studies of people thrown off the rolls became a staple of the hearings. John Harris, the President of the National Council of Social Security Field Office Locals, brought some of these cases to the Ways and Means Committee. He told the story of Charles. His review began in May and, although he was hospitalized in August, September, and October, he lost his benefits in November. Eleven days later Charles entered a Minneapolis area mental hospital, threatening to kill himself because his inner voices were telling him to do so. The case made the administration look particularly callous.[29]

The Media Picks Up the Story

The media publicized the hearings and the court cases and also uncovered horror stories that became fodder for the hearings. Only a few days after the March 1982 hearings in the Social Security Subcommittee of the Ways and Means Committee, the *Los Angeles Times* ran an unusually long story that introduced its readers to the continuing disability reviews. It led with the experience of an Ohio woman with severe heart and lung diseases who required a portable oxygen machine around the clock. Her doctor wrote that she "is just barely alive, let alone able to work." Nonetheless, she lost her benefits. A suburban Chicago social worker complained that nothing she or colleagues said about people's conditions to the state authorities made any difference. Instead, as one Wisconsin disability examiner put it, "the current adjudicative climate . . . seems to be one of deny, deny, deny." The *LA Times* article told the story making the rounds about Hubert Tuttle, a forty-six-year-old resident of Lansing, Michigan. When the former machine shop foreman heard he was being cut from the rolls, he drove to the local Social Security office and shot himself with a 16-gauge shotgun. He left behind a note that said, "They are playing God."[30]

The *New York Times* soon published a more tempered story that reported that the Reagan administration had removed 106,000 people from the disability rolls, "including some who are almost certainly entitled to them." The *Times* also wrote about how the media covered the disability reviews. It noted that stories about the disability cutoffs were appearing in papers across the nation and showing up on local television broadcasts and network documentaries as well.[31]

Such stories only fed the demand for more Congressional hearings. The administration did what it could to defend the process and to temper its most severe effects, yet Congress clearly wanted to express its displeasure with the reviews in ways that voters understood. Commissioner Svahn tried to correct a story in the *New York Times* by sending a letter to the editor, just as his predecessor Arthur Hess had done during the controversy over the implementation of SSI in 1974. Svahn pressed the point that the disability reviews should not be called "Reagan's cutoff" but, rather, a "Congressionally mandated crackdown on ineligibility which the General Accounting Office, Congress's own audit agency, tells us is draining $2 billion yearly from the nearly bankrupt Social Security trust funds."[32] In a way, Svahn and the other Reagan officials felt ambushed. Joseph Califano and Stan Ross, key officials in the Carter administration, had worried about the rising costs of the disability programs and laid the groundwork for the disability reviews.

The story played in the press not as an inherited blunder from the hapless Carter administration but, rather, as an example of the Reagan administration's insensitive efforts to cut the federal budget. Many observers perceived the decision to accelerate the disability reviews as part of the Reagan administration's efforts to cut the federal budget. With this framing, every misstep or problem that arose acquired the most cynical interpretation possible and provided more evidence of a heartless administration that tried to balance the federal budget "on the backs of the disabled." Prominent among the disabled were the people on SSI. The failure on the part of the Reagan administration to anticipate negative public reactions proved to be a major blunder.

The media, as always, ran stories that seemed to fit the mood of the times. In the late seventies up through the consideration of the 1980 legislation, the newspapers and television networks heavily played up stories of undeserving disability beneficiaries who were cheating the system. In this master narrative, beneficiaries ripped off the taxpayers, and the bureaucracy failed to stop the abuse. Then the story changed. In 1981 it switched to the government conducting a raid on humble and worthy disabled citizens, again with the bureaucracy failing to stop the abuse. It was a cycle that would play itself out over the entire history of the SSI program. Even at the time, one prominent Reagan administration official observed, "It's really a cyclical turn and five years from now there will again be a lot of concern about all the ineligibles on the DI rolls. . . . Five years from now they'll be back to writing stories about how Johnny is getting disability while chopping wood out in his backyard."[33]

In a sense, the media itself was not just a passive observer but, rather, part of the problem. In the early eighties, for example, the media contributed misleading narratives to the coverage of the CDI reviews. The emphasis on the "horror stories" produced a distorted image of the reality of the reviews. Quality assurance studies found an error rate in the reviews of only about 3 percent, but, as Commissioner Svahn observed, "Three percent . . . [is] enough to keep one horror story on the front page of every newspaper in the country every week."[34] Moreover, the bias of the media for the sensational story over the thoughtful think-piece meant that the stories were one-sided. Nothing an administration spokesperson said in a one- or two-sentence quote could possibly add an appropriate context to an extended profile of the sufferings of a terminated beneficiary. The media seldom corrected the false claims of mistreatment and refrained from printing or televising stories that featured obviously ineligible persons who were cheating the system.[35]

The media's biggest error came in failing to convey the complex dynamics of disability policymaking. All of the emphasis on the coldhearted Reagan administration and its changing the rules to purge the disability rolls obscured the fact that most of the problems turned up by the reviews were problems that had been inherent in the disability programs since their creation. The media thereby missed an opportunity to educate their publics about disability in general and disability in SSI in particular. Instead, they recycled old shop-worn prejudices, which made for good headlines and dramatic TV stories, but which undermined sensible public policymaking in SSI and disability policy more generally.

The Problem of the Mentally Ill

People with mental impairments posed special problems from the very beginning of the review process. Even before the reviews began, the Carter administration decided in 1979 to tighten up the mental impairment listings and make it more difficult to obtain disability benefits based on a mental impairment. This change had the dual effect of making it harder to qualify in the first place and easier to be removed from the rolls in a CDI. Early in the controversy, New York's Social Service Commissioner worried that many mentally ill beneficiaries failed to return the paperwork that would either forestall a review or, if they were dropped from the rolls, initiate a review of their case. She ordered the New York State Disability Determination Office not to drop mentally disabled recipients from the rolls if they failed to mail back the recertification form. From a state and local government perspective, dropping people from the rolls made their welfare a state rather than a federal responsibility. In this manner the reviews undid the SSI reforms that had federalized state welfare programs and provided income support for the deinstitutionalization movement.[36]

In 1983 the treatment of the mentally ill became a flash point. On February 8, 1983, the state and city of New York filed a federal lawsuit. In the words of city official Carol Bellamy, the suit sought to "restore benefits to more than 5,200 mentally impaired New Yorkers and to protect the rights of more than 60,000 others who could lose benefits within the next 5 years if the eligibility standards and procedures are not changed." The suit, believed to be the first class action suit filed by state and local governments, charged the SSA with "imposing unlawfully restrictive eligibility standards" on the mentally disabled.[37]

The New York lawsuit marked a broadening of the protest against the disability reviews. It focused on SSI, rather than SSDI, and it concerned not just the conduct of the reviews but the very rules of the disability determination process that governed both programs. In other words, more than the continuing disability review process needed to be reformed. Instead, broad changes in such things as the rules that defined mental disability needed to be made.

Congressional hearings on the mentally disabled ensued, conducted not by the proprietary Ways and Means and Finance Committees but, rather, by the Senate's Special Committee on Aging. As always, the testimony contained lots of case studies, most of which concerned SSI. During the hearings, the Chairman of the Orange County Board of Commissioners in Florida brought up a matter related to that county's efforts at deinstitutionalization. Florida lagged behind other states in deinstitutionalizing the mentally ill. As people with mental disabilities made their way into the community, the authorities simply assumed that they would be eligible for SSI. They discovered that, because of the tight eligibility criteria, only about half of the applicants for benefits were accepted, even after the denied applicants appealed the decisions. That left the county with some $300,000 in unreimbursed health and welfare costs and no real way to support the deinstitutionalized mentally ill.[38]

The controversy raised the question of whether the definition of disability should be the same for SSI and SSDI in cases involving mental health. At one hearing Allen Jensen, a Ways and Means staffer, asked experts in the field whether it made sense for both SSI and SSDI to define a disabling mental illness in the same way. Perhaps SSI, the fallback welfare program, should cast its net wider than SSDI, the program that gave workers a ticket out of the labor force.[39] Such a division would ease the problem of a person cut off from SSDI who could not fall back upon SSI because of the common definition for disability in the two programs. But advocates for the mentally ill and the mentally retarded resisted the suggestion to separate SSI and SSDI. One noted, "I really don't think you can separate the definition for disability, depending on whether a person had worked in the past."[40] Elizabeth Boggs, a prominent figure among advocates representing the interests of developmentally disabled individuals, said that "many of us who speak for the disabled see (SSDI, SSI, Medicare, and Medicaid) as inevitably intertwined and mutually supportive, and we want to resist any tendency that might arise to disassociate those systems."[41] In other words, the link between Social Security and public assistance through SSI brought a sort of dignity to groups that had been mistreated in the past. Advocates for those groups wanted to retain the connection, even though it stretched the holes in the safety net. They argued that if the definition of disability for the mentally ill and the mentally retarded needed to be changed, those changes should cover both SSDI and SSI.

Legal Advocates Widen the Scope of the Investigation

Legal advocates, such as Jonathan Stein of the Community Legal Services Corporation in Philadelphia, played an important role in exposing the problems of the continuing disability investigations. Not only did Stein send letters to key newspapers such as the *New York Times* in an attempt to influence public opinion and counteract the efforts of administration officials, he also kept the *Philadelphia Inquirer* supplied with information that demonstrated the hardships and injustices of the disability reviews. Stein commented, "They've run reckless with denials." "Unless you are totally bedridden," he continued, "and unable to move even an eyeball, you're not disabled." He called it a "shameful misrepresentation of the law." He made sure that lawyers in his office informed Senator John Heinz (R-Pennsylvania), who served on the Senate Special Committee on Aging, about the situation. Heinz, in turn, asked GAO investigators, in the words of his staffer Frank McArdle, to "look at what's going on in Pennsylvania." Stein, meanwhile, filed a class action suit on behalf of those in Pennsylvania who were removed from the rolls without sufficient inquiry into whether their condition had improved. The *Inquirer*, in turn, reported on all of those things.[42]

These experiences marked the start of an important relationship between Stein and the SSI program that would leave a significant imprint on the program. Stein and his colleagues pressed to end the review process as it was being conducted. Stein argued that it was impossible for the state disability determination agencies to review as many as 540,000 cases in 1982 and 540,000 cases in 1983. He charged that Social Security had narrowed the definition of disability without consulting or gaining approval from Congress and that state disability examiners routinely ignored evidence from treating physicians in favor of "cursory, one-shot consultative examinations." They gave little credence to complaints of pain, and they treated the review cases de novo, rather than looking to see if there had been medical improvement in a particular case. Stein and his legal aid colleagues therefore welcomed the chance for the House Select Committee on Aging and the Senate Government Affairs Committee, neither of which was implicated in passing the 1980 law or carrying out its flawed implementation, to enter the discussion.[43]

Stein and his legal aid colleagues, who defended both SSI and SSDI beneficiaries, helped broaden the terms of the discussion. As a result of their efforts, the cases of more SSI, rather than SSDI, recipients began to show up in the Congressional hearings. Almost always, though, the Congressional committees billed the hearing as being about the Social Security Disability Insurance Program. Cutting people off the SSDI rolls generated more political outrage than terminating someone from SSI rolls because the people on the SSDI rolls had established a work history before qualifying for benefits. They were invariably referred to as SSDI beneficiaries. By way of contrast, people on SSI—usually referred to as recipients rather than beneficiaries—were more likely never to have worked, a fact that made them more needy but less politically appealing. As one former SSDI recipient who had been removed from the rolls told the *Philadelphia Inquirer*, "This is my money. I'm not asking them for anything. I'm not one of those people who worked today and not tomorrow."[44] Senator Carl Levin (D), who, like his Michigan colleague Riegle, played a leading role in publicizing the disability reviews, began a Subcommittee on Oversight of Government Management hearing on the subject by telling the audience, "What we should remember about the disability program is that it is not a charity program, it is not a handout." No one bothered to point out that SSI was a charity program and a handout for which taxpayers, not the affected workers, had paid. SSI cases were simply lumped together with SSDI cases.[45]

For that reason, among others, the discussion of the continuing disability reviews at the Congressional hearings and in the press seldom included statistics that separated SSDI and SSI recipients. Fragmentary data presented to Congress by the Disability Evaluation Division in California suggested in that state at least that the number of continuing disability reviews in 1982 involved twice as many SSDI cases as SSI cases: 48,008 compared with 24,832. The cessation rate was slightly higher for SSDI than for SSI, 39.9 percent compared with 37.9 percent. The data also showed lengthening periods of time to process individual cases, increasing workloads for disability examiners, and longer backlogs—all attributable to the large numbers of continuing disability reviews being done in California. An increase of 36 percent in the number of disability examiners could not compensate for the onslaught of cases.[46]

Chaos in the Courts

In the first two years of the reviews, most of the policy pressure came from Congress. In 1983 and 1984, the SSA received more pressure from the states and the courts. In a typical year, the federal courts received about 2,000 Social Security-related cases. In fiscal year 1983, however, plaintiffs filed 23,690 new lawsuits, creating a backlog in excess of 37,000 Social Security cases by the end of the year (Figure 5-3). Many of these cases involved thousands of litigants bound together in a class action. Indeed, at the peak in 1984, Social Security cases comprised 27 percent of the district courts civil caseload and 19 percent of the circuit courts caseload in cases in which the United States was a party.[47]

The courts ruled against the government's position on virtually all of the key policy issues involved in the CDIs. For example, in the Ninth Circuit case of *Finnegan v. Matthews*, the court held that SSI benefits for grandfathered recipients (people admitted to the federal SSI rolls from the old state rolls) could not be terminated unless the original decision to put them on the state rolls was demonstrably wrong or unless their medical condition had improved.[48] The same court broadened the decision to apply to nongrandfathered SSI recipients, ruling

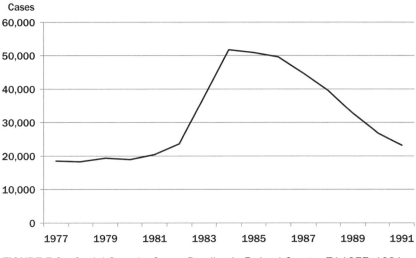

FIGURE 5-3 Social Security Cases Pending in Federal Courts, FY 1977–1991

that such people could not be removed from the rolls unless their medical condition had improved.

On January 11, 1984, federal Judge Jack B. Weinstein ruled on the case brought by the city and state of New York concerning people with mental disabilities. He held that the federal government had not followed proper standards in conducting the disability reviews on people with mental disabilities. Instead, the court held, the SSA followed a "covert policy" that was "contrary to legal requirements in assessing the ability of the mentally ill to work." Judge Weinstein therefore ordered that those people whose benefits had been terminated be reinstated "until the claimant's eligibility is properly determined." As many as 62,000 people would need to have their cases reconsidered.[49]

The SSA refused to let the courts make policy in this manner. To this end, it promulgated formal rulings of "non-acquiescence," which directed its components to ignore federal court decisions with which the agency disagreed. The SSA would grant the relief the courts demanded to the particular litigants in the case, but it refused to extend the court's rulings to other individuals in the district or circuit or to modify its policies nationwide. In a June 1983 Senate hearing, SSA executive Lou Hays defended the practice by claiming that "the Social Security Administration has . . . a longstanding practice . . . of publishing a ruling stating that it will not adopt a particular court decision as agency policy. There are seven such rulings in effect now."[50] What Hays did not make clear was that only three such rulings were issued prior to the 1980 disability legislation, two of those in 1979, and none had anything to do with disability.[51]

As a result of the SSA's policy of nonacquiescence, a whole new group of law-suits challenged the administration on the issue of nonacquiescence itself. In the Ninth Circuit class-action SSI case of *Lopez v. Heckler*, the plaintiffs sought to force the SSA to follow the rulings in *Finnegan* and other related cases. The Court agreed with *Lopez* and ordered the SSA to reinstate the benefits of every SSI recipient it had ceased during the previous three years. Since the Circuit covered California and other western states, the order applied to as many as 78,000 people.[52]

The SSA issued its rulings of "non-acquiescence" in eight major lawsuits that involved the core policy issues in the disability reviews. It deliberately chose not to appeal any of these cases and in this manner to avoid the possibility of the Supreme Court forcing it to change its nationwide policies. As a Los Angeles Legal Aid attorney complained in one class-action lawsuit: "So there's no possi-ble way to get to the Supreme Court because they won't appeal."[53]

The courts, in general, took a dim view of the practice of nonacquiescence. One Circuit Court Judge called the SSA's legal position the equivalent of the South's doctrine of nullification on the eve of the Civil War. "The word arro-gance comes to mind," said U.S. District Judge William P. Gray, the judge over-seeing the *Lopez* case.[54] Another ruling suggested that the SSA's position violated the principles of *Marbury v. Madison* and hinted at the potential for a constitu-tional crisis. In the case of *Hillhouse v. Harris*, the Eighth Circuit Court became so angry about the government's posture of nonacquiescence that it threatened to bring personal contempt charges against the Secretary of the Department of Health and Human Services (HHS).[55]

The Department of Justice (DOJ) also grew concerned about the SSA's nonac-quiescence policy. In a September 1983 confidential memorandum, Assistant Attorney General J. Paul McGrath counseled HHS that its nonacquiescence policy was counterproductive. McGrath observed, "In Lopez v. Heckler . . . the district court . . . imposed extraordinarily broad and burdensome obligations on the agency, obligations that probably would not have been imposed but for the court's obvious negative reaction to the agency's policy." The Justice Department directed HHS that no future nonacquiescence rulings could be issued by the SSA "without prior written approval from DOJ."[56] In response to the avalanche of court cases and the government's rapidly deteriorating posture in the federal courts, several U.S. attorneys served notice that they were no longer willing to defend every Social Security case brought in their jurisdiction.

In addition to the actions of the U.S. attorneys, the SSA's ALJs brought a fed-eral lawsuit against the agency to force the SSA to stop the "Bellmon reviews" mandated by the 1980 amendments.

Since the concern was with the possibility of Administrative Law Judge (ALJ) allowance rates being too high, the SSA targeted the reviews to those ALJs whose allowance rates were on the high end of the distribution. Once again a perfectly sensible idea from the perspective of good public administration turned out to be bad politics. The ALJs viewed the decision to "target" high-allowance ALJs as an implicit attempt to pressure them to deny more claims. It fed into the growing narrative that the administration was engaged in a wholesale "purge" of the disability rolls to generate budget savings. The case embarrassed the SSA and brought unwanted attention on both the high reversal rates in the CDI process and on the issue of lack of uniformity in disability determinations. The case was eventually settled, but the damage had been done.

Rebellion in the States

Under the stress of these rulings, the entire disability determination system threatened to collapse. By October 1984 the SSA operated under eighteen different class action lawsuits in various areas of the country on the issue of medical improvement alone. This situation led to a crisis in federalism in the form of a rebellion by the states. DDS administrators and the Governors of the states, aware of the media "horror stories" and of the adverse court rulings, began to feel under siege. The pressure of the massively rising CDI workloads wore them down. The legal decisions, in turn, put the state disability determination units in a bind. They faced the choice of following the SSA's guidelines, which they were contractually obligated to do, or following the legal opinions in their circuit.

Within the bureaucracy, DDS officials felt themselves squeezed between two opposing forces. On the one end, SSA policymakers created an adjudicative climate in which fewer disability claims were allowed and more current beneficiaries removed from the rolls. On the other end, the ALJs reversed an extremely high percentage of the DDS CDI terminations—66 percent in the early months of the reviews. The DDS officials complained they were being discouraged from allowing cases and the ALJs that they were being pressured to deny more cases. These complaints fit the narrative of an ongoing purge of the disability rolls.

As a result of all this turmoil, state agencies began to rebel against the SSA's policies. Despite the fact that the states worked for the SSA under contract and the fact that the SSA paid their salaries and all their operating costs, some DDS administrators decided to disregard the orders they received from the SSA. By March 1983, a total of eighteen states refused to follow federal regulations in the CDI process. By that October, a total of thirty states had stopped terminating disability benefits, either due to court cases or state policy decisions. By January 1984, nine states, containing 28 percent of the total national workload, had stopped processing CDI cases altogether, often under orders from their state governors. In Alabama, Governor George Wallace issued an executive order placing a moratorium on the state DDS making any more terminations of disability benefits. As Wallace recalled, "I felt that the SSA had overstepped their authority and that as a result, citizens of Alabama would be taken off disability benefit rolls . . . [and] would likely never be put back on the rolls to receive the assistance to which they were entitled."[57] Governor James Hunt of North Carolina, the only other southern governor to impose a moratorium, explained, "My examination of the law led me to conclude . . . that . . . the federal agency had misinterpreted the mandate of the Congress and that the state had the power to change the policy. We did so."[58]

This rebellion in the states presented a major problem for the administration, and it threatened to bring the entire CDI process to a halt. The judicial and state actions meant that there was a wide lack of uniformity from state to state in the SSDI and SSI programs—programs that were supposed to be national in nature and uniform in administration. As an illustration of how bad matters had become, the Secretary of HHS sent a letter to the governors of all the states on December 7, 1983, imposing a temporary moratorium on sending out any new termination notices. On January 24, 1984, HHS lifted the moratorium, but Secretary Heckler had to send *four different versions* of her letter to the states announcing the resumption of case processing. One version of the letter went to the states that had imposed their own state moratoria (eight states) ordering them to resume processing under the HHS rules. One version of the letter went to the states where HHS wanted the governors to resume processing of cases under the HHS rules but not send any termination notices pending the outcome of a pending court case (six states). One version went to the states operating under court orders that mandated ignoring certain of the HHS rules (twelve states), telling them to follow the courts' rules. And one version of the letter went to those states that had continued to process their workloads according to the HHS standards (twenty-four states). The SSA became so frustrated that it contemplated establishing a federal DDS in Baltimore and taking over case processing from nonconforming states. Although the agency developed a detailed plan, nothing came of this idea at the time.[59]

Administration Attempts at Limited Reform

With pressure from Congress growing, the states rebelling, the courts making policy, and the administration losing control of the policy agenda, the last thing the administration wanted was a new set of legislative mandates. Throughout the process, therefore, the administration undertook self-initiated reforms to fore-stall more drastic Congressional action.

In early September 1982, as the problems with the CDIs increased, HHS Sec-retary Richard Schweiker and SSA Commissioner John Svahn jointly announced a set of sixteen reforms that they hoped would quell the rising chorus of com-plaints about the CDIs. Starting on October 1, 1982, all CDI cases would com-mence with a face-to-face interview with the beneficiary in an SSA field office. This procedure allowed the agency to weed out people who were clearly dis-abled, in the expectation that potential "horror stories" could be caught and corrected before they developed. The SSA also softened the collection of back payments by ruling that a person's disability stopped when he was notified that his benefits were terminated rather than when he had originally recovered. It made the process more sympathetic to the beneficiary by having state disability determination offices review all of the medical evidence available for the past year. It doubled the number of quality reviews it performed on cases in which the state agency recommended that a person be removed from the rolls. In this way, the agency hoped to reduce the number of mistakes in the process. At the same time, the SSA refined the selection process for disability reviews, so that more people were considered permanently disabled and therefore exempt from the reviews. Finally, the administration also endorsed two reform provisions then being considered in Congress: face-to-face interviews at the reconsidera-tion stage and permitting payment continuation for up to six months during the lengthy appeals process.[60]

In May 1983 the SSA developed a second set of reform proposals it hoped would alleviate the clamor for legislation and forwarded them to Margaret Heck-ler, the new HHS Secretary and former Republican Congresswoman from Mas-sachusetts. The proposals, the SSA told the Secretary, "promise a revolution-ary impact on the CDI program and should lead to a marked reduction in the 'horror stories' flowing from it."[61] On June 7, 1983, Heckler announced what she described as "a package of major reforms," adopting most of the SSA rec-ommendations.[62]

The June 1983 reforms improved administrative procedures, without conced-ing much on the underlying policy issues. They increased the number of cases exempted from review by 200,000. They placed two-thirds of the pending men-tal illness cases under a moratorium until new mental impairment standards could be developed. The targeting of reviews on those most likely to recover ended. Heckler rejected the SSA's recommendation to announce some retreat on the issue of a medical improvement standard. She said that the package of reforms she announced would mean the loss of one-third to one-half of the savings projected from the CDIs. She added, "President Reagan fully shares my concerns. He has personally approved the reforms I am announcing today."[63]

Despite the best efforts of the administration to prevent Congress from legislating in the midst of the disability reviews, all of the attention from so many different sources meant that some sort of legislation remained likely. Passing a law that embodied the Congressional concerns about the continuing disability reviews proved difficult, however, because of the many conflicting interests involved. The Ways and Means and Senate Finance Committees, for example, wanted to correct what its members saw as the excesses in the process, but also hoped to make changes in SSI and SSDI that fit a more general, long-term agenda. Other Congressmen simply wanted to end a particular injustice that they had helped expose. Advocacy groups representing the disabled contemplated using the legislative process to give more procedural rights to people on the disability rolls and make it harder to remove people from the rolls. The Reagan administration portrayed itself as concerned for vulnerable individuals but wanted to avoid burdening the continuing disability process with too many rules or too much oversight. Administration officials favored administrative actions, over which they had substantial control, rather than legislation. They wanted to be the agents who redressed the problem, rather than allowing Congress to gain credit for correcting the administration's mistakes.

The legislative process lasted from 1982 to 1984, even as the issues developed in the courts and the states. Representative Jake Pickle's Social Security Subcommittee first brought a comprehensive bill before the full Ways and Means Committee at the end of April 1982. This bill allowed recipients of Social Security disability benefits to keep their benefits during the first level of appeal, something that SSI recipients were already allowed to do. It also instituted a face-to-face hearing at the first level of appeal between state disability examiners and the person whose disability benefits were being reviewed.

Beyond these responses to the disability reviews, the Subcommittee had a broader agenda for changing both SSI and SSDI: it wanted to make the disability standards the same from one level of appeal to the other. Along these lines, the Subcommittee suggested that the record be closed at the reconsideration level, so that the ALJs would consider the same evidence as state disability examiners. That provision, which would have the effect of tightening rather than loosening the disability programs, turned out to be controversial enough to delay the acceptance of Pickle's bill by the full Ways and Means Committee—the first of many delays in the process.[64]

After another month, the full Ways and Means Committee approved a bill, which became known as the Disability Amendments of 1982. The very existence of the bill was an admission on the part of the Committee that the 1980 law would no longer suffice. Instead the bill proposed both permanent and temporary adjustments to the continuing disability reviews. It tried to ease the disability review process without derailing the reform process that had begun in 1980. The Committee hoped to send the message that the disability reviews should "not be done in a precipitous manner" and that proper attention should be paid to people who had "their benefits terminated abruptly" and as a result faced a "difficult time adjusting" and the threat of "financial hardship." It also wanted to end a system in which the ALJs reversed about 60 percent of the state agency decisions on appeal, in part because the state disability determination offices and the ALJs were making decisions based on "different criteria."

Like other Ways and Means bills on these subjects, the details became quite technical in nature, exactly the sort of thing that the media had trouble reporting to the general public. For example, the Committee proposed a face-to-face hearing at the reconsideration level for someone who was terminated from the rolls for medical reasons and lengthened the amount of time someone had to appeal his case from sixty days to six months. Under the Committee's bill, a terminated person's benefits would continue until the reconsideration phase (the first level of appeal). Someone who had been on the disability rolls for three years and whose benefits were cut off because they no longer qualified as disabled would receive "adjustment" benefits for an additional four months. Since the Ways and Means saw the problems with continuing reviews as temporary in nature, limited to the start-up phase of the operation, it "sunset" these new "adjustment" benefits so that they ended in December 1984.[65]

In ordinary times, such legal and procedural arcania would have been left to the Ways and Means Committee, with the House of Representatives following the Committee's wishes. In this case, the Committee knew that it was dealing with controversial matters. When the bill reached the Rules Committee, Congressmen associated with the House Select Committee on Aging offered their own amendments. Congressman John Paul Hammerschmidt (R-Arkansas) wanted, for example, to continue benefits in continuing disability reviews through the ALJ decision—the next level of appeal after the reconsideration phase—rather than through reconsideration as the Ways and Means Committee recommended. Before the Rules Committee could decide the matter, the Ways and Means Committee asked to postpone the floor debate on the bill, so as to incorporate suggestions from the many subcommittees in the House and Senate that were considering the matter. That put the matter off into the late summer of 1982.

Meanwhile, Senators William Cohen (R-Maine) and Carl Levin intended to offer an amendment to a pending debt ceiling bill requiring that benefits be paid through the ALJ decision. Senator Howard Metzenbaum (D-Ohio) and nine other Senators said that they, too, would offer an amendment to the debt ceiling bill. Their amendment would require that someone's condition have medically improved before he could be taken off the rolls.[66]

The question of medical improvement became central to the debate over the continuing disability reviews. The Committee on Ways and Means opposed a medical improvement standard. Liberals such as Senator Metzenbaum thought such a standard essential to end the abuses of the disability reviews. The adverse publicity caused by the "disability purge" reinforced the interest in a medical improvement standard for people on the rolls, even though the Ways and Means Committee continued to resist it.[67]

The issue involved a fundamental choice. On one side stood those who believed that a uniform definition of disability should be applied through all of the many levels of the disability determination process and, more fundamentally, that the definition of disability should be the same for someone who wanted to enter the rolls and someone already on the rolls. On the other side, many thought that putting someone on the rolls and then taking him off, even though his medical condition had not improved, was unfair. It smacked of "changing the rules in the middle of the game." So these people wanted a different set of rules to apply to those already on the rolls. They proposed alternate standards to cover cases where people already on the rolls were being reviewed. Some thought that those on the rolls should simply be put there for life or until they reached the regular retirement age. Others thought that the test of disability for someone already on the rolls should be the inability to perform one's past work, rather than all work. Almost everyone felt that the SSA should have to show through objective medical measures that a person's condition had improved.

Members of the Ways and Means Committee objected to the way that Senator Metzenbaum and others were usurping the Committee's right to make this choice. At the very least, the Committee favored "thorough" Congressional consideration of the issue, with full consideration by "the committees of appropriate jurisdiction." The important matter should not be left, as the Committee put it, to "the budget reconciliation process, miscellaneous floor amendments, or other procedures which do not facilitate full congressional discussion."[68]

In the narratives that the Ways and Means Committee, the Committee on Governmental Affairs, and other Congressional entities developed to explain the continuing disability review issue, SSI played a secondary, but nonetheless important, role. The stories always mentioned the fact that in January 1974 some 1.3 million blind and disabled people left the state rolls and entered the SSI rolls. These rolls continued to grow as SSI became much more of a disability program and much less of an old age program. The state disability determination offices acted as processing centers for both SSDI and SSI disability cases. During the onslaught, there was simply no time to check to see if people on the rolls remained disabled and less time to make sure that the decision to place a given person on the rolls was the correct one.[69]

While comprehensive legislation continued to be elusive, Congress decided to allow a few noncontroversial rule changes to go through on a piece of legislation involving the tax treatment of income earned in the Virgin Islands. This narrow bill, which originated in the House, became the unlikely vehicle for the first post-1980 disability legislation. In January 1983, President Reagan signed this interim legislation that, although it did not deal with the major policy issues, did make at least some small changes in the disability reviews. The legislation allowed the SSA to slow down the disability reviews by lifting the requirement that it review "non-permanently" beneficiaries once every three years. Although reviews needed to continue, their number could be determined by such things as the backlog of reviews, the number of new applications for benefits, and the staffing levels at the state DDS. The new law also established "face-to-face evidentiary hearings" prior to the reconsideration level for people whose benefits were to be terminated. At the urging of the Senate, the law also contained a provision that required the government "to make every reasonable effort to seek and obtain all relevant medical information."[70]

Two months after President Reagan approved the "stop-gap" disability bill, he signed major bipartisan legislation addressing the financial solvency of the Social Security system.[71] Passage of this bill laid to rest, for the next decade or so, the issue of Social Security financing as a major point of partisan political contention. The disability issue now rose to the top of the Social Security policy agenda, and perhaps, as a result of the Social Security rescue legislation, the Reagan administration gained more freedom to negotiate over the continuing disability reviews. Clearly, also, the administration hoped the issue would be off the table by the 1984 election.

Still, as late as the end of January 1984, the administration hoped that its self-initiated reforms would deter Congress from legislating. At a Senate Finance Committee hearing on January 25, Acting Commissioner Martha McSteen opened her testimony by telling the Committee: "I would like to make clear at the outset that the administration opposes enactment of disability legislation." She noted that the administration "strongly opposed" the use of any type of medical improvement standard. Likewise, the administration "strongly opposed" any change in its nonacquiescence practices. "We think the . . . steps that have been taken to date have improved and strengthened the disability process, and the proposed legislative changes . . . are not needed," she concluded.[72]

That simply did not satisfy Representative Pickle. In response he arranged for the new round of hearings to publicize horror stories and put renewed pressure on the administration to bargain with Congress. "What we have now is a mess," he said, and "If indeed we are in a mess today, then we need to send this message loud and clear to the administration."[73]

In the winter and spring of 1984, Congressman Pickle took his Social Security Subcommittee on a barnstorming tour of the nation. At a February session in Dallas he said he was sorry "that these hearings are necessary at all." Until the beginning of 1984, he had clung to the hope that Congress and the administration would agree on permanent legislation to end the continuing disability review crisis. His subcommittee had worked up a new bill in July and August 1983, and the Subcommittee on Public Assistance added its input on SSI, but the administration backed away from the process.[74] Pickle's bill dealt with the matters of medical improvement and established new standards for multiple impairments and mental disabilities, as well as making permanent the continuation of benefits upon appeal (a feature from the 1983 interim disability legislation that had already been extended by an October 1983 law to run until the end of 1983).

Demonstrating that the demands on the administration came from Republicans as well as Democrats, Senator John Heinz joined Pickle at the Dallas hearing. He said that he and Congressman Pickle decided to hold the hearings across the nation because the problem of the disability reviews "must receive national attention. It must be brought to the president's attention in a forceful and urgent way." He urged the administration to sit down with the key players, who included Pickle, Heinz, Senator Levin, and Senator Cohen, and "work out a legislative solution." Heinz believed that fairness would be a big issue for the President's opponents in the 1984 election and "frankly, I don't want to see my President hurt because of an insensitive bureaucracy running out of control." The problem went beyond the odd case that Congressmen and Senators could handle on their own as routine casework. Instead, it involved "tens of thousands being thrown off the rolls who genuinely cannot work."[75]

At the hearings in Dallas and elsewhere, Pickle touched base both with the victims of the disability reviews and with local politicians who wanted to put their indignation on the record and gain media attention. Texas Governor Mark White entered a formal statement into the record of the Dallas hearing. He characterized the state of the federal disability program as one of "complete confusion." At a time of record unemployment in Texas, the disability reviews had removed 9,700 Texans from the beneficiary rolls since March 1981. "We are talking about disrupting the lives of people who have worked and earned their disability entitlement, individuals some of whom have been disabled for a decade, are suddenly informed that without any improvement in their condition, they are no longer eligible," the Governor said, conveniently leaving SSI out of the discussion. The Governor noted that many of his colleagues in other state houses were simply not administering the review on the Social Security Administration's terms. Since Texas was not one of those states, the Governor faced a situation "in which my constituents are being held to a stricter, more arbitrary policy than their counterparts in States under executive or court orders." The Governor strongly supported legislative reforms that would alleviate the situation. Without it, "chaos will only worsen here."[76]

By the time Pickle and his subcommittee got to Atlanta in March 1984, the Congressman reported that "the program [presumably SSDI] is operating in a state of administrative uncertainty and chaos which works untold hardship on thousands of beneficiaries." He noted that progress was being made in the House, with the House passing a rule that cleared the way for floor action on the Committee's disability bill that had languished since the summer. According to Pickle, the fact that "some 29 to 30 states" had removed themselves from the review process made the administration's claim that it could handle the problem administratively untenable.[77]

As the political realities set in, the administration realized it was on the losing end of this political battle. Administration officials quietly dropped their strident opposition to legislation. When the Pickle hearings reached Miami at the end of April, the Congressman noted that although the problems of the disability program had occupied his subcommittee for over a year, he sensed that the situation was changing. On March 27, the House passed a disability bill by a vote of 410 to 1. The leadership of the Republican-controlled Senate, presumably in touch with the administration, agreed to act on a disability bill. Once this agreement was reached, HHS Secretary Heckler ordered a suspension of the disability review process on April 13, 1984, until final legislation could be passed and implemented. Pickle hoped that the legislation would "bring a measure of order and fairness to this program."[78]

As always, SSI hitchhiked on the back of SSDI in the disability controversy. Social Security politics, not welfare politics, drove the process. Even so, SSI remained an important part of the controversy over the continuing disability reviews. At the Miami hearing, as in the previous hearings on Pickle's national tour, the case studies presented often concerned SSI.

Just as deliberations over the 1980 disability law intruded far into that year's presidential election campaign, so did the 1984 law. On May 22, the Senate passed its version by the unanimous vote of 96 to 0. In July a conference committee met to reconcile the House and Senate versions of the bill. It reached agreement quickly on a number of key items but then adjourned and did not reconvene until after the political party conventions on September 14. The final bill passed both houses of Congress by unanimous votes. President Reagan signed the Social Security Disability Benefits Reform Act of 1984 (often referred to by its acronym, DBRA) into law on October 9.[79]

In his signing statement, President Reagan characteristically put a rosy gloss on the history of this period. "This legislation," he said, "has been formulated with the support of the administration." "When I took office on January 20, 1981," he reminded his audience, "my administration inherited the task of implementing the continuing disability investigations . . . which had been enacted and signed into law in the previous administration." According to the President, by the spring of 1984, "it became apparent that legislation was needed to end the debate and confusion." At that point, his administration "worked with the Congress to develop this consensus legislation."[80]

The Disability Benefits Reform Act of 1984

The new law shifted the terms of the policy discussion from the concern over high benefit levels and uncontrollable growth of the disability rolls in 1980 to the protection of people on the rolls in 1984. The 1980 law attempted to reduce program costs and improve work incentives for SSI and SSDI beneficiaries. The 1984 law focused on procedural safeguards that would protect people on the rolls from summary removal, matters that inevitably involved lawyers and the legal process. It also concentrated on areas of the disability determination process—mental impairments in particular—that did not reflect an up-to-date understanding of particular impairments or did not comprehend the difficulties that chronic pain imposed on an individual. These sorts of matters involved the expertise of the doctors and other medical professionals who treated people with disabilities.

In a political sense, the 1984 law marked a resolution of the political tension among members of the proprietary committees, administration officials, and other members of Congress, such as Senators Levin and Heinz, who, with the help of legal advocates and their own constituents, had "discovered" a particular flaw in the continuing disability review process and wanted to put their stamp on the law. Although the conference committee functioned largely as a direct negotiation between Congressman Pickle of the Ways and Means Committee and Senator Dole of the Senate Finance Committee, the law itself became a compendium of issues raised during the period between 1981 and 1984.[81]

Much of the law affected SSI, but only one section concerned SSI directly. It involved the provisions to extend benefits and Medicaid to disabled beneficiaries of SSI who engaged in "substantial gainful activity." Even though the Reagan administration had argued against this measure, both the House and Senate included it in their versions of the bill. The conference committee took the more liberal of the two versions, allowing the continuation of the special provisions originally enacted in 1980 through June 30, 1987. Little evidence showed that people actually used these provisions. Nonetheless, Congress decided to retain these social experiments from the Carter era.[82]

The bulk of the law dealt with matters that had acquired political meaning in the continuing disability review controversy, including medical improvement, multiple impairments, pain, continuing benefits through the appeals process, and mental impairments. The influence of legal aid officials and other advocates, who had pushed so many of the issues to the courts, showed in the very lawyerly language of the law. The issue of medical improvement involved the most negotiation among the interested parties. In the House version of the legislation, a person could be terminated from the disability rolls only if there was substantial evidence that the beneficiary could perform substantial gainful activity (SGA) as a result of a medical improvement in his condition or improvements in medicine meant that the condition that had put him on the rolls was no longer disabling. In the Senate version, the burden of proof lay with the claimant. As the conference committee explained, in the sort of legal rhetoric that was typical of the law, "for benefits to be continued on this basis, individual must state and evidence in file must show that medical condition is the same as or worse than at time of last decision." The law as enacted permitted the government to remove people from the rolls on the basis of no longer being disabled only if substantial evidence demonstrated that medical improvement had occurred and the individual was able to engage in SGA. In the absence of medical improvement, the government could still take someone off the rolls, if the previous decision to put the person on the rolls was "clearly erroneous" or made in error. If a person could not be located or did not follow prescribed treatment, he could also be removed from the rolls.

The portion of the law that dealt with medical improvement also contained provisions related to the many court cases on the subject. Congress required cases that involved legal disputes over the issue of medical improvement be remanded back to the SSA for review. The SSA had an obligation to notify people involved in these cases that they could request a review of their case. Individuals found to be disabled under the new standard could receive retroactive benefits that covered the period in which they had been off the rolls; individuals whose cases were being reviewed under the new procedure would receive benefits until a new determination had been made. All in all, the law attempted to balance between allowing a person to remain on the rolls indefinitely and protecting against "arbitrary termination decisions." And Congress made it clear that these new standards and rules applied both to SSDI and SSI.[83]

On most matters, Congress indicated its displeasure with the way the administration handled the disability reviews, ordered changes, or commissioned a study, but left it to the SSA to figure out how to implement the changes. It referred the matter of how to evaluate an applicant's complaints of pain to a group of outside experts, appointed through the Institute of Medicine. On the question of evaluating multiple impairments, Congress ordered the SSA to take the combined effect of the impairments into consideration but did not say how to do so. As for mental impairments, Congress required that the SSA publish "revised impairment criteria" designed "to realistically evaluate the person's ability to engage in SGA in a competitive workplace environment." Until such criteria became effective, it mandated a delay in further disability reviews of people with impairments.

Congress retained many of the changes in the continuing disability review process that had been improvised by the administration during the political controversy. In particular, it made permanent the provision that SSI recipients cut from the rolls could retain their benefits through the decision of an ALJ. In the conduct of the reviews, Congress demanded new regulations to determine when consultative medical examinations needed to be obtained and required the SSA to make "every reasonable effort" to obtain information from an individual's treating physician.[84] It also required the SSA to issue new regulations that would determine the frequency of continuing eligibility reviews.[85]

Finally, on the matter of "non-acquiescence," or not following the orders of the courts, Congress made no new law and instead issued a statement of legislative intent. The conferees suggested that the policy of nonacquiescence be followed only in cases where the SSA brought the matter to the Supreme Court to decide. In cases where the SSA could not decide on the right policy to follow, the conferees urged that it seek a legislative remedy from Congress.[86]

Implementing the 1984 Law

With the passage of legislation and the safe reelection of President Reagan, the policy action shifted back to the executive branch, although Congress, with its growing number of subcommittees and expanding staffs, kept a close eye on the implementation process. The year 1985 became the key one for putting the DBRA into operation. Acting Commissioner McSteen told her executive staff that implementation of the new law "is one of the highest priorities of the agency" to which she was devoting "a major portion" of her time "because of the complexity and sensitivity of the issues involved and the extremely high level of interest from outside SSA."[87]

In February 1985, McSteen announced that her agency would send out notices to some 175,000 people (the exact number remained unclear) who had been on the disability rolls, gotten taken off the rolls, and then became part of class action suits or other legal actions. This action followed the provisions in the 1984 law to remand court cases back to the agency for review under the new medical improvement standard. By June, McSteen could report that most of the cases had been remanded back to the SSA and that 133,000 members of the first fourteen remanded classes had been notified of their rights.[88]

The SSA also made an effort to reach individuals with mental impairments who had received unfavorable decisions since the beginning of the disability reviews on March 1, 1981. The idea was to inform these individuals that they had the right to reapply for benefits and have their cases reviewed with the new mental impairment standard mandated by Congress. The "Important Message to People with Mental Impairments" declared that "a change in the law may make you eligible for disability benefits" if "you believe you are disabled because of a mental impairment" and "your SSDI or SSI claim was denied" or "your disability checks were stopped for medical reasons." The notice invited those affected to contact a local Social Security office and file a new application for benefits.[89]

At the end of April 1985, HHS Secretary Margaret Heckler proposed new regulations to govern the disability review process that, she said, would lay the groundwork to administer the disability program "fairly, compassionately and on a uniform national basis." She emphasized that the new rules closely adhered to Congress's intent that the agency not remove people from the disability rolls "unless medical improvement has occurred."[90]

The draft regulations included specific examples of what constituted medical improvement. In one such example, someone with a back problem, who could not lift anything over ten pounds, had gone on the disability rolls. After a successful operation on his back, the weakness in his legs, which had prevented him from standing for more than a half hour at a time, decreased, and the person could now lift fifteen pounds frequently and twenty-five pounds occasionally. Under the proposed new rules, medical improvement had occurred, and the person was no longer disabled for SSI or SSDI purposes.[91] As these examples made clear, medical improvement, like disability itself, remained a concept over which reasonable people might disagree.

Next on the agenda came the vexing issue of nonacquiescence. In June, Secretary Heckler said that the SSA would begin to apply—at the ALJ and higher levels of appeal—appeals court rulings to all similar cases of people who lived within that court's jurisdiction. That meant, however, that the state DDS agencies would not apply the circuit court decisions because, according to Martha McSteen, they were "heavily involved in implementing the 1984 disability legislation."[92] Heckler added that the SSA would withhold benefits and seek new court reviews in cases where the agency believed that the court was in error. HHS Under Secretary

Charles Baker said that the exception would occur only "in those few cases that the agency, after consultation with the Department of Justice, has determined are appropriate 'test' cases for relitigation." Even so, advocates such as Carl Loewenson, national staff counsel for the American Civil Liberties Union, worried that the SSA had only moved "part-way toward recognizing that the executive branch should follow binding appeals court decisions." But the executive branch of the government, rather than the judiciary, still wanted "to have the final say over what the law means."[93]

The network of advocates and others that had formed in the years of the continuing disability reviews soon took up the matter of how the SSA should go about implementing the nonacquiescence parts of the 1984 law. It was a good illustration of how the control of the SSA and the proprietary Congressional committees had been permanently breached in the matter of disability policy (and hence of SSI policy). Congress now provided a forum for advocates to register their criticisms of the new policy. Former HEW Secretary Arthur S. Flemming, the co-chair of the coalition to protect Social Security that had been formed to protest the Carter disability cuts, appeared with Eileen Sweeney of the National Senior Citizens Law Center before a subcommittee of the House Judiciary Committee. Flemming urged Congress to do more to bring the SSA into compliance with court decisions. Sweeney, a national leader among the legal advocates, complained that the new SSA policy on nonacquiescence was the same as the old policy. She criticized in particular the SSA's decision to ignore circuit precedents at the initial and reconsideration levels of review. The policy forced people to pursue their claim to the ALJ level, which raised due process questions. Sweeney believed that the matter required a new legislative remedy. In nonacquiescence, as in medical improvement, the 1984 law solved part, but not all, of the problem.[94]

On June 6, 1985, Martha McSteen appeared before the House Social Security Subcommittee at an oversight hearing on the implementation of the 1984 law. She gave an upbeat assessment of the process. She reported that work on regulations concerning medical improvement, multiple impairments, mental impairment reviews, the continuation of benefits during appeal, and the frequency of disability reviews was well underway. The commission to investigate the question of pain had begun to meet.[95]

Despite McSteen's confidence in her agency, the hearing provided a forum for the agency's critics. "In my opinion, the situation remains disastrous," said New York Attorney General Robert Abrams. A representative of Massachusetts Governor Michael Dukakis, who three years later would win the Democratic nomination for President, lamented, "Sadly we are now faced with a set of proposals that threaten again to terminate truly disabled people from the rolls." Barney Frank, the still relatively junior Massachusetts Congressman, played upon current stories about wasteful Pentagon expenditures. "If the Department of Human Services would show about one-third the compassion for the disabled the Pentagon shows for ashtrays and toilet seats, I think we would all think we had had a very good year," he said. Eileen Sweeney, a seemingly ubiquitous figure at these types of hearings, accused the administration of "creating the illusion of change (while) carefully and fairly creatively orchestrating maintenance of the status quo."[96]

Specific criticisms from the witnesses included the charge that the SSA had failed to notify all members of the class in legal suits concerning their rights to reapply for benefits. Other witnesses expressed concern that the multiple impairment regulations were not sympathetic enough to people applying for benefits. Nearly all of the nonadministration witnesses criticized the SSA's proposed medical improvement regulations and the newly announced SSA policy on nonacquiescence.[97]

In the meantime, the administration lifted its self-imposed moratorium in 1985, and the states began to be inundated with cases to process. Deferred cases and cases held in limbo all came spilling forth. The release of the pent-up cases contributed to another surge in CDIs after 1985. Many of the complaints about processing delays reemerged. A cycle appeared to be at work, one that repeated itself in 1994. Legislation of that year introduced a statutory requirement that a significant percentage of SSI cases had to be reviewed each year. As a consequence, CDIs once again reached high levels, and the GAO once again issued critical reports about unprocessed CDI backlogs.[98]

All of these things meant that the 1984 law did not completely mollify the legal advocates, state officials, and others who criticized the SSA on its handling of disability reviews. These critics maintained their stance as watchdogs over the process, ready to file their grievances in court or make their complaints known to members of Congress. They realized that they had brought about real change to the disability determination process. For one thing, they had forced the CDI cessation rate back down to about one-fourth the level of the early eighties, although the volume of annual CDIs was soon back to the eighties level.

One of the key results of their work came in the new regulations on mental impairments, which Secretary Heckler announced at the end of August 1985. She called the new regulations "a new approach for people with mental disorders, giving special attention to the seriously mentally disabled population with psychotic disorders." She lauded the newly calibrated relationship between the severity of a mental impairment and a person's functional capacity to work. She expressed confidence that the new standards, based on "state-of-the-art mental-impairment evaluation," reflected modern medical knowledge and would produce the "best and fairest possible decisions" in a difficult area.[99]

The mental impairment standards had a particular importance for SSI, because of the prevalence of people with mental disabilities on the SSI rolls. They provided a good example of how the political furor over the disability reviews ended up making real changes in the administration of the program.

Conclusion

The founding legislation in 1972 established the basic rules and standards for the SSI program; the 1980 disability law moved the program in the direction of encouraging work among its disabled beneficiaries; and now the 1984 law provided procedural safeguards to protect people on the rolls and laid the groundwork for changes in the disability standards that applied to SSI beneficiaries. The sequence of these three laws reflected the growing importance of disability in the SSI caseload.

The controversies over the disability reviews escalated into a legislative process that produced a major new law in 1984. It also helped strengthen the web of interest groups that formed to protect the interests of people on the rolls and gave them a permanent voice in SSI policy. The existence of this web meant that after 1984 perceived injustices in the disability review process would be exposed quickly and addressed by the courts and Congress, as the future fight over childhood disability benefits would demonstrate.

The 1984 legislation, on balance, reliberalized the disability programs. It sent the opposite policy signal from the one in the 1980 law. Program administrators felt whipsawed by the events of the period 1980–1984. They understood their legislative marching orders in 1980 to be to tighten up on the disability program and reduce the size of the rolls. When this effort became controversial, the Congress in effect told the administrators to turn around and march as fast as possible in the opposite direction. This sort of inconsistency in a policymaking process influenced so much by public opinion and media coverage reinforced the natural tendency of bureaucrats to be cautious and risk-averse.

The entire episode underscored the fact that the disability program—whether attached to SSI or to SSDI—came bundled with inherent difficulties. Every effort to push one place produced an unwanted bulge someplace else.

In terms of disability policy, the 1984 law helped change what policy insiders termed the adjudicative climate. After the 1980 law, the presumption among those who made disability determinations was that policymakers wanted the law to be strictly applied. The 1984 law helped change that presumption and loosen up the process. The return to a more "liberal" policy environment invited a return to the concerns that the rolls were growing too fast and led to remedial legislation that pushed in the opposite direction once again.

As for SSI, the controversy over the disability reviews helped cement the program's identity as a disability, rather than an old age, program. It also showed the positive and negative effects of the link between SSI and SSDI. The link helped bring attention to SSI recipients. It also put policy in a sort of straitjacket. A tightening of the SSDI rolls inevitably meant a tightening of the SSI rolls as well, weakening the safety net for those thrown off the SSDI rolls. Nonetheless, the link remained as strong as ever after 1984, as the SSI program faced its next round of challenges.

THE COURTS AND OTHER SOURCES OF PROGRAM GROWTH

How the Program Expanded in
a Conservative Age

During the Reagan and first Bush years, Supplemental Security Income (SSI) operated in a manner that was out of sync with prevailing political sentiment. The program continued to grow in an era characterized by concern over the rising government debt and welfare dependency. The era culminated in spectacular growth in the number of children on the SSI rolls, the product of forces unleashed by the 1984 amendments and a 1990 Supreme Court decision.

Growth of the SSI Rolls

When General Accounting Office (GAO) official Jane Ross testified before the Senate Special Committee on Aging in 1995, she emphasized the decade-long growth in the disability rolls. She noted that, in 1985, some 4.2 million blind and disabled persons under age sixty-five received either Social Security Disability Insurance (SSDI) or SSI benefits, including 1.6 million blind and disabled adults and children on the SSI rolls. By 1994 the number of people on the disability rolls had increased by 70 percent to reach 7.2 million people. Although the SSDI rolls grew by 41 percent, the SSI rolls more than doubled, with much of the growth taking place after 1990.[1] Children accounted for much of the rise. In the three-year period from December 1989 to December 1992, for example, the number of children ages twenty-one years or younger increased from about 293,00 to 614,000.[2]

The expansion of the SSI program began as a reaction against the disability reviews and Social Security reforms of the early eighties. In 1983 Congress passed the Social Security rescue legislation that included a provision for a six-month delay in the cost of living adjustment (COLA). In the same legislation, it took steps to ensure that SSI beneficiaries were not unduly harmed by the delay. The legislation increased SSI payments by $20 a month for individuals and $30 a month for couples, effective July 1, 1983. These increases followed from the advice of the National Social Security Commission (the Greenspan Commission) that low income Social Security recipients needed protection against the loss of income caused by the COLA delay. Although Congress followed this advice, it also made sure that all SSI recipients, not just those who also received Social Security, benefited.[3]

Congress took the opportunity of the Social Security rescue bill to make other adjustments in SSI. It ordered that the federal government increase its outreach activities so that more Social Security beneficiaries knew they could also receive SSI payments. The legislation also made it possible for residents of private emergency shelters to become eligible for SSI, and it ruled that in-kind assistance from a private nonprofit organization be disregarded in determining the level of a person's SSI benefits. These were small changes, but they pointed in a liberal direction. By the time this legislation was enacted—in April 1983—the disability program was at the peak of the controversy described in the previous chapter. This political climate undoubtedly inclined Congress to look at the administration's policy preferences more critically and to move these social programs in a more liberal direction.

The 1984 Disability Benefits Reform Act, which established the medical improvement standard for the continuing disability reviews, also made SSI more generous. The new listings for mental health, for example, expanded the number of people with mental illness who were potentially eligible for disability, including SSI. In general, the 1984 law influenced what policymakers called the adjudicative climate and sent the signal that the states and the federal government should be more lenient in admitting people to the disability rolls than they had been during the disability "purge" of the early eighties. A loosening of the disability rolls inevitably meant an expansion of SSI.

Reagan and the Bigger Picture

During the second term, the Reagan administration continued the President's efforts to overhaul the social welfare system and restrain the growth of the welfare state. Despite strenuous public relations efforts, the resulting legislative proposals failed to gain traction in Congress. Just as big ticket, expansive social welfare programs of the Medicare or Family Assistance Plan variety appeared to be off the political agenda, so aggressive and visible efforts to make the welfare state more conservative met with failure.[4]

Each year, it seemed, President Reagan wanted to make major changes in the nation's welfare programs. Early in 1986, for example, he gave a radio address in which he talked about "misguided welfare programs." Echoing the line of thought popularized by Charles Murray in his influential book *Losing Ground* (1984), Reagan said, "We're in danger of creating a permanent culture of poverty as inescapable as any chain or bond." In a sign of the policy mood of the time, Office of Management and Budget's Counsel Michael Horowitz publicly praised the book in ads for the publisher, and the Office of Personnel Management held an Executive Forum where Murray spoke to an assembly of top Reagan administration officials, each of whom received a free copy of his book.

Reagan urged his Domestic Policy Council to come up with something better, and he explicitly included SSI in the mandate for change. The Council created a proposal that would limit the total amount of assistance that low income people could receive from federal programs—a sort of super cap on welfare. Another feature of the measure included granting more power to the states to experiment with ways of encouraging work among welfare beneficiaries and to set their own eligibility rules. Launched with great fanfare, the proposal influenced the tone of the social welfare debate but never came close to passage.[5]

Upheaval at the Social Security Administration

One of the Reagan administration's more successful initiatives took the form of the 1984 report by the *President's Private Sector Survey on Cost Control*, commonly known as the Grace Commission. In the name of eliminating waste, fraud, and inefficiency, the Grace Commission suggested dumping large parts of the federal enterprise. Along with a general critique of government and its wasteful ways, the Commission conducted in-depth reviews of selected federal agencies, including the Social Security Administration (SSA). The Commission dispatched a team to the SSA and devoted one of its thirteen volumes to the SSA and its programs. In the Commission's most radical proposal, it recommended that the SSA close most of its 1,343 field offices and all of its Teleservice Centers, which would leave it with no more than five hundred offices nationwide. The proposal, of course, stood no chance of being implemented. Republicans and Democrats, liberals and conservatives, responded as one when the SSA proposed closing a local field office—not in my district.[6]

The suggestion that the SSA close many of its offices paved the way for the Commission to propose a massive staffing reduction. In particular, the Commission recommended that the SSA reduce total staffing by 19,791 positions. As it became clear that the office closings would never happen, the Commission lowered the target to 17,791 positions. The Reagan administration embraced the Grace report and directed the SSA to cut its staff by over 17,000.

The arbitrary demand to cut the agency's staff, at the very time Congress was increasing its workloads by liberalizing the disability program and encouraging more SSI outreach, troubled Acting Commissioner and career bureaucrat Martha McSteen. She assigned Deputy Commissioner for Operations, Herbert Doggette Jr., as the agency's liaison to the Grace team. Doggette recalled that the head of the team from the Grace Commission took him aside and told him, "Herb, I want you to know how impressed we are with the work you are doing at SSA. I don't know of any private sector firm that could do anywhere near as efficient a job with all the constraints you operate under. But of course, we cannot say any of this in our report. We have to say SSA is wasteful and inefficient. But I want you to know, that I know it isn't true."[7]

As the administration worked at the macro level to make big changes in the nation's social welfare laws, it also made changes at the micro level to influence the way in which the laws were administered. In the summer of 1986, the Reagan administration announced that Dorcas R. Hardy, who had worked with Reagan in California, would become the new Commissioner of Social Security. She replaced McSteen, who had made a concerted attempt to mediate between the administration and the Social Security loyalists. The press described Hardy, by way of contrast, as a "conservative Reagan loyalist with a reputation as a tough—some say harsh—administrator." Hardy took as her mandate to downsize the Social Security workforce, implementing the Grace recommendations.[8] She believed in and actively pursued the Grace Commission recommendations on staffing levels.

No one quite knew how Hardy would handle the SSI part of her portfolio. An early incident offered a clue. Soon after arriving at the SSA, Hardy was scheduled to make a speech to an outside group. Her speechwriter at the time dutifully prepared the usual boilerplate talk, describing the agency's work and pledging her best efforts. Among the twenty or so pages of the draft speech he included a brief paragraph on SSI, noting it as one of the SSA's core responsibilities. Hardy returned the speech to the speechwriter with the entire SSI paragraph deleted, and in the large, emphatic hand that characterized her comments on draft documents, she wrote in red ink, "No mention of SSI in my speeches! I am NOT the welfare queen."[9]

Another sign of Hardy's attitude toward SSI came in the publication of the SSA's first modern Agency Strategic Plan, one of her proudest accomplishments as Commissioner. The strategic initiatives included a thinly veiled indication that Hardy wanted to return the SSI program back to the states. The head of the SSI program at the SSA at the time later lamented that "Dorcas Hardy's attitude toward SSI was that it belonged back in the states." Hardy's posture also reinforced the negative attitude of the SSA field offices toward SSI, characterized by the SSI program head as "We hate this program, we hate the people that it brings into our offices, we hate the caseload." Now, with Hardy's arrival, these disgruntled employees knew, "gee, the Commissioner hates it too."[10] There was no indication, however, that Hardy's desire to turn SSI back to the states ever found a receptive audience any higher in the Reagan administration.

Hardy was, in the opinion of most, an able and effective administrator. In such key areas as automation, telephone service, and strategic planning, she moved the agency forward. Her manner and management style, however, were often perceived as abrasive. The rank and file employees did not much like her, and her relations with federal employee unions were troubled. Hardy had contempt for the unions, and they returned the sentiment.[11] On the day her resignation was announced, members of the AFGE Union Local 123 at SSA headquarters in Baltimore assembled on the lawn in front of the headquarters complex and marched in a circle, round and round, loudly chanting, "Ding dong, the witch is dead."[12]

A Changed Policy Climate

As Commissioner Hardy pursued her mission to make the SSA operate more efficiently, she encountered resistance from various units within the bureaucracy. The experience with the disability reviews had created avenues of communication between these bureaucrats and members of Congress. Hence internal administrative moves by the Commissioner that might have gone undetected in earlier eras elicited Congressional protests. The subtext of these protests was that the problems of the disability reviews should not be repeated in shortsighted attempts to save money. When the SSA asked the state Disability Determination Services (DDS) to boost the workloads of its employees by 20 percent in 1987, David MacCabe, Deputy Director of the Texas Disability Determination office, promptly replied, "They are asking us to speed up determinations without enough resources. . . . We haven't really implemented what Congress wanted us to do." Representative Barney Frank, alerted to the situation by Massachusetts state officials, drafted a letter on behalf of the Massachusetts Congressional delegation that warned "a drastic speedup in case processing at this point threatened a return to the situation we faced in 1981."[13]

Similar administrative moves by Reagan officials met with similar forms of resistance. In October 1987, the press learned that the Reagan administration had decided to put aside the 1983 provision that in-kind assistance, such as free food, shelter, firewood, or winter clothing, be disregarded as received income in the SSI program. The measure, which had been part of the Social Security rescue legislation, expired on September 30, 1987, and Congress had taken no action to renew it. The administration stepped into the void, without making a public announcement, by rescinding the prior policy. Word of the administration's action soon reached the advocacy groups and members of Congress who had established links with SSI recipients during the crisis over the continuing disability reviews. "For every bag of groceries, we give these poor people, the Government will reduce their benefit checks," said Sharon Daly of the United States Catholic Conference. Representative Ron Wyden (D-Oregon) said he had heard the complaints of his constituents who had been receiving gifts of food from nonprofit groups. Wyden noted that the administration urged the private sector to take care of poor people's needs but then threw roadblocks in the way. He added, "The Administration appears to be grasping at technicalities to force further cutbacks in programs that serve domestic needs as we go into the cold winter months." At a time of national concern over homeless individuals, the administration's actions appeared not efficient but rather cruel.[14]

The administration recognized that it was on the losing side of the issue and in the face of the criticism retreated. Dr. Otis Bowen, the Indiana physician and former governor who served as President Reagan's Secretary of the Department of Health and Human Services (HHS), announced that he would take administrative action to prevent the reduction of benefits. He expected that Congress would soon pass corrective legislation. He said that the President had known nothing of the new policy, and administration officials blamed Congress, now controlled by the Democrats in both the House and the Senate as a result of the 1986 election, for letting the law lapse. Democrats took exception to this charge. Senator Moynihan called the Reagan administration's actions "sneaky, mean and contemptible," done "in the dark of the night."[15]

Homelessness and AIDS

Homelessness became a newly visible issue in the eighties that required some sort of policy response. In a large omnibus bill approved at the end of 1987, Congress included special grants to the states for projects to create procedures and services "to ensure that homeless individuals are provided SSI and other benefits under the Social Security Act to which they are entitled and receive assistance in using such benefits to obtain permanent housing, food, and health care." The legislation authorized the establishment of SSI outreach teams, composed of social workers, doctors, and officials from the state DDS, to bring the homeless who lived in shelters into contact with the program and put them on the rolls. The measure was just one item among thousands in a budget reconciliation bill, but it, like much of the legislation of the period, marked an expansion of the SSI program.[16]

Even more important in shaping the social policy of the era was the AIDS epidemic, which came upon the American scene in 1981 and caught public health providers unprepared. At the time, health care authorities thought the problem of infectious disease had largely been solved and that sexually transmitted diseases, once a major public health priority, occupied a low position among the hierarchy of public health problems. As it became clear that the disease affected homosexuals and intravenous drug users in disproportionate numbers, and in an era when people were being urged to take personal control of their health problems, government only slowly came to the cause of investing in AIDS research and taking care of AIDS patients. Conservative commentator William Buckley wrote in the *New York Times* that "everyone detected with AIDS should be tattooed on the upper forearm, to protect common needle users, and on the buttocks, to prevent the victimization of other homosexuals."[17] President Reagan, who often used denial to cope with social and personal problems, did not even mention AIDS until January 1986. Then even he conceded that AIDS constituted "one of the highest public health priorities." In 1987, at the same time Congress mandated outreach to the homeless, it took steps to increase the AIDS budget of the research-oriented National Institutes of Health.[18]

AIDS, like homelessness, was a multidimensional problem in which SSI had a part in nearly any proposed solution. Homeless people and people with AIDS needed money and medical care. SSI, with its links to disability benefits and Medicaid, served as an available source of such help. In recognition of that fact, the SSA took steps in July 1987 to broaden the definition of AIDS so that SSI reached more of the affected population. Adopting guidelines from the Centers for Disease Control, the new definition allowed people with the AIDS virus who had either dementia or wasting syndrome to qualify for benefits. Unlike SSDI, SSI brought health insurance benefits immediately, compared with a two-year waiting period for Medicare in SSDI. In addition, SSI, which did not require a person to have a previous work history, had more flexibility in its admissions conditions than did SSDI. This flexibility might help relatively young intravenous drug users and others who did not have sufficient work credits to qualify for SSDI. Here again was a force that pushed for the liberalization of the program in a conservative age.[19]

Incremental Reform

Small, incremental measures came easier than larger, big ticket items. At the end of the Reagan presidency, Congress did manage to pass two major social welfare issues on which the Democratic Congress and the Republican President reached consensus. One, the Medicare Catastrophic Coverage Act, expanded the Medicare program to put a limit on medical expenditures and to extend Medicare's coverage to include prescription drugs. Although the law contained Medicaid provisions, such as requiring states to provide pregnancy-related services to pregnant women with incomes below the poverty line, it focused on the more popular Medicare program. Even then, its financing provisions, which put the increased costs of the program partly on the elderly themselves, soon produced a reaction that led to the measure's repeal in the next Congress.[20]

The second major measure, the Family Support Act of 1988, signed by President Reagan in October 1988, represented the latest iteration of welfare reform. In keeping with the social welfare style of the era, it relied heavily on state, rather than federal, initiatives to create programs that would encourage welfare mothers to work. The measure contained sops for liberals in the form of social services and other supports for welfare mothers that enabled it to get through the Democratic Congress. At the same time, in the words of *Time* magazine, it recognized "the importance of such conservative values as family, responsibility, and work," part of the "tough, tight fisted" style of the Reagan era. Nearly all of its provisions centered on Aid to Families with Dependent Children, not SSI. That meant that the two major social welfare measures of the era largely bypassed SSI.[21]

Still, SSI had its Congressional defenders who managed to expand the program using large pieces of legislation, such as the annual budget reconciliation acts, as vehicles. In legislation containing hundreds of costly items, SSI features attracted little attention. The SSI situation resembled that of Medicaid, another program in which, as one advocate put it, "No enhancement of Medicaid can get through Congress on its own as a separate, free-standing measure these days." The chances were much better for success when Medicaid measures were wrapped up in a big comprehensive bill. Sara Rosenbaum, Director of health programs for the Children's Defense Fund, said, "We learned to turn Reagan's legislative ploy back on him. Just as he used the reconciliation process to advance his agenda cutting social programs, people in Congress learned how to use that process to expand and improve social programs."[22]

The Congressional supporters of SSI expansion included the members of a subcommittee on retirement income and employment of the House Select Committee on Aging. Although this subcommittee was neither the most important nor the most influential one on Capitol Hill, it included Edward Roybal (D-California), who served in the House from the era of John F. Kennedy through the era of the first George Bush. As a member of the appropriations committee, he enjoyed some legislative clout. Roybal's subcommittee held hearings and issued reports on SSI, with the objective of creating demand for the program's expansion and liberalization. A 1988 report noted, for example, that the subcommittee's witnesses recommended such things as increasing the SSI benefit level to the annual poverty guideline and adjusting the asset test that limited program eligibility to the level of inflation (increase it, in other words, so that more people qualified as poor enough to get SSI). The suggestions even included proposals to extend SSI beyond old age and disability to cover people who were chronically unemployed or illiterate.

Congressman Roybal introduced a bill that proposed to raise the federal benefit standard to the annual poverty guideline, with further changes tied to the inflation rate. The bill would also raise the asset test to $4,208 for an individual and $6,311 for a couple and permanently exclude in-kind assistance from the definition of income. Under Roybal's bill, a person who was homeless, over the age of fifty with no history of work in the previous five years, or was chronically dependent on welfare would be eligible for SSI. In other words, Roybal wanted to make SSI benefits more generous and more available, so that the program became more like a general anti-poverty program and less a program reserved for the deserving poor.[23]

Although Roybal was a powerful Congressman, his bill stood no chance of passage. It did become one of a number of liberal proposals to expand the SSI program that together created support for incremental changes in the program. The Disability Advisory Council, which issued its report in 1988, came at the problem of reforming SSI from a different direction. It recommended that "the DI and SSI programs should be restructured so as to assign a higher priority to encouraging beneficiaries to work than to declaring them unable to work." A product of the tradition within Social Security to use advisory councils as vehicles to discuss policy problems and float policy proposals and of the recent concern over the disability reviews, the Council noted that the SSI program already contained strong work incentives. It urged the SSA to employ "intense marketing techniques" so that more SSI beneficiaries, advocates, and employers knew about these provisions. In other words, although the Council was concerned mainly with things like improving the disability determination process, it made recommendations to expand the SSI program though outreach activities.[24]

In 1989 the Ford Foundation, an organization that started out with ties to the conservative Ford family of motor car fame but had become a dependable advocate of liberal causes, issued a report on social welfare policy. Under the title "The Common Good: Social Welfare and the American Future," the report, written or at least signed by a panel of experts and dignitaries appointed by the Foundation and chaired by Du Pont executive Irving Shapiro, recommended major expansions of the American welfare state. It urged, for example, that treatment be available on demand for those with alcohol or drug problems and that new programs pay for the long-term care of the elderly. SSI figured in the panel's recommendations, which included the suggestion that federal SSI funding be increased by $2.5 billion a year. Although the Ford Foundation had little or no clout in the realm of government policy, the report hoped to pick up on the possibilities for change presented by the arrival of George H. W. Bush in office, presumably more of a liberal Republican than his predecessor.[25]

Congress contained other pockets of support for the expansion of SSI, such as the Subcommittee on Human Resources, the successor to the Subcommittee on Public Assistance, of the Ways and Means Committee. In 1989 this subcommittee marked up a bill that included $583 million to make more severely disabled children eligible for SSI—part of a more general concern for the welfare of children that was popular at the time. Representative Henry Waxman (D-California) headed a subcommittee of the Energy and Commerce Committee that came at the SSI program through Medicaid. Waxman's subcommittee suggested in 1989 that the federal government help the states fund expanded home care services for the mentally retarded and the frail elderly who were eligible for Medicaid. The rationale was that such services enabled people to live at home, rather than in institutions.[26]

Perhaps the ultimate statement of the case for SSI expansion came just before the 1992 presidential election with the report of the SSI Modernization Project. Arthur S. Flemming, a Republican who nonetheless was a strong liberal on Social Security (he was head of Save Our Security) and civil rights issues (he was former head of the Commission on Civil Rights) and who carried prestige as a former Secretary of Health, Education, and Welfare, headed the group that produced the report. Flemming was a man of unquestioned integrity who spoke with evangelistic fervor in a booming voice about the needs of the poor and the disadvantaged. The group also contained a solid core of advocates, such as attorney Eileen Sweeney, and others who wanted to make changes in the SSI program so that it paid higher benefits to more people.

According to the panel, the SSI program needed to be modernized or updated but not changed in a fundamental way. The disabled and the elderly, simply put, deserved better treatment by their fellow citizens. The better off needed to share more of their resources with the less well off. SSI might not have been the perfect vehicle to effect that transfer, but it operated as the nation's major program for that purpose. As Flemming put it, "This is the wealthiest nation in the world. We have the money. It is only fair to ask the upper 1 percent to share a portion of their wealth with the poorest of the poor."[27]

The panel urged the SSA to increase staffing levels so that SSI beneficiaries received better service and applicants waited less time for government authorities to process their cases. The panel wanted to increase the federal benefit rate and make the means test that determined whether or not a person was poor enough to qualify for benefits reflect the current cost of living. The same income that would have sufficed to maintain someone in relative comfort in 1972 no longer met the basic living needs of someone in 1992.[28]

The Bush Administration

The Bush administration objected to these proposals on the grounds of cost. At the same time, the new administration presented a more sympathetic face to the SSI program than did the Reagan administration. Gwendolyn King, who had experience working on the Hill with Senator John Heinz, succeeded Dorcas Hardy as Social Security Commissioner in 1989. Although she had solid Republican credentials, she nonetheless took more liberal positions than her predecessor. An African American, King, in the words of an experienced SSA staffer, "positioned herself to look very different from Dorcas Hardy and that included the public face around SSI. So she was a great supporter of the SSI program."[29]

A good indication of the changed attitude toward SSI at the SSA came at the end of 1989. An internal SSA report revealed that, as a result of heavy agency workloads, many SSI beneficiaries had been mistakenly dropped from the rolls. The problem concerned the failure of beneficiaries to return financial information to the SSA in a timely manner. Agency staff members, who were not supposed to drop anyone from the rolls without calling or visiting the recipient, did so anyway. According to the report, "In many cases involving recipients who are of advanced age or who have a language barrier or impairments that might make it difficult to comply with agency requests, field officers suspend benefits without first making the follow-up telephone or personal contact required by the Program Operations Manual System." As a consequence, the number of people dropped from the rolls for failure to cooperate with the agency's efforts rose from 80,000 in 1987 to 105,000 in 1988.[30]

Although the report itself might not have been much of a surprise, the agency's response revealed its new attitude toward such problems. A spokesman immediately put out word that the agency was "extremely concerned" because it was suspending payments to "some of the most vulnerable people, the elderly and the disabled." The agency sent out a corrective order in which it admonished fieldworkers to "be careful to make sure that SSI benefits are not improperly suspended for failure to provide information."[31] As if that were not enough, Commissioner King gave a scolding talk on the subject that was broadcast to all 1,300 Social Security field offices, in which she said that the findings of the study "deeply troubled" her. "Let me say this in the most direct, unambiguous way," she continued, "I will not tolerate this happening again. If one, just one, beneficiary is wrongly denied his or her benefits, that is a tragedy, nothing less. We will not permit such tragedy to take place."[32]

Gwendolyn King made SSI an agency priority for the first time since the troubled implementation period in 1974. She endorsed outreach efforts to sign up more people for the program. Setting a personal example, she even joined SSA fieldworkers in Baltimore who approached homeless people and tried to persuade them to come to a shelter where they could apply for SSI benefits. "These are people who may not speak to anyone else during the day unless somebody goes by to talk to them," she said. Ron Pollack, the Executive Director of the Families USA Foundation and a frequent critic of the SSA during the days of the disability purges, noted that, under King, the agency demonstrated "greater sensitivity." "I think she genuinely would like to work to improve services," he said. He added that many people still did not know about the program and hence he welcomed the new outreach efforts. As many as two million people might not have been getting the SSI benefits for which they were qualified.[33]

It was difficult to evaluate the results of such efforts. Analysts often cited increased outreach as one reason among many for the expansion of the SSI rolls. The Bush administration also resisted efforts during the budget planning season in late 1989 to cut the SSA workforce, from 63,000 to 58,800; it had once numbered 80,000. The action or lack of action meant that more people were available to work with SSI applicants than the agency had originally planned. The downsizing era appeared to be over, at least for a time. Commissioner King said that the agency needed "a period of stability" and what she called "a more human-oriented approach." She hoped in this manner to arrest the decline in the morale of SSA employees that many agency observers attributed to the cuts in the workforce.[34]

In keeping with the incremental pattern of SSI reform, the Omnibus Budget Reconciliation Act of 1990 contained a number of small changes in the program, such as excluding victim compensation payments as income for program purposes or requiring the agency to make every reasonable effort to see that a pediatrician or other qualified specialist evaluate a child's eligibility for SSI. The bill also doubled the period of time—from three to six months—a person could receive "presumptive disability" benefits (for certain impairments) while his or her application was being processed. And the applicant did not have to return the payments should he or she be denied benefits. None of these things amounted to a major change of the sort that made headlines, yet each helped expand the program.[35]

The *Zebley* Case

In 1990 a Supreme Court decision altered the relatively placid pattern of SSI's post-1984 development. The decision affected how the SSA evaluated children who applied to the disability program. The case arose from the disability reviews of the early eighties that first brought the attention of legal advocates to the disability determination process. It provided a perfect illustration of how at a time when Congress was little inclined to make major changes the courts provided an alternative avenue to bring those changes about.

In a manner typical of legal disputes, the case developed over a long period of time. On July 13, 1978, four years after the implementation of SSI, Brian Zebley was born in Upland Pennsylvania, near the city of Chester, outside of Philadelphia. At birth he manifested brain damage, and as a result he suffered from mental retardation, visual problems, and partial paralysis.[36] As a handicapped child, he became a candidate for SSI, which, unlike SSDI, had special provisions for children. Social Security coverage of working parents did not include benefits for their disabled children, so SSI was the program that covered Brian's situation: a desperate need for the money and services necessary to sustain his life.

Zebley went on the SSI rolls from 1980 to 1983 and then, in the era of the disability purges, the state disability determination office in Harrisburg removed him from the rolls. His case became part of a class action against the government that began in July 1983. Three years later, the United States district court for the Eastern District of Pennsylvania dismissed the suit. On appeal, however, the Third Circuit Court vacated the district court's dismissal in August 1988. It remanded the case back to the district court. The SSA appealed the decision to the Supreme Court, which heard oral arguments at the end of November 1989.

Then, on February 20, 1990, the Supreme Court, by a vote of 7 to 2, decided in Zebley's favor.

Zebley's lawyers included Richard Weishaupt and Jonathan Stein of the Philadelphia Community Legal Services offices. They took on the case because it originated in the Philadelphia area and because it involved issues on which they had become engaged during the controversy over the disability reviews. Weishaupt, a native of Queens, New York, who had attended Catholic schools before going to Harvard Law School and then taking a job with Philadelphia Community Legal Services in the fall of 1974, delivered the oral argument before the Supreme Court. He worked closely with his colleague Stein and other lawyers who represented the many organizations that filed *amici* briefs. The impressive list included the attorney generals of many of the states and professional organizations such as the American Academy of Child and Adolescent Psychiatry and the American Medical Association (AMA). The presence of the AMA and other groups added to the weight of a case that had been brought by lawyers from a Community Legal Services office.

Understanding the case required an understanding of the SSI disability determination process. The process for adults differed from the process for children in ways that, according to the plaintiffs, discriminated against the children. The problem went back to the original SSI statute in which the Ways and Means Committee had added disabled children's benefits to the traditional adult benefits in the public assistance programs that had preceded SSI. Despite the addition of this new group, the SSI program inherited its definition of disability and its disability determination process from the SSDI program. The SSA did its disability business through institutions already developed for SSDI.

The basic idea behind the original SSDI law in 1956 (and an even earlier law in 1954 that established a rudimentary disability program) was that Social Security paid benefits to wage earners who could no longer work because of a physical or mental impairment that was expected to last indefinitely or result in death. The inability to engage in substantial gainful activity, to use the legalistic language, became the key test of disability. When SSI came along, this definition had somehow to be applied to children who by law were not allowed to work in the labor force. Their impairments had to be of "comparable severity" for them to receive SSI benefits.

Between the beginnings of disability insurance in the fifties and the implementation of SSI in the seventies, the disability determination process became more transparent in that applicants had access to its rules and regulations. When disability insurance became law in 1956, the SSA did not publish its medical listings or disability determination procedures. The unpublished regulations contained a "listing of impairments" that were prima facie evidence of the presence

of a disability. The medical advisory board for the SSA insisted that it was unde-
sirable for "examining physicians throughout the country to have available to
them exactly what it is that makes it possible for a person to qualify." Armed
with this information, it was feared that physicians would game the system in
favor of the applicants. Lawyers, who quickly became involved in the disability
process, thought that such rules put them at an impossible disadvantage. Congress, legal advocates, and the prevailing sentiment in favor of "sunshine" in the
regulatory process combined to produce a more open process. By 1979 the SSA
had published both the "medical listings," which included the specific numerical
values of clinical tests required for disability benefits, and a specific set of rules
that explained the application of vocational considerations to disability determination. The rules for getting disability insurance became part of the public
record.[37]

The problem in *Zebley* concerned the disparities in the processes used for
adults and children. The SSA used a five-stage process for adult cases. It asked if
an applicant was working. If not, the second question concerned the existence of
a severe impairment. If such an impairment existed, the third question became
whether the impairment met or equaled the medical listings. If so, the person
received benefits. If not, the process continued, and the examiners asked if the
impairment prevented the applicants from meeting the demands of past relevant work. If so, the fifth and final question in the sequence involved whether
the impairment prevented the applicant from doing other work. To answer this
question, state disability examiners used a table that matched a person's "residual functional capacity" with his age, education, and past work experience. For
example, a person limited to light sedentary work qualified for benefits if he was
fifty years old, had less than a high school education, and had no skilled work
experience.

Children received a different treatment. Examiners determined if they were
working, a relatively easy question to answer. If not, they then asked if the child
had a severe impairment. If so, then they proceeded to the question of whether
the impairment met or equaled the medical listings. If so, the child received benefits. The process for children did not go on to steps four and five, since the SSA
did not think that questions related to the demands of past relevant work or
other work applied to children. To be sure, the medical listings for children,
which first appeared in 1977, added a category for growth impairment and contained special details related to the evaluation of children. The lawyers for Zebley
argued that even with these additions and refinements the process unfairly discriminated against children.

Justice Blackmun agreed with the plaintiffs.[38] He wrote, "While adults who
do not qualify under the listings still have the opportunity to show they are dis-

abled at the last stages of the Secretary's test, no similar opportunities exist for children, who are denied benefits even if their impairments are of 'comparable severity' to one that would actually (though not presumptively) disable adults." The secretary's regulatory process nullified "the congressional choice to link the child-disability standard to the more liberal test applied to adult disability claims."

The opinion stated that even though a vocational analysis was inapplicable to children that "does not mean that a functional analysis cannot be applied to them, since an inquiry into an impairment's impact on a child's normal daily activities is no more amorphous or unmanageable than an inquiry into the impact of an adult's impairments on his ability to perform any kind of substantial gainful work that exists in the national economy." The medical listings, Justice Blackmun noted, "obviously do not cover all illnesses and abnormalities that can actually be disabling." The listings excluded people who could not work "because of pain, consequences of medication, and other symptoms that vary greatly with the individual." The process rectified these omissions for adults in the "final, vocational steps of the Secretary's test," but for children "there is no similar opportunity." "Children whose impairments are not quite severe enough to rise to the presumptively disabling level set by the listings, children with impairments that might not disable any and all children, but which actually disable them, due to symptomatic effects such as pain, nausea, side effects of medication, etc., or due to their particular age, educational background, and circumstances, and children with unlisted impairments or combinations of impairments that are not equivalent to any one listing—all of these categories of child claimants are simply denied benefits, even if their impairments are of 'comparable severity' to one that would actually . . . render an adult disabled."

The government argued that the solution to the problem was to build better listings and that such an approach was the only practical one to the problem. To do an individual, functional assessment of each child applicant was not feasible because children did not work and there was "no available measure of their functional abilities analogous to an adult's ability to work." Blackmun stated that the listings could never be made complete or comprehensive enough. As he put it, "No decision process restricted to comparing medical evidence to a fixed, finite set of medical criteria can respond adequately to the infinite variety of medical conditions and combinations thereof, the varying impact of such conditions due to the claimant's individual characteristics, and the constant evolution of medical diagnostic techniques." Instead, the SSA needed to undertake a functional analysis of children. According to Blackmun, "An inquiry into the impact of an impairment on the normal daily activities of a child of the claimant's age—speaking, walking, dressing, feeding oneself, going to school, playing, etc.—is, in our view, no more amorphous or unmanageable than an inquiry into the impact of an adult's impairment on his ability to perform 'any other kind of substantial gainful work which exists in the national economy.' "

Only Justices White and Rehnquist disagreed with Blackmun's opinion. Justice White noted that the Court had traditionally given the Secretary "exceptionally broad authority" to make regulations for the evaluation of disability. Congress had not expressed a clear intent on the matter and therefore the court should defer "to the agency's interpretation."[39] Blackmun's opinion did not give the Secretary of HHS the deference he deserved on this matter.

Implementing *Zebley*

The *Zebley* decision posed a major challenge to the way that the SSA conducted the SSI program. As Linda Greenhouse reported in the *New York Times*, it represented a major victory for advocates of the disabled.[40] Jonathan Stein said, "This decision ends 16 years of a federal safety net program that has never worked as intended." He believed it would lead to two major developments. All future child applicants would be judged by new standards, and up to a quarter of a million children rejected since 1980 would have their cases reopened. The SSA faced what by any measure would be a daunting task, one that was not nearly as simple as Justice Blackmun implied in his decision. Louis Enoff, the SSA deputy commissioner who functioned as the chief operating officer, told the press, "We now have a decision and we are going to implement this as quickly as we can, working with experts and those who have an interest in providing benefits to these very needy children."[41]

A Supreme Court decision sent the same sort of signals to the SSA that a law passed by Congress did. In both cases, the agency knew it had to follow the decision made by another branch of government. Because the decision came from the Supreme Court, not a district court, the SSA could not simply give Brian Zebley and the others in the class action their benefits and continue business as usual for children who applied for SSI. In other words, a Supreme Court decision had the same effect on the SSA as a law passed by Congress. In both cases, however, the agency needed to figure out a way to implement a decision made by an outside agency for which the practical details of public administration were not a high priority.[42] The presence of interested onlookers, such as the lawyers who tried the *Zebley* case and members of Congress who took an interest in the issue, meant that the implementation process would be marked by a high degree of public scrutiny. It more closely resembled a negotiation than a formal bureaucratic exercise.

In this spirit, the SSA convened a group of experts in April 1990 to help formulate new regulations that used age-appropriate functional criteria in the determination of a child's application for disability benefits. As might be expected, the group included people with expertise in the field of child development, such as pediatricians and child psychologists, as well as experts in the sorts of disabilities that the SSA had largely neglected, such as learning disorders. Significantly, however, legal advocates from Community Legal Services in Philadelphia and the Mental Health Law Project also participated in the meetings. They wanted to be sure that the regulations that the SSA adopted met the letter of the law or, even better, interpreted the law in as broad a way as possible, so the maximum number of children received relief. In a sense, then, these meetings marked an extension of the case itself.[43]

Not surprisingly, conflicts developed in framing the regulations. Jean Hinckley, the director of the litigation support staff at the SSA, noted that the *Zebley* case was "unprecedented in scope" and presented overwhelming administrative problems. A major issue concerned whether the SSA would have to go back and retrieve the files of all children denied benefits. It could be "a massive undertaking" according to Hinckley, since the government denied or terminated benefits for 283,360 children from May 1983 to February 1990. As the matter dragged on, members of Congress, such as Senator John Heinz, expressed their impatience that, "Not one denial has been reversed, not one check mailed, not one child helped." The legal advocates uncovered cases of children still denied benefits because the SSA refused to follow the standards mandated by the Supreme Court. A staff member of Tennessee's Rural Legal Services said, "The Tennessee disability agency, under instructions from Social Security, is still applying Federal criteria in a narrow, restrictive way so that children are excluded." From the Bush administration's point of view, the problem concerned the back payments that children might receive for the time they were improperly excluded from the rolls. These payments could amount to a substantial amount of money. As a White House official noted, "Nobody in the Administration wants to hurt poor and disabled children, but we don't want to give them a financial windfall."[44]

By February 1991 the SSA had new regulations ready, although even these did not stop the controversies over *Zebley*. A February 1991 joint letter from thirty-one Democratic members of the House complained about the *Zebley* implementation. It was typical of the type of mixed signals that Congress often sent agencies trying to implement legislation. The letter complained that the SSA was not paying enough *Zebley* class members fast enough. Still, one of its five proposals called for extending the comment period for the new *Zebley* regulations from sixty days to "at least six months," thereby delaying the processing of any cases that much longer.

The thirty-one Democrats also objected "strongly to the addition of a 'severity step' to the SSI eligibility determination process." "This additional step," the members continued, "applied before any of the *required* eligibility tests, would result in frequent and inaccurate denials of claims judged 'not severe' enough to qualify for SSI benefits." The group said of the severity test: "This gratuitous addition to the regulations is not required by the *Zebley* decision. . . . In fact, the 'severity step' runs counter to the *Zebley* decision, which seeks to eliminate rather than to establish barriers to the payment of benefits to needy, disabled children."[45]

Beyond the occasional intervention by concerned members of Congress, battles continued between Jonathan Stein and the administration on pretty much every step of the implementation. Stein and his colleagues at the Philadelphia Community Legal Services formed a special Zebley Implementation Project to communicate their concerns. Typical of the types of issues the Project raised was a dispute involving quality assurance reviews of *Zebley* cases. The Project wanted the SSA to devote all its quality assurance resources to reviewing denied cases and not allowances.

The relationship between advocates like Stein and the administration was often adversarial. A memo written by an SSA executive after one June 1991 conference call among the SSA, Stein, and officials of the federal agency responsible for Medicaid captured the spirit of their interactions: "There was considerable acrimony between Stein and [Medicaid officials] and little indication of any 'give' on either side. . . . As the conversation went on, Jonathan threatened further court action seeking (e.g., a contempt citation against the Secretary), which tended to undercut any efforts at more reasoned discussions of the issues."[46]

One particular issue that threatened for a time to become a serious controversy for the SSA concerned the destruction of documents. The SSA typically disposed of around four million folders of material each year—first by moving the folder to one of the government's twelve Federal Records Centers and then by having the National Archives destroy the material according to its retention schedule. The *Zebley* ruling required the SSA to reopen childhood cases back to January 1980 and obliged the SSA to retain material going back this far. Stein and his colleagues wanted the SSA to reopen all childhood cases back to the start of the program in January 1974. In this manner a dispute over policy became entangled in a dispute about the procedures for retaining old records. As the *Washington Post*'s Spencer Rich, explained: "The dispute illustrated what often happens when the Supreme Court enunciates a large principle, leaving lesser bodies to sort out the details."[47]

Zebley's attorneys lobbied Congress and the courts to intervene. In June 1990, Senator Heinz wrote HHS Secretary Sullivan to express his alarm "over the potential destruction of SSI children's disability files by SSA field offices and federal records centers." The next month the federal district court overseeing the *Zebley* implementation issued a Protective Order forbidding the SSA from destroying any case folders with potential *Zebley* material. Commissioner King decided to respond by placing a moratorium on the destruction of any case folders. This moratorium stayed in effect for one year, until all the *Zebley* cases had been electronically flagged. Commissioner King then informed Stein and Congress that routine folder destruction would resume.[48]

The New Childhood Disability Regulations

Despite all the attendant controversies over implementation procedures, the new regulations did take effect. The new regulations broadened the disability determination for children to consider the effect of their medical conditions on their ability to walk, eat, dress themselves, and undertake other regular activities.[49] Under the new rules, a child with a severe impairment who did not meet or equal the medical listings would undergo an Individualized Functional Assessment to determine whether his impairments substantially limited his (or her) "ability to function, independently, appropriately, and effectively in an age-appropriate manner." The use of the adverbs that resisted precise definition and the concept of "age-appropriate" behavior indicated just how hard the new regulations would be to administer.[50]

The SSA tried to clarify the concepts. A disabling impairment needed to reduce substantially "the child's ability to grow, develop, or mature physically, mentally or emotionally to the extent that it limits his or her ability to (1) attain age appropriate developmental milestones or (2) attain age appropriate daily activities at home, school, work, or play or (3) acquire the skills needed to assume adult roles." To get at these things for children not automatically declared disabled by virtue of their impairment, the agency now needed to assess the child's "social, communication, cognitive, personal and behavioral, and motor skills, as well as his or her responsiveness to stimuli and ability to concentrate, persist at tasks at hand and keep pace." All of that needed to be done in an age-appropriate manner, and some of the tests were not applicable to all children. For example, a child needed to be at least three years old before the agency would try to assess his ability to concentrate.[51] In addition, the scoring of the various findings was complex, and the process involved getting data from teachers, parents, and others with knowledge of a child's ability to function from day to day. If the Individualized Functional Assessment showed that a child had a moderate limitation in three areas of functioning or a marked limitation in one area and a moderate limitation in another, the child received benefits.[52]

Gwendolyn King and other SSA officials blessed the new regulations. The Commissioner said that the changes brought "Social Security's evaluation of childhood disability into line with state-of-the-art practice in pediatric and adolescent medicine." She expressed the hope that SSI would now be able to reach the entire population of children with disabilities "it was intended to reach."[53]

Despite these sentiments, disputes over the *Zebley* case dragged on past the date that regulations were issued. The issue of just how many old cases would need to be reviewed remained unresolved, a source of considerable conflict between Zebley's lawyers and the SSA. In March 1991 the Bush administration announced a compromise agreement under which the government would consider rejected applications dating from January 1, 1980. The SSA put the number of applications in this category at between 400,000 and 450,000.[54] Even then, it took the SSA until July to gear up the process and send notices to affected children.[55] And even at that point, problems persisted because the legal advocates, in their watchdog roles, charged that the DDS made mistakes in applying the new rules.

Childhood Mental Disability

During the negotiations over the *Zebley* case, the SSA issued new childhood mental disability listings in December 1990. These listings, like the *Zebley* decision, had a major impact on how the SSA evaluated childhood disability. The 1984 Disability Benefits Reform Act had required a revision of the rules used for the evaluation of mental impairments. The revisions that appeared at the end of August 1985 affected only the adult part of the listings. Nonetheless, they demonstrated the expansive nature of the mental health category. The number of major mental health impairments, for example, doubled from four to eight. The adult listings marked the SSA's attempt to satisfy the Congressional desire that the revised standards should "realistically evaluate the ability of a mentally impaired individual to work in a competitive environment."[56]

Congress said nothing about how such a concept should apply to children. When the listings for children appeared on December 12, 1990, they reflected the terminology of a new edition of the American Psychiatric Association's *Diagnostic and Statistical Manual of Mental Disorders*. The number of major mental health impairments increased from four in 1977 to eleven, four more than in the adult mental health listings, in 1990. The listings included such new entities as anxiety disorders, autistic and other pervasive developmental disorders, and attention deficit hyperactivity disorder (ADHD). The new childhood disability listings were much more specific and detailed than the former standards that had been issued in 1977. They contained a more explicit emphasis on the age of the child. In the works before the *Zebley* decision, the new mental health listings for children nonetheless reflected its emphasis on Individualized Functional Assessments.[57]

In a sense, both the *Zebley* decision and the new childhood mental disability listings were the products of the disputes over the continuing disability reviews in the early eighties. Because the reviews targeted younger disability beneficiaries with nonpermanent disabilities, they exposed the special problems of making disability determinations for the mentally ill. Congress intervened to call attention to the problem and insist that the SSA revise its procedures. Because SSI included benefits for children as well as adults, the process required that the SSA inquire into mental impairments that were unique to children. The delay between 1984 and 1990 in issuing the regulations for children meant that these listings, when they finally appeared, reflected newly defined categories of childhood mental impairments, such as ADHD. The *Zebley* case also followed from the disability reviews. In the key development, attorneys Stein and Weishaupt agreed to take on Zebley's case as part of their work representing the victims of what they considered to be the disability purges. In looking for a legal argument to make before the Supreme Court, they came upon the disparities between the disability determination processes for adults and children. They never met Zebley personally, but their association with his case had a major impact on his life and on the lives of many children in similar circumstances. The train of developments that began with the Carter administration's disability law in 1980, setting the continuing disability review process into motion, continued at full speed into the nineties.

Consequences—The SSI Expansion

The *Zebley* case and the new childhood mental disability listings, combined with the SSA's more tolerant attitude toward SSI in Gwendolyn King's tenure as Commissioner, increased formal outreach activities at SSI. The start of a new baby boom as baby boomers had children of their own and the onset of a recession in the late eighties all came together to produce a major surge in the SSI rolls. Between 1984 and 1996, the SSI beneficiary population grew by 59 percent, and this rise was entirely due to disability cases (see Figure 6-1). The overall increase was greater among the adult disabled than among children (50 to 22 percent), but the increase in children was quite dramatic when compared to its pre-*Zebley* baseline (see Figure 6-2).[58]

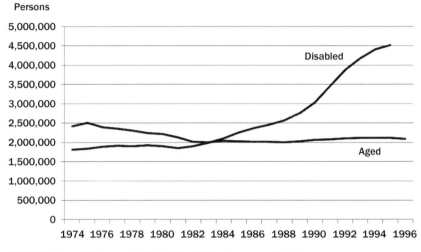

FIGURE 6-1   SSI Growth, FY 1974–1996, Aged vs. Disabled

Although Congress might not have been able to enact major legislation to expand SSI, these delayed reactions to the previous legislation and external economic factors produced the same effects as if Congress had passed what it might have called the SSI Childhood Disability Act.

Predictably, as the pendulum shifted in the liberal direction, Congress suddenly shifted gears and once again became concerned with the problem of too many people being on disability, not too few. In 1992 and 1994, the Congressional Research Service, in response to "various congressional requests," released two studies of the rising tide of disability.[59] In 1994 the GAO reported, with some alarm, that the number of children receiving disability benefits from SSI had more than doubled between 1990 and 1994. Thirty percent of these new awards came as a result of the Individualized Functional Assessments that had been mandated by the *Zebley* case. As much as two-thirds of the new awards involved children with mental impairments. At the end of 1993, 770,500 children received SSI childhood disability benefits. In 1989 such children made up 11.5 percent of the SSI caseload; at the end of 1993, one in five people on the rolls was a disabled child.[60]

A 1995 report from the GAO noted further increases in the trends. The number of children on the SSI rolls now approached 900,000, at a cost of some $4 billion annually. The GAO reported that the changes in the regulations induced by the *Zebley* decision were responsible for 200,000 of these children being on the rolls. Eighty-four percent of those children presented mental impairments as their primary limitation, including 14.8 percent with ADHD, which had become shorthand for a group of children on the rolls that some members of Congress began to

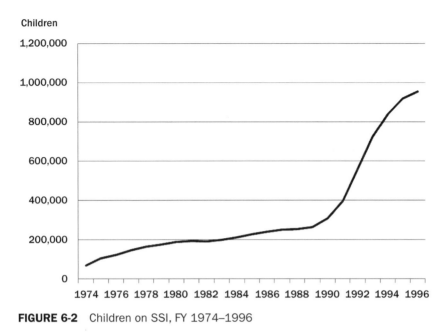

FIGURE 6-2   Children on SSI, FY 1974–1996

view with some suspicion. Hyperactivity, it came to be believed, was a symptom that children, coached by parents anxious to get the benefits, could fake. These sentiments revealed that the surge in the SSI rolls contained elements that alerted authorities to apply pressure in the opposite direction, continuing a dynamic process that had always characterized the Social Security disability programs.[61]

A check of the childhood disability rolls in December 1994 revealed that most qualified on the basis of mental retardation, just as they had from the beginnings of the SSI program. Respiratory disorders, by way of contrast, accounted for only 3 percent of the children on SSI. Childhood impairments were sensitive to age. For example, more than half of the newborns and toddlers who received SSI benefits did so on the basis of congenital anomalies, such as Down syndrome or very low birth weight. As the children aged, different factors came into play. Most of the growth in the rolls came not from mental retardation but, rather, from mental disabilities. In particular, ADHD rose from 7 to 11 percent of the caseload between 1990 and 1994.[62]

Conclusion

In this manner a period in SSI's history that began rather sedately after the great excitement of the disability purges ended with the great rise in the childhood disability rolls. The politics of this period featured three distinct ways in which the rolls were expanded. Congress made changes in the SSI program through little noticed additions to large omnibus bills, drawing on the advice of interested advocates for the disabled who testified before one of the growing number of Congressional subcommittees. The SSA made important regulatory changes in the law, such as the new childhood disability mental health listings, that were the result of legislation from a previous period. The federal courts expanded the program by using the legal system to order changes in the program that Congress was not otherwise prepared to make. These various mechanisms of expansion did not exist independently of the historical forces that defined the era. Health and welfare benefits for children and disability rights were already popular causes of the time, as the expansion of the Medicaid program and the passage of the Americans with Disabilities Act in 1990 indicated. Still, the great expansion in child disability benefits came about through indirection—discrete and disparate changes in the policy environment reinforced one another to produce a consistent trend.

The expansion of the child disability rolls had an important feature that made it different from previous surges in the disability rolls. The great rise in the rolls during the seventies involved first SSDI and then SSI, and politicians viewed the rise through the lens of the Social Security program. This lens blurred SSI and SSDI beneficiaries together, so that the policy response was tempered by the positive reputation of the Social Security program. The great rise in the childhood disability rolls affected SSI but not SSDI rolls. Its excesses could therefore be addressed under the rubric of welfare reform, almost guaranteeing a different and more punitive response.

THE WELFARE REFORM OF 1996

How the Program Became Swept Up in the
Narrative of Welfare Fraud and Abuse

In 1994 the Republicans gained full control of Congress for the first time since 1952. Only two years later, Bill Clinton became the first Democratic president since Franklin Roosevelt to win a second term in office. In those three eventful political years, Supplemental Security Income (SSI) emerged as an object of political controversy that centered on three groups whose receipt of benefits came under public scrutiny. The presence of children with behavioral disabilities, substance abusers, and immigrants on the SSI rolls tarnished SSI's image as a refuge for the deserving poor. Each of these groups figured in the extended discussion of welfare reform that took place in those years, and Congress made each of those groups the targets of significant cuts in the SSI program. A program launched in a liberal era of welfare reform, that had endured controversies related to its identity as a disability program, now battled for its survival in a conservative era of welfare reform.

Exposing the Children on SSI

At the beginning of 1994, the *Washington Post* ran a series of feature stories about social programs that threatened to bust the federal budget. Thanks to the efforts of Congressman like Henry Waxman (D-California), Medicaid had expanded so much that it now loomed as "a fiscal 'Time Bomb.'" Like many social programs, it exemplified the phenomenon of mission creep. As recently as the eighties, Medicaid, according to the *Post's* Dan Morgan, "was a no frills government insurance program." By 1994 it had morphed into a mini national health insurance program that paid the medical bills of "millions of children and women in working families, illegal immigrants seeking care in emergency rooms . . . AIDS sufferers and some elderly nursing home patients with middle-class spouses or children." Accompanying charts illustrated the "rocketing costs of an entitlement." Among those who drove up Medicaid's costs were the severely disabled, and the hospitals that treated them were "increasingly aggressive in using the SSI program to qualify for Medicaid." Hence an expose of Medicaid was also an expose of SSI, the gateway program to Medicaid.[1]

Soon after its series on Medicaid, the *Post* turned its attention to the disabled children on SSI. On February 4, 1994, it ran a long story co-authored by Bob Woodward, perhaps America's most famous investigative print reporter of the post-Watergate era. In many ways, the themes of the story repeated those in the series on Medicaid. In both cases, a program had grown out of control, and costs began to soar as it took on new clientele. In both cases, the process of program expansion occurred largely out of sight from public scrutiny and presented the public with a fait accompli.

If Congressman Waxman had worked the interstices of the legislative process to expand Medicaid, then Tom Joe, the relatively obscure official in the Nixon era welfare bureaucracy, had manipulated the process to slip disabled children into the legislation that created SSI. The relevant part of the legislation consisted of twenty-six words inserted into the Social Security Amendments of 1972. "It wasn't thought of as a big deal," said Social Security Administration (SSA) staffer Frank Crowley. "It was one of those annoying little details." Tom Joe, with characteristic arrogance leavened by humor, added, "This is a good example of democracy not at work." In both cases something that started out small and relatively insignificant became large and veered out of control. As in the Medicaid story, a graph accompanied the SSI story, under the heading "Soaring Costs."[2]

The official statistics told a different story rather than one of soaring costs (Figure 7-1).[3] The December 1973 conversion to the state rolls brought 2,278 children onto the new federal program. In SSI's first year of operation (1974), the federal government awarded benefits to 66,699 additional children. The number of new awards hovered around the 50,000 level until the 1990 *Zebley* decision, when the number of awards skyrocketed, but the rate then fell off.

The Woodward story focused not so much on the soaring costs but instead on whether the children who received SSI really deserved the benefits. It featured a Pennsylvania pediatrician and state Disability Determination Services (DDS) employee who examined the files of SSI applicants and told Woodward that "children who curse teachers, fight with classmates, perform poorly in school or display characteristics of routine rebellion are often diagnosed with behavioral

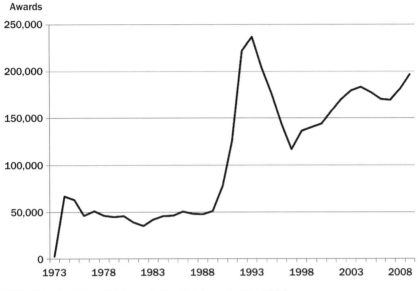

FIGURE 7-1   New SSI Awards for Children, 1973–2009

disorders and therefore qualify for the program's cash benefits, which average $400 a month."

It was not a case of bad kids so much as bad parents. The kids suffered from what psychologist Kenneth Carroll called "parental neglect and abuse." Parents were being rewarded for their children's shortcomings. Even if these payments were awarded to deserving children, they in fact went into the pockets of often profligate parents. The parents could spend the money as they pleased because of lax and permissive program supervision. Some bought television sets, video games, or cars. Lump sum payments that some parents received as a result of the settlement of the *Zebley* case put even more money in their hands and increased the temptation to make ill advised purchases. In this way, the SSI parents came to resemble the irresponsible "welfare queens" on Aid to Families with Dependent Children (AFDC) who, according to popular stereotypes, drove Cadillacs and had illegitimate children on the public's nickel.

Woodward's story damaged SSI by putting it in bad company at just the time when the Clinton administration was figuring out what sort of welfare reform package it should send to Congress. Journalists forgot or never knew of the historical association between SSI and Social Security and instead portrayed it as a welfare program that was as bad as any other. Although Woodward's story did not include a malevolent welfare queen, it did feature the case of Beverly Smith of Greensville, Kentucky, who in 1992 received a back payment of $13,000 for her eleven-year-old hyperactive son. It was more than a year and half's worth of her wages as a custodial worker at a bank. Faced with this windfall, she went on a shopping spree and bought a car, a washer and dryer, a refrigerator, a stove, a computer, and three jogging suits for her son. In other words she made some of the purchases that she could otherwise not afford. Although these purchases undoubtedly benefited her son as well as her, they seemed like an extravagant use of public money that, in some people's opinion, Beverly Smith should have earned herself.[4]

Stories such as Woodward's had a compounding effect as other journalists investigated SSI's problems. In what might be considered piling on, curmudgeonly *Post* columnist Jonathan Yardley quoted the passage about children with behavioral problems receiving benefits. He said the phenomenon exemplified America's "It Isn't My Fault Society" in which children vilify "teachers and pull knives on classmates" and then receive disability benefits on the basis of age-inappropriate behavior.[5] SSI, in other words, condoned and even encouraged bad behavior.

The *Post* had influence in Congress because it was perceived as a liberal paper. If such a paper was willing to attack SSI, then that attack must be merited. The *Post* also exerted influence because television producers read it and used it to generate story ideas for the evening newscasts and the prime time news magazines produced by the news divisions of the networks. In this manner, ABC's *Prime Time* picked up on the *Post* story and ran a piece on SSI in October 1994. A Congressional subcommittee screened the piece at a hearing, and several members cited it in Congressional debate. If the *Post* brought Bob Woodward to the project, ABC News offered the stellar combination of Mike Wallace's son Chris, future network anchor Diane Sawyer, and well-known White House correspondent Sam Donaldson. Donaldson offered a comment about "how easy it is get on the receiving end of what some are calling 'crazy checks.'"

ABC News went back to the Pennsylvania pediatrician featured in Woodward's story for an interview. She told the producers who put the story together that fewer than 30 percent of the children on SSI actually deserved their benefits. She implied that a family of disabled children could "buy a Mercedes" with their benefits. That caused Chris Wallace to comment that, "If Porter's estimates are anywhere near accurate," then SSI was "a massive taxpayer-funded scam." Most of the pediatrician's points, including the obviously inaccurate one about the Mercedes, went unchallenged. The interviews of white teachers and politicians in the Arkansas delta reinforced the popular stereotype of black welfare recipients as undeserving frauds. It was nonetheless a powerful piece that influenced the tone of Congressional debate.[6]

Exposing the Substance Abusers

Senator William S. Cohen of Maine (R) came at the program from a different direction. He released an investigative report from the minority staff of his Sub-committee of the Senate Special Committee on Aging with the arresting title "Tax Dollars Aiding and Abetting Addiction." The report had a lurid tone, reading more like a journalistic expose than the usual committee print. Cohen reported, "that the 'word on the street' is that SSI benefits are an easy source of cash for drugs and alcohol," and that loose administration of the program allowed the "widespread manipulation of this system by addicts and alcoholics." Cohen took care to implicate both Social Security Disability Insurance (SSDI) and SSI in his indictment that "taxpayer dollars are being used directly to subsidize and perpetuate drug and alcoholic abuse." Yet most, if not all, of the examples in the report came from SSI.

Prior to a 1991 change in the medical listings, the SSA's policy held that a sub-stance abuser had to have a serious additional medical impairment (such as ir-reversible organ damage, or a demonstrable mental illness) to qualify as disabled. Starting with the 1991 change, if the substance abuser had no such additional im-pairment, the DDS would continue with the determination process, performing the residual functional assessment step in the sequential evaluation process and then assessing whether the substance abuse itself was sufficient to make the per-son disabled. The possibility therefore arose that people with no other impair-ment, other than their drug addiction or alcoholism, might qualify as disabled under SSI or SSDI. In a straightforward way, this change made policy sense, since alcoholics and drug addicts were often so impaired by their habits that they could not work. But awarding disability benefits to such an unsavory cohort of people proved to be very unpopular.

Controls that Congress put in the law to protect the public from being ripped off by irresponsible drug addicts and alcoholics failed to take hold. In SSI, for example, alcoholics and drug addicts needed to receive their benefits through a representative payee, and all drug addicts and alcoholics needed to participate in an approved substance control program. These regulatory safeguards had never worked effectively. In the frenzied period of SSI implementation, for example, the SSA had little time to vet representative payees or treatment programs.

The result was a public relations disaster for the SSI program. Cohen's report told of a director of a Denver homeless shelter who called SSI "suicide on the installment plan." On the first day of the month, when the addicts received their checks, they binged on drugs and alcohol and only returned to the shelter and any modicum of supervision when the money was gone. In Bakersfield, California, an SSI applicant received thousands of dollars worth of unrestricted retroactive benefits and died of a lethal drug overdose. Another California resident, who used a check for $18,000 in retroactive SSI and SSDI benefits to go on a drinking binge, purchased a car, got arrested for drunk driving, and ended up in jail.[7]

The report sent the message that cuts could be made in SSI by restricting or eliminating benefits to drug addicts and alcoholics. Such a move, far from depriving the recipients of a necessary welfare benefit, would actually eliminate some of the reckless behavior that their consumption of drugs and alcohol induced. Addicts, cut off from the money they used to purchase their supply, would alter their behavior in a publically beneficial way. None of that was certain, of course. An SSI cutoff might, for example, lead to more criminal activities and acts of violence as desperate addicts sought new sources of money to feed their habits. The report made it clear, however, that the present system was a failure.

In early 1994, Cohen pursued his crusade, and the Clinton administration considered plausible cuts in welfare programs. By the end of February 1994, Cohen had a bill, which he called the "Social Security Disability and Rehabilitation Act of 1994," ready to introduce in Congress. The bill garnered an impressive list of cosponsors, such as Senator Robert Dole, the Republican leader who was being vetted by the press and his party as a possible presidential nominee in 1996. Cohen portrayed his bill—which he also publicized through an op-ed piece in the *Washington Post* with the provocative title "Playing Social Security for a Sucker"—as a humane response to the problem. Under the present system, a Denver liquor store owner served as a representative payee for scores of hardcore alcoholics. He used the $160,000 he received in this manner to "run a tab for 40 alcoholics who are supposed to be using the government money to get help for their problem." Cohen wanted to get cash out of the hands of substance abusers and put it under the care of an "institution or approved agency" to manage. He proposed the abolition of lump sum retroactive payments to substance abusers until they had a chance to complete treatment and could spend the money responsibly. He suggested that more disability reviews be conducted on alcoholic or drug addicted SSI or SSDI recipients. He also wanted to remove people who used their benefits for illegal activities such as drug dealing from the rolls and increase the penalties for those who defrauded the programs.[8]

Cohen's campaign helped make the administration's task of producing a welfare reform bill a little easier. The administration faced a dilemma. It wanted to accompany welfare reform with expanded work and job training programs. To pay for those new programs, it needed to suggest offsetting cuts in entitlement programs, and nearly all of the potential cuts were politically controversial. Cohen had made the problem easier by finding a loophole in SSI that could be eliminated, saving the government money without appearing to harm welfare recipients.[9]

Exposing the Noncitizens

Since the start of the SSI program, aliens admitted to the United States for permanent residence qualified for SSI on the same basis as American citizens. The law barred illegal aliens, often referred to as undocumented workers, and aliens not admitted on a permanent basis from receiving SSI. Like the situation with children the presence of noncitizens on SSI, who generally composed less than 10 percent of the SSI population, provoked little notice, at least at first. Unlike the rest of the SSI caseload, however, the majority of noncitizens on SSI qualified on the basis of age rather than disability. By 1994 nearly a third of the aged people who received SSI were noncitizens. As a result, elderly noncitizens on SSI became more visible as a cohort than their overall percentage in the SSI population (11 percent) would otherwise suggest.

This differing profile reflected the immigration patterns of the foreign born. A young person would come to the United States and then decide to bring over his aged parents. The younger immigrant tended to be able-bodied, and the older immigrant often came to this country without substantial resources and no Social Security. This process produced a ready-made market for aged noncitizens to get SSI, even though the statistics showed that noncitizens on SSI were a small and relatively steady population, compared with a large and growing population of U.S. citizens (Figure 7-2).[10]

In the speculation over the Clinton recommendations on welfare reform, legal aliens figured prominently. The issue concerned whether elderly noncitizens should be allowed to go on the SSI rolls. Cutting off noncitizens from benefits figured to make some $2 billion available for the other aspects of welfare reform. Could immigrants claim SSI benefits on the basis of old age, even though they were not citizens? The law said yes, but the Clinton administration decided that a person should become a citizen before he or she could claim benefits. Many Republicans appeared to agree and suggested that the administration not limit cuts to people applying for new benefits but also take benefits away from legal aliens already on the rolls. This more stringent Republican strategy would yield as much as $7 billion in savings. The Republican position gave protective political cover to the Clinton administration. It could argue that it was following the more humane and prudent course and, at the same time, wringing some money out of SSI. If cuts needed to be made in welfare programs, then limiting the benefits of noncitizens appeared to be a distasteful but politically viable option.[11]

Cutting benefits for immigrants was not without controversy. Most Americans, who in almost all cases could trace their ancestry back to someone who immigrated to America, identified with the abstract category "immigrant." As an anthropologist might say, the immigrant was not the other but us. To be sure,

Persons

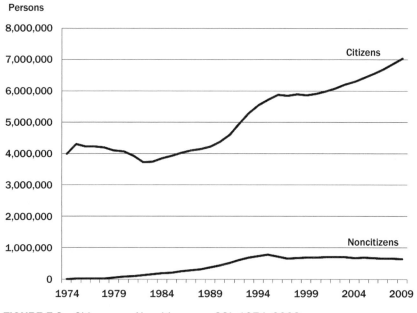

FIGURE 7-2   Citizens vs. Noncitizens on SSI, 1974–2008

the changing face of immigration changed the ethnicity of the typical immigrant. No longer did people come to America from Italy, Russia, Poland, or Greece as they did in the great immigration at the end of the nineteenth century. The descendants of the older immigration regarded themselves as Americans as much as they considered themselves Irish, Italian, or Jewish. When their forbearers had arrived in America, the welfare system contained neither Social Security nor Supplemental Security Income. The new immigrant was more likely to be Hispanic or Asian. These new immigrants arrived in a country with a much more well developed welfare state than did the old immigrants, and often the new immigrants came from countries with rudimentary provisions for old age pensions. All of those things greased the skids, so to speak, for the newer immigrants to claim benefits that were not available to the older immigrants. That seemed like an unfair advantage to some, who much after the fact viewed the immigration experience through a romantic and nostalgic haze. They tended to forget the hostility of each immigrant group for the ones following them.[12]

The liberal *Washington Post* warned that the debate over welfare reform not become "an exercise in immigrant bashing." The paper noted that the number of lawfully resident aliens who received SSI had increased from 3 to 10 percent of the caseload over the past ten years. It nonetheless objected to the charge that immigrants "who get here, reach back for their parents, [and] support the parents only for the minimum legal interval and slough them onto the rolls" abused the system. Such a view failed to recognize that a fourth of the legal aliens on the rolls were refugees, such as Soviet Jews or people fleeing from oppression in Vietnam, Cambodia, or Cuba. Another fifth of the legal aliens had resided in the country for ten years before claiming SSI benefits. It also did not take into account the fact that the immigrants bringing their parents to this country were themselves already American citizens. To deny their benefits to their parents discriminated among groups of American citizens on the basis of nationality.[13]

The conservative *Wall Street Journal* lumped the immigrant problem and the childhood disability problem together. It reported on immigrants being coached to "fake craziness to get on the rolls of the Supplemental Security Income . . . program" and also decried the fact that 10 percent of the people on the SSI rolls were not citizens. The paper noted, however, that the problem extended beyond immigrants to include the "fuzzy world of mental disorder." This problem tended to get swept under the rug by the iron triangle of "Congress, social service advocates and the pliant press." That unfortunate tendency put the country at risk to have "the almighty deficit" "swell again."[14]

Through its editorial and op-ed pieces, the *Journal* pressed the point that SSI not be left behind in welfare reform. According to conservative economist Carolyn Weaver, a resident scholar at the American Enterprise Institute who had worked for Robert Dole on the Senate Finance Committee and served on the staff of the Greenspan Commission, SSI was growing more rapidly than AFDC and would soon overtake it as America's most costly welfare program. As the gateway to Food Stamps and Medicaid, a growing SSI program could produce adverse consequences that reverberated throughout the nation's social welfare programs. Weaver believed that, although SSI enjoyed considerable support on Capitol Hill, it was nonetheless a deeply flawed program that created strong disincentives to work. By giving aid "with no strings attached," it perpetuated "the very conditions (alcoholism, drug addiction, or certain forms of mental illness, for example) that preclude work and promote dependency." SSI, therefore, had many of the same imperfections as AFDC, and therefore Congress should put it on the table in the welfare reform debate.[15]

In the spring of 1994, as the debate heated up, a growing coalition of conservative House Democrats and Republicans supported eliminating welfare benefits for noncitizens.[16] The Mainstream Forum, a group of some ninety self-described moderate Democrats, introduced a welfare reform bill that contained cuts in welfare benefits for immigrants. Although the Democrat-controlled House Ways and Means Committee voted down a measure to deny SSI benefits to immigrants, the vote was close, and Representative Harold Ford, the Chairman of the welfare subcommittee, abstained. This sort of division among Democrats on key points of policy delayed the administration's welfare reform efforts and, although no one knew it at the time, the 1994 election would take control of the issue out of the administration's hands.[17]

Legislation in 1994

If the administration wanted a demonstration of the difficulties of welfare reform, it could observe how advocates reacted to the Woodward story in the *Washington Post*. On the one hand, Gerald D. Kleczka, a Democratic Congressman from Wisconsin, argued that the SSI program had "considerable flaws" and wasted taxpayer money. He and fellow Wisconsin delegation member Senator Herb Kohl (D) promised to introduce legislation that would deal with both childhood disability and substance abuse. On the other hand, the Executive Director of the Bazelon Center for Mental Health Law chided the paper for running "an unfortunate caricature" of SSI. Far from being the program gone haywire of Woodward's story, SSI in fact encouraged low income families to remain together and promoted work. A child could not get SSI benefits just by acting out and becoming a disciplinary problem. The rules, written "by a panel of the nation's pediatric and mental health experts," were too stringent for that. SSI deserved praise for the way it enabled "parents to meet the complex needs of a child with severe disability," not the ridicule of *Post* reporters. Martha "Marty" Ford, an influential Washington advocate on behalf of children with disabilities, added that SSI provided only "basic, minimum support to qualified people."[18]

With welfare reform moving slowly, the campaign to make the SSA an independent agency became the vehicle for SSI reform in 1994. The drive to take the SSA out of the Department of Health and Human Services (HHS) went back to the seventies, but the idea gained serious momentum in the disability review era of the early eighties. The 1981 Social Security Commission and the 1982–1983 Greenspan "rescue" Commission both endorsed the idea of an independent agency, and the Greenspan report recommended the creation of another commission to study its feasibility. This commission reported favorably in 1984, and the legislative drive to make the SSA independent began in earnest. Over the years, the proposal received support, but it faced potential presidential vetoes and never commanded enough interest to move to the top of the Social Security agenda. Other issues always intervened that prevented the measure from gaining full legislative approval.[19]

Senators like Daniel Patrick Moynihan (D-New York) kept alive the idea of making the agency independent. He believed that making the agency independent would arrest the agency's decline. The narrative of the agency's decline centered on incidents that related to SSI. The accelerated disability reviews reflected inappropriate political influence over the agency's affairs with disastrous public relations results. The attempt to automate the agency's operations had gone badly in the mid-eighties and resulted in declining service to SSA beneficiaries. During the nineties, serious backlogs of disability claims continued to discredit the agency. Congress hoped that the creation of an independent agency would reverse what the Ways and Means Committee called "the marked decline in the agency's performance over the past 15 years." When President Clinton gave Moynihan his approval, it appeared certain that the campaign would end in victory.[20]

A legislative package that was headed toward passage attracted the interest of Congressmen who wanted to attach other features to it. In the spring of 1994, the issue of the misuse of SSI benefits by drug addicts and alcoholics remained hot. If independence for the SSA was in some sense a liberal measure, then a provision related to substance addiction in SSI and SSDI might give it some conservative counterbalance and increase its appeal. In this spirit the Ways and Means Committee added provisions to restrict payments to alcoholics and drug addicts to the measure on agency independence that Senator Moynihan had already introduced in the Senate.[21]

With the Democrats still in charge of Congress, the Ways and Means Committee took pains to cast the parts of the legislation related to substance addiction in positive, rather than punitive, terms. The stated goal was to restructure the SSDI and SSI programs "to offer transitional, time-limited assistance to alcoholics and drug addicts who are seeking to regain control of their lives." As such, the legislation required that addicts seek treatment and not use their SSI or SSDI benefits to buy drugs or alcohol. An alcoholic or drug addict would be required to receive his payments through a representative payee, who was neither a family member nor a friend but, rather, a qualified organization. A strict three-year limit would be established on the eligibility of substance abusers for SSI or SSDI, and retroactive benefits would be paid in installments rather than as a lump sum.[22]

Advocates for people with disabilities objected to the three-year limit, pushed by Representative Kleczka in the House and Senator Cohen in the Senate, as a way of throwing substance abusers "to the wolves." The encouragement of treatment programs—the classic rehabilitation approach to the disability problem—was fine, but real benefit cuts attracted real opposition.[23] The fact that the Clinton administration supported the substance abuse parts of the independent agency legislation helped temper some of the criticism, although the administration recommended that the three-year limit should apply only to those who had the opportunity to get treatment. The administration also endorsed conducting disability reviews in the SSI program, particularly for those receiving childhood disability benefits.[24]

In the Congressional debate on the measure, the substance abuse provisions attracted more attention than the independent agency features of the bill. Reporting on House passage of the measure, the *New York Times* noted that most of the speeches "were aimed at the provisions affecting 119,000 substance abusers" receiving SSI or SSDI.[25] Representative Kleczka, who claimed pride of author ship in these provisions, told his colleagues that in recent months SSI had become "the subject of widespread public outrage," with reports of "alcoholics and drug addicts using taxpayer money to finance their habits." Kleczka said that he put the thirty-six-month limit on disability benefits for substance abusers to send "a clear message that Federal assistance cannot last forever" and to save the taxpayers some $940 million over five years. He claimed his efforts would make it much harder for drug addicts and alcoholics to abuse the system. He also lauded the disability reviews that would be done for children as they approached adulthood. These would make sure that the children met the adult criteria for disability, a first step toward dealing with the vast explosion in childhood disability benefits.[26]

Representative Bill Thomas, a Republican from California, joined Democrat Kleczka in supporting the measure that would "stop drug addicts and alcoholics from abusing the Social Security disability and Supplemental Security income program." His constituents, he said, were "outraged to find that addicts who were supposed to be getting treatment to end their addiction were able to use taxpayer dollars to subsidize their habits."[27]

With Senator Cohen and Representative Kleczka spearheading the fight, the provision to put a three-year limit on SSDI and SSI benefits for substance abusers cleared both the House and the Senate. As the measure went to conference, disability advocates did what they could to prevent the three-year limit from becoming law. George Washington University psychiatrist Roger Meyer described alcohol and drug addiction as "chronic relapsing disorders" that could not be resolved in three years. Joe Manes of the Bazelon Mental Health Law Center described the cutoff as "quite vindictive."[28]

The conference committee tempered some but not all of the disputed aspects of the measure. The conferees made a distinction between SSI and SSDI. Drug addicted and alcoholic SSI beneficiaries would lose their cash benefits after thirty-six months. Drug addicted and alcoholic beneficiaries on SSDI could remain on the rolls if they were not receiving treatment. Their three-year eligibility clock would only start after treatment began. For both SSI and SSDI beneficiaries, health insurance benefits could continue after thirty-six months "so long as the terminated individual continues to be disabled." The conferees offered no rationale for distinguishing between SSI and SSDI recipients, a distinction that did not escape notice.[29] Senator Cohen's version of the legislation, for example, would have treated SSI and SSDI recipients the same way and not started the thirty-six-month clock until treatment became available. He admitted, however, that it was too late to change the legislation and that on balance the legislation marked "a major step toward restoring the public's confidence and integrity in our Nation's disability program."[30]

Even before the Republican victory in the 1994 elections, therefore, Congress had chosen to make a significant cut in the SSI program and to treat SSI differently from SSDI. In doing so, it reinforced the perceptions that the SSI program had serious flaws and the notion that Social Security beneficiaries had a greater right to cash disability benefits than did SSI beneficiaries. When President Clinton signed the legislation on August 15, 1994, the day after the fifty-ninth anniversary of the Social Security Act, he used Franklin Roosevelt's pen from 1935. Clinton emphasized the independent agency aspects of the legislation, and he praised Senator Moynihan for his persistent work on that issue. The President spoke of "reinventing our Government to streamline our operations so that we can serve the American people better." Clinton mentioned the provisions "designed to strengthen the integrity of the disability programs," including the thirty-six month limit on benefits for substance abusers, only in a brief written statement.[31]

The 1994 Election

As the legislation to create an independent agency reached its last stages, the Clinton administration continued planning for a comprehensive welfare reform bill. By late spring, 1994, the President's advisers came to a consensus on the plan. The President agreed to introduce a welfare reform bill in June that would make AFDC a "two year transitional benefit." Although the welfare reform debate centered on AFDC, SSI still figured into the discussion. Clinton would, for example, finance his $9.3 billion bill in part through $3.5 billion that would be realized by cutting benefits to elderly immigrants receiving SSI benefits. Under the President's proposal, a person would have to be in the country for five years before he could claim SSI. By one estimate, as much as a third of the cost of the Clinton welfare reform plan would be financed through SSI cutbacks. Ending welfare as we know it—the popular political mantra of the era—apparently also meant changing SSI as we know it as well.[32]

President Clinton introduced welfare much too late in the session for Congress to act in 1994. He had decided to put national health insurance ahead of welfare reform. Then the Republican landslide in November 1994 changed the terms of the discussion.

Incoming House Speaker Newt Gingrich (R-Georgia), who touted his party's "Contract with America," now became a party to the negotiations. Gingrich hoped to use Congress, rather than the White House, as a base from which to control the nation's public agenda.[33] In terms of the party structure of government, the situation resembled that of 1947, in which a weak Democratic president faced a newly elected Republican Congress. In 1947 the Republicans put the reform of labor law at the top of their agenda and produced the Taft-Hartley Act modifying many of the provisions of FDR's pro-union National Labor Relations Act (the Wagner Act). In 1995 the Republicans wanted to do many things, but welfare reform, repealing one of the provisions of FDR's Social Security Act, stood near the top of the agenda.[34]

In the wake of the Republican victory, President Clinton instinctively sought common ground. He said, for example, that his version of welfare reform was in fact quite similar to one that the Republicans had proposed. Gingrich pushed back against such statements. Welfare programs, he said, "ruin the poor." His colleague Jim Talent (R-Missouri) contemplated passing a law that would deny welfare benefits to children born of mothers who were less than twenty-six years old. Gingrich himself entertained the notion of reinvigorating the orphanage as an alternative to welfare.[35]

Clinton had already demonstrated that he was willing to make cuts in Supplemental Security Income. The Republican leadership went further and contemplated ending the SSI program as a federal entitlement and putting a cap on SSI expenditures. If the money ran out, then successful program applicants would be placed on a waiting list. Unlike Clinton, Republicans favored "block granting" the Food Stamps and the School Lunch programs, so that the states, rather than the federal government, determined the nation's social welfare priorities.[36]

Despite these differences between the parties, the discussions of 1994 helped lay the groundwork for the legislative proposals of 1995. The idea of cutting benefits to immigrants appealed to both Republicans and Democrats. The GOP took the idea further than did the Democrats, floating the proposal that legal immigrants not be allowed to receive benefits from some sixty federal programs. The list included not only SSI but also federal initiatives related to public health and nutrition, such as free childhood immunizations and subsidized school lunches. It also recognized the political reality that legal aliens did not have the right to vote, thus softening the political impact of the measure. Opponents argued that the Republicans were picking on a politically vulnerable group as an indirect means to carry out their attack on the social programs they opposed. A spokesman for the libertarian Cato Institute implicitly agreed. He said that his organization believed that "nobody should get these programs, but if welfare is not going to be eliminated outright, then . . . it should be for citizens only." Representative Rick Santorum (R-Pennsylvania) argued that the Republicans were not anti-immigrant but that they wanted the kinds of immigrants who "will take responsibility for themselves and not rely on the federal government."[37]

The tangled nature of immigration policy made the issue even more complicated. Foreigners who possessed "green cards," certifying them as permanent residents, became eligible for citizenship after five years in the United States. Many found the tests of citizenship to be daunting and simply maintained their status as permanent residents. As permanent residents, they qualified for SSI and other welfare programs, without the stress of having to show that they could speak English and have a general knowledge of U.S. government and history. Hence the growing ranks of SSI recipients included such people as seventy-three-year-old Chinese immigrant Suichi Mock, who, along with her husband, had lived and worked in the United States for a combined total of forty years and paid U.S. income taxes during those years. Neither she nor her husband had acquired a retirement pension; no longer able to work, they depended on SSI. She said her SSI check meant "food for us" and that she was not able to pass the citizenship test, in part because she could not speak English and apparently did not need to do so in her New York Chinatown neighborhood. She had long passed the period in which the sponsor who had brought her to the United States had an obligation to support her and keep her from becoming a public charge.[38]

The welfare reform debate left open the question of what would happen to Suichi Mock if she lost her SSI benefits. The GOP entertained the idea of an escape clause that would allow her to receive welfare benefits at age seventy-five. That still left two years in which she would have to fend for herself. Perhaps necessity would drive her to get a job, although the labor market for people her age with physical limitations was not promising, or to acquire the necessary knowledge to pass the citizenship test. Or perhaps she would leave her New York neighborhood and return to China. In other words, the welfare reform debate had the potential not just to weed out undesirables or compel socially desirable behavior but also to allow hardworking people to slip through the safety net.

Children on the SSI rolls became another holdover from the 1994 discussion who figured in the welfare reform discussions of 1995. At the end of 1994, the incoming Republican leadership in the House drafted a measure that essentially would put an end to these benefits. They floated the idea of replacing cash payments with vouchers that could only be used for medical expenses and equipment. Louisiana Republican Jim McCrery took the lead on the initiative.

Advocates for children with disabilities tried to burst the trial balloon. One mother of a nine-year-old with Down syndrome predicted that vouchers would increase the number of children with disabilities who were institutionalized. She worried about what would happen to her son who, she said, "can't cross the street, has no concept of danger, is not toilet-trained and does not know how to dress himself." Another parent of a child with spina bifida and mild mental retardation admonished that the Republican proposal would send the message to parents that "Government doesn't trust families to decide how best to use the money for their children."[39]

In the Christmas season, Carolyn Weaver, the conservative economist from the American Enterprise Institute, appeared on National Public Radio's flagship news broadcast *All Things Considered*. An articulate and personable spokesperson for the conservative point of view, she noted that SSI's difficulties might stem from the assumption that all policy problems had solutions. Although she did not claim to have the answers to the rising SSI rolls, she suggested that policymakers should experiment with time-limited benefits that would help "target resources on the most disabled."[40]

If Carolyn Weaver, although definitely a partisan figure, spoke in academic tones about SSI, the *Wall Street Journal* was less temperate in its attacks on the program. Early in 1995 it ran an opinion piece on SSI by Heather Mac Donald of the Manhattan Institute. Mac Donald picked up on Weaver's earlier work and acknowledged that SSI was the nation's fastest-growing welfare program. Since its beginnings in 1974 through 1993, the number of beneficiaries had tripled to reach 4.5 million. Mac Donald said the reason lay in a fundamental shift in the concept of disability. Where once the program had supported people with medical impairments, it now aided people "with social handicaps that no doctor could cure—drug abuse, a chaotic upbringing and a lack of education and work ethic."

Mac Donald had no desire to be politically correct, maybe because she sensed that with the Republican victory standards of political correctness were changing. She cited the rise in people classified with mental impairments and argued, "The beast that lies beneath the entire mental impairment caseload is substance abuse." Classifying addiction and alcoholism as disabilities had "appalling consequences," but the group that had led the rise in the disability category was "children with behavioral problems." She questioned whether disability payments were even appropriate for children and observed that SSI rewarded "the worst kind of parenting." She advised that SSI expenditures not be capped, as some Republicans wanted, but rather they should be cut "by adopting a more reasonable definition of disability."[41]

The Republicans and Welfare Reform

The new Republican House Ways and Means Committee wasted no time in taking up the matter of welfare reform. Voting along partisan lines, the Ways and
Means subcommittee concerned with welfare approved a proposal to turn AFDC
from a federal entitlement to a block grant that allowed the states to run their
own programs. No federal money would be allowed to go to unmarried mothers
below the age of eighteen. SSI became an important topic of the subcommittee's
discussions. On February 15, 1995, it considered childhood SSI benefits. The subcommittee recommended, along 8 to 5 party lines, that the process for awarding
benefits to children be changed so that all eligible children met or equaled the
medical listings. They eliminated the post-*Zebley* "individualized functional
assessments" that attempted to ascertain whether children engaged in age-
appropriate activities. Representative McCrery said that the change would end
the pernicious practice of parents coaching their children to act crazy in order to
get benefits. Sander Levin (D-Michigan) countered, "We're talking about the
most vulnerable children in America," and that the Republicans were moving in
lock step without thinking of the consequences of their actions.[42]

Liberals did what they could to rally their supporters. Anthony Lewis of the
New York Times wrote a column with the headline "Visigoths at the Gates."
One of the planned attacks of the new barbarians that Lewis cited was on "payments for children with disabilities under the Supplemental Security Income"
program. If successful, the initiative could damage the lives of "900,000 poor
children suffering from cerebral palsy, mental illness or other conditions." It
was a battle between Lewis's deserving poster children and McCrery's devious
welfare cheats.[43]

The liberals knew they were defeated in the House. They did their best to
obstruct the efforts of Ways and Means Chairman Bill Archer (D-Texas) but
realized they did not have the votes. A new partisan fervor that had been building since the departure of Wilbur Mills gripped the once staid committee. Archer said that the efforts of Democrats like Jim McDermott (D-Washington)
and Pete Stark (D-California) to block the legislation reflected "the dying hyste-
ria of Democrats trying to defend the welfare state." Democrats chose to ignore
the overwhelming volume of evidence of abuse in the SSI program. Stark countered that Archer "was in a hurry to ram this through because he has a schedule
handed down" by Speaker Gingrich. According to Stark, Republicans pushed
measures that would cause real hardship for children.[44]

The House Ways and Means Committee released the outlines of the "Personal
Responsibility Act" at the beginning of March 1995. It represented the Gingrich-
era Republican vision for SSI in its purest form. It restricted welfare for noncitizens

by making them ineligible for thirty-five federal welfare programs, including SSI and Medicaid. The exceptions, such as permitting legal permanent residents over seventy-five years old who had been in the United States for five years to collect benefits, were few. It eliminated SSI benefits for drug abusers and alcoholics, although those who could qualify on the basis of another disabling condition could still receive benefits. The legislation also contained the proviso that $100 million of the savings from cutting off drug abusers and alcoholics would be spent on drug treatment and drug abuse research. It changed the procedure for determining benefits for children to eliminate individualized functional assessments. Children already on the rolls who met or equaled the medical listings could remain on the rolls. Children filing new claims had to have an impairment that met or equaled the medical listings *and* were either in a hospital or similar facility or were severely disabled enough that they would be placed in such a facility if they were not receiving personal assistance. It mandated continuing disability reviews for children with nonpermanent impairments every three years and for low birth weight children after they had been on the rolls for a year. It established a new program of block grants to the states for children with disabilities in order to provide medical and other services, but not cash grants, to children who met or equaled the medical listings. In other words, it contained nearly everything the Republicans had promised for SSI and more.[45]

With the exception of the provisions related to immigrants, almost all of the SSI parts of the bill concerned disability. The disability category, far more than the adult category, was vulnerable to charges that it could be manipulated so that the undeserving poor received benefits. Immigrants tended to qualify for benefits on the basis of old age, but it was not the category that came under attack so much as the worthiness of immigrants themselves to receive any sort of benefits. For the most part, though, it was the link between SSI and disability that produced the program's political liabilities.

The Republicans defended their proposals with explanations that drew on the contemporary critiques of SSI. They argued that the program contained perverse incentives that needed to be changed. Giving benefits to addicts and alcoholics who did not work "affronts working taxpayers and fails to serve the interests of addicts and alcoholics, many of whom use their disability checks to purchase drugs and alcohol." Changing the rules for childhood disability prevented parents from exploiting lax rules and coaching their children to get benefits. Creating block grants assured that "taxpayers are protected from continuing abuse of the current SSI cash payment, which is not always spent on improving the condition of disabled children." Continuing disability reviews protected "taxpayers against abuse" and encouraged "children whose condition improves to become free of government dependence."[46]

In the increasingly partisan debate, the Democrats on the Ways and Means Committee countered that the proposals put SSI beneficiaries at risk. The Republican bill provided "states with wide latitude to deny services to disabled children regardless of the severity of their impairment." It denied cash benefits "to severely disabled children." It made legal immigrants ineligible for SSI so that, for example, "a hard working employee in a restaurant, who has lived here four years, has paid his income and payroll taxes and is hit by a truck crossing the street would be ineligible for SSI benefits." The Democrats took a "yes, but" approach by framing alternative proposals that recognized abuses in the program but still provided protection to SSI beneficiaries. For example, they, like the Republicans, would deny SSI benefits to drug addicts and alcoholics but the Democrats would place more of the money saved into the treatment of the SSI population.[47]

The Democrats wanted to do something similar regarding immigrants. The issue involved a practice known as "deeming." From the beginnings of the program, SSI counted income/assets of a person living with an SSI child beneficiary or the income/assets of an ineligible spouse living with an SSI beneficiary to determine whether an applicant qualified for SSI. As part of the 1980 disability legislation, Congress added Sponsor to Alien Deeming. Under this new provision, the income/assets of a sponsor counted in determining the SSI eligibility of an alien applicant for three years. Subsequent legislation extended the Sponsor to Alien deeming period from three to five years. In 1995 the Democrats proposed not to cut immigrants off from benefits completely but, rather, to extend the deeming period until the immigrant became a U.S. citizen. The Democrats hoped to limit the number of immigrants on the rolls, without dropping them from the rolls completely.

The formal debate in the House took place between March 21 and March 24, 1995. Congressman Levin established the Democratic position when he said, "There is some abuse in the program, but do not punish truly handicapped children because of the abuse of some families." In a similar manner, he commented on the immigration issue by saying, "There needs to be reform but there does not need to be a drastic, drastic kind of reform."[48] Levin's tempered rhetoric reflected his position as a member of the Ways and Means Committee. Cardiss Collins (D-Illinois) presented a less restrained view of how the Republican proposal looked from her inner-city district in Chicago. The veteran Congresswoman and former head of the black caucus said that Attila the Hun "would be delighted with this bill." She described the Personal Responsibility Act "as the most callous, coldhearted, and mean-spirited attack on this country's children that I have ever seen in my life."[49]

By way of contrast, Congressman Clay Shaw (R-Florida), who chaired the Ways and Means Human Resources Subcommittee, announced that he and his fellow Republicans were "taking the final steps to revolutionize welfare." Drug addicts would no longer "receive monthly disability checks because of their addiction" and refocusing childhood disability benefits would provide "more help to severely disabled children, while protecting taxpayers against fraud and abuse."[50]

Representative McCrery, only the sixth Republican to represent Louisiana since Reconstruction, carried the burden of the argument on childhood disability. He portrayed SSI as "the most sought after welfare program in America," because it paid the most generous benefits of any welfare program. The *Zebley* decision had altered this program for the worse because it "radically liberalized the criteria" under which children qualified for benefits. He quoted an Arkansas state official to the effect that many children who received SSI checks were not disabled at all. He talked about a psychologist in a Louisiana parish who told authorities about parents coaching their children to do poorly, dooming them to failure. According to McCrery, an abused program begged for reform. The solution was to overturn the *Zebley* decision and to limit cash payments to only the most severely disabled children who otherwise would be institutionalized. Less disabled children would receive services designed to cope with their disability. All in all the legislation would "restore integrity to this out of control federal program."[51] "God help the family that has a truly disabled child," Barbara Kennelly (D-Connecticut) replied.[52]

The Republicans maintained party discipline on the bill, which passed the House on March 24 by a vote of 234 to 199. Almost all of the major SSI provisions passed intact. When Republican Ileana Ros-Lehtinen of Florida (herself a Cuban immigrant) wanted to offer an amendment that would permit legal immigrants to remain eligible for benefits, the Republican leadership prevented it from coming to a vote.[53]

Debating the Program in the Gingrich Era

As the Senate Finance Committee took up the measure, journalists and policy analysts in think tanks wrote pieces in an attempt to influence the debate. The *New York Times*, no friend to the new Republican majority, nonetheless contributed a piece on how SSI had affected elderly immigrants. It told the story of a seventy-four-year-old Chinese garment worker who learned from her coworkers that, even though she lived with her son, she could qualify for SSI. After waiting for the third anniversary of her residence in the United States, she quit her job and applied for SSI. "Everybody knows about this," she said. "I was hoping my children would take care of me when I got old," she added. "But they all have their own families. It's the American style."

The *Times* described SSI as "something akin to a retirement system for elderly immigrants, who in many cases come from countries that have meager or nonexistent retirement systems." A professor at UC Davis commented, "Everybody knows that this is free money." He claimed that SSI was destroying the old traditions of caring for the aged. The paper reported that advocates for immigrants believed that the program protected one of America's most vulnerable groups, but the piece contained no quotation or other evidence in support of that claim. It left little doubt that the prudent course was to close a gaping loophole in the law.[54]

At just about the same time, the libertarian Cato Institute issued a report by Christopher Lloyd, a lawyer who worked in northern Virginia, that collected all of the evidence against SSI in one place and outlined a conservative alternative to the program. The predominant motif of the report was that SSI sucked up money and functioned as one of Washington's "fiscal black holes." Without serious reform, policymakers would never be able to "curtail SSI's skyrocketing costs."[55]

The actual cost data showed a program with rising costs, but the rate of that rise was steady over time, at least prior to the *Zebley* decision.[56] Until the *Zebley* decision, the cost of the SSI program rose at a rate of 10 percent a year. Although the decision produced a spike, cost increases returned to their historic levels by 1995.[57] Whether those increases represented skyrocketing costs that created fiscal black holes, as the Cato Institute analysis claimed, was a matter of opinion.

Christopher Lloyd, the Cato Institute analyst, offered a historical narrative that explained how the program became unglued. Sold as a program for seniors who needed modest additions to their Social Security checks, SSI instead became a program of generous benefits for the blind and disabled. The SSA maintained a missionary approach toward the program, spending $8 million a year to find new beneficiaries—as required by the 1983 and 1987 legislation. After years of neglect, the problems with SSI finally came into public view because of "media horror stories." Lloyd relayed the story of a man in Wisconsin, himself on SSI and SSDI, who coached his daughter "to put gum in her hair, to act up in the classroom, and to earn bad grades." The family used the money it received from her SSI benefit to buy a car and take a vacation in Florida. His report also cited the story of a Cambodian resident of Orange County, California, who offered his services coaching Cambodian immigrants on how to get benefits. He advised them to tell authorities that Communists had killed their families, to avoid eye contact, and to look sad.

The Cato report identified four fatal flaws in the SSI program. It discouraged substance abusers from seeking rehabilitation and treatment. It offered cash assistance to disabled children for which there was no convincing rationale. It functioned as an open-ended entitlement with limitless costs. Finally, in a manner similar to other disability programs, it failed to distinguish between those who could and those who could not work.

Although the 1994 law marked a start toward patching up the program, Lloyd believed that more needed to be done. He endorsed the reforms in the 1995 Republican bill and suggested many more. Among other things, he proposed that the program's cost of living adjustments be eliminated, a cap on SSI enrollment be established, federally funded outreach activities be eliminated, and disability protection be privatized. Until the government took these steps to undo the historical legacy of the SSI program, SSI would continue as a fiscal black hole, and the back door of the welfare state would remain open.[58]

Not so fast, countered Mary Somoza, a member of the New York State Advisory Council on developmental disabilities and the mother of twins born prematurely and diagnosed with cerebral palsy. SSI and Medicaid kept her family together. She pointed to her situation and questioned whether families really coached children to "act crazy" in order to get benefits. She and her family had never been on welfare before the birth of her twins, and she and her husband found the application process so difficult and daunting that they almost gave up in despair. It took four months of intense investigation for her application to be approved. She persevered because she did not want her children to go to an institution, and she feared that the Republican proposal would break up many families such as hers.[59]

The Senate Finance Committee announced its version of the bill on May 26, 1995. The measure passed in Committee by a vote of 12 to 8, with Democrat Max Baucus of Montana, up for reelection in 1996, voting with the Republicans. Administration officials expressed relief that the legislation eliminated, in the words of HHS Secretary Donna Shalala, "some of the extreme and punitive measures" of the House bill. The officials even suggested that President Clinton might sign a welfare reform bill similar to the one from the Senate Finance Committee.[60] In general, the Committee softened some of the features of the House bill. Noncitizens, for example, would be barred from receiving SSI, but with the proviso that they could collect benefits if they had worked in the United States for a sufficient time to qualify for SSDI benefits. The Senate proposed a new, restrictive definition of childhood disability benefits but kept cash childhood disability benefits intact. Someone under eighteen would be considered disabled if he or she had a "medically determinable physical or mental impairment, which results in marked, pervasive, and severe functional limitations, which can be expected to result in death or which has lasted or can be expected to last for a continuous period of not less than 12 months." The bill directed the SSA to eliminate the category of "maladaptive behavior" from its consideration of personal and behavioral functioning and to end individualized functional assessments for children. In a bow to the rehabilitation tradition in welfare reform, the bill also required disabled children on SSI to have a treatment plan.[61]

The Senate debated the bill during the dog days of summer and passed it by the beginning of fall. The "Work Opportunity Act of 1995" received eighty-seven votes on final passage, with only twelve senators voting against it. As in the House, the Senate devoted a lot of attention to SSI, although some of the details became garbled. Senator Bob Packwood (R-Oregon) explained, for example, that SSI "is totally a Federal program. No state money and no state administration is involved in this at all"—conveniently forgetting about the extensive system of state supplementation. The Senator clearly wanted to keep things simple. He said that the Finance Committee simply wanted to establish three categories that would no longer be eligible for SSI benefits: people with drug or alcohol addiction, noncitizens, and children with modest disabilities. These points no longer seemed particularly controversial.[62]

In this spirit, Rick Santorum, who had begun the welfare reform debate in the House and who had moved to the Senate, took the lead in presenting the SSI proposals. Like Senator Packwood, the new Senator from Pennsylvania got the occasional detail wrong, as in his description of SSI as a program created in 1974. He said that SSI was one area on which the Senate could come to an agreement. He noted that in more than half of the states the average SSI payment for one child was more than the AFDC payments for a family of four. He told a story about a welfare queen named Eulalia Rivers, whose sixteen children and their eighty-nine grandchildren collected between $750,000 to $1 million a year in federal benefits, mostly from SSI. He said that in the Rivers family and in others across America, SSI put "marginally disabled or nondisabled children on the dole for life" and hid the real problem of abusive and neglectful parenting. SSI, in short, was a program that harmed children. It also paid adults to be drug addicts, and the government even paid workers to "go into the homeless shelters, to go into the clinics, to go into the streets and alleys and find drug addicts and alcoholics so that we can give them money."[63]

To be sure that his colleagues got the point, Santorum inserted a story from the *Baltimore Sun* into the record, the latest in a series of media attacks on SSI. That it came from the *Sun*, a newspaper from a Democratic state that routinely supported Democratic candidates for president and a paper likely to be read by Social Security employees in Baltimore, added to the story's punch. It told the story of Delmont Williams, who was found dead in a Baltimore alley, with enough alcohol and heroin in his body to "intoxicate three men." "And you paid for it," the paper added, just part of the $1.4 billion spent on drug abusers in SSI. The story went on to educate readers about the SSI program, with the skewed information that was becoming common. The paper claimed that Congress created SSI "with little deliberation or debate" in order to "provide food, shelter, and clothing to disabled poor people."[64]

Summarizing from the article, Santorum asked if SSI was a program that was helping people. "The answer is, obviously, no," he answered. Subsidies for drug addicts needed to be ended. He then turned to the delicate matter of benefits for noncitizens. The issue was a poignant one for him because his father was an immigrant who came to America in the thirties and worked in the Pennsylvania coal mines. No one wanted to deter people from coming to the country and reaping the benefits of the fastest growing economy in the world, but "it should not be the role of the American taxpayers to be the retirement home for millions of people who want to bring their parents to this country to retire with them." All of these things seemed self-evident to Santorum, who was confident that the changes in SSI were things that could bring the parties together and on which they could find "consensus and agreement."[65]

Although Santorum spoke for a group of newly elected conservative Republicans who wanted the Senate to follow the lead of the House, his remarks made some more liberal Republicans squeamish.[66] Senator Allan Simpson (R-Wyoming) praised the Senate for writing a more humane bill than the House. Alcoholics and drug abusers needed treatment. The evidence that parents coached their children in order to receive SSI payments was anecdotal and should not be used "as an excuse for carrying out some wholesale purge of children from the SSI rolls."[67] Senator Chafe of Rhode Island (R) portrayed SSI as a program that provided "important assistance to families by replacing a portion of the income that is lost when a parent must care for a disabled child." "No doubt about it," agreed Senator Dole, "for some families with a severely disabled child, SSI can be a lifesaver."[68]

It came down to distinguishing between the program's legitimate purposes and the fraud and abuse that characterized the program at least in part. Senator Cohen, for example, realized that "fraud and abuse should not be the only cause for reform of the disability programs." Still, he took the lead in exposing such things as the misuse of SSI benefits by drug addicts and alcoholics and, in his latest expose, of detailing how translators helped immigrants get SSI by "coaching them on medical symptoms and providing false information on their medical histories." But beyond ending such obviously fraudulent practices, effective welfare reform required policies that distinguished between "those Americans who have fallen on hard times and need a helping hand" and "those who simply refused to act in a disciplined and responsible manner."[69] No one quite knew how to do that. It was far easier to go after the drug addicts committing slow motion suicide, the children feigning madness, and the immigrants playing on America's generosity.

The Outcome of the 1995 Debate

The children feigning madness became a point of contention in the conference committee that convened on October 24. The House wanted to end the entitlement for children in SSI, and the Senate wanted to retain the entitlement but make it harder for children to qualify for benefits. At the same time, liberals conducted a media campaign to discredit the reports that children were being coached in bad behavior in order to receive SSI benefits. In September, Christopher George, a *Wall Street Journal* reporter, published an article in a magazine read mainly by other journalists. He argued that the attack on SSI children represented a "media crusade gone haywire." The *Washington Post*, *Boston Globe*, and ABC News all gave undue credence to dubious sources, despite the existence of four major studies that showed "no evidence of widespread fraud or abuse in the program."[70] Molly Ivins, the Texas-based columnist with a national following, charged that "the culprits in the case are some of the most distinguished names in journalism," such as Bob Woodward and Chris Wallace. Ivins made the point that the lurid stories just did not mesh with a program that rejected two out of three applicants in 1994 and that paid more than 60 percent of its childhood benefits to kids with serious physical handicaps, such as not being able to walk, or kids who were severely mentally retarded. Ivins admitted that there was some fraud in the program, citing an SSA study that found thirteen cases of possible cheating among 617 applicants. She felt that in the name of ending a very small amount of fraud, Congress was choosing to make the lives of 300,000 crippled poor children more miserable, all as a result of "some careless, thoughtless, one-sided reporting by journalists who should know better."[71]

At this point welfare reform became part of a high-stakes political game that involved passing legislation that would enable the Republicans to say that they had enacted their Contract with America, allowing President Clinton to say that he had honored his campaign pledge to "end welfare as we know it," and providing Senate majority leader Dole with a credible record on which to run for President in 1996. Before a final welfare reform bill would be signed into law in August 1996, the President would veto two welfare reform bills. Although SSI was not the single most important point of difference in these disputes, it nonetheless

influenced the debate. Childhood disability and benefits for immigrants continued to be areas of disagreement.

After completing work on their welfare reform bill, Republican leaders in the
House and Senate met to come up with a compromise measure that they hoped
President Clinton would sign or alternatively would inflict political damage on
the President for not signing. There came word on November 10, 1995, that senior Republican leaders had reached an agreement on welfare reform as part of
a larger budget package. In general, the measure, as the *Times* reported, retained
many of the elements in the House plan but softened them somewhat to con-
form to the wishes of Senator Dole and his Republican colleagues.[72]

One example concerned childhood disability benefits. Cash childhood SSI
benefits would be retained but with a new, more stringent definition of disability
along the lines of the Senate bill. The bill created a new distinction among children based on their need for personal assistance. In particular, children under
six with a medical impairment that severely limited their ability to function in an
age-appropriate manner and who in the absence of special personal assistance
would require specialized care outside of the home would receive 100 percent
of the SSI benefit promised by the current law. Children six or older needed to
meet more stringent criteria to get a full benefit. If the child required personal
care assistance with at least two activities of daily living, continual supervision
to avoid injuring or harming himself, or the administration of medical treatment and who would require full- or part-time specialized care outside of the
home without such assistance, he would be eligible for a full benefit. All other
disabled children who qualified for benefits would receive 75 percent of the SSI
benefit.[73]

It was easy to see that this formulation came from blending elements of the
Senate and House versions of welfare reform related to SSI. In this case, as in so
many others, the need to come up with an acceptable compromise trumped any
desire to produce a law that would be easy to administer. Nothing in the history
of the SSA's disability programs suggested that these new childhood disability
rules, once put into operation, would be administered in a manner free from
controversy or that would end the periodic surges in the disability rolls. Instead,
Republican legislators asked beleaguered state officials in the disability determination offices to make extraordinarily complex decisions, all in the name of ending fraud and abuse.

Something of the same desire to please could be found in the provisions related to noncitizens in the Republican proposal. Most noncitizens would be
ineligible for SSI, but the Republican leaders made what they considered to be
politically acceptable exceptions. These included refugees and asylees, who fell

into a category that might be called the deserving immigrants. The House Republicans accepted the provision in the Senate bill that also tried to define politically deserving immigrants. It permitted immigrants lawfully admitted for permanent residence who received credit for forty qualifying quarters of Social Security coverage and, in an interesting twist, did not receive any federal means-tested benefits during any of these quarters to qualify for SSI. In other words, SSI would become an ersatz form of Social Security for this group, a reward for working for ten years and not accepting welfare during this period.[74]

Although the Republican proposal was artful, President Clinton decided to veto it anyway. Most of the reasons concerned programs only tangentially related to SSI. Leon Panetta, then serving as the President's Chief of Staff, said that the Republicans were "cutting school lunches" and child care, actions that he termed "unacceptable" and grounds for a veto. Just as the Republicans needed to reconcile differences between party factions, so the President and Democrats faced considerable internal pressures. Administration officials remained divided on the Republican welfare proposal, pointing to such things as the SSI provisions for disabled children and the treatment of immigrants as problems. Antipoverty groups, who were natural allies of the administration, also pressured Clinton to reject the Republican proposal. Sharon Daly of Catholic Charities USA said that the Republican bill would "tear apart the nation's safety net for poor children."[75]

In the highly fluid situation, the Republicans were not certain how best to package their welfare proposals. They decided to include them in two different legislative vehicles. One was the comprehensive budget bill, and the other would be a freestanding welfare bill, which had already passed both Houses of Congress but still needed to be reconciled between the House and the Senate. The Republicans hoped that this legislative strategy would put maximum pressure on President Clinton and deny him the chance to end welfare as we know it.[76]

On December 6, 1995, the President vetoed the budget bill, and, as a result, the second federal government shutdown of the year began. Congress then proceeded with the freestanding welfare reform bill as modified by the conference committee. The debate on acceptance of the conference report that took place just before Christmas reprised many of the themes in the debate.[77] Representative McCrery pointed out that the provisions on SSI for children represented a compromise. As he put it, "Those of us who wanted to replace cash benefits with services to disabled children agreed to continue cash." Some Democrats, of course, still objected to the measure, since under its terms fewer children would qualify for SSI. McCrery argued that something was wrong with a program whose caseload tripled in six years. (The child beneficiary caseload did nearly triple from 1990 to 1995, but the rest of the SSI caseload increased only about

TABLE 7-1   Growth in SSI Caseloads, 1990–1995, by Age Cohort

YEAR	CHILDREN	ADULTS
1990	308,589	4,508,538
1991	397,162	4,721,308
1992	556,470	5,009,719
1993	722,678	5,261,652
1994	841,474	5,454,312
1995	917,048	5,597,086

Source: Social Security Administration, *SSI Annual Statistical Report 2002,* Table 3: Recipients, by age, December 1974–2002, p. 19.

24 percent during this period [see Table 7-1].) Representative Bruce Vento (D-Minnesota) countered that the proposal was harsh, because "funding to aid children with Down syndrome, cerebral palsy, AIDS, muscular dystrophy, and cystic fibrosis under SSI would be cut 25 percent." For the Republicans many of the kids on SSI fell into the nebulous category of people who were not truly disabled but sought benefits anyway. The Democrats chose to label these kids with their medical diagnosis and in that manner portray them as members of the deserving poor.[78]

The provisions for childhood SSI benefits ran into more opposition in the Senate than in the House. Liberals like Barbara Boxer (D-California) argued that cuts in SSI benefits would "have a dramatic impact on low-income families who use SSI to help pay for their disabled children's needs." Senator Chafee noted that SSI "took a big bite" in the Senate's original welfare reform bill, and the conference agreement only made the problem worse. He said that the distinctions "in this two-tiered program are arbitrary and make no practical difference to a family where one parent must give up his or her job to remain at home with a severely disabled child."[79]

At this point in the debate, such comments served only to put the Senators on record as objecting to a particular proposal in a larger bill that was destined to pass anyway. The measure cleared Congress on December 22, and President Clinton vetoed it on January 9, 1996, at the beginning of a presidential election year. He took the position that he would continue to work with Congress "to enact real, bipartisan welfare reform" but that H.R. 4, the "Personal Responsibility and Work Opportunity Act of 1995," fell short of that goal. Instead of sending him an effective welfare reform vehicle, the President charged, Congress had instead produced a measure "to meet an arbitrary budget target." The President specifically mentioned budget cuts and structural changes in "help for disabled children" as objectionable features of the bill.[80]

1996—Bipartisan Legislation on Substance Abuse

Congress returned to the task of welfare reform. Before it could produce a new comprehensive proposal, it passed and the President signed a measure that dealt with the substance abuse part of the SSI reform agenda. The drive for this legislation began in 1995 and culminated in 1996. It received bipartisan support, even from liberals such as Earl Pomeroy (D-North Dakota), because it included a provision that increased the earnings limit under Social Security.

The legislation carried the attractive title "Senior Citizens Right to Work Act." The idea was that a Social Security recipient would be able to earn as much as $30,000 a year with no reduction in his Social Security benefits. Although the SSI substance abuse provision had little relationship to a senior citizen's right to work, it nonetheless got included in the legislation. It was undoubtedly the most popular part of the triumvirate of cuts for immigrants, disabled children, and substance abusers, and, as in other measures of the era, it provided a cost-saving conservative counterweight to an otherwise liberal piece of legislation. It also applied not just to SSI but to SSDI as well, freeing it from the possible stigma of being part of welfare reform. Its appeal could be stated quite directly. As one Congressman put it, "This should put an end to having disability being misused by drug and alcohol addicts to support their habits."[81]

Both conservative and liberal Senators put their blessings on the substance abuse part of the legislation. Senator John McCain (R-Arizona), who entertained presidential ambitions, noted that only those whose sole disabling condition was drug addiction or alcoholism would be cut from the rolls. Those alcoholics or drug addicts who had another disabling condition could still receive benefits. The legislation also contained the sweetener that some $50 million would be added to the Substance Abuse Prevention and Treatment Block Grant to help those with substance abuse problems. The bill would not just cut people off from benefits; it would also get them into treatment. Still, some conservatives, while supporting the bill, worried that it would not end the spectacle of drug addicts and alcoholics funding their habits with SSI benefits, because they might still qualify by claiming some other disability.[82]

The Senior Citizens Right to Work Act eventually became part of a larger bill. Although President Clinton could hardly have approved of the bill's new title, he signed the "Contract with America Advancement Act of 1996" into law at the end of March 1996. No one at the SSA or in the administration raised objections to the requirements regarding alcoholics and drug addicts, since the Clinton administration had made the same request as part of the FY 1997 budget. The new law prohibited SSDI or SSI eligibility "to individuals whose drug addiction and/or alcoholism is a contributing factor material to the finding of disability." For those who qualified by virtue of some other disabling impairment, but were still drug addicts or alcoholics, the law required that they have a representative payee. Such payees could receive a $50 fee for their efforts. The law also authorized funds for continuing disability reviews. In this manner, policymakers disposed of the substance addiction part of the SSI reform agenda. It was a measure so popular that Congress had chosen to legislate on it both in 1994 and 1996.[83]

For the first time in the forty-year history of the disability program, Congress singled out a particular disabling impairment as not qualifying for benefits. In the past, a person with a disabling impairment qualified for benefits, regardless of how that impairment originated. The morbidly obese person, the applicant with smoking-related lung cancer, and even the unsuccessful suicide attempt all qualified for disability benefits. Republican Congressman and future Chairman of the Social Security Subcommittee Clay Shaw of Florida seemed unaware of this policy history when he said, "Most of the American people would be outraged to find . . . that someone is even receiving disability when they inflict it on themselves."[84] But policymakers considered drug addiction and alcoholism to be unsavory forms of impairment and took special steps to exclude drug addicts and alcoholics from the public welfare rolls.

1996—A New Welfare Law

The question of whether or not AFDC would be retained as an entitlement stood at the heart of the welfare reform debate. SSI nonetheless remained important as a source of revenue to pay for welfare reform and as a test of the political system's responsiveness to the problems in the program related to children and immigrants receiving benefits. It appeared likely that any welfare reform legislation would include a provision concerning children's SSI benefits and another that addressed the rights of noncitizens to welfare benefits such as SSI. In both cases, the Republicans in Congress wanted to go further in the sense of cutting off more people from benefits than did the Democrat in the White House.

One measure of the support for limiting childhood SSI benefits came in the National Governors Association February 1996 policy statement. The Governors, from whom both parties sought approval for legislation that would change the balance between state and federal power, favored ending cash benefits to about a fourth of the childhood SSI caseload. They wanted to base entitlement to benefits more on medical evidence and less on an individual functionalized assessment of a child's ability to perform daily activities.[85]

The struggle over welfare reform lasted into the summer. Rumors surfaced in July that the White House might accept the latest Republican version of welfare reform, despite deep divisions in the party and among White House staff members over the issue. The end of AFDC as an entitlement supported in large part by federal money was in sight. "The entitlement appears to be a lost proposition," one Democratic Congressional aide said. Some politically savvy observers believed that the Republicans might be able to assemble a veto proof majority over the issue. An official with La Raza, a Hispanic civil rights organization interested in retaining welfare eligibility for legal immigrants, added, "It's been made clear to us that the White House wants to sign a welfare reform bill at all costs."[86]

In July 1996 both houses of Congress passed the latest version of welfare reform, convened a conference committee, and completed action on the first day of August. The debate provided a final opportunity for the members to put themselves on the record on one of the defining issues of the times. Representative Clay Shaw once again informed his colleagues that aliens over age sixty-five were five times more likely to go on SSI than citizens over age sixty-five. "We have got to stop making welfare available for citizens of other countries. It is that simple," he said.[87] Senator Alfonse D'Amato (R-New York) proudly stated that he was the grandson of immigrants and that immigration "contributed to the strength of America." Nonetheless, the fact that the 3 percent of the population over age sixty-five who were immigrants claimed 30 percent of the SSI benefits indicated that something was "terribly wrong." According to Senator Pete Domenici (R-Colorado), newly naturalized citizens were bringing over their parents and promising to support them only to find out that the government would do nothing if they stopped supporting them. The rolls were becoming crowded with immigrants.[88]

Liberals pushed back, but it was clear that they did not have the votes to stop the bill and were trying instead to give the President ammunition to veto the legislation. Senator Kennedy charged the Republicans with pulling "back the welcome mat for legal immigrants who enter this country under our laws, play by the rules, pay taxes and contribute to our communities. . . . If you are a legal immigrant and you fall on hard times, you are out of luck."[89] The provisions related to children's benefits also received vituperative criticism. Senator Carol Moseley-Braun (D-Illinois) said that the Republicans were doing "violence to poor children, putting millions of them into poverty who were not in poverty before." Senator Kennedy added that 300,000 children with serious disabilities, such as mental retardation, tuberculosis, autism, and head injuries, would be cut from the SSI rolls.

The liberals played on politically resonant symbols. Each of the diseases that Senator Kennedy mentioned, for example, had large charitable followings and enjoyed significant government support. Americans still related to their immigrant past. In 1996, however, the appeal of welfare reform transcended the political causes of helping crippled children or providing a welcoming environment for immigrants. By a count of 52 to 46, for example, the Senate voted to uphold the provisions in the bill banning SSI and other forms of public assistance for legal immigrants.[90]

As the bill waited the outcome of a conference committee and approached final passage, liberal groups, such as the National Urban League, the Children's Defense Fund, the National Conference of Catholic Bishops, and the Union of American Hebrew Congregations, lined up against the legislation. They urged President Clinton to veto it. The benefit rights of immigrants remained a key issue. One Democratic Congressional aide noted that, in conference, the Republicans would sand "down the rough edges, except in the area of restricting benefits for legal immigrants, where they perceive no political disadvantage in being barbaric." A Republican Congressional aide countered that "under no circumstances will we allow handouts—cash welfare—to go to non-citizens."[91]

House Majority Leader Dick Armey framed the welfare reform issue in a way that Republicans found congenial. "In the end," he said, "the president is going to have to make a determination whether or not he's going to sign this bill and satisfy the American people, while he alienates his left-wing political base, or if he's going to veto the bill in order to satisfy the left wing of the Democratic party and thereby alienate the American people."[92]

The President spoke to the press on the issue of welfare reform on July 31, 1996, in what was the climactic moment of the debate. He announced that the latest version of welfare reform was a great improvement over the previous versions, pointing out that it dropped some of the deep cuts for disabled children. He expressed his disappointment that the Congressional leadership "insisted on attaching to this extraordinarily important bill a provision that will hurt legal immigrants in America, people who work hard for their families, pay taxes, serve in our military. This provision has nothing to do with welfare reform. It is simply a budget-saving measure and it is not right." He nonetheless felt that "this is the best chance we will have for a long, long time to complete the work of ending welfare as we know it by moving people from welfare to work, demanding responsibility and doing better by children." He announced that he would sign the bill.[93]

The final version of "The Personal Responsibility and Work Opportunity Reconciliation Act of 1996" contained variations on the SSI provisions that had been developed in the past two years. It prohibited SSI eligibility to all noncitizens, with the exception of refugees and asylees for the first five years after their arrival to the United States and active duty armed forces personnel and honorably discharged veterans (as well as their spouses and dependent children). The law therefore honored the nation's obligations toward veterans by creating another entitlement for them that was not available to civilians. The law also made an exception for lawful permanent residents who had earned forty quarters of coverage for Social Security purposes and, by extension, for their children under eighteen, although a quarter in which the person received public assistance would not count as one of the forty. In this manner, the law gave noncitizens who had worked in the United States and paid taxes more rights than other noncitizens, another bow to the nation's social welfare traditions. Still, the provision meant that the SSA would redetermine the eligibility of all noncitizens on the SSI rolls, and if they did not fall into one of the approved categories their benefits would end.

The new law also changed the definition of childhood disability as it applied to SSI, effectively repealing the *Zebley* decision through legislation. It eliminated the comparable severity standard in the original SSI law and provided instead that a child would be considered disabled if the child had a medically determinable impairment that resulted in marked and severe functional limitations and that could be expected to result in death or to last for at least twelve months. It directed the SSA to take out references to maladaptive behavior in the Listing of Impairments for Children and to discontinue the use of individualized functional assessments. It required the SSA to redetermine the eligibility of all childhood disability recipients within a year and to drop those who failed to meet the new standard from the rolls. Children on the rolls would also be subject to continuing disability reviews once every three years.

Although the law backed away from the distinctions in the earlier version of the bill that would have limited some children to only three-quarters of the benefit to which they were entitled and from ending cash SSI benefits for other children altogether, it nonetheless marked a concerted attempt to cut down on the number of children on the rolls.[94]

Conclusion

As these matters indicated, passage of the 1996 laws marked not the end of the development of SSI as much as a point of change that was likely to produce its own consequences. The 1996 law did, however, settle for the foreseeable future the question of whether SSI would remain a federal entitlement. Unlike AFDC, it would. It received special treatment from the welfare reform process in that regard. At the same time, it formed an important part of the welfare reform package. The earlier 1996 law dealing with substance abuse took what might be called a traditional approach, bundling SSI with Social Security and mixing the expansion of Social Security with measures designed to correct a problem in SSI. The major welfare reform law of the year that President Clinton signed in the summer applied nearly exclusively to SSI rather than Social Security. It put the program in the company of other welfare programs, such as Food Stamps and AFDC, and it made major cuts in the program.

Reflecting the opinion of many liberals, lawyer and advocate Jonathan Stein said that the new rules for childhood disability were based on "an assumption of problems" that did not exist. Congressmen watched a tape from the TV program *Prime Time* that focused on "two families in Louisiana" who appeared to be cheating. "There was no other evidence," Stein said.[95]

Whether or not that was true, it pointed to the dynamic that produced the changes in the 1996 law related to SSI. In a sense, the changes followed a very old reform model in which investigators uncovered an outrage and Congress responded. Senator Cohen helped expose the drug addicts. Bob Woodward and ABC News, among others, publicized the children whose parents coached them on how to deceive the authorities. Other journalists exposed the existence of noncitizens using SSI as a makeshift retirement program. Each of these things invited actions that were compatible with the prevailing view that the existing welfare system was a failure that provided too many incentives for fraud and deceit and that allowed too many undeserving beneficiaries to be on the rolls. Each offered cost-savings in a legislative effort that depended on such savings. Hence, the SSI cuts, although not exactly compatible with the other parts of the law that emphasized the importance of work over welfare, became part of the larger reform process.

When SSI began, an inner circle of Congressmen on proprietary committees and bureaucrats from the still widely respected Social Security Administration influenced its development. Public exposure of SSI's problems that demanded Congressional response began in 1974 with the many stories of SSI's failed implementation. These stories focused not on deceitful SSI beneficiaries as much as on beleaguered SSI applicants facing a flawed system run by indifferent bureaucrats and computers that failed to function properly. The horror stories of the eighties also helped open up the policymaking process beyond the tight circle of Congressmen on proprietary committees and federal bureaucrats to include advocates for the beneficiaries. Once again the press focused on the injustices done to SSI recipients. The pattern changed in the nineties. Despite the existence of a wide circle of people who defended the rights of SSI beneficiaries and used the courts and the budgetary process to expand the program, the stories from the media now put the spotlight on fraud and abuse. The bureaucrats in the SSA and even the Congressmen on the Ways and Means and Finance Committees played a secondary role to the Republican leadership in the House and the members of the media who influenced the public perception of the problem.

The politics of SSI had shifted from the Social Security and disability arenas into the much less ruly realm of welfare reform. In 1972 the contrast between SSI and other welfare programs had been helpful in launching the program and expanding the American welfare state. In 1996 the similarities between SSI and other welfare programs resulted in significant cuts in the program. The program's identity as a welfare program had overshadowed its pedigree as an offshoot of Social Security.

POST-1996 DEVELOPMENTS

A Brief Postscript

Although the 1996 welfare reforms marked a point of real change in America's welfare state, Congress soon scaled back the changes in Supplemental Security Income (SSI). Congress experienced buyers' remorse with respect to childhood disability benefits and benefits for noncitizens. Then the cycle repeated itself so that by early 2011 policymakers again raised concerns about too many undeserving children on the SSI rolls. One might argue that the SSI program went around in circles, but, as the concluding chapter of this book demonstrates, SSI developed in distinctive ways that reflected the trajectory of the welfare state in recent America.

Implementing Welfare Reform

With the 1996 welfare reform on the books, the action shifted, at least at first, from Congress to the bureaucracy. As usual, much depended on how the new law would be implemented. Representative Sander M. Levin (D-Michigan) said, "We're going to have to carefully watch the implementation. . . . No one is quite sure how this is going to work out."[1] The process of implementation began relatively soon after President Clinton's landslide victory over Senator Dole in the 1996 election. The parents of more than a quarter million children on SSI received letters informing them that their cases would be reviewed. The law gave the executive branch considerable discretion in writing regulations and permitted those on the rolls to receive benefits through June 1997 (a year after enactment of the law). Senator Tom Daschle (D-South Dakota), the Majority Leader who had voted against the final bill in the Senate, noted that "Congress provided the executive branch with wide latitude to interpret the statute." Marty Ford, a lobbyist for ARC (the organization for retarded citizens), put it more directly. "The power to hurt these children or to assist them is completely in President Clinton's hands," she said.[2]

A Social Security Administration (SSA) spokesman estimated that some 100,000 to 200,000 children would be dropped from the rolls. The variance indicated how much depended on how the government defined "marked and severe functional limitations." So with Congress moving on to other topics, advocates and bureaucrats geared up for the challenges ahead. It remained to be seen whether impaired children—such as seven-year-old Eugene Wheeler who had chronic asthma that required him to take three different medications during the day and that had delayed his development—would stay on the rolls. Advocates such as Jonathan Stein wondered if the federal government would be able to handle all of the redeterminations that the new law required it to perform. Past efforts had resulted in many mistakes. The effect of the new law on the SSA hearings and appeals system was also unclear since people removed from the rolls had the right to appeal the decision. The part of the law dealing with noncitizens posed only slightly less difficult challenges.[3]

Purging the Children

The 1996 law tightened the requirements for disabled children who applied to the program, mandated a review of the benefit rolls, and required the SSA to remove from the rolls any child not qualifying under the tighter rules. In other words, Congress wanted to get tough on kids who acted out in school to get the "crazy checks" that supplemented family incomes. This policy mood lasted barely long enough for the administrators of the program to start the actual process of getting tough. Once the reality of the shift in policy set in, policymakers backed off their earlier resolve and, in a series of administrative and legislative steps, reversed much of what they had done in 1996.

The first order of business in implementing the new regime for children on SSI consisted of promulgating new regulations that removed any references to the "comparable severity" standard established by the *Zebley* decision. This process, which involved revisions in both policy and procedures, required the government to go through the formal rule-making process. The revised regulations appeared in the Federal Register in February 1997. The SSA estimated that 288,000 of the approximately 880,000 children on SSI in 1997 would be subject to review.[4] An initial round of review notices went out in March 1997, just as SSA Commissioner Shirley Chater, a Clinton appointee, stepped down and career Health and Human Services official John J. Callahan became Acting Commissioner.

The appointment of Kenneth Apfel as permanent SSA Commissioner in September 1997 marked the beginning of a new policy regime with regard to SSI and children. At Apfel's confirmation hearing, Senators asked him critical questions about the childhood reviews. In response, Apfel pledged to conduct a "top-to-bottom" review of the disability review process for children.

Apfel's top-to-bottom review came in the context of the initial round of reviews of disabled children on the rolls. By the middle of August 1997, some 170,300 cases had been reviewed, and 56 percent of the reviews resulted in terminations. These terminations of flesh-and-blood children provoked the usual reactions in the usual places. Jonathan Stein told the *New York Times* that "Congress set a somewhat stricter standard, but the Administration has misinterpreted it and applied it in an arbitrary, anarchic way." Eunice Kennedy Shriver called the terminations "unfair to children with mental retardation." A paralegal in a Louisiana legal services office told the *Times*, "Children are not being evaluated fairly. . . . Almost as soon as parents submit information requested by the Social Security Administration, they get back letters saying their children are no longer disabled."[5]

Senators John Chafee (R-Rhode Island) and Kent Conrad (D-North Dakota) sent a letter to President Clinton complaining that the eligibility criteria being used were "far more severe than is required." They told Clinton that "the Administration has misinterpreted the intent of Congress in reforming the Supplemental Security Income program for their children."[6] The *Times* reported that parents had been dissuaded from pursuing appeals after their children had been terminated from the rolls. One Wheeling, West Virginia, parent said that Social Security employees made it clear "they didn't want us to appeal."[7] SSA employees explained to him and other parents that if their appeals were unsuccessful, they would have to repay the government for any benefits received by electing to continue payments through the appeal process.

Apfel began his promised top-to-bottom review promptly and released the results on December 17, 1997. He identified three problem areas, and he proposed solutions to each of the problems. First, the SSA promised to readjudicate all cessations involving mental retardation (about 42,000 cases) and to extend this review to all new claims filed since the August 22, 1996, date of passage of the welfare reform law. Second, in about 5 percent of the cessations, the SSA terminated benefits because the parents refused to cooperate with the reviews and provide the requested information about their children. The SSA promised to reopen these cases, making sure the parents were given ample opportunity to cooperate and granting them full appeal rights with payment continuation and back pay for any months of terminated benefits. Finally, the SSA pledged to contact the parents in all cases where the cessation action was not appealed (about 86,000 cases) and give them another opportunity to file an appeal. The SSA estimated that these actions would reduce the ultimate number of children terminated from SSI from the original estimate of 135,000 to about 100,000.[8]

Although the number of children on SSI decreased by 11 percent between 1996 and 2000, three years later the number rebounded to its 1996 level. From 2003 to 2009, the number rose another 25 percent beyond the 1996 level. By 2009, the number of kids on SSI was 25 percent higher than it had been at the start of the 1996 reform effort aimed at reducing the rolls (see Figure 8-1).[9] On the one hand, the *Zebley* ruling produced a dramatic rise in the child SSI population of 210 percent. On the other hand, Congress's effort to repeal *Zebley* resulted in a mere 11 percent reduction, and that reduction proved to be only temporary. In the long run, the trend line continued upward from the much higher baseline established by the *Zebley* case. Children comprised 14.4 percent of the overall SSI population in 1996 and 15.6 percent in 2009. In terms of program costs, the annual federal expenditures for child SSI recipients rose by 80 percent from its 1996 level of $5 billion to its 2009 level of $9 billion.[10]

Nor did the 1996 legislation have much of an impact on the prevalence of mental disorders among children on SSI. In 1990, before the *Zebley* decision, 48 percent of the children on SSI had mental disorders.[11] By the end of 1993, that

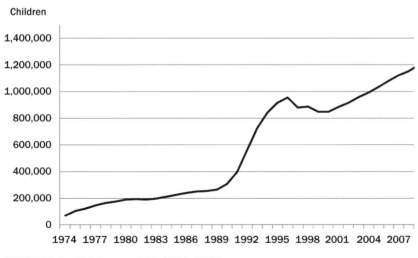

FIGURE 8-1   Children on SSI, 1974–2008

figure rose to 59 percent.[12] In 1996, when Congress attempted to reverse the *Zebley* decision, 62 percent of children on SSI qualified on the basis of mental disorders.[13] In 2009, that percentage reached 66 percent.[14] Despite the 1996 changes in the definitions of disability for children, the overwhelming preponderance of children on SSI in 2009 entered the rolls because of mental disabilities. The next largest diagnostic group—"nervous system and sensory disorders"—accounted for only 8 percent of the cases.[15]

Other policy reversals from the 1996 law followed. One year after enactment of the welfare reform bill, Congress passed P.L. 105-33, which required continuing Medicaid coverage for terminated SSI children who did not meet the revised disability standards established in the welfare reform law. This change voided the major budget savings that might have been realized from the 1996 law. Since the average SSI recipient's Medicaid costs were more than twice the cost of his or her cash benefits, the measure erased at least two-thirds of those savings.

Backpedaling on Aliens

In 1996, many members of Congress, particularly in the House, wanted to cut aliens off entirely from SSI. The law that emerged granted three categories of exceptions to the general rule that lawfully admitted aliens could not receive SSI for the first five years of their residence in the United States. The exceptions included aliens who were admitted as refugees or asylees, aliens who were serving or who had served honorably in the U.S. military, and aliens who had been employed in the United States, paid their taxes, and earned the equivalent of forty quarters of coverage under Social Security. Aliens in the first two categories could only receive SSI for five years. Policymakers expected that aliens in the third category would qualify for Social Security benefits and therefore have little need for SSI.

Aliens in these three categories became known as "qualified aliens," in contrast to the unqualified ones whose benefits would be terminated. The new law required the SSA to review the cases of all aliens on SSI to determine whether they qualified under the more restrictive eligibility rules and, if not, to terminate their benefits. The law became effective upon passage in August 1996, although the SSA had until March 1997 to notify all aliens of the pending review of their eligibility. No more than a third of the aliens on SSI in 1996 fell into one of the protected categories. Of 725,000 aliens on SSI, therefore, 500,000 might be ineligible under the 1996 law.[16]

Even before the bill was signed, some pushback against the provisions for aliens occurred. Officials in states like California realized that legal aliens dropped from the SSI rolls might migrate to the state welfare rolls. In early August, for example, the *Los Angeles Times* reported that 93,000 Los Angeles County residents would lose their SSI, shifting costs of $236 million to the County. County Supervisor Gloria Molina said, "This is going to probably bankrupt us."[17] Regional papers throughout California featured stories predicting a high local impact of the SSI cuts.[18] A similar reaction occurred in New York. "Unkind Cuts: The Welfare Overhaul May Save Washington Money, but It Will Cost New York Plenty" headlined Long Island's *Newsday*.[19] In October 1996 New York City Mayor Rudy Giuliani (R) brought a federal lawsuit against the government to prevent implementation of the alien-related provisions of the welfare reform law and a subsequently passed immigration law.[20]

In the immediate aftermath of the November presidential election, House Ways and Means Committee Chairman Bill Archer (R-Texas) warned the President against trying to change the SSI alien rules.[21] Archer's warning had little effect. Barely a month after the original welfare reform bill passed, Congress amended it to add battered spouses and their eligible children to the list of qualified aliens. In June 1997, Congress extended benefits for terminated aliens until September 30, 1997, even if the review determined them to be ineligible. The Balanced Budget Act of 1997 further liberalized the SSI alien rules. In particular, it expanded the scope of the "battered" recipient exemption, granted Cuban and Haitian immigrants categorical status as "qualified aliens" regardless of their actual immigration status, increased to seven years the period for which time-limited qualified aliens could receive SSI, and extended the eligibility of terminated aliens until September 30, 1998. The climax of this reconsideration process came in 1998 with the passage of a relatively obscure law that granted permanent eligibility for SSI to all aliens who had been on the rolls when the welfare reform bill was enacted in August 1996.

Even after this 1998 law, Congress continued to soften the rules denying SSI to aliens. A 2000 law extended refugee status to victims of human trafficking. In 2007, Iraqi and Afghan aliens received special status that permitted them to receive SSI for up to six months, and then by virtue of a 2008 law, up to eight months. Another law lengthened the seven-year period for SSI receipt to nine years for those in refugee or asylee status and made this extension retroactive. The law also lifted time limits for anyone who had a citizenship application pending.

As a result of all these changes, nowhere near the expected 500,000 noncitizens left the rolls. Instead, the results were more modest. The trend line in the number of aliens on SSI dipped slightly after 1996 and did not return to 1996 levels (see Figure 8-2).[22] As a percentage of the overall SSI population, aliens declined from 11.0 percent in 1996 to 8.4 percent in 2009.

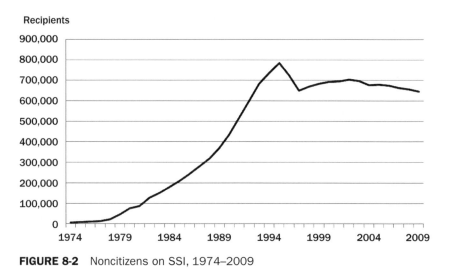

Recipients

FIGURE 8-2   Noncitizens on SSI, 1974–2009

Tweaks, Here and There

Most of the changes after 1996 made SSI more liberal. Only criminals and people who had committed fraud belonged to a class of individuals for whom neither liberals nor conservatives wanted to do favors. By way of contrast, Congress rewarded Iraqi and Afghan immigrants "who have provided service to the United States" with special immigration status in 2007 and allowed them to collect SSI benefits for six months. The following year, Congress extended the six-month period to eight months and then in 2009 eliminated the eight-month limit for the Iraqi and Afghan immigrants and placed them on the same footing as other humanitarian immigrants.

In a similar manner, special policy initiatives or favored programs and activities also moved SSI in a liberal direction. For example, in 2009, as part of the Obama administration's fiscal stimulus program, one-time payments of $250 went to Social Security and SSI beneficiaries. This money received a special exclusion in the SSI program, so that recipients did not have to claim it as income that might reduce their benefits. A 1998 law excluded from countable income/resources for SSI purposes any payments made under the Ricky Ray Hemophilia Relief Fund. A 2010 provision in law sheltered the first $2,000 received by an SSI recipient for participating in clinical trials for rare diseases. These exclusions functioned almost like hidden tax expenditures within the welfare state.[23]

Chasing the Dream of Program Simplification

At the same time as Congress loaded the law with exceptions, the Social Security Administration made a concerted effort to simplify the SSI program. At the beginning of the new millennium, it issued three reports that described the problems and proposed solutions.[24] The SSI population amounted to less than 15 percent of the Old Age, Survivors, and Disability Insurance population, yet SSI consumed 37 percent of the agency's administrative resources.[25] Complexity in SSI contributed to errors in payments, caused hardship and frustration for beneficiaries, and added unduly to the agency's workload. To remedy these problems, the SSA suggested such things as averaging wages over a calendar year rather than offsetting actual wages against SSI payments every month. It also recommended that the income and resource thresholds be updated to reflect modern price levels and that income and resource levels be indexed to inflation. On a smaller scale, the agency advocated cutting down on the number of exclusions by consolidating resource exclusions from burial expenses, burial plots, and burial insurance.[26]

Since each of these simplifications cost money in the short term, they proved difficult to enact in an era of deepening budget deficits. The push for simplification at the turn of the millennium went the way of nearly a dozen previous efforts, which yielded many recommendations but few resultant changes.

The Policy Cycle Repeats?

If the welfare measures of 1996 marked an important moment in the recent history of SSI, so too did a much less publicized 1993 Congressional action that ended the option of having the federal government pay the administrative costs of the state supplements. As a direct result, federal administration of state supplementation became less of a good deal for the states, and more states began to administer the supplements on their own. At the start of the program, the SSA administered state supplements for thirty states and the District of Columbia; by 2010, it did so for only fifteen states.[27] This trend appeared to indicate that the states, contrary to the wishes and expectations of SSI's founders, were becoming more important in SSI. A counter trend, however, pushed toward more federal and less state involvement in SSI.[28] By the end of 2009, only one-third of SSI beneficiaries received supplemental benefits, compared with 54 percent in 1974, and in 2010, federally administered state supplements constituted only 7 percent of total SSI expenditures, down from 25 percent in 1974.[29]

Post millennial economic exigencies further altered the path of SSI's development. As the recession of 2007 lingered, many states, particularly those with large SSI supplemental benefits, cut SSI to save money. Those cuts, in turn, prompted the media to write stories about the harmful effects on SSI recipients. The *Chapel Hill* (North Carolina) *Herald* lamented the fate of families with disabled children who were "struggling to keep food on the table, a roof over their heads and to pay for needed health and dental care."[30] In February 2010, the *Philadelphia Inquirer* criticized Governor Ed Rendell's proposed cuts to the state supplementation of SSI benefits. Jonathan Stein called for a rally at the State Capitol to protest the SSI cuts.[31] Despite the protests, the cuts proceeded. In 2009, California eliminated its state supplement for SSI couples, and in 2011, it cut out supplements for most individuals. In 2010, New Jersey decided to decrease its state supplements by 9.2 percent, in a year when its SSI population went up 4 percent.[32]

The state cuts and the ensuing publicity put pressure on the federal government to spend more on SSI. That, in turn, revived concerns about people who were using SSI to rip off the government. The media had it both ways, producing some stories about the adverse effects of the SSI cuts on recipients and other stories about how SSI recipients exploited American taxpayers. The *Boston Globe* took pride of place in its SSI coverage. In 2009, the paper reported on the Bonilla family, "one of the thousands of low-income families who will suffer from steep budget cuts."[33] The next year the same paper ran stories that featured case studies of families using their children to obtain SSI benefits to which they were not entitled.[34]

Globe reporter Patricia Wen wrote about Geneva Fielding, a single mother of three boys living in the projects in Roxbury, who managed to keep her household solvent by getting her youngest child on SSI for his "impulsiveness." Her two older sons were denied SSI, she told Wen, because they were not on medication. "To get the check," Fielding said, "you've got to medicate the child." Wen also reported the case of Yessina, who had failed to get her seven-year-old on SSI in two previous tries, until she finally persuaded his doctor to put him on medication for attention deficit hyperactivity disorder (ADHD). Although none of the more than two dozen parents Wen interviewed admitted that they coached their kids to exaggerate their symptoms to get them on SSI, all said they knew a lot of other people who did. Wen told the obligatory "horror story" of a Boston area couple who got themselves and their three children on SSI as disabled and then overdosed their four-year-old daughter with ADHD meds, causing her death.

The second installment in the series highlighted the case of Roxanne Roman, whose eighteen-month-old infant had not yet learned to speak in complete sentences. Diagnosed with "speech delay," this infant became a very young SSI beneficiary. According to Wen, children on SSI due to a diagnosis of speech delay had increased twelvefold since 1997. Children under five were now the fastest-growing age group qualifying for SSI; roughly 40 percent of new SSI beneficiaries were under age five.[35]

Wen indicted the government for failing to do sufficient disability reviews of children on the rolls and the SSI program itself for discouraging work. She reported on families whose teenage children on SSI avoided working because their work would reduce the SSI check that provided the family's main source of income. As one SSI mother put it, "You got to do more to get into the program, but once you do, it's an easier and better form of welfare. You get more money, and they don't check up on you."[36] The *Globe* report concluded that the SSI "disability program has gone seriously astray, becoming an alternative welfare system with troubling built-in incentives that risk harm to children."[37] A lucrative industry helped kids qualify for SSI. Hospitals and insurance companies hired companies to put children on SSI in an effort to get on Medicaid and shift costs to the federal government. States also made efforts to get children off state welfare programs and on the federal SSI program.

The *Globe* series stirred up a great deal of controversy.[38] A professor of policy at Brandeis defended SSI and argued against "Draconian cuts." The President of the major federal employees union lobbied for more money for the SSA to conduct more disability reviews.[39] Jonathan Stein complained that the series was "reminiscent of a similar media frenzy in the mid-1990s" that resulted in "hundreds of thousands of disabled children" losing their SSI benefits.[40] Democratic Congressman Richie Neal of Springfield called for hearings on the issues raised in the series. Scott Brown (R), the heir to Edward's Kennedy seat, wanted the Senate to hold its own hearings. Ways and Means Subcommittee Chairman Geoff Davis (R-Kentucky) asked the General Accounting Office to investigate the *Globe* allegations.

SSA Commissioner Michael Astrue, a Boston native who maintained many personal and professional connections to Massachusetts, sat down with the *Globe* editorial board for an in-depth interview about the series. Astrue conceded many of the problems. He said that reforms were needed in what he characterized as "an admirable, but flawed, program." He worried, though, that the debate about reforming the program would too easily be "consumed by emotionally pitched partisan strife, often led by disability advocates and taxpayer groups." To prevent this outcome, Astrue called for a review to be done by the Institute of Medicine. "Too much legislation happens by sound bite and anecdote," he said. "When you see how shrill the advocates are, and then you see what we are getting from the other side of the fence too, what kind of legislation is this going to look like if we're not careful?"[41]

It all made for an unedifying public policy process. In 1990, the Supreme Court in the *Zebley* case wanted to make the disability determination system more equitable for children, and in the process it made it more subjective and more susceptible to fraud and abuse. The *Zebley* ruling also launched a huge upsurge in the number of children on SSI, transforming a small, little-noticed part of the SSI system into a highly visible and controversial component. In 1996, Congress wanted to eliminate fraud and abuse in the SSI program and constrain its growth, so it made the disability determination process more stringent. In 1997, when politicians and the public realized that a more stringent disability determination process meant thousands of actual children being dropped from the rolls, they backed off their earlier resolve and began to blame the administrators, alluding to flawed procedures. The administrators tried to deflect blame by halting the reviews and announcing a review of the reviews. After all these moves and countermoves, the number of children receiving SSI benefits once again reached its pre-1996 levels.

In a somewhat similar manner, noncitizens on SSI came to be associated with other "undeserving" welfare recipients in the early nineties. As a result, aliens on SSI became a particular target of the 1996 reforms. Within two years, however, Congress quietly returned the law to the *status quo ante*. Constant change, rather than equilibrium, appeared to be the norm.

Conclusion

The creators of Supplemental Security Income (SSI), a triumvirate of Nixon administration officials, Social Security Administration (SSA) employees, and Congressional staff members, envisioned a program that would bring the dignity of the Social Security approach to elderly and disabled people who lived in poverty. The new program had a means test, and it obtained its funding from general revenues, not a payroll tax specially designated for its use. In these regards, it remained a welfare program. Unlike other welfare programs, however, it offered a uniform benefit, payable across the country, at federal expense. Furthermore, the federal government would pay that benefit itself, rather than entrusting the states to be its agent. As such, the program represented an unprecedented federal takeover of previously state-run welfare programs. Furthermore, a recipient did not have to undergo the sort of intensive interaction with caseworkers that characterized other welfare programs. Instead, a person who qualified for the program received a gold-colored check from the federal treasury every month.

Like all social programs, SSI reflected the conventional wisdom of the era of its creation. Policymakers, frustrated by the results achieved by President Johnson's War on Poverty, doubted the efficacy of social services and hoped to avoid the racial disputes that characterized the social policy of the times. President Nixon, in particular, saw social services as instruments of the Democratic Party. Cash grants might better serve his political purposes.

The creators of SSI took as a given that their new program should cover the people in the adult categories. Although they concentrated their attention on the

231

elderly, the program ended up serving primarily people with disabilities and secondarily the elderly. If SSI had limited its focus to the elderly, it might have developed into a well-received program for the deserving poor that decreased in importance over time as the level of Social Security benefits rose. The adult categories, however, came bundled with the blind, a relatively minor concern, and people with disabilities, a much more important group.

Having the SSA run SSI meant that the new program would inherit institutional structures from existing programs and in particular the Social Security Disability Insurance (SSDI) program. The states, not the federal government, ran the disability determination offices. Once again, history influenced the course of public policy in ways that few people even recognized A system of disability determination that was the product of a long chain of historical events grew to include new responsibilities under SSI. The state disability determination offices dated back to Congressional debates over a disability bill in 1952. A short-term compromise to the political problems of that year became a permanent solution. The terms of the 1952 agreement and the 1956 law that followed it became the basis for the definition of disability in SSI and for the bureaucratic structure used to decide if someone met that definition.

In other words, SSI reflected the conventional wisdom of 1972 but also the accumulated wisdom of previous eras. Aid to the blind and aid to the elderly came from the 1935 Social Security Act. Aid to the disabled originated in the 1950 Social Security amendments. The disability determination system started in political deliberations that took place in 1952, 1954, and 1956. All figured in the history of SSI.

In the decade between 1975 and 1985, the history of SSI merged with the history of SSDI. Generous SSDI benefits paid during a period of high unemployment encouraged people to apply for disability benefits and discouraged labor force participation. The response to this problem took the form of 1980 legislation that reduced the level of disability benefits for some applicants and attempted to create work incentives in both SSI and SSDI. The Reagan administration's implementation of these 1980 amendments produced a firestorm of protest that deserving people were being cut from the rolls. Congress reacted by passing new legislation in 1984 that made it easier for people already on the disability rolls to remain there. Although policymakers concentrated on SSDI throughout these episodes, their actions affected the disability category in SSI. It became easier for people with mental impairments to qualify for SSI, for example.

The dispute over childhood benefits came in the more permissive post-1984 atmosphere. Since childhood benefits were unique to SSI, they did not enjoy the same political protection as benefits for disabled adults on SSDI. Still, an alternative avenue for program expansion existed in the form of the courts. In particular, courts concerned with civil rights expanded the entitlements of such groups as the residents of mental hospitals and, in a 1990 Supreme Court decision, children who applied for disability benefits. This decision effectively changed the law related to childhood disability benefits, so that more children who applied for SSI received benefits. As with other expansions of the disability rolls, this one produced a strong reaction in Congress. In 1996 Congress effectively overturned the 1990 Supreme Court decision through legislation.

With the 1996 legislation, SSI entered another stage in its history. The controlling context shifted from disability back to welfare reform. One pervasive critique of welfare programs was that they contained perverse incentives. Aid to Families with Dependent Children (AFDC), for example, paid benefits to dependent children, leading some to believe that it encouraged women to have children out of wedlock. SSI, devoted to the deserving poor, nonetheless developed what some people perceived as incentives for people to engage in socially unproductive behavior. As with AFDC, SSI's association with bad behavior invited a punitive legislative response.

The Modern Policymaking System for Social Welfare

If nothing else, then, the history of SSI demonstrates that historians make a mistake when they sharply differentiate SSI from AFDC. SSI, just like AFDC, was a welfare program and just like AFDC it paid benefits to groups that many believed were unworthy of aid. The groups that engendered controversy in SSI included noncitizens, substance abusers, and children. These groups did not break down neatly on racial and gendered lines. If anything the categories reflected new groups that had risen to public prominence in the post–Great Society era, such as immigrants, drug addicts, and children with learning disabilities, attention deficit disorders, and other behavioral problems.

Policymakers created SSI in the shadow of Social Security, yet the policymaking system for SSI was quite different from the one that nurtured the Social Security program in its years of growth and expansion between 1950 and 1972. The policy actors and forces described by Martha Derthick in her 1979 book on Social Security no longer sufficed to explain the development of the SSI program. Fundamental American institutions, like Congress and courts, functioned differently and played different roles in SSI than they did in Social Security.

The Congress that legislated SSI policy differed from the one that had passed disability insurance in 1956, Medicare in 1965, and even SSI in 1972. Ways and

Means remained the single most important Congressional committee for both Social Security and SSI. Until the mid-seventies, however, Ways and Means operated as a committee of the whole when it made Social Security law. For most of Social Security's postwar run, Wilbur Mills presided over the Committee and tried to keep policy consistent from year to year, control the favors granted to lobbyists, and restrain the growth of program costs. After 1975, Mills left, turnover in the Committee's chair became more frequent, and the Committee acquired permanent subcommittees. SSI became the responsibility of the subcommittee concerned with public assistance. At the same time, the staff available to the Committee expanded, so that the Congressmen no longer needed to depend on executive agencies, such as the SSA and ancillary organizations, such as the Congressional Research Service, to mark up its laws. The Subcommittee on Public Assistance, for example, employed a staffer who specialized in SSI.

Another significant Congressional development was an increase in its oversight of federal programs. When disability insurance ran into controversy in the late fifties, Ways and Means formed a temporary subcommittee to investigate the problems. When SSI and disability insurance encountered difficulties in the eighties, an array of Congressional committees, such as those concerned with government operations and public policy toward the aged, held hearings and became a party to the legislation passed in 1984. An expanded policy system increased the number of actors who could influence legislation, undermining the consistency and coherence of policy.

Although Congress's operational capacity was expanding in the SSI era, making for an often unwieldy policy system, it did not have a monopoly of control over the system. Instead, the courts played a significant role in shaping the program. Like Congress, the courts were an enduring American institution. The creators of Social Security, aware of the Supreme Court's power of judicial review, wrote the 1935 legislation with the Court very much in mind. As expected, private employers challenged the Social Security law in court. Once the Supreme Court ruled favorably in 1937, its influence over the program waned. SSI did not face a similar challenge to its existence. Instead, a different pattern of court involvement in the program developed. Instead of invoking the court's power of judicial review over legislation, the court became involved in SSI procedures related to the fundamental rights of beneficiaries. Where the thirties court was a conservative influence on policy, the post-1972 SSI court was a liberal influence on policy. Where the thirties cases often came from businessmen eager to limit the government's power to tax, the SSI cases came from a new group of legal advocates who filed class-action suits on behalf of people on the SSI rolls in a conscious effort to make benefits more broadly available. The earlier court, once it had decided the constitutionality of the Social Security program, tended to defer to the executive branch and Congress on questions of policy. The later court intervened far more in the day-to-day administration of SSI policy, not hesitating, for example, to get involved on questions related to gender equity, the rights of children, and the basic rights of welfare recipients. As a result, the courts influenced SSI far more than Social Security.

The media kept a closer eye on Congress and the courts in the SSI era than in the era of the great Social Security expansion. In the era of Social Security's creation, people remained in touch with current events by reading the local newspaper and listening to commentators on the radio. Washington insiders read newspapers with national, rather than merely local, audiences, such as the *New York Times*. Such newspapers tried to give readers the inside story on Washington developments, such as reporting in 1935 on rumors that the Social Security bill was running into trouble in the Ways and Means Committee. In the era of SSI, the reach of the media expanded to include nightly newscasts on television and televised news magazines, such as *60 Minutes*, that offered long features on particular aspects of the news. Newspapers remained important, but in the post-Watergate television era these newspapers no longer reported on current events as much as they tried to get the story within the story. In a manner similar to the news magazines on television, they conducted investigations of programs like SSI, and like the news magazines they made an effort to separate the good guys from the bad guys.

In the era of Social Security expansion, the media tended to let the SSA frame the story. A typical feature highlighted the first disability insurance beneficiary or the difference that Social Security made for long-term recipients. The stories often took a respectful attitude toward government authorities, such as the SSA. In the post-Watergate era, these authorities often became the bad guys, as in stories about the bungled implementation of SSI, with people forced to sit in waiting rooms or even buses for days as they tried to straighten out why they were not receiving a check or why their check was made out for the wrong amount. Later in SSI's history, the stories centered on the cruelty of the Reagan administration in throwing disabled people off the rolls, and still later the stories highlighted parents coaching their children to act crazy in order to qualify for benefits and substance abusers feeding their habits with the money they received from SSI. The stories had no consistent bias in terms of expanding or contracting the program. If the stories portrayed people not receiving the benefits to which they were entitled, then they suggested the program be expanded. If the stories featured people using their benefits to engage in destructive behavior, then they argued in favor of program contraction. The only common thread was that the stories portrayed the government as incompetent, a fundamental change from the stories of Social Security's expansion.

To be sure, welfare programs never received the same good press as did the post-1950 Social Security program, even in the fifties and early sixties. By the end of the fifties, stories about welfare queens shirking work and having babies out of wedlock were not uncommon, and these stories not only had an anti-welfare slant but also a racial bias in their association of black people with welfare abuse. And in the seventies, the press began to write negative stories about the solvency of the Social Security program. Needy geezers became greedy geezers. Nonetheless, unlike the earlier welfare programs and the Social Security program, SSI was never free of media criticism. That criticism in turn often acted as an influence over public policy, as in the 1980 disability legislation, the 1984 disability rescue legislation, and the 1996 welfare reform act.

Because the policymaking system for SSI was different than the one that prevailed in Social Security between 1950 and 1972, SSI policy did not have the same clear direction as Social Security. The courts, Congress, the executive branch of the government, and the media all collaborated in a well-orchestrated expansion of Social Security with a clear sequence of priorities: raise benefits, expand coverage, cover disability, finance health care, and protect benefits against inflation. A similar collaboration was simply not possible in SSI. That program contended with the bad economy, rising distrust of government, a decentralized committee system in Congress, a rights-centered activist court, and a fickle media. These various forces prevented SSI from having a clear direction and instead caused it to lurch from one initiative to another. The 1980 legislation marked an effort to cut the rolls; the 1984 legislation marked an expansion of the rolls; the *Zebley* decision expanded the number of children on SSI; and the 1996 welfare reform legislation marked a concerted effort to cut the rolls.

Policy Erosion

A good example of the lack of firm direction in the program concerned the casual way in which Congress and the states legislated changes in what constituted income for SSI beneficiaries. A fundamental tenet of SSI held that the program functioned as a supplement to other income sources a recipient might have to bring his total income up to a minimally acceptable level. When the program began in 1974, Congress set the federal benefit rate at $140 for an individual and $210 for a couple. In theory but not, as we shall see, in practice, if an individual recipient had $100 in monthly income from another source, the individual's SSI supplement would be $40, so that the person's total income reached the federal benefit level of $140. In a similar manner, receipt of outside income of $139 yielded an SSI supplement of one dollar. The concept appeared straightforward enough. When someone received other income, the program reduced the person's benefits so that the person's total income did not exceed the federal benefit rate.

The political objectives of the moment complicated this simple concept. In the first place, the states exercised their option to raise benefit levels above the federal benefit rate and to set the rules for permissible income and resource levels that applied to benefits paid from state funds. In the second place, SSI existed in the shadow of the Family Assistance Plan (FAP), and an explicit object of FAP was to create work incentives for welfare beneficiaries. A system that took away every dollar that a person earned by reducing the person's welfare benefit by the amount of a person's wages offered little encouragement for a person to take a paid job. The FAP, therefore, in the manner of the day, contained various disregards designed to make work more attractive. Although SSI was intended for a different group, for whom employment was not as important a policy goal, it nonetheless contained similar work disregards. At the end of 1998—and in spite of numerous programmatic efforts to generate work incentives—the portion of SSI recipients with earned income barely reached 4.5 percent.[1] Nevertheless, the program contained a general exclusion for earned income of $65 per month and one-half of the remainder. In addition, there were two "special" exclusions related to work incentives: income required for a plan for achieving self-support and work expenses for the blind were not counted in figuring the SSI payment.

The program also featured a general exclusion for *unearned* income of $60 per month, and a collection of six additional "special exclusions." The special exclusions included educational scholarships, property tax rebates, payment for foster care, one-third of support received from an absent parent, certain earnings of an eligible child attending an educational institution, and irregular or infrequent income up to $30 per quarter if unearned and $60 per quarter if earned.

Thus the initial SSI program contained a total of ten exceptions to the general principle that receipt of other income reduced the amount of the SSI payment. Over time, however, policymakers included an array of additional exceptions to the income rules. In the incremental style that applied to many social welfare programs, Congress excluded restitution payments to Japanese internees and relocated Aleutians and payments from the Agent Orange Settlement and the Radiation Exposure Act from income that reduced SSI benefits. Other exclusions included reparations to victims of Nazi persecution, payments to American Indians under the Claims Resettlement Act of 2010, and payments made by the Ricky Ray Hemophilia Relief Fund. Still other exclusions applied to the first $2,000 in cash gifts to individuals under age eighteen with life-threatening medical conditions. The value of an uncashed domestic airline ticket did not count as income nor did benefits paid through the Earned Income Tax Credit or the incentives received by a recipient for participating in a program for the Prevention of Chronic Diseases in Medicaid. In all, the list of "special exclusions" grew from eight to fifty-three.

Few, if any, of these additional exclusions related to the creation of work incentives or other identifiable policy objectives. Not examples of straightforward incremental policymaking, they did not lead to a defined goal because an undisciplined Congress gave them no clear direction. Instead, these changes represented ad hoc attempts to fit other policy goals into the framework of the SSI program or to recognize the special needs of small segments of the SSI population. Taken as a group, they made the system more generous, but they affected a relatively small number of recipients who were deemed worthy of special treatment. This type of irregular incremental policymaking might therefore best be described as *policy erosion*, defined as the slow, erratic, incremental retreat from foundational policy principles.

A similar pattern prevailed regarding the resource limits. The 1972 law set the general resource limit at $1,500 in assets for an individual and $2,250 for a couple and included four general exclusions of assets that would not count toward these limits. By the end of 2010, the law contained sixteen general exclusions and an additional thirty special exclusions.

In addition to the incremental expansion that led to policy erosion, SSI followed a common pattern in which a policy, initially adopted as a temporary expedient of some kind, became permanent. The policies related to home energy assistance exemplified the general phenomenon. In 1981, Congress created the Low Income Energy Assistance Program (LIEAP), which provided cash benefits to poor persons who needed help with their winter energy bills. In late December 1982, Congress enacted a law excluding from countable income for SSI purposes any payments received under the LIEAP. In a sense, the law resembled state and local efforts to help welfare recipients meet the rising costs of home heating. The law set September 30, 1983, as the expiration date for this temporary provision. Two weeks later, however, Congress passed another bill that extended the duration of the exclusion until September 1984. In July 1984, a third bill became law that kept the temporary exclusion alive until October 1987. In December 1987, Congress made the exclusion of LIEAP payments permanent, retroactive to October. All in all, of the seven temporary exclusions from countable income introduced into the SSI program, all but the two most recent became permanent parts of the law.[2]

Disguised Federalism

So the SSI policymaking system lacked the clear direction and what might be called the legislative discipline of the system that had operated during the days of the Social Security expansion. In these regards, it represented something new among the programs under the control of the SSA. At the same time, the program also felt the weight of the past. The history of SSI demonstrated that one could not simply wipe the historical slate clean and, for example, create new categories of welfare recipients who, by participating in a program with links to Social Security, escaped the stigma associated with welfare. Many Americans viewed welfare beneficiaries with suspicion as people who somehow could not manage their own affairs. These people, according to the conventional wisdom, often fell victim to the perverse incentives that the welfare system offered and indulged in destructive behavior, as was the case with substance abusers. Alternatively, they corrupted their children, as was the case with childhood disability benefits, or abused America' generosity, as did immigrants who put their parents on SSI. The emergence of these stigmatized groups in the SSI program reinforced the old Social Security adage that programs for poor people made poor programs.

Nor did SSI represent a clean break from the past by taking over state programs and turning them into a national program administered by the federal government in Washington. Instead, the new SSI contained vestiges of the old programs in the form of what might be called "hidden federalism." The states, far from disappearing, played important roles in the SSI program. Furthermore, the imprint of state practices with regard to the aged, the blind, and the disabled remained in the SSI program and preserved differences from state to state that SSI was explicitly intended to abolish.

One place where the states remained visible was the state disability determination system. The person who investigated a case to certify an applicant as disabled worked for the state, not the federal government. State influence also persisted in the program's system of state supplementation. States, counties, cities, and other localities all played important roles in the supplementation system. The sheer numbers were impressive. In 1983, 130 different state supplementation payment categories existed in the federally administered part of the SSI program and another 158 different payment categories in the state-administered supplements. Adding these to the various federal payment categories yielded 300 different payment levels within SSI.

One might wonder how such a situation arose in a program that offered the states the convenience of federal administration and payments that came from the U.S. Treasury and featured rules intended to promote national uniformity.

Once again, historical particulars and initial choices mattered. In 1972 Congress included the option of state supplements because of a legitimate concern that no recipient of aid under the old state programs should suffer a decrease in benefits due to the conversion to the new federal program. That fit the political instincts of Congress and the expansive spirit of the age. The federal government had neither the means nor the desire to raise benefit levels in all states to the levels of high-benefit states. The fact that the states had already administered the adult welfare categories for at least thirty-two years, and in many cases longer, created a wide disparity in the benefit levels by 1972 that the federal government could not completely overcome. Hence, it permitted states to supplement the federal benefit but gave the states the option of administering such supplements themselves or having the federal government administer the supplements at federal expense. Later, Congress reconsidered the matter and *required* that states supplement benefits for people whose SSI benefit would be below their old state welfare benefit. That requirement meant that the program ultimately contained both mandatory and optional supplementation and that some states administered their supplements themselves and others allowed the federal government to administer the supplements. Many administrative problems resulted from this tangled arrangement.

As the law was implemented, it became clear that the federal government had no policy or administrative control over any aspect of the state-administered supplements. Nineteen states exercised their option to administer the state supplements themselves, even though this decision increased state administrative costs. Perhaps a desire to keep employees on the state payrolls motivated this decision, or perhaps the decision stemmed from a reluctance to accept uniformity under federal guidelines. Over time, more states decided to administer the supplements themselves, so that the total reached twenty-nine.

In a reform effort whose main aims were simplification, unification, and streamlining, the system of state supplementation marked a move in the opposite direction. When the states created their supplement programs, they used their existing programs as models. The federal government, faced with an inflexible deadline to start the SSI program on January 1, 1974, lacked leverage in its negotiations with the states. Many of the political executives in charge had changed between the passage of the law in October 1972 and its implementation in 1974. The Department of Health, Education, and Welfare in particular went from a strong supporter of national welfare benefits to a defender of the states' freedom to experiment in social welfare policy. The process resulted in the creation of an unwieldy, complex, and politically contentious state superstructure over a federal program. Because policymakers proved unwilling to implement a pure and simple federal system to replace the old state-based adult welfare programs, they allowed the states considerable leeway. The result was more hidden federalism.

The state of New York, under the control of a liberal Republican governor, opted for a state supplement system that maintained geographic distinctions of the sort that SSI was supposed to eliminate. Although the federal SSI benefit was uniform throughout the state of New York and the nation, the state's supplement program differentiated among people living in New York City, the suburban counties close to the city, and those in the rest of the state. The decision reflected the fact that the counties already paid different welfare benefits according to the contributions that they added to federal and state revenues. The state also made finer distinctions among the beneficiary's living arrangement than did the federal government, preserving special arrangements for people with mental retardation. California maintained the advantages that it offered to the blind in its state supplement arrangement, which also included a hard-to-administer distinction between someone who lived in a place with cooking facilities and someone living where no cooking facilities were available. States put different rules about the resources and income that affected a person's eligibility for SSI and the person's benefit level into their programs and further undermined the uniformity that the new program was supposed to create.

Final Thoughts

SSI offered a vision of social policy in which the federal government handled the problems of income maintenance for the nation's citizens and the states and localities offered social services that responded to people's particular problems that required personal interaction. The federal government wrote checks, and the localities hired social workers to counsel people on their problems and to match needy people with available local resources. The federal government utilized the wide sweep of its tax system to make transfer payments that sustained people and enabled them to survive their personal vicissitudes and the impersonal effects of economic fluctuations. The local governments capitalized on their proximity to an individual to help him make the necessary adjustments to overcome his problems and receive personal attention and care from the local support system. The state supplement system complicated the federal end of this arrangement and prevented the vision from being realized.

The SSI program, already compromised by the system of state supplementation put in place in 1972 and burdened by the need to administer disability benefits to children, moved further from its original vision over the course of its history. The federal program of 1972 became the object of a round of reforms in

1996 that sought to restore power to the states. The program's emergence as a disability program complicated the achievement of its policy goals. The reaction against welfare recipients who seemed to be exploiting the vulnerabilities of the system led to measures designed to cut benefits. Even in the face of these fundamental policy trends, however, SSI also exhibited patterns of incremental policy-making that expanded particular aspects of the program, and it never devolved back into a state program of the sort that existed before 1972.

Incremental change produced a steady erosion in the policy principles that governed the program, and temporary changes tended to become permanent. In these regards SSI functioned in a manner similar to most social programs. At the same time, SSI developed in unexpected ways because policymakers in 1972 could not see into the future. They could not know that disability rolls would rise and that disability would become a controversial area of public policy. They could not anticipate the series of events that would make SSI the major income support for the deinstitutionalized mentally ill.

As with all programs, initial choices mattered because the program was most malleable in the era of its creation, before all of the incremental and temporarily permanent changes and before unintended and unforeseen policy developments influenced the program. The choice to include childhood disability benefits and the initial decision to make SSI a federal entitlement but also to include optional and mandatory state supplements established the basic direction the program would follow. The political context of the program's creation helped define its fundamental identity. That identity persisted into the future even as the political context in which the program operated changed.

The program's history illustrated how yesterday's solutions become today's problems, a common theme in policy history. SSI never developed into the type of respectable welfare program for which its founders hoped. It failed to become as politically acceptable or popular as Social Security and instead became a more typical welfare program, complete with groups accused of ripping off the government. Nonetheless, it persisted from 1974 to the present day, as a permanent memorial to the last vestiges of the expansive welfare state of the Great Society era and a powerful reminder of the forces that shaped social welfare policy at the end of the twentieth century.

Notes

PREFACE

1. See Edward Berkowitz, *Disabled Policy: America's Programs for the Handicapped* (Cambridge: Cambridge University Press, 1987); *Mr. Social Security: The Life of Wilbur J. Cohen* (Lawrence: University Press of Kansas, 1995); *Robert Ball and the Politics of Social Security* (Madison: University of Wisconsin Press, 2003); *America's Welfare State: From Roosevelt to Reagan* (Baltimore: Johns Hopkins University Press, 1991); President's Commission for a National Agenda, *A National Agenda for the Eighties* (New York: New American Library, 1981).

2. Fortunately, the history office of the Social Security Administration has housed the Congressional documents related to Social Security and SSI in one convenient place, and much of the archival material is available to researchers through the Social Security history website, http://www.socialsecurity.gov/history.

3. But welfare rights nonetheless figures as an important topic. See Felicia Kornbluh, *The Battle for Welfare Rights: Politics and Poverty in Modern America* (Philadelphia: University of Pennsylvania Press, 2007).

INTRODUCTION

1. *The 2004 Green Book*, Background Material and Data on the Programs within the Jurisdiction of the Committee on Ways and Means, U.S. House of Representatives (Washington, DC: Government Printing Office, 2004), p. 3-2.

2. *Congressional Record*, Senate, September 29, 1972, p. S16303.

3. "Welfare Program for Aged, Blind, and Disabled Overpaid $403-Million in First 18 Months," *New York Times*, August 16, 1975, p. 26.

4. Social Security Administration, "SSI Annual Statistical Supplement, 2010," Washington, DC, 2011, Tables 2 and 3, pp. 16, 18.

5. Joanne L. Goodwin, *Gender and the Politics of Welfare Reform: Pensions in Chicago, 1911–1929* (Chicago: University of Chicago Press, 1997); Linda Gordon, *Pitied but Not Entitled: Single Mothers and the History of Welfare 1890–1935* (New York: Free Press, 1998); Theda Skocpol, *Protecting Soldiers and Mothers: The Political Origins of Social Policy in the United States* (Cambridge, MA: Harvard University Press, 1995).

6. Carole Haber and Brian Gratton, *Old Age and the Search for Security* (Bloomington: Indiana University Press, 1994).

7. Abraham Epstein, *Insecurity: A Challenge to America,* 2nd rev. ed. (New York: Agathon Press, 1968), pp. 534–35.

8. Edwin E. Witte, *The Development of the Social Security Act* (Madison: University of Wisconsin Press, 1963), pp. 190–92.

9. Statement of Robert B. Irwin, Executive Director of the American Foundation for the Blind, Senate Finance Committee, *Hearings on the Economic Security Act*, 1935, p. 726.

10. Statement of S. Merwin Sinclair, President of Executives of State Commissions and State Agencies for the Blind and Pennsylvania Council for the Blind, Senate Finance Committee, *Hearings on the Economic Security Act*, 1935, p. 778.

11. Senator Pat Harrison, *Congressional Record*, Senate, June 14, 1935, p. 9267.

12. Ibid., p. 9269.

13. Witte, *The Development of the Social Security Act*; Arthur J. Altmeyer, *The Formative Years of Social Security* (Madison: University of Wisconsin Press, 1968).

14. For a short overview of the legislative history of Social Security, see Edward D. Berkowitz, "The Historical Development of Social Security in the United States," in *Social Security in the 21st Century*, ed. Eric R. Kingson and James H. Schulz (New York: Oxford University Press), pp. 22–38.

15. Vincent Burke and Vee Burke, *Nixon's Good Deed: Welfare Reform* (New York: Columbia University Press, 1974); Daniel Patrick Moynihan, *The Politics of a Guaranteed Income* (New York: Random House, 1973); Molly C. Michelmore, *Tax and Spend: The Welfare State, Tax Politics, and the Limits of American Liberalism* (Philadelphia: University of Pennsylvania Press, 2012); Brian Steensland, *The Failed Revolution: America's Struggle over a Guaranteed Income* (Princeton, NJ: Princeton University Press, 2007).

16. Gordon, *Pitied but Not Entitled*, p. 5.

17. Marisa Chappell, *The War on Welfare: Family, Poverty, and Politics in Modern America* (Philadelphia: University of Pennsylvania Press, 2010), pp. 93, 107.

18. Initially this resource limit was set at $1,500, and it was not raised until 1985. The present limit of $2,000 has not been increased since 1989.

19. A change in the law in 2000 permits persons who have attained their Full Retirement Age as defined by Social Security to receive a retirement benefit without having to meet any retirement test. The retirement test still applies, however, to anyone who selects early retirement.

20. Kimberly J. Morgan and Andrea Louise Morgan, *The Delegated Welfare State: Medicare, Markets, and Governance of Social Policy* (New York: Oxford University Press, 2011); Steven Rathgeb Smith and Michael Lipsky, *Nonprofits for Hire: The Welfare State in the Age of Contracting* (Cambridge, MA: Harvard University Press, 1993); Jacob S. Hacker, *The Divided Welfare State: The Battle over Public and Private Social Benefits in the United States* (New York: Cambridge University Press, 2001); Jennifer Klein, *For All These Rights: Business, Labor, and the Shaping of America's Public-Private Welfare State* (Princeton, NJ: Princeton University Press, 2003); Christopher Howard, *The Hidden Welfare State: Tax Expenditures and Social Policy in the United States* (Princeton, NJ: Princeton University Press, 1997); Christopher Howard, *The Welfare State Nobody Knows: Debunking Myths about U.S. Social Policy* (Princeton, NJ: Princeton University Press, 2007); Suzanne Mettler, *The Submerged State: How Invisible Government Policies Undermine American Democracy* (Chicago: University of Chicago Press, 2011).

21. Edwin Amenta, *When Movements Matter: The Townsend Plan and the Rise of Social Security* (Princeton, NJ: Princeton University Press, 2008).

22. Edward D. Berkowitz, *Something Happened: A Political and Cultural Overview of the Seventies* (New York: Columbia University Press, 2006).

23. Deborah Stone, *The Disabled State* (Philadelphia: Temple University Press, 1984).

24. See Edward D. Berkowitz, *Disabled Policy: America's Programs for the Handicapped* (New York: Cambridge University Press, 1989).

25. Martha Derthick, *Policymaking for Social Security* (Washington, DC: Brookings Institution, 1979).

26. Daniel T. Rogers, *The Age of Fracture* (Cambridge, MA: Harvard University Press, 2011).

27. When Derthick turned her attention to the implementation of SSI and the disability reviews of the Reagan era, the institutional focus of her study shifted to include the courts and the other things mentioned here. See Martha Derthick, *Agency under Stress* (Washington, DC: Brookings Institution, 1990).

28. Joan Vennochi, "Blame It on the Sixties, Man," *Boston Globe*, May 29, 2011.

29. "Tax Dollars Aiding and Abetting Addiction: Social Security Disability and SSI Cash Benefits to Drug Addicts and Alcoholics," Investigative Staff Report of Senator William S. Cohen, February 7, 1994.

30. Thomas M. Parrott, Lenna D. Kennedy, and Charles G. Scott, "Noncitizens and the Supplemental Security Program," *Social Security Bulletin* 61 (1998): 3–31.

31. See Paul Pierson, *Politics in Time: History, Institutions, and Social Analysis* (Princeton, NJ: Princeton University Press, 2004); Stephen Skowronek and Karen Orren, *The Search for American Political Development* (New York: Cambridge University Press, 2004).

CHAPTER 1

1. Daniel Patrick Moynihan, Memorandum for the President, June 6, 1969, in *Daniel Patrick Moynihan: A Portrait in Letters of an American Visionary*, ed. Steven R. Weisman (New York: Public Affairs, 2010), pp. 192–93.

2. Along with a $60 a month work disregard and a 50 percent tax on earnings beyond that amount (that is to say, the benefits would be reduced $1 for each $2 earned by work).

3. Daniel Patrick Moynihan, *The Politics of a Guaranteed Income: The Nixon Administration and the Family Assistance Plan* (New York: Vintage Books, 1973), pp. 222–26.

4. Edward Berkowitz, *Mr. Social Security: The Life of Wilbur J. Cohen* (Lawrence: University Press of Kansas, 1995).

5. Included in Richard Nixon to Robert Finch, February 11, 1969, Robert Ball Papers, Wisconsin State Historical Society, Madison, Wisconsin.

6. Testimony by Robert Finch, "Social Security and Welfare Proposals," House Report No. H 781-1, Part 1 of 7, October 15 and 16, 1969, *Ways and Means Hearings* (Washington, DC: U.S. Government Printing Office, 1970), p. 52.

7. Ibid., p. 113.

8. Ibid., p. 120.

9. Source: Social Security Administration, *Annual Statistical Supplement 1972*, Table 138, p. 146.

10. House Report No. H 781-1, p. 119; Vincent J. and Vee Burke, *Nixon's Good Deed: Welfare Reform* (New York: Columbia University Press), p. 90.

11. "Nixon's New Federalism Offers Hope," *Portland Oregonian*, August 12, 1969.

12. Supplemental Statement of John F. Nagle, Chief, Washington Office, National Federation of the Blind, *House Hearings*, 1969 (see note 6), p. 994.

13. Most Social Security beneficiaries acquired their rights to those benefits through the payroll contributions that they and their employers had made on their behalf. Those on welfare rolls might not have made such contributions, and in those cases Lourie proposed that these contributions come from general revenues. See testimony of Norman Lourie, NASW, House Report No. H 781-1, p. 1541.

14. Testimony of Steven Minter, Director, Cuyohoga County Welfare Department, House Report No. H 781-1, p. 1959.

15. Robert M. Ball to the Under Secretary, December 5, 1969, Robert Ball Papers, Wisconsin State Historical Society; Julian Zelizer, *Taxing America: Wilbur D. Mills, Congress, and the State, 1945–1975* (New York: Cambridge University, 1999), p. 324; Robert M. Ball, "Social Security Amendments of 1972: Summary and Legislative History," *Social Security Bulletin* 36 (March 1973): 4–5.

16. "Family Assistance Act of 1970, Report of the Committee on Ways and Means on HR 16311," Report No. 91-904, pp. 3, 9, 39, 40.

17. Wilbur Mills, *Congressional Record*, House, April 15, 1970, pp. H3081–84.

18. Edward D. Berkowitz, *America's Welfare State* (Baltimore: Johns Hopkins Press, 1991), pp. 131–32.

19. Martha Derthick, *Agency under Stress: The Social Security Administration in American Government* (Washington, DC: Brookings Institution, 1990), p. 133.

20. Felicia Kornbluh, *The Battle for Welfare Rights: Politics and Poverty in Modern America* (Philadelphia: University of Pennsylvania Press, 2007), pp. 29–30.

21. John Jacobs, *A Rage for Justice: The Passion and Politics of Phillip Burton* (Berkeley: University of California Press, 1995).

22. Barry Kalb, "Angry Welfare Group Holds Hill Sit-In," *Washington Star*, September 3, 1986, p. 3; Eve Edstrom, "Irate Welfare Mothers Hold Wait-In," *Washington Post*, September 20, 1967, p. 1; Tom Wicker, "Still No Room at the Inn," *New York Times*, September 24, 1967, p. E13.

23. HEW Secretary Elliott Richardson to Robert Ball, August 18, 1970, Social Security Administration (SSA) History Archives, Baltimore, Maryland.

24. Robert M. Ball, "Social Security Amendments of 1972: Summary and Legislative History," *Social Security Bulletin* (March 1973): 8.

25. See, more generally, Edward Berkowitz, *Robert Ball and the Politics of Social Security* (Madison: Wisconsin University Press, 2003); Martha Derthick, *Policymaking for Social Security* (Washington, DC: Brookings Institution, 1979).

26. Quoted by Derthick, *Agency under Stress*, p. 98.

27. Christopher Howard, "Workers' Compensation, Federalism, and the Heavy Hand of History," *Studies in American Political Development* 16 (2002): 28–47; Edward D. Berkowitz and Monroe Berkowitz, "The Survival of Workers' Compensation," *Social Service Review* (June 1984): 259–80; Paul A. Raushenbush and Elizabeth Brandeis Raushenbush, "Our 'U.C.' Story," Madison, Wisconsin, 1979.

28. Jerry Cates, *Insuring Inequality: Administrative Leadership in Social Security, 1935–1954* (Ann Arbor: University of Michigan Press, 1983); Berkowitz, *Mr. Social Security*, pp. 145–53; Berkowitz, *Robert Ball and the Politics of Social Security*, pp. 121–26.

29. Jennifer Mittelstadt, *From Welfare to Workfare: The Unintended Consequences of Liberal Reform, 1945–1965* (Chapel Hill: University of North Carolina Press, 2005).

30. "The History of FAP Planning," May 6, 1970, Nixon Library.

31. Ball to Arthur J. Altmeyer, May 11, 1971, Arthur Altmeyer Papers, Wisconsin State Historical Society, Madison, Wisconsin.

32. "Specifications for a Federal Assistance Program for the Adult Categories," Ida Merriam to Robert Ball, March 1, 1971, SSI Papers, SSA History Archives.

33. Ball to Ida Merriam, March 1, 1971, SSI Papers, SSA History Archives.

34. Ibid.

35. Robert Ball to Jack Futterman, March 1, 1971, SSI Papers, SSA History Archives.

36. Jack Futterman to Arthur E. Hess, March 4, 1971, SSI Papers, SSA History Archives.

37. "Administering the Adult Assistance Program—Mr. McKenna's Memorandum of May 17, 1971," Futterman to Ball, May 25, 1971, SSI Papers, SSA History Archives.

38. "Social Security Amendments of 1971," House Report No. 92-231, May 26, 1971.

39. "Social Security Amendments of 1971," p. 2.

40. Ibid., pp. 4–5; the states now must reimburse the federal government for the administrative costs involved. In FY 2010 the SSA received about $160 million in fees from the states for this service.

41. Renato Anthony DiPentima, "The Supplemental Security Income Program: A Study of Implementation" (doctoral dissertation, University of Maryland, 1984), p. 3.

42. *Social Security Bulletin, Annual Statistical Supplement, 1968* (U.S. Social Security Administration), Table 134, p. 133.

43. "Social Security Amendments of 1971," *Hearings Before the Senate Committee on Finance* (Washington, DC: U.S. Government Printing Office, July 27–August 3, 1971), p. 32.

44. Ibid., pp. 146–47.

45. Ibid., p. 198.

46. Ibid., pp. 157–58.

47. Ibid., p. 199.

48. Ibid., p. 200.

49. Ibid., p. 148; Edward D. Berkowitz, *Disabled Policy: America's Programs for the Handicapped* (New York: Cambridge University Press, 1987); Deborah A. Stone, *The Disabled State* (Philadelphia: Temple University Press, 1985).

50. Lawmakers stated their aim as creating "incentives and opportunities for those able to work or to be rehabilitated that will enable them to escape from their dependent situations." See "Social Security Amendments of 1971," p. 147.

51. For a brief overview of the development of the 1954–1956 program, see Larry DeWitt, "The Development of Social Security in America," *Social Security Bulletin* 70, no. 3 (2010): 12–13. For more detail, see Larry DeWitt, Daniel Beland, and Edward D. Berkowitz, *Social Security: A Documentary History* (Washington, DC: Congressional Quarterly Press, 2008), pp. 181–220.

52. "Social Security Amendments of 1971," pp. 147–48.

53. Jennifer L. Erkulwater, *Disability Rights and the American Social Safety Net* (Ithaca, NY: Cornell University Press, 2006), p. 83.

54. "Social Security Amendments of 1971," p. 149.

55. Mills, *Congressional Record*, House, June 21, 1971, p. H5542.

56. *Congressional Record*, House, June 21, 1971, p. H5533.

57. Ibid., p. H5609.

58. See Committee on Finance, "Social Security and Welfare Reform: Summary of the Principal Provisions of H.R. 1 as Determined by the Committee on Finance," June 13, 1972, 92nd Congress, 2nd Session.

59. "Senator Long Releases Text of Opening Statement to Be Given July 27 at Committee Hearings on H.R. 1," Committee on Finance Press Release, July 26, 1971, Robert Ball Papers.

60. Quoted in Erkulwater, *Disability Rights and the American Social Safety Net*, p. 79.

61. *Congressional Record*, March 16, 1971, p. 6732.

62. Statement by the President, White House press release, May 18, 1971, Robert Ball Papers.

63. "Social Security Amendments of 1971," *Hearings Before the Committee on Finance*, United States Senate, Ninety-Second Congress, First Session on H.R. 1 (Washington, DC: GPO, 1971), p. 270.

64. Ibid., p. 756.

65. Testimony of Warren S. Richardson, General Counsel, Liberty Lobby, Washington, DC, in ibid., p. 770.

66. Testimony of James A. Gavin, Legislative Director of the National Federation of Independent Business, ibid., p. 915; Testimony of Paul Henkel, Chairman of the Social Security Committee, Council of State Chambers of Commerce, ibid., p. 754.

67. Ibid., p. 1730.

68. Ibid., pp. 1032–33.

69. Ibid., pp. 1088–89, 1113.

70. Ibid., Testimony of Governor Oglivie, pp. 1044–46, 1058.

71. Ibid., p. 2000.

72. Ibid., p. 1915.

73. Berkowitz, *Robert Ball and the Politics of Social Security*, pp. 199–206.

74. "Social Security and Welfare Reform, Summary of the Principal Provisions of H.R. 1 as Determined by the Committee on Finance," June 13, 1972, p. 54.

75. "Social Security Amendments of 1972," Senate Report No. 92-1230, September 26, 1972, p. 75.

76. Ibid., p. 393.

77. Ibid., pp. 147–48.

78. Ibid., p. 385.

79. *Congressional Record*, Senate, September 28, 1972, p. S16244.

80. *Congressional Record*, Senate, September 28, 1972, p. S16246.

81. Quoted in *Robert Ball and the Politics of Social Security*, p. 207.

82. *Congressional Record*, Senate, September 29, 1972, p. S16303.

83. These original resource limits would not be increased until 1985. Since 1989 they have been $2,000 and $3,000, respectively.

84. Social Security Administration, "Summary of the Provisions of HR 1 as Passed by the Congress and Sent to the President," pp. 32–37, SSI Papers, SSA History Archives.

85. Available online at http://www.presidency.ucsb.edu/ws/index.php?pid=3673&st=H.R.+1&st1=.

86. Philip Burton, *Congressional Record*, House, October 17, 1972, H10209.

CHAPTER 2

1. "Address by Robert M. Ball," Delivered to Social Security Employees, Baltimore, November 20, 1972, Robert Ball Papers, Wisconsin State Historical Society, Madison, Wisconsin.

2. Quoted in Edward Berkowitz, *Robert Ball and the Politics of Social Security* (Madison: University of Wisconsin Press, 2003), p. 211.

3. "Address by Robert M. Ball," November 20, 1972.

4. Richard D. Lyons, "Nixon Signs $5-Billion Bill Expanding Social Security," *New York Times*, October 31, 1972, p. 1.

5. Thomas E. Mullaney, "Economic Upturn through Decade Appears Possible," *New York Times*, January 17, 1973, p. 177.

6. Edwin L. Dale Jr., "Personal Income in U.S. Climbed 8.6% Last Year," *New York Times*, January 19, 1973, p. 41.

7. Caspar W. Weinberger, with Gretchen Roberts, *In the Arena: A Memoir of the 20th Century* (Washington, DC: Regenery Publishing, 2001).

8. The speech is available online at http://www.ssa.gov/history/bobball.html; see also Berkowitz, *Robert Ball and the Politics of Social Security*, pp. 215–22.

9. Richard P. Nathan, "Rethinking Welfare Reform," *New York Times*, January 18, 1973, p. 41; James Welsh, "Welfare Reform: Born, Aug. 8, 1969; Died, October 4, 1972," *New York Times*, January 7, 1973, p. 312.

10. Memorandum, from Jerry Boyd to Jack S. Futterman, September 3, 1971, SSI Papers, SSA History Archives.

11. Robert Ball, "Commissioner's Bulletin," February 7, 1973, Number 130, SSA History Archives.

12. "Strategy for Implementation of the SSI Program for the Aged, Blind, and Disabled," February 8, 1973, SSI Papers, SSA History Archives.

13. Robert Ball to Division Heads, November 3, 1972, SSA History Archives; Robert Ball to Stuart H. Clarke, Office of the Secretary, Department of Health, Education, and Welfare, December 11, 1972, SSA History Archives.

14. Emma Brown, "Sumner G. Whittier, Ex Head of VA, Dies at 98," *Washington Post*, January 18, 2010, p. B04.

15. "Strategy for Implementation of the SSI Program," SSI Papers, SSA History Archives.

16. Peter M. Wheeler, Assistant Executive Secretary, Department of Health, Education, and Welfare to Social Security Administration, July 26, 1973, SSI Papers, SSA History Archives; Sumner Whittier to Arthur E. Hess, "Proposed Policy for Disposition of Resources under Title XVI," May 22, 1973, SSI Papers, SSA History Archives; Acting Commissioner of Social Security to the Secretary (through the Under Secretary and the Executive Secretary), July 9, 1973, SSI Papers, SSA History Archives.

17. See Acting Commissioner of Social Security to the Secretary, "Proposed Policy under Title SVI regarding the Reasonable Value of an Excludable Home," n.d., but early July 1973, SSI Papers, SSA History Archives.

18. Assistant Secretary, Comptroller, to the Secretary, July 16, 1973, SSI Papers; Peter M. Wheeler to Arthur Hess, July 24, 1973, SSI Papers, SSA History Archives. It should be added that this policy applied to the program in its very early years. Eventually, program officials realized that the concept of a "reasonable value" of a home resisted precise quantification and allowed people living in their homes to keep those homes, no matter their market value, and still receive SSI.

19. "Report of Telephone Conversation between Harry Overs and Les Plumly, Director, Operations Planning and Research Staff," July 18, 1973, SSI Papers, SSA History Archives, with enclosures.

20. Berkowitz, *Robert Ball and the Politics of Social Security*, pp. 142–46.

21. See Arthur J. Altmeyer, *The Formative Years of Social Security* (Madison: University of Wisconsin Press, 1968), pp. 105–9.

22. Commissioner of Social Security to the Secretary, "SSI Screening Project—INFORMATION MEMORANDUM," March 7, 1973, SSI Papers, SSA History Archives.

23. Jill Quadagno and Madonna Harrington Meyer, "Organized Labor, State Structures, and Social Policy Development: A Case Study of Old-Age Assistance in Ohio, 1916–1940," *Social Problems* 36 (April 1989): 181–96.

24. "Many Are Facing Food Stamp Loss," *New York Times*, May 31, 1973, p. 15.

25. Jack Jones, "Welfare Reform: Some Gains but More Needed," *Los Angeles Times*, June 10, 1973, p. B1.

26. Gary W. Bickel and David Wilcock, *The Supplemental Security Income Program: Estimated Impact by State* (Washington, DC: Bureau of Social Science Research, January 1974), p. 18.

27. Ibid., p. 32.

28. Quoted in Eileen Shanahan, "Senate Approves 11% Pension Rise, Tax Help for the Poor," *New York Times*, December 1, 1973, p. 1.

29. Committee on Finance, United States Senate, "Continuation of Existing Temporary Increase in the Public Debt Limit," Senate Report No. 93-249, June 25, 1973.

30. Senator Ribicoff, *Congressional Record*, Senate, June 29, 1973, p. S15287.

31. Wilbur Mills, *Congressional Record*, House, June 30, 1973, p. H5789.

32. Senator Long, *Congressional Record*, Senate, June 30, 1973, p. S12718; Richard L. Madden, "Social Security Increase Is Approved by Congress," *New York Times*, July 1, 1973, p. 1.

33. "U.S. to Aid Disabled," *Chicago Defender*, July 3, 1973, p. 2.

34. "Implementing the 1972 Amendments," *SSA Commissioner's Bulletin*, February 7, 1973, SSA History Archives.

35. In all, the SSA had to sign formal contracts with seventy-two state and local agencies, representing 1,350 distinct organizations handling the adult categories in the states.

36. Arthur E. Hess, "Getting the SSI Program Underway," *Commissioner's Bulletin* 136, August 14, 1973, SSA History Archives.

37. Renato DiPenitima, "The Supplemental Security Income Program: A Study of Implementation" (doctoral dissertation, University of Maryland, 1984), p. 189.

38. "A Rise in Social Security Checks Approved 13-12 by House Panel," *New York Times*, November 7, 1973, p. 20; Eileen Shanahan, "House Panel Backs Two-Step Social Security Rise Totaling 11% Next Year," *New York Times*, November 8, 1973, p. 31; "Pension Approval Made Final in Panel," *New York Times*, November 9, 1973, p. 4.

39. "Social Security Benefit Increase," House of Representatives, Report No. 93-627, November 9, 1973, p. 3.

40. Ibid., p. 9.

41. Representative Ullman, *Congressional Record*, House, November 14, 1973, pp. H9986–87.

42. Martha Griffiths, *Congressional Record*, House, November 14, 1973, pp. H9990–91. It is interesting to note that Michigan was in fact one of the nine states that would benefit from this provision. Even so, Griffiths opposed the provision. The fact that 70 percent of the money went to two states, neither of which was Michigan, may have influenced her decision.

43. Representative Abzug, *Congressional Record*, House, November 14, 1973, p. H9997.

44. Representative Corman, *Congressional Record*, House, November 14, 1973, p. H9998.

45. *Congressional Record*, House, November 15, 1973, p. H10072.

46. Richard L. Madden, "House Approves a 2-Step, 11% Rise in Social Security," *New York Times*, November 16, 1973, p. 1.

47. Shanahan, "Senate Approves 11% Pension Rise, Tax Help for the Poor," p. 1.

48. Richard L. Madden, "Congress Passes 11% Benefits Rise," *New York Times*, December 22, 1973, p. 51; "Supplemental Security Income Provisions," *Commissioner's Bulletin*, December 27, 1973, SSI Papers, SSA History Archives.

49. Generally, the SSI program had more "liberal" general eligibility rules and more stringent disability rules than the states. So state beneficiaries, who might not qualify as disabled under SSI, could be grandfathered into the federal system if they were certified as disabled by the states prior to the conversion. In this manner, states could "dump" a portion of their caseloads on the federal government.

50. Peter Kihss, "Senate Proposal Sets Relief Test," *New York Times*, November 18, 1973, p. 55.

51. Statement by the President, January 3, 1974, Office of the White House Press Secretary, SSA History Archives.

52. Nelson Rockefeller to Caspar Weinberger, October 12, 1973, Record Group 47, Records of the Social Security Administration, Bureau of Supplemental Security Income, State Supplemental Agreements, 1974–1977, Box 2, File 2 of 2, New York Supplementation, National Archives II, College Park, Maryland.

53. Idem.

54. Walker W. Evans to Dave Tomlinson, October 16, 1973, RG 47, Bureau of Supplemental Security Income, State Supplemental Agreements, 1974–1977, Box 2, File 2 of 2, New York Supplementation.

55. Renny DiPentima to David Tomlinson, October 18, 1973, in ibid.

56. David T. Tomlinson to Arthur F. Simermeyer, October 24, 1973, in ibid.

57. "Agreement between the Secretary of Health, Education, and Welfare and the State of New York," signed November 13, 1973, NARA II, RG 47, Social Security Administration, Bureau of Supplemental Security Income, State Supplemental Agreements, 1974–1977, Box 2, File 1 of 2, New York Supplementation.

58. Press Release, Department of Social Services (Albany, New York), December 24, 1973, NARA II, RG 47, Social Security Administration, Bureau of Supplemental Security Income, State Supplemental Agreements, 1974–1977, Box 2, File 2 of 2, New York State Supplementation.

59. Sumner Whittier to Elliot A. Kirschbaum, "Outstanding Issues concerning California," July 31, 1973, and State Relations Staff, "Status of California Issues," August 8, 1973, in NARA II, RG 47, Social Security Administration, Bureau of Supplemental Security Income, State Supplemental Agreements 1974–1977, Box 7, File 2 of 2, California Supplementation.

60. John L. Burton to John F. Richardson, Regional Commissioner, SSA, San Francisco, September 21, 1973, NARA II, RG 47, Social Security Administration, Bureau of Supplemental Security Income, State Supplemental Agreements, 1974–1977, Box 7, File 2 of 2, California Supplementation.

61. "Proposed Variations for Federally Administered Optional State Supplemental Payments for State of California," September 25, 1973, in ibid.

62. "Agreement between the Secretary of Health, Education, and Welfare and the State of California," December 5, 1973, NARA II, RG 47, Social Security Administration, Bureau of Supplemental Security Income, State Supplemental Agreements, 1974–1977, Box 7, File 1 of 2, California Supplementation.

63. Felicia Kornbluh, "Disability, Antiprofessionalism and Civil Rights: The National Federation of the Blind and the 'Right to Organize' in the 1950s," *Journal of American History* 97 (March 2011): 1023–47.

64. Ralph Santiago Abascal to Caspar W. Weinberger, December 26, 1973, NARA II, RG 47, Bureau of Supplemental Security Income, State Supplemental Agreements, 1974–1977, Box 7, File 2 of 2, California Supplementation; Edward Berkowitz, *Disabled Policy: America's Programs for the Handicapped* (New York: Cambridge University Press, 1987), pp. 193–207.

65. "Modification No. 1 to the California State Supplemental Security Income Agreement," December 17, 1973, NARA II, RG 47, Social Security Administration, Bureau of Supplemental Security Income, State Supplemental Agreements, 1974–1977, Box 7, File 1 of 2, California Supplementation.

66. "Report of Audit, State of California, Department of Social Welfare, Supplemental Security Income Program Adjust Payment Level for January 1972," February 6, 1974, and Herbert Wit, Regional Audit Director, to William L. Henry Jr., Assistant Director, Division of Social Security Audits, March 25, 1974, NARA II, RG 47, Social Security Administration, Bureau of Supplemental Security Income, State Supplemental Agreements 1974–1977, Box 7, File 1 of 2, California Supplementation.

67. David T. Tomlinson, State Programs Manager, to Renny DiPentima, Deputy Assistant Bureau Director for Systems, January 15, 1975, NARA II, RG 47, Social Security Administration, Bureau of Supplemental Security Income, State Supplemental Agreements, 1974–1977, Box 2, File New Jersey Supplementation.

68. The state of Texas argued that a provision of its state constitution precluded even mandatory supplemental payments, and this contention was allowed to stand. So Texas paid no state supplement. The result was that some residents of Texas who were converted from the old state programs did in fact suffer a decrease in their benefit amounts owing to their movement to the federal program.

69. Peter Kihss, "City Opens a Drive to Find Elderly Poor," *New York Times*, November 20, 1973, p. 43; "Metropolitan Briefs—City Opens Hunt for Elderly Poor," *New York Times*, November 20, 1973, p. 85.

70. Peter Kihss, "Two-Name Checks for Needy to End," *New York Times*, December 4, 1973, p. 73.

71. Paul Houston, "650,000 More May Be Eligible for Welfare, *Los Angeles Times*, December 2, 1973, p. B1.

72. Craig Palmer, "3 Million Set to Receive U.S. Checks," *Baltimore Afro American*, December 1, 1973, p. 3.

73. Bureau of District Office Operations to All Regional Representatives, All District, Branch and Teleservice Center Managers, "Our State of Readiness for January," December 17, 1973, SSI Papers, SSA History Archives.

CHAPTER 3

1. Jack S. Futterman, "A Two Level Review: SSA Organization for Administering SSI, SSA's Organization as a Whole," March 1, 1974, mimeo, SSI Papers, SSA History Archives.

2. Robert Ball, "Talk Delivered on July 7 1966 to the Employees of the Social Security Administration," Robert Ball Papers, Wisconsin State Historical Society, Madison, Wisconsin; Robert Ball to Lyndon Johnson, October 14, 1966, Ball Papers.

3. "It Took a Giant-Sized Effort," *OASIS* (March 1974): 6–10; "Our 'Excellent Service' Recognized," *OASIS* (March 1974): 5. Copies in SSA History Archives.

4. Futterman, "A Two Level Review," pp. 14–15.

5. Ibid.

6. Peter Kihss, "Banks Here Shun New Aid Checks," *New York Times*, January 1, 1974, p. 23; "System to Cash Relief Checks Is Set Up under New Program," *New York Times*, January 2, 1974, p. 41; "U.S. Offers a Plan on Benefit Checks," *New York Times*, January 3, 1974, p. 38.

7. Robert D. McFadden, "Welfare Shift Is Accompanied by Bureaucratic Turmoil," *New York Times*, January 8, 1974, p. 37.

8. Laurie Johnston, "Long Lines as City Welfare Clients Shift to U.S. Program," *New York Times*, January 9, 1974, p. 39.

9. "US Approves Plan to Replace Checks for Social Security," *New York Times*, January 13, 1974, p. 31.

10. "Buses Warm Elderly at Social Security," *New York Times*, January 10, 1974, p. 41.

11. Deidre Carmody, "Courage and Dignity of Elderly Poor Surface during Project to Aid Them," *New York Times*, February 25, 1974, p. 29.

12. McCandlish Phillips, "For the Elderly Nowadays a Lamb Shank Is a 'Treat,'" *New York Times*, October 14, 1974, p. 35.

13. Peter Kihss, "State Welfare Rolls Rise First Time in 19 Months," *New York Times*, July 3, 1974, p. 35.

14. "On the Long Line," *New York Times*, January 12, 1974, p. 32.

15. "A Dream Miscarries," *New York Times*, October 1, 1974, p. 40.

16. "Propping Family Income," *New York Times*, January 8, 1975, p. 26.

17. Alfonso Navarez, "State Bill for Needy Held Inadequate," *New York Times*, April 17, 1974, p. 46.

18. Max H. Seigel, "Relief Cuts Evict Old and Disabled," *New York Times*, September 30, 1974, p. 1.

19. Will Lissner, "State Supports a Plan to Augment US Supplemental-Income Aid," *New York Times*, October 26, 1974, p. 35.

20. Peter Kihss, "Supplemental Aid to Poor Assailed," *New York Times*, August 11, 1974, p. 53.

21. Testimony of James Cardwell, "Supplemental Security Income Program," *Hearings Before the Subcommittee on Public Assistance of the Committee on Ways and Means*, Ninety-Fourth Congress, First Session, June 3, 1975, p. 37.

22. Mike Goodman, "Check Delays Create Hardships for State's Aged, Blind, Disabled," *Los Angeles Times*, June 16, 1974, p. A1.

23. Ursula Vils, "The Social Insecurity of Mrs. E. S.," *Los Angeles Times*, August 13, 1974, p. G1.

24. Leslie Berman, "Woman, 83, Gets Plenty of Promises but No 'Gold Checks,'" *Los Angeles Times*, September 29, 1974, p. OC1.

25. Kathleen Hendrix, "Social Security: And the Wait Goes On," *Los Angeles Times*, December 13, 1974, p. H1.

26. "Emergency Benefits for Helpless Sought," *New York Times*, January 12, 1974, p. A10.

27. James Cardwell, "Progress Report—Supplemental Security Income for the Aged, Blind, and Disabled," Memorandum for Members of the House of Representatives, January 28, 1974, SSI Papers, SSA History Archives.

28. "Supplementary Income Checks Delayed Again," *Los Angeles Times*, February 14, 1974, p. OC2.

29. "It Took a Giant-Sized Effort," *OASIS* (March 1974): 6. Copy in SSA History Archives.

30. Peter Kihss, "US May Stop Aid to 40,000 in State," *New York Times*, March 7, 1974, p. 43.

31. "Extension of Time for Determination of Disability for Supplemental Security Income Purposes in Certain Cases Added to State Programs between July 1973 and December 1973," House Report No. 93-871, March 4, 1974.

32. *Congressional Record*, House, March 5, 1974, pp. H1404–5.

33. "Hearings Ordered before Recipients Lose Disability Aid," *New York Times*, October 18, 1974, p. 38.

34. William F. Doherty, "45-Day Limit Set for SSI Processing," *Boston Globe*, May 15, 1975.

35. "Nixon Asks Built-In Aged Aid Boosts," *Los Angeles Times*, May 24, 1974, p. 2.

36. *Congressional Record*, Senate, June 25, 1974, pp. S11494–95.

37. See Social Security Administration, "Commissioners Bulletin," Number 140, August 9, 1974, SSA History Archives. Note that the *resource limits* of $1,500 for an individual and $2,250 for a couple were not raised automatically.

38. Judy Lee Mann, "Elderly Riled by Greenspan Remark," *Washington Post*, September 20, 1974, p. A2.

39. See "SSA Program Circular," Public Information, No. 63, January 28, 1975, Assistant Commissioner for Program Evaluation and Planning, Social Security Administration, Legislative Report, November 12, 1974, SSA History Archives.

40. William C. Rempel, "Elderly Battle the Bureaucracy Circuit," *Los Angeles Times*, March 2, 1975, p. CS1; Anne H. Reese, "Social Security Check Delays," *Washington Post*, March 11, 1975, p. A15; Elaine Barrow, "Elderly Seek Financial Relief," *New York Times*, March 9, 1975, p. 100.

41. Craig A. Palmer, "Criticize Social Security 'Nightmares,'" *Chicago Defender*, May 6, 1975, p. 10.

42. See Julian E. Zelizer, *On Capitol Hill: The Struggle to Reform Congress and Its Consequences* (New York: Cambridge University Press, 2004).

43. Testimony of James Cardwell, "Supplemental Security Income," *Hearings Before the Subcommittee on Public Assistance of the Committee on Ways and Means*, June 3–6, 9–12, 1975, pp. 16, 23; Volume 2, p. 496.

44. Sumner Whittier, "Administration of the Supplemental Security Income Program," *Hearings Before the Subcommittee on Oversight of the Committee on Ways and Means*, September 8, 1975, p. 20.

45. "Administration of the Supplemental Security Income Program," *Hearings Before the Subcommittee on Oversight of the House Committee on Ways and Means*, September 8, 1975, p. 33.

46. "8 Pct. Boost in Security Benefits Set," *Washington Post*, April 26, 1975, p. A2; "8% Hike in Social Security Benefits to Begin in June," *Los Angeles Times*, May 15, 1975, p. A2; Edward Berkowitz, *Robert Ball and the Politics of Social Security* (Madison: University of Wisconsin Press, 2003), p. 234.

47. "8% Hike," *Los Angeles Times*.

48. A. H. Raskin, "New York's Desperation Reflects That of Its Poor," *New York Times*, May 18, 1975.

49. "State Expected to Get No Benefit in a Supplemental Security Rise," *New York Times*, June 5, 1975, p. 40; Peter Kihss, "Official Decries U.S. Supplemental-Income Plan," *New York Times*, June 8, 1975, p. 45; Peter Kihss, "People in Income Program to Get Cost-of-Living Rise," *New York Times*, June 17, 1975, p. 71. What New York was doing was simply lowering their optional state supplement by the same amount that the federal government increased the SSI benefit. The net result was that the beneficiaries saw no increase in their payment but the state lowered its expenditures for SSI. By refusing to "pass-along" the federal benefit increase, the state was in effect using federal money to replace state money in its state supplement.

50. Linda Greenhouse, "Legislature Increases Aid for Elderly; Longest Session since 1911 Is Ended," *New York Times*, July 13, 1975, p. 1.

51. Stuart Auerbach, "Welfare Review Planned," August 13, 1975, *Washington Post*, August 13, 1975, p. A1.

52. "Welfare Program for Aged, Blind, and Disabled Overpaid $403-Million in First 18 Months," *New York Times*, August 16, 1975, p. 26 (the *Times* ran the *Washington Star* story); Austin Scott, "403.8 Million in Welfare Overpaid," *Washington Post*, August 16, 1975, p. A1.

53. "27 States Withholding $206 Million in Dispute with Social Security Agency," *New York Times*, August 19, 1975, p. 24 (this story originally appeared in the *Washington Star*).

54. "Delays, Unfair Denials Hurt Supplemental Benefits Plan," *Washington Post*, August 27, 1975, p. D5.

55. Eugene L. Meyer, "Court Orders Advance Notice in Security Income Cutbacks," *Washington Post*, August 29, 1975, p. A1; "Ruling Restricts Welfare Aid Recovery," *Los Angeles Times*, August 29, 1975, p. B21.

56. "Ford Asks Review of Welfare Agency," *New York Times*, August 28, 1975, p. 41.

57. "Payments Awaiting Blind and Disabled," *New York Times*, March 3, 1974, p. 74; Judy Luce Mann, "Aged, Blind, Disabled Eligible for US Aid Haven't Applied," *Washington Post*, March 15, 1974, p. C6; Ted Watson, "Thousands Eligible for State Aid," *Chicago Defender*, April 10, 1974, p. 2.

58. Within two years, the SSA found itself administering 408 different state supplementation payment types. See Committee on Finance, *Hearing on the Supplemental Security Income Program* (Washington, DC: U.S. Government Printing Office, June 12, 1973), Tables 8, 9, pp. 248–54.

59. Ibid., p. 156.

60. For staffing levels, see *SSA Annual Report to Congress*, FY 1976, p. 49; *House Committee on Ways and Means Report*, WMCP 95-27; *SSA Annual Report to Congress*, 1978, p. 65 (Washington, DC: U.S. Social Security Administration, 1978). Staffing levels are full-time permanent staff. For number of offices, see *SSA, The Year in Review*, 1972, p. iii; *SSA Annual Report to Congress* (Washington, DC: U.S. Social Security Administration, 1977), p. 7. All of these documents are available in the SSA History Archives.

61. Martha Derthick, *Agency under Stress: The Social Security Administration in American Government* (Washington, DC: Brookings Institution, 1990), p. 27.

62. Ibid., p. 30.

63. Ibid., p. 29.

64. Personal experience of one of the authors.

65. Renato Anthony DiPentima, "The Supplemental Security Income Program: A Study of Implementation" (doctoral dissertation, University of Maryland, 1984), pp. 203–17.

66. Oral history interview with Renny DiPentima, June 20, 1995, Social Security Administration Oral Histories, available at http://www.ssa.gov/history/renny.html.

67. Derthick, *Agency under Stress*, p. 26.

68. This probably was a function of the higher other income of the aged, and perhaps in part of differential state supplements favoring the disabled and blind. See James C. Callison, "Early Experience under the Supplemental Security Income Program," *Social Security Bulletin* 37 (June 1974): 3–11, Table 1.

69. Ibid., Tables 7, 8.

70. The tiny exception being payments for the blind in three jurisdictions: California; Washington, DC; and Montana.

71. "The SSI Fiasco," *Washington Post*, August 23, 1975, p. A14.

72. Arthur E. Hess, "Supplemental Security Income: The Achievements," *Washington Post*, September 2, 1975, p. A15.

CHAPTER 4

1. Statement of Joseph Kelly, Regional Commissioner, Social Security Administration, in "Administration of the Supplemental Security Income Program," *Hearings Before the Subcommittee on Oversight of the House Committee on Ways and Means*, September 17, 1976, pp. 38–39.

2. Statement of James Cardwell, in ibid., p. 109.

3. Edward Berkowitz and Kim McQuaid, "Social Security and the American Welfare State," in *The Vital One: Essays in Honor of Jonathan Hughes (Research in Economic History, Supplement 6)*, ed. Joel Mokyr (Greenwich, CT: JAI Press, 1991), pp. 169–90.

4. Statement of Philip J. Rutledge, "Administration of the Supplemental Security Income Program," *Hearings Before the Subcommittee on Oversight of the House Committee on Ways and Means*, October 20, 1976, p. 24.

5. Ibid., p. 19.

6. Statement of James Cardwell, in ibid., p. 109.

7. We base this discussion on and take the statistical references from *Staff Data and Materials on Supplemental Security Income (SSI) Disability Proposals*, prepared for the Subcommittee on Public Assistance of the Senate Committee on Finance, September 1978.

8. This discussion is taken from Table 8, "Number of Persons Receiving Federally Administered SSI Payments, by Reason for Eligibility and State, June 1978," in ibid., pp. 17–18.

9. *The Supplemental Security Income Program*, Report of the Staff to the Committee on Finance, April 1977, p. 119.

10. Edward Berkowitz, *Disabled Policy: America's Programs for the Handicapped* (New York: Cambridge University Press, 1987), pp. 111–12.

11. Ibid., p. 86.

12. Ibid., p. 90.

13. *The Supplemental Security Income Program*, Senate Staff Report, p. 119.

14. "The Beneficent Monster," *Time*, June 29, 1978.

15. Nancy Hicks, "Increase Noted in Permanently Disabled Who Seek Assistance," *New York Times*, February 27, 1976, p. 12.

16. Committee on Finance, *Staff Data and Materials Related to the Social Security Act Disability Programs*, September 1983, pp. 12, 19.

17. Gerald Grob, *The Mad among Us: A History of the Care of America's Mentally Ill*, (Cambridge, MA: Harvard University Press, 1994), p. 255.

18. Edward Berkowitz, *Mr. Social Security* (Lawrence: University Press of Kansas, 1995), pp. 156–57; "The Politics of Mental Retardation during the Kennedy Administration," *Social Science Quarterly* 61 (June 1980): 128–43.

19. Jennifer L. Erkulwater, *Disability Rights and the American Social Safety Net* (Ithaca, NY: Cornell University Press, 2006), p. 90; Grob, *The Mad among Us*, pp. 266, 290–91.

20. Peter Koenig, "The Problem That Can't Be Tranquilized," *New York Times*, May 21, 1978, p. SM4.

21. Robin Herman, "Some Freed Mental Patients Make It, Some Do Not," *New York Times*, November 19, 1979, p. B1.

22. "Court Bars Closing in Adult-Home Case," *New York Times*, February 3, 1978, p. A20.

23. Donald Janson, "Aged in Boarding Homes Are Cheated, Panel Says," *New York Times*, February 11, 1978, p. 47.

24. Glenn Fowler, "Panel Told of Fear and Abuse in 'Adult Homes,'" *New York Times*, February 3, 1979, p. 21.

25. "Ex State Mental Patients Live in Neglect in Queens," *New York Times*, August 28, 1979, p. B3.

26. Antonio G. Olivieri, "Mentally Ill, 'Dumped' and Isolated," *New York Times*, March 11, 1978, p. 23.

27. Sheila Rule, "Carey Announces Plan on Adult-Care," *New York Times*, March 31, 1978, p. A18.

28. Martin Waldron, "Blind Woman, 62, Tells State Panel of Abuse by Boarding Home Owner," *New York Times*, June 27, 1978, p. NJ20.

29. David J. Rothman and Sheila M. Rothman, *The Willowbrook Wars* (New York: Harper and Row, 1984).

30. Frances Cerra, "More Long Island Residences for Retarded Are Planned Despite Community Hostility," *New York Times*, January 28, 1979, p. BK56.

31. Frank Del Olmo, "Federal Ban on Old-Age Assistance to Illegal Immigrants under Attack," *Los Angeles Times*, February 16, 1976, p. A19; Thomas M. Parrott, Lena D. Kennedy, and Charles G. Scott, "Non-citizens and the Supplemental Security Income Program," *Social Security Bulletin* 61 (1998): 4–5.

32. Kennedy and Scott, "Non-citizens and the Supplemental Security Income Program," p. 5; Charles H. Percy, "An Unfair Welfare Handout," *Los Angeles Times*, December 20, 1977, p. D5.

33. Percy, "An Unfair Welfare Handout," p. D5.

34. See, for example, Grace Jeanmee Yoo, "Constructing Deservedness: Federal Welfare Reform, Supplemental Security Income and Elderly Immigrants" (doctoral dissertation, University of California, San Francisco, 1999).

35. Martha Wellman, "SSI Losers May Be Rescued," *Los Angeles Times*, August 26, 1976, p. SF1; Edward Berkowitz, *Something Happened: A Political and Cultural Overview of the Seventies* (New York: Columbia University Press, 2006), p. 169.

36. "Welfare Aid Overpaid by $547 Million," *Los Angeles Times*, January 21, 1976, p. B2; "U.S. Overpayments in Welfare Grants Hit $547,000,000," *New York Times*, January 21, 1976, p. 11.

37. "$197 Million Overpaid to Old, Disabled, Audit Finds," *Los Angeles Times*, February 24, 1976, p. A2; "$197 Million in Aid to Elderly, Blind Overpaid," *Los Angeles Times*, April 8, 1976, p. B19.

38. "SSI Errors Remain High, Official Says," *Washington Post*, April 10, 1976, p. A9; "Welfare Error Rate Declines," *Washington Post*, April 23, 1976, p. A4; "Pensioners Found to Have Received a Billion Too Much," *New York Times*, November 21, 1976, p. 29; "Overpayments to Elderly Hit by GAO," *Washington Post*, November 20, 1976, p. B6.

39. Haynes Johnson, "The Bureaucracy: Days of Endless Struggle, Drowning in a Sea of Paper," *Washington Post*, March 27, 1977, p. 1.

40. "Cardwell: View from the Top," *Washington Post*, March 28, 1977, p. A8.

41. Haynes Johnson, "Social Security: U.S. Umbilical Cord," *Washington Post*, March 28, 1977, p. A1.

42. Ibid.

43. "Extension of Interim Assistance and Food Stamps for SSI Beneficiaries and Continuation of Federal-State Matching Funds for Non-welfare Recipient Children," *Executive Hearing Before the Subcommittee on Public Assistance of the Committee on Ways and Means*, June 10, 1976; "Bill Extending Benefits to Aged, Blind, and Disabled Sent to Ford," *Los Angeles Times*, July 3, 1976, p. A18.

44. The quotes in this paragraph from Hale Champion and Stanford Ross derive from oral interviews conducted by Edward Berkowitz for the Centers for Medicare and Medicaid Services and are available on the CMS website.

45. Chris Connell, "Carter Picks D.C. Lawyer to Head Social Security," *Washington Post*, August 25, 1978, p. A2.

46. See Edward Berkowitz, *Robert Ball and the Politics of Social Security* (Madison: University of Wisconsin Press, 1991), p. 258; Joseph A. Califano Jr., *Governing America: An Insider's Report from the White House and the Cabinet* (New York: Simon and Schuster, 1981), pp. 43–45.

47. Richard P. Nathan, "Modernize the System, Don't Wholly Discard It," *Los Angeles Times*, February 27, 1977, p. H3; Grayson Mitchell, "Welfare Plan to Stress Jobs for Those Who Can Work Aid for Those Who Can't," *Los Angeles Times*, August 1, 1977, p. B18. On the Carter welfare proposal, see Califano, *Governing America*, pp. 320–68; James Patterson, "Jimmy Carter and Welfare Reform," in *The Carter Presidency: Policy Choices in the Post-New Deal Era*, ed. Gary M. Fink and Hugh Davis Graham (Lawrence: University Press of Kansas, 1998), pp. 117–36. On the Earned Income Tax Credit, see Christopher Howard, *The Hidden Welfare State: Tax Expenditures and Social Policy in the United States* (Princeton, NJ: Princeton University Press, 1997).

48. Welfare Reform Committee of the Committee on Agriculture, Committee on Education and Labor, Committee on Ways and Means, *Explanatory Material to Accompany HR 109950*, March 24, 1978. The Welfare Reform Committee was a special ad hoc creation designed to streamline the welfare reform legislative process by bringing members of the interested committee in the House together in one group—an effort to circumvent the balkanized legislative process.

49. "Presumptive Disability under SSI Program," House Report No. 95-1289, June 13, 1978, pp. 2–4.

50. "Presumptive Disability for Supplemental Security Income," Senate Report No. 95-1311, October 9, 1978.

51. "Elimination of Work Disincentives under SSI Programs," House Report No. 95-1345, July 12, 1978, pp. 2, 16–17.

52. Ibid., p. 29.

53. Statement of Hale Zukas, "Supplemental Security Income Disability Program," *Hearing Before the Subcommittee on Public Assistance, Committee on Finance*, September 26, 1978, p. 33.

54. Ibid., pp. 14–17.

55. Table 175, *1984–85 SSA Annual Statistical Supplement*, p. 241.

56. "GAO Letter to Secretary Califano on the SSI Disability Program," April 18, 1978, excerpted in Larry DeWitt, Daniel Beland, and Edward D. Berkowitz, *Social Security: A Documentary History* (Washington, DC: Congressional Quarterly Press, 2008), pp. 371–72.

57. DeWitt et alia, *Social Security: A Documentary History*, pp. 373–74.

58. *SSA Key Workload Indicators Report*, 1993, p. 1.

59. The ALJs allowed 48 percent of the previously denied claims that were appealed to them. Not all denied claims were appealed.

60. See Berkowitz, *Mr. Social Security*, pp. 301–4; Berkowitz, *Robert Ball and the Politics of Social Security*, pp. 260–64; Califano, *Governing America*, pp. 388–97.

61. Steven Rattner, "Califano Seeks Approval for Plan to Trim Disabled Workers' Pay," *New York Times*, February 23, 1979, p. A21.

62. "Supplemental Security Income Disability Amendments of 1979," House Report No. 96-104, April 25, 1979.

63. *Congressional Record*, House, June 4, 1979, pp. H4021–24, H4105.

64. *Congressional Record*, Senate, December 5, 1979, p. S17789; January 30, 1980, p. S609.

65. "Social Security Amendments of 1979," Report No. 96-408, November 8, 1979, pp. 2–5.

66. *Congressional Record*, Senate, December 5, 1979, pp. S17777–78.

67. "Social Security Disability Amendments of 1980: Legislative History and Summary of Provisions," *Social Security Bulletin* (April 1981): 14–31.

CHAPTER 5

1. Spencer Rich, "Inside: Health and Human Services," *Washington Post*, August 25, 1983, p. A19.

2. David Broder, "Hill, Reagan Aides Eye Painful Cuts," *Washington Post*, January 2, 1981, p. A1.

3. *SSI Annual Statistical Supplement*, 2000, Table 2.

4. The Continuing Disability Investigations were later renamed Continuing Disability Reviews as one of the cosmetic changes thought to soften the image of the review process after it became highly controversial. For most of the period covered here they were known as CDIs, but the terms are interchangeable.

5. The other proposals were to change the insured status rules to make fewer people eligible for disability in the first instance and to institute a cap on total income for disabled beneficiaries. Together these two proposals were estimated to reduce program expenditures by more than $5 billion over the first six years.

6. *America's New Beginning: A Program for Economic Recovery* (Washington, DC: Government Printing Office, February 18, 1981), pp. 1–10.

7. Memorandum, from Larry DeWitt, Field Representative Phoenix District Office, Subject: Briefing Paper for Select Session III, 4/1/85, available in the Social Security Administration History Archives, L1, folder "Disability: Continuing Disability Reviews."

8. "Reagan's '7 Untouchables,'" *Los Angeles Times*, February 10, 1981, p. A1.

9. Howell Raines, "Reagan Won't Cut 7 Social Programs That Aid 80 Million," *New York Times*, February 11, 1981, p. A1.

10. Bernard Weinraub, "U.S. Limit on Medicaid Would Shift Burden to States," *New York Times*, April 6, 1981, p. B12.

11. Ronald Reagan, "Address to the Nation on the Program for Economic Recovery," September 24, 1981, *Public Papers of the Presidents, Ronald Reagan, 1981* (Washington, DC: Government Printing Office, 1982), p. 835.

12. The government's position, however, was undermined by its own policy history. Prior to 1969 the reviews were de novo, but from 1969 to 1976 the SSA required a finding of medical improvement before ceasing benefits. By 1976 the press of disability workloads—thanks in significant part to the coming of SSI—was such that the state DDS administrators were pressuring the SSA to return to the old policy, which it did. See *Social Security Continuing Disability Investigation Program: Background and Legislative Issue Paper*, House Subcommittee on Social Security, Report 97-37, September 20, 1982, pp. 24–27.

13. Again the policy history here told a more conflicted tale. Prior to 1979, claims were processed to conclusion (including looking at educational and vocational factors) even if the person had no severe medical impairment. The SSA's post-1979 policy statement on this issue gave over twenty examples of potentially nonsevere impairments (such as arthritis, loss of one eye, hypertension, epilepsy, liver disease, diabetes, etc.). Thus a person could be suffering from all twenty diseases and still be found not to be disabled. Moreover, if the person had at least one *severe* impairment, the government *would* consider the sum of all his or her nonsevere impairments when making the disability assessment. See DeWitt, "Disability: Continuing Disability Reviews," p. 7.

14. Routine, rather than accelerated reviews, continued, however, which meant that SSI beneficiaries would be involved in the initial review process, even if at lower levels than the SSDI population.

15. Oral interview with Rhoda Davis, conducted by Larry DeWitt on February 5, 1996, SSA History Collection, pp. 24–28.

16. Herbert R. Doggette Jr., letter to Jim Demer, dated April 16, 1991, copy in SSA History Archives.

17. Oral interview with Rhoda Davis, February 5, 1996, pp. 24–28.

18. *Social Security Disability: SSA Is Making Progress toward Eliminating Continuing Disability Review Backlogs*, GAO Testimony, GAO-/T-HEHS-97-222, September 25, 1997, Table 1, p. 3.

19. The data shown in Figure 5-1 and in subsequent graphs include both the standard reviews and the mandated reviews from the 1980 legislation.

20. Ibid.

21. Peter Kihss, "New Yorkers Notified of Aid Loss in Review of U.S. Disability Cases," *New York Times*, September 28, 1981, p. A1.

22. Testimony of Lou Hays, "Social Security Appeals and Case Review Process," *Hearings Before the Subcommittee on Social Security of the Ways and Means Committee*, October 23 and 28, 1981, pp. 12–13.

23. David S. Broder, "Aid Shift to States Reported," *Washington Post*, January 19, 1982, p. A1.

24. Spencer Rich, "Budget Knife Aimed at Disability Benefits," *Washington Post*, March 5, 1982, p. A25. Similar proposals affecting SSDI had been part of the ill-fated 1981 administration proposals. The suspicion here was that the administration was trying to introduce these policies in SSI and then move them to SSDI.

25. "Welfare Benefits Tied to Tax Form," *New York Times*, June 8, 1982, p. A25.

26. "Judge Asked to Save Benefits," *New York Times*, June 15, 1982, p. B7; "Court Bars Social Security Benefit Cutoffs," *Los Angeles Times*, June 15, 1982, p. A2; Robert Pear, "Welfare Cutoffs Blocked after Plea of Tax Privacy," *New York Times*, June 16, 1982, p. D19; "Agency's Right to Review Welfare Tax Data Upheld," *Los Angeles Times*, July 7, 1982, p. OC15.

27. Testimony of Lou Hays, "Social Security Appeals and Case Review Process," p. 17.

28. "Disability Amendments of 1982," *Hearings Before the Subcommittee on Social Security of the Committee on Ways and Means*, March 16 and 17, 1982, pp. 21–27.

29. Ibid., p. 96.

30. David Treadwell and Marlene Cimons, "Disability Purge Ruinous to Many," *Los Angeles Times*, March 21, 1982, p. A1.

31. Robert Pear, "Fairness of Reagan's Cutoffs of Disability Aid Questioned," *New York Times*, May 9, 1982, p. 1.

32. John A. Svahn, "Disability Benefit Reviews: Fairness Counts," *New York Times*, May 20, 1982.

33. Quoted in David Whitman, "Television and the 1981–84 Purge of the Disability Rolls," Center for Press, Politics and Public Policy, Kennedy School of Government, 1984, p. 7, SSA History Archives.

34. Ibid., p. 18.

35. Ibid.

36. Robin Herman, "Easing of U.S. Rules on Aid for Disabled Is Sought," *New York Times*, February 8, 1982, p. B2.

37. Testimony of Carol Bellamy, "Social Security Reviews of the Mentally Disabled," *Hearings Before the Special Committee on Aging*, United States Senate, April 7 and 8, 1983, pp. 92–93; "Dumping the Disabled," editorial, *New York Times*, February 19, 1983, p. 22.

38. Testimony of Louis O. Treadway representing the National Association of Counties, "Social Security Reviews of the Mentally Disabled," p. 85.

39. "SSI Disability Issues," *Hearing Before the Subcommittee on Public Assistance and Unemployment Compensation*, June 6 (Washington, DC: U.S. Government Printing Office, 1983), p. 28.

40. Testimony of Dan Jordan, Executive Director, Mental Health Advocates, Oakland, in ibid., p. 19.

41. Testimony of Elizabeth Boggs, in "Supplemental Security Legislation," *Hearing Before the Subcommittee on Public Assistance and Unemployment Compensation*, August 3, 1983, p. 81.

42. Mary Jane Fine, "Witnessing the Worst Thing Social Security Has Done," *Philadelphia Inquirer*, April 11, 1982.

43. Jonathan M. Stein, "A Disability Benefits Review Program That Has Gone Awry," letter to the editor, *New York Times*, May 22, 1982, p. 26.

44. Fine, "Witnessing the Worst Thing."

45. "Oversight of Social Security Disability Benefits Termination," *Hearing Before the Subcommittee on Oversight of Government Management of the Committee on Governmental Affairs*, U.S. Senate, May 25, 1982.

46. Ibid., p. 97.

47. David Koitz, "Status of the Disability Programs of the Social Security Administration," *Congressional Research Service Report for Congress*, 92-691 EPW, September 8, 1992, pp. 154–55. Note that these are end-of-year pending levels and they include all Social Security cases, not just disability-related cases, but disability-related cases comprised 95 to 96 percent of the cases. Also note that the federal government's fiscal year runs from October through the following September.

48. Finnegan v. Matthews, 641 F 2nd 1340, Court of Appeals, 9th Circuit, 1981.

49. Joseph P. Fried, "Social Security Aid for the Mentally Ill Reinstated by Judge," *New York Times*, January 12, 1984, p. B2.

50. "Social Security Disability Reviews: The Role of the Administrative Law Judge," *Hearing Before the Senate Subcommittee on Oversight of Government Management*, June 8 (Washington, DC: U.S. Government Printing Office, 1983), p. 21.

51. Ibid., p. 238. The first nonacquiescence ruling cited by Hays was issued in 1967, involving how earnings are to be credited when a husband and wife jointly own a business. On the legal issues involved in nonacquiescence, see Susan Gluck Mezey, *No Longer*

Disabled: The Federal Courts and the Politics of Social Security Disability (Westport, CT: Greenwood Press, 1988).

52. Patti v. Schweiker, 669 F2d582, 587 (9th Circuit 1982); Lopez v. Heckler, 713 F2nd 1432, Court of Appeals 9th Circuit, 1983.

53. Dorothy Townsend, "U.S. Sued over Social Security," *Los Angeles Times*, December 30, 1982, p. C1.

54. Dan Morain, "Judge to Order Some Disability Pay Restored," *Los Angeles Times*, June 7, 1981; Dan Morain, "72,800 May Regain Disability Benefits," *Los Angeles Times*, June 19, 1983, p. A31; Dan Morain, "78,000 May Refile for Revoked Benefits," *Los Angeles Times*, August 14, 1983, p. OCA6.

55. Hillhouse v. Harris, 715 F2d 428, Court of Appeals, 8th Circuit, 1983.

56. J. Paul McGrath, Assistant Attorney General, to Juan A. del Real, General Counsel, Department of Health and Human Services, September 9, 1983, in Mary Ross Papers, Box 60, SSA History Archives.

57. George C. Wallace to James Demer, February 6, 1991, SSA History Archives.

58. James B. Hunt Jr. to James Demer, February 19, 1991, SSA History Archives.

59. A federal DDS unit was eventually established in Baltimore in 1987.

60. HHS Press Release, September 8, 1982, in Mary Ross Papers, Box 60, Social Security History Archives.

61. John A. Svahn to the Secretary, May 25, 1983, in Mary Ross Papers, Box 60.

62. HHS Press Release, June 7, 1983, in Downey Book Collection, Social Security Disability Benefits Reform Act of 1984 and Related Amendments, SSA History Archives.

63. Svahn to the Secretary, May 25, 1983.

64. "Ways and Means Talks on Disability Bill Fail," *Washington Post*, April 30, 1982, p. A7.

65. "House Unit Backs Bid to Soften Impact of Disability Aid Cutoffs," *Los Angeles Times*, May 20, 1982, p. B11; "Disability Amendments of 1982," House Report No. 97-588, May 26, 1982, pp. 4–6.

66. *Social Security Continuing Disability Investigation Program: Background and Legislative Issue Paper*, September 20, 1982, Ways and Means Committee, Print 97-37, pp. 3–4.

67. Ibid., pp. 24–26.

68. Ibid., p. 2.

69. *Oversight of the Social Security Administration Disability Reviews*, a report prepared by the Subcommittee on Oversight of Government Management of the Committee on Governmental Affairs, United States Senate, August 1982, p. 11.

70. "Taxes on Virgin Island Source Income; Disability Benefits," House Report No. 97-985, December 21, 1982. This bill became PL 97-455, *An Act Relating to Taxes on Virgin Island Source Income and Social Security Disability Benefits*, signed into law on January 12, 1983.

71. Paul Light, *Artful Work: The Politics of Social Security Reform* (New York: McGraw Hill, 1995); W. Andrew Achenbaum, *Social Security: Visions and Revisions* (New York: Cambridge University Press, 1988).

72. "Social Security Disability Insurance Program," *Hearing Before the Committee on Finance*, January 25, 1984, pp. 93–107.

73. "Social Security Disability Reviews: The Human Costs," *Joint Hearing Before the Special Committee on Aging, United States Senate, and the Committee on Ways and Means*, February 17, 1984, pp. 2–3.

74. For a good summary of the history that led to disability legislation in 1984, as well as information on the relevant legal cases and the actions by the states, see Katharine P. Collins and Anne Erfle, "Social Security Disability Benefits Reform Act of 1984: Legislative History and Summary of Provisions," *Social Security Bulletin* 48 (April 1985): 5–32.

The SSI parts of the legislation were similar to the SSDI parts. For example, they asserted that the revision of regulatory criteria related to mental impairments would apply to SSI as well as to SSDI.

75. Senator Heinz in "Social Security Disability Reviews: The Human Costs," *Joint Hearing Before the Special Committee on Aging, United States Senate, and the Committee on Ways and Means*, February 17, 1984, p. 5.

76. Statement of Robert McPherson, Austin, Texas, Director of Planning, Office of the Governor, State of Texas, in ibid., pp. 23–24.

77. "Status of Continuing Disability Reviews," *Hearing Before the Subcommittee on Social Security of the Committee on Ways and Means*, Atlanta, Georgia, March 23, 1984, pp. 2–3, 17.

78. "Status of Continuing Disability Reviews: Social Security Disability Cutoffs Controversy," *Joint Hearing Before the Subcommittee on Social Security of the Committee on Ways and Means and the Subcommittee on Health and Long-Term Care of the Select Committee on Aging*, House of Representatives, Miami, Florida, April 30, 1984, p. 4.

79. Here, as elsewhere, Collins and Erfle, "Social Security Disability Benefits Reform Act of 1984," contains the complete details.

80. *Public Papers of the Presidents: Ronald Reagan, 1984, Vol. II* (Washington, DC: Government Printing Office, 1987), pp. 1477–78.

81. Spencer Rich, "Hill Conferees Agree on Tougher Rules for Disability Reviews," *Washington Post*, September 15, 1984, p. A15.

82. For comprehensive descriptions of the law, we rely on "Social Security Disability Benefits Reform Act of 1984," *Legislative Report*, 98th Congress, Number 2, September 21, 1984, SSA History Archives; "Social Security Disability Benefits Reform Act of 1984," House Report No. 98-1039, September 19, 1984.

83. House Report No. 98-1039, pp. 23–28.

84. Ibid., pp. 33–36.

85. Ibid., p. 42. Congress also enacted a provision *requiring* the SSA to federalize the operations of any state DDS that refused to follow federal guidelines in making disability determinations.

86. Ibid., pp. 36–37.

87. Martha A. McSteen to All Executive Staff, March 1, 1985, SSA History Archives.

88. "SSA Invites Ex-Recipients to Apply Again," *Baltimore Sun*, February 15, 1985; "Soc. Sec. May Re-Enroll 175,000," *USA Today*, February 15, 1985; "Report of Hearing, House Committee on Ways and Means, Subcommittee on Social Security," June 6, 1985, SSA History Archives.

89. "Important Message," February 26, 1985, SSA History Archives.

90. "HHS News," April 29, 1985, SSA History Archives.

91. "U.S. Proposes New Rules for Reviews on Disability Benefits," *New York Times*, April 30, 1985, p. A15.

92. "Report of Hearing, House Committee on the Judiciary, Subcommittee on Administrative Law and Governmental Relations," July 25, 1985, SSA History Archives.

93. "HHS Broadens Social Security Appeal Rulings," *Toledo Blade*, June 4, 1985; "Heckler Bows to Courts on Policy Issues," *Los Angeles Times*, June 3, 1985, p. 2.

94. "Report of Hearing," July 25, 1985.

95. Statement by Martha A. McSteen, "Oversight Hearing Implementation of 1984 Disability Amendments," June 6, 1985, in *Report of Hearing House Committee on Ways and Means Subcommittee on Social Security*, June 6, 1985, SSA History Archives.

96. Spencer Rich, "State Officials Attack New Disability Rules," *Washington Post*, June 7, 1985; AP news story filed by Christopher Connell and UPI story filed by Dana Walker, pulled from the wires by the SSA Press Office, SSA History Archives.

97. *Report of Hearing, Subcommittee on Social Security*, June 6, 1985.

98. *Social Security Disability: SSA Is Making Progress toward Eliminating Continuing Disability Review Backlogs*, GAO Testimony, GAO-/T-HEHS-97-222, September 25, 1997.

99. "Rule Published on Mental-Impairment Aid," *Washington Post*, August 28, 1985, p. A17.

CHAPTER 6

1. Jane L. Ross, Testimony, *Social Security—Federal Disability Programs Face Major Issues*, March 2, 1995, for the Special Committee on Aging, U.S. Senate, p. 3.

2. Lenna Kennedy, "Children Receiving SSI Payments, December 1992," *Social Security Bulletin* 56 (Summer 1993): 77.

3. "Social Security Amendments of 1983," *Report of the Committee on Ways and Means on HR 1900*, March 4, 1983, p. 106.

4. Gareth Davies, "The Welfare State," in *The Reagan Presidency: Pragmatic Conservatism and Its Legacies*, ed. W. Elliot Brownlee and Hugh Davis Graham (Lawrence: University Press of Kansas, 2003), pp. 209–32. See also Martha Derthick and Steven M. Teles, "Riding the Third Rail: Social Security Reform," pp. 182–208 in the same volume.

5. Robert Pear, "President Reported Ready to Propose Overhaul of Social Welfare System," *New York Times*, February 1, 1986, p. 12; Bernard Weinraub, "Reagan Is Pushing the Welfare Issue," *New York Times*, February 16, 1986, p. 17; Robert Pear, "Reagan Aide Wants Lid on Benefits for Poor," *New York Times*, March 2, 1986, p. 1; "Reagan Seeks Change in Welfare System," *New York Times*, December 13, 1986, p. 12.

6. "President's Private Sector Survey on Cost Control: A Report to the President," January 15, 1984, available online at http://www.uhuh.com/taxstuff/gracecom.htm.

7. Personal conversation with one of the authors.

8. Spencer Rich, "Dorcas R. Hardy in Control at Social Security, a Tough New Administrator," *Washington Post*, July 28, 1986, p. A9.

9. One of the authors was, for a brief time, one of Hardy's speechwriters where he witnessed this incident.

10. Rhoda Davis interview conducted by Larry DeWitt, SSA History Archives, p. 37.

11. Early in her tenure, Hardy barred union officials from appearing in public with her even on purely ceremonial occasions and refused to meet with the union official representing SSA headquarters employees. The union's newsletters during the Hardy tenure were filled with scathing and sometimes quite personal criticisms of the Commissioner.

12. Personal observation by one of the authors.

13. Spencer Rich, "States Asked to Increase Disability Caseload," *Washington Post*, September 13, 1986, p. A9.

14. Robert Pear, "New Reagan Policy to Cut Benefits for the Aged, Blind, and Disabled," *New York Times*, October 16, 1987, p. A1.

15. Robert Pear, "U.S., Facing Criticism, Drops Plan to Cut Benefits for the Poor," *New York Times*, October 17, 1987, p. 1.

16. Section 9117 of P.L. 100-203, the Omnibus Budget Reconciliation Act of 1987, approved December 27, 1987.

17. William F. Buckley Jr., "Identify All the Carriers," *New York Times*, Tuesday, March 18, 1986, p. A27.

18. Daniel M. Fox, "AIDS and the American Health Polity: The History and Prospects of a Crisis in Authority," in *AIDS: The Burdens of History*, ed. Elizabeth Fee and Daniel M. Fox (Berkeley: University of California Press, 1988), pp. 316–43.

19. Spencer Rich, "New Definition to Widen AIDS Disability Benefits," *Washington Post*, July 28, 1987, p. A4.

20. Spencer Rich, "Provisions of 'Catastrophic' Insurance Act," *Washington Post*, July 1, 1988, p. A21; T. Rice, K. Desmond, and J. Gabel, "The Medicare Catastrophic Coverage Act: A Post-Mortem," *Health Affairs* 9 (1990): 75–87.

21. Edward Berkowitz, *America's Welfare State* (Baltimore: Johns Hopkins University Press: 1991), pp. 145–47; see also the essays in Richard W. Coughlin, ed., *Reforming Welfare: Lessons, Limits and Choices* (Albuquerque: University of New Mexico Press, 1989); for a longer-term perspective, see R. Kent Weaver, *Ending Welfare as We Know It* (Washington, DC: Brookings Institution, 2000).

22. Robert Pear, "Expanded Right to Medicaid Shatters the Link to Welfare," *New York Times*, March 6, 1988, p. 1.

23. *Supplemental Security Income (SSI): Current Program Characteristics and Alternatives for Future Reform*, A Background Paper by the Subcommittee on Retirement Income and Employment, Select Commission on Aging, August 1988, Committee Publication 100-669.

24. See Executive Summary, *Report of the Disability Advisory Council*, 1988.

25. Kathleen Teltsch, "Ford Foundation Urges Big Changes in U.S. Social Programs," *New York Times*, May 11, 1989, p. A22.

26. Martin Tolchin, "Congress Begins Work on Programs for Poor Children," *New York Times*, June 16, 1989, p. A10; Spencer Rich, "Medicaid, Welfare Expansions Gain Support," *Washington Post*, July 16, 1989, p. A5.

27. "Supplemental Social Security Change Urged," *Washington Post*, September 5, 1992, p. A11.

28. *Supplemental Security Income Modernization Project, Final Report of the Experts*, August 1992, SSA History Archives.

29. Rhoda Davis interview, p. 44. King restored relations with the unions and was much liked by the rank and file employees, as observed by one of the authors, who was on her staff during King's tenure as Commissioner.

30. Martin Tolchin, "Many Wrongly Losing U.S. Payments," *New York Times*, December 8, 1989, p. A20.

31. "Payments to Elderly, Disabled Wrongly Cut Off, Agency Says," *Washington Post*, December 9, 1989, p. A7.

32. Martin Tolchin, "Social Security Chief Scolds Staff over Handling of Disability Cases," *New York Times*, December 19, 1989, p. B10.

33. Martin Tolchin, "Social Security Chief Seeks to Expand a U.S. Welfare Program," *New York Times*, December 29, 1989, p. A14.

34. Martin Tolchin, "Bush Bars Reduction in Social Security Staff," *New York Times*, December 15, 1989, p. A20.

35. "Congress Agrees to Budget Reconciliation Bill," SSA Administration, *Legislative Bulletin*, 101-23, October 31, 1990, SSA History Archives.

36. Jennifer L. Erkulwater, *Disability Rights and the American Safety Net* (Ithaca, NY: Cornell University Press, 2006), p. 132. We have relied on Erkulwater for this description of the case, as well as on an oral interview we conducted on February 16, 2011, in Philadelphia with Richard Weishaupt and Jonathan Stein of Community Legal Services, who wrote the brief and argued the case.

37. See Edward Berkowitz, *Disabled Policy: America's Programs for the Handicapped* (New York: Cambridge University Press, 1987), pp. 101–3.

38. Sullivan v. Zebley, 493 521 (1990), argued November 28, 1989, decided February 20, 1990. Majority opinion by Justice Blackmun joined by Justices Brennan, Marshall, Stevens, O'Connor, and Kennedy. Justice White filed a dissenting opinion, joined by Justice Rehnquist. The text of the decision is available online at

http://webcache.googleusercontent.com/search?q=cache:zgZ1zwjFspgJ:laws.lp.find-law.com/getcase/US/493/521.html+sullivan+v+zebley&cd=2&hl=en&ct=clnk&gl=us&source=www.google.com. We used the online version of the decision.

39. Sullivan v. Zebley, 493 US 521 (1990).

40. Linda Greenhouse, "Justices Limit Parent's Rights in Child Abuse Case," *New York Times*, February 21, 1990, p. A20.

41. Spencer Rich, "Thousands of Children in Line for Aid," *Washington Post*, March 1, 1990, p. A23.

42. This is the major theme of Martha Derthick's *Agency under Stress: The Social Security Administration in American Government* (Washington, DC: Brookings Institution, 1990).

43. General Accounting Office, *Social Security—New Functional Assessments for Children Raise Eligibility Questions*, March 1995, p. 8.

44. Robert Pear, "Despite Order, U.S. Stalls Aid to Poor Children," *New York Times*, November 19, 1990, p. A1.

45. Letter to Honorable Gwendolyn S. King, dated February 20, 1991, copy in SSA History Archives, Unit L1, file "Zebley."

46. Mary Ross, "Note for the Records," dated June 28, 1991, SSA History Archives, Mary Ross Papers, box MR-42.

47. Spencer Rich, "Benefit of Court Win Eludes Children," *Washington Post*, June 28, 1990, A23.

48. Letters to various members of Congress and Jonathan Stein, from Commissioner Gwendolyn S. King, August 12, 1991, copies in SSA History Archives, L1, folder: Zebley.

49. "More Poor Children Eligible for Disability Benefits," *New York Times*, February 11, 1991, p. B8.

50. "Restructuring the SSI Disability Program for Children and Adolescents," *Report of the Committee on Childhood Disability of the Disability Policy Panel*, National Academy of Social Insurance, 1996, p. 12.

51. General Accounting Office, *Social Security: Rapid Rise in Children on SSI Disability Rolls Follows New Regulations*, 1994, p. 7.

52. General Accounting Office, *Social Security: New Functional Assessments for Children Raise Eligibility Questions*, March 1995, p. 9.

53. "More Poor Children Eligible for Disability Benefits," p. B8.

54. "U.S. in Accord on Child Benefits," *New York Times*, March 17, 1991, p. 24.

55. U.S. to Begin Reviewing Claims of Children Rejected for Benefits," *New York Times*, July 9, 1991, p. A17.

56. General Accounting Office, *Social Security: Rapid Rise in Children on SSI Disability Rolls*, p. 8.

57. *Restructuring the SSI Disability Program for Children and Adolescents*, p. 12; monograph on disability listings available at SSA History Archives.

58. *SSI Annual Statistical Supplement*, 2003, Table 3, p. 21.

59. David Koitz and Geoffrey Kollmann, Congressional Research Service, "Status of the Social Security Administration's Disability Programs," April 7, 1994, Social Security History Archives.

60. General Accounting Office, *Social Security: Rapid Rise in Children on SSI Disability Rolls*, pp. 2–3, 9.

61. *New Functional Assessments for Children Raise Eligibility Questions*," pp. 1, 2, 9.

62. *Restructuring the SSI Disability Program for Children and Adolescents*, pp. 1, 10, 23.

CHAPTER 7

1. Dan Morgan, "Medicaid Costs Balloon into Fiscal 'Time Bomb,'" *Washington Post*, January 30, 1994, p. A 1; Dan Morgan, "When Long Term Means Lifetime," *Washington Post*, February 1, 1994, p. A13.

2. Bob Woodward and Benjamin Weiser, "Costs Soar for Children's Disability Program," *Washington Post*, February 4, 1994, p. A1.

3. *SSA Annual Statistical Supplement, 2010*, Table 7.A8.

4. Woodward and Weiser, "Costs Soar for Children's Disability Program," p. A1.

5. Jonathan Yardley, "America's Faultless Performance," *Washington Post*, February 7, 1994, p. C2.

6. Ken Silverstein and Alexander Cockburn, "How Rich Journalists Stole Crutches from Crippled Children," *Counterpunch*, July 15, 1995, pp. 1–3.

7. "Tax Dollars Aiding and Abetting Addiction: Social Security Disability and SSI Cash Benefits to Drug Addicts and Alcoholics," *Investigative Staff Report of Senator William S. Cohen*, February 7, 1994, "Executive Summary," and pp. 1–7.

8. Bill S. 1863, 103rd Congress, 2nd Session, February 23, 1994; William S. Cohen, "Playing Social Security for a Sucker," *Washington Post*, February 23, 1994, p. A17; Cohen, "Reform of the Social Security Disability Program," *Congressional Record*, Senate, February 24, 1994, pp. S1794–995.

9. Jason DeParle, "Clinton Considers Taxing Aid to Poor to Pay for Reform," *New York Times*, February 13, 1994.

10. *SSI Annual Statistical Supplement*, various years, Social Security Administration, Tables 4 and 29.

11. Ron Suskind, "Clinton Weighs Cuts to Finance Welfare Reform—Some Immigrants' Benefits as Well as Housing Aid Are Said to Be Targets," *Wall Street Journal*, February 14, 1994, p. 2; Jason DeParle, "Democrats Face Hard Choices in Welfare Overhaul," *New York Times*, February 22, 1994, p. A16.

12. Oscar Handlin, *The Uprooted: The Epic Story of the Great Migrations That Made the American People, Second Edition* (Philadelphia: University of Pennsylvania Press, 2002); Nathan Glazer and Daniel P. Moynihan, *Beyond the Melting Pot, Second Edition: The Negroes, Puerto Ricans, Jews, Italians and Irish of New York City* (Cambridge, MA: MIT Press, 1970); John Higham, *Strangers in the Land: Patterns of American Nativism, 1860–1925* (New Brunswick, NJ: Rutgers University Press, 2002); Matthew Jacobson, *Whiteness of a Different Color: European Immigrants and the Alchemy of Race* (Cambridge, MA: Harvard University Press, 1999).

13. "Leave the Immigrants Be," *Washington Post*, February 20, 1994, p. C6.

14. "Spending Impaired," *Wall Street Journal*, March 8, 1994, p. A1.

15. Carolyn L. Weaver, "Welfare Reform Is Likely to Leave This Monster Intact," *Wall Street Journal*, April 6, 1994, p. A14.

16. William Claiborne, "Immigrants' Benefits at Risk," *Washington Post*, March 24, 1994, p. A1.

17. Jason DeParle, "Welfare Plan Seeks Limit on Benefits," *New York Times*, May 12, 1994, p. A22; "On Not Blaming Immigrants First," *Washington Post*, May 9, 1994, p. A16.

18. Leonard S. Rubenstein, "Unfair Portrayal of a Good Program," *Washington Post*, February 26, 1994, p. A24; "Contention over Children's Benefits," letters to the editor from George E. Ayers, Gerald D. Kleczka, Martha E. Ford, and Rhoda Schulzinger, *Washington Post*, March 2, 1994, p. A16.

19. An independent agency bill passed the House in 1986 but was not considered by the Senate.

20. See HR Report No. 103-506, May 12, 1994, pp. 44–46.

21. Ibid., p. 44.

22. Ibid., pp. 44, 47.

23. Spencer Rich, "After Impending Divorce, Rocky Honeymoon Likely," *Washington Post*, May 12, 1994, p. A25.

24. "Statement of Administration Policy on HR 4277—Social Security Administrative Reform Act of 1994," May 17, 1994, SSA History Archives.

25. Michael Wines, "House Backs Independence for Social Security Agency," *New York Times*, May 18, 1994, p. A16.

26. *Congressional Record*, House, May 17, 1994, p. H3449.

27. Ibid., p. H3451.

28. Spencer Rich, "Panel Backs Independence for Social Security," *Washington Post*, July 21, 1994, p. A29.

29. "Social Security Administrative Reform Act of 1994," House No. Report 103-670, August 4, 1994, p. 116.

30. *Congressional Record*, Senate, August 5, 1994, p. S10874.

31. "Remarks on Signing the Social Security Independence and Program Improvements Act of 1994," August 15, 1994, and "Statement on Signing the Social Security Independence and Program Improvement Act of 1994," *Public Papers of William Clinton, 1994*, pp. 1675–76.

32. Jason DeParle, "Clinton Agrees to Welfare Financing," *New York Times*, May 26, 1994, p. A14; Eric Pianin and Ruth Marcus, "Clinton to Offer $9.3 Billion Welfare Bill," *Washington Post*, June 10, 1994, p. A18.

33. Linda Killian, *The Freshmen: What Happened to the Republican Revolution* (New York: Basic Books, 1999).

34. Harry A. Brown and Emily Clark Millis, *From the Wagner Act to Taft-Hartley: A Study of National Labor Policy and Labor Relations* (Chicago: University of Chicago Press, 1965).

35. Richard Cohen, "Orphanages: Giving Gingrich the Dickens," *Washington Post*, December 6, 1994, p. A19.

36. Jason DeParle, "Momentum Builds for Cutting Back Welfare System," *New York Times*, November 13, 1994, p. 1; Robert Pear, "G.O.P. Proposal Would Overhaul Welfare System," *New York Times*, November 22, 1994, p. A1; Barbara Vobedja, "GOP Welfare Bill Would Deny Benefits to Millions, Report Says," *Washington Post*, November 23, 1994, p. A14.

37. Robert Suro, "GOP Would Deny Legal Immigrants Many U.S. Benefits," *Washington Post*, December 24, 1994, p. A1.

38. Ibid.; Robert Pear, "Deciding Who Gets What in America," *New York Times*, November 27, 1994, p. E5.

39. Robert Pear, "Republican Bill Would Trim Aid for Poor Children Who Are Ill or Disabled," *New York Times*, December 29, 1994, p. A16.

40. "Supplemental Security Income Payments on the Rise," NPR, *All Things Considered*, Washington, DC, December 26, 1994.

41. Heather Mac Donald, "SSI Fosters a Disabling Dependency," *Wall Street Journal*, January 20, 1995, p. A12.

42. Robert Pear, "House Panel Takes Step 1 in Plan to Revamp Welfare," *New York Times*, February 16, 1995, p. D22.

43. Anthony Lewis, "Visigoths at the Gate," *New York Times*, February 27, 1995, p. A15.

44. Robert Pear, "House Committee Completes Plan to Overhaul Welfare," *New York Times*, March 4, 1995, p. 9.

45. "House Committee on Ways and Means Markup of Welfare Reform Proposal," *Legislative Bulletin* 104-1, March 7, 1995, SSA History Archives.

46. "Welfare Transformation Act of 1995," House Report No. 104-81, March 15, 1995, pp. 47–55.

47. Ibid., pp. 372–79.

48. *Congressional Record*, House, March 21, 1995, p. H3348.

49. Ibid.

50. Ibid., p. H3356.

51. Ibid., p. H3357.

52. Ibid., p. H3362.

53. Robert Pear, "House Bill Links Licenses to Child-Support Payment," *New York Times*, March 24, 1995, p. A22; "House Passes H.R. 4, The Personal Responsibility Act of 1995," *Legislative Bulletin*, 104-4, March 27, 1995, SSA History Archives.

54. Ashley Dunn, "For Elderly Immigrants, a Retirement Plan for U.S.," *New York Times*, April 16, 1995, p. 1.

55. Christopher M. Wright, "SSI: The Black Hole of the Welfare State," Cato Policy Analysis No. 224, April 27, 1995, Cato Institute, Washington, DC.

56. *SSI Annual Statistical Supplement, 2010*, Social Security Administration, Table 2.

57. Ibid., authors' calculations.

58. Christopher M. Wright, "SSI: The Black Hole of the Welfare State," Cato Policy Analysis No. 224, April 27, 1995, Cato Institute, Washington, DC.

59. Mary Somoza, "Broken by the Budget?" *New York Times*, May 27, 1995, p. 19.

60. Robert Pear, "Senate Committee Approves a Vast Overhaul of Welfare," *New York Times*, May 27, 1995, p. 1.

61. "The Senate Finance Committee Reports a Welfare Reform Bill, the 'Family Self-Sufficiency Act of 1995,'" *Legislative Bulletin*, 104-6, June 2, 1995, SSA Archives.

62. *Congressional Record*, Senate, August 7, 1995, p. S11739.

63. Ibid., pp. S11770–71.

64. Ibid., pp. S11772–74.

65. Ibid., pp. S11774–75.

66. *Congressional Record*, Senate, September 8, 1995, p. S12924.

67. *Congressional Record*, Senate, August 8, 1995, p. S11807.

68. *Congressional Record*, Senate, September 14, 1995, p. S13613.

69. *Congressional Record*, Senate, September 19, 1995, pp. S13781–82; "Agency Is Faulted for Fraud in Disability Payments to Immigrants," *New York Times*, September 5, 1995, p. D9.

70. Christopher George, "A Media Crusade Gone Haywire," *Forbes Media Critic*, September 1995, pp. 66–71.

71. Molly Ivins, "The Media Fueled Assault on Funding for Disabled Kids," *Philadelphia Daily News*, September 25, 1995, p. 22.

72. Robert Pear, "House and Senate Leaders Compromise to Soften Welfare Bill," *New York Times*, November 11, 1995, p. 11.

73. "Provisions of the Balanced Budget Act of 1995 (HR 2491) as Vetoed by the President on December 6, 1995," *Legislative Bulletin*, 104-18, February 2, 1996, SSA Archives.

74. Ibid.

75. Robert Pear, "As Welfare Compromise Emerges, Clinton Aide Says Veto Is Certain," *New York Times*, November 13, 1995, p. A1.

76. Robert Pear, "Republicans in Accord on Welfare Bill," *New York Times*, November 15, 1995, p. B10.

77. This discussion benefits from a time line of the 1996 welfare reform law prepared by the American Public Welfare Association and available online at http://www.apwa.org/reform/timeline.htm.

78. *Congressional Record*, House, December 21, 1995, pp. H15520, H15526, H15530.

79. *Congressional Record*, Senate, December 22, 1995, pp. S19168, S19174.

80. "Message to the House of Representatives Returning without Approval Legislation on the Welfare System," January 9, 1996, *Public Papers of the Presidents, William J. Clinton, 1996* (Washington, DC: Government Printing Office, 1997), pp. 22–23.

81. *Congressional Record*, House, December 5, 1995, p. H13970.

82. *Congressional Record*, Senate, March 28, 1996, pp. S3018, S3117, S3119.

83. "The President Signs H.R. 3136, The "Contract with America Advancement Act of 1996," *Legislative Bulletin*, 104-22, April 9, 1996, SSA History Archives; Shirley S. Chater, Commissioner of Social Security, to William J. Clinton, March 28, 1996, SSA History Archives.

84. Committee on Ways and Means, *Exploring Means of Achieving Higher Rates of Treatment and Rehabilitation among Alcoholics and Drug Addicts Receiving Federal Disability Benefit*, p. 61.

85. Robert Pear, "On Social Policy, Governors Quietly Split the Difference," *New York Times*, February 8, 1996, p. A1.

86. Robert Pear, "White House Is Optimistic about Chances of Welfare Bill with New G.O.P. Moves," *New York Times*, July 13, 1996, p. 10.

87. *Congressional Record*, House, July 18, 1996, p. H17675.

88. Ibid., p. S8092.

89. Ibid., p. S17956.

90. Ibid., p. S8106; Robert Pear, "Big Role to States," *New York Times*, July 24, 1996, p. A1.

91. Robert Pear, "Agreement Struck on Most Elements for Welfare Bill," *New York Times*, July 30, 1996, p. A1.

92. "Playing 'Gotcha!' on Welfare Reform," *Chicago Tribune*, July 21, 1996.

93. Statement by the President, The White House, July 31, 1966; see Maeve Quaid, *Workfare: Why Good Social Policy Ideas Go Bad* (Toronto: University of Toronto Press, 1992); CNN, "Clinton Says He'll Sign GOP Welfare Bill," available online at http://articles.cnn.com/1996-07-31/us/9607_31_clinton.welfare_1_gop-welfare-welfare-reform-legal-immigrants?_s=PM:US.

94. "Congress Reaches Agreement on H.R. 3734, The Personal Responsibility and Work Opportunity Reconciliation Act of 1996," *Legislative Bulletin*, 104-30, August 2, 1996, SSA History Archives. Other features relevant to SSI included incentive payments from SSI program funds to state and local penal institutions for furnishing information to the SSA that results in suspension of SSI benefits; installment payments of large past-due SSI payments; the establishment of a dedicated savings account to maintain retroactive SSI benefits; the denial of SSI benefits for any month in which an individual is fleeing prosecution, a fugitive felon, or violating a condition of prohibition and parole; and the denial of SSI benefits for ten years to individuals who have misrepresented residence in order to obtain benefits in two or more states.

95. Source interview with Jonathan Stein.

CHAPTER 8

1. Joyce Purnick, "Throwing Out the Disabled or the Fraud?" *New York Times*, August 8, 1996, p. B1.

2. Michael Janofsky, "Disabled Children's Families Brace for Benefit Cuts," *New York Times*, December 23, 1996, p. A12.

3. Daisy Fried, "Thousands of Sick Children Will Soon Be Purged from Federal Disability Rolls," *Philadelphia City Paper*, November 21–26, 1996.

4. Ibid.

5. Robert Pear, "After a Review, 95,180 Children Will Lose Cash Disability Benefits," *New York Times*, August 15, 1997.

6. Ibid.

7. Ibid.

8. Social Security Administration, "Review of SSA's Implementation of New SSI Childhood Disability Legislation," December 17, 1997, SSA History Archives. A fourth area of concern involved quality assurance procedures internal to the bureaucratic process that would not be visible to the public.

9. *SSI Annual Statistical Report, 2008* (Social Security Administration), Table 4.

10. *SSI Annual Statistical Report, 2011* (Social Security Administration), Table IV.C1.

11. *SSA Annual Statistical Supplement*, 1990 edition, Table 9F1, p. 309 (data as of December 1989). (This includes mental retardation and mental disorders other than retardation—the two standard categories of mental disorders in the disability listings.)

12. *SSA Annual Statistical Supplement*, 1994 edition, Table 7F2, p. 301 (data as of December 1993).

13. *SSA Annual Statistical Supplement*, 1996 edition, Table 7F, p. 318 (data as of December 1995).

14. *SSI Annual Statistical Report, 2009* (Social Security Administration), Table 21.

15. Ibid. (The miscellaneous category of "other" was 9.7 percent.)

16. Data on these features of the SSI population are not regularly reported by the SSA. The number of SSI-receiving aliens who were in the military or were veterans is unknown, but it was probably very small. Indeed, this category was more symbolic than real. A 1980 special study of aliens on SSI found that only about 20 percent of alien beneficiaries were "dually entitled," meaning receiving Social Security and SSI, and not all of these were receiving Social Security because they had forty quarters of coverage on their own work history. Many were family members of Social Security beneficiaries and eligible for Social Security on that basis. The percentage of the SSI alien cohort in the United States as refugees or asylum seekers is also unknown from the period, but that same 1980 study suggested that in 1979 only about 13 percent of SSI aliens were in the country as refugees (the percentage of asylum seekers is not given, but it would be less than the refugee category). Even if we assume that these two categories have no overlap (which was likely not the case), at most 33 percent of aliens on SSI would clearly fall into the excluded categories. See Lenna Kennedy and Jack Schmulowitz, "SSI Payments to Lawfully Resident Aliens, 1978–1979," *Social Security Bulletin* 43 (March 1980): 3–10.

17. Jeffrey L. Rabin and Patrick J. McDonnell, "Reform Bill Assailed as Nightmare for County," *Los Angeles Times*, August 1, 1996, p. 1.

18. Anastasia Hendrix, "Welfare Changes in County 'Costly' Millions to Offset Loss of Federal Money," *The Fresno Bee*, August 15, 1996, p. A1; Ryan McCarthy, "County Bridles under Welfare Burden," *The Sacramento Bee*, September 8, 1996, p. N3.

19. "Unkind Cuts: The Welfare Overhaul May Save Washington Money, but It Will Cost New York Plenty," *Newsday*, August 5, 1996, p. A30; Julie Shaver, "What the Welfare Law May Mean for Certain Recipients," *New York Times*, August 23, 1996, p. A22.

20. "Mayor Giuliani Makes Cases for Immigration in Lawsuit," *Washington Post*, October 12, 1996, p. A11.

21. "Archer Warns against Trying to Grant Welfare to Non-citizens," *Washington Times*, November 23, 1996, p. A4.

22. *SSI Annual Statistical Report, 2009* (Social Security Administration), Table 29.

23. Christopher Howard, *The Hidden Welfare State* (Princeton, NJ: Princeton University Press, 1997); and *The Welfare State Nobody Knows* (Princeton, NJ: Princeton University Press, 2006).

24. *Social Security Administration's Report on Supplemental Security Income and Resource Exclusions and Disability Insurance Earnings-Related Provisions*, Social Security Administration, March 2000; *The SSI Program at the Millennium*, SSA, November 2000; *Simplifying the Supplemental Security Income Program: Challenges and Opportunities*, SSA, December 2000, all in SSA History Archives.

25. The remaining 15 percent of the administrative budget was devoted to workloads involving Medicare. See *SSI Program at the Millennium*, p. 41.

26. Ibid., p. 15.

27. http://mwww.ba.ssa.gov/policy/docs/statcomps/supplement/2010/7b.html.

28. *SSI Annual Statistical Report, 2011* (Social Security Administration), Table IV.C4, p. 49.

29. http://mwww.ba.ssa.gov/policy/docs/statcomps/supplement/2010/7b.html.

30. "Recent Economic Slump Hitting the Disabled Hard: Food, Housing and Health Care Costs Put Strain on Families," *Herald Sun* with *Chapel Hill Herald*, August 23, 2008, p. CH1.

31. Amy Worden, "Fears That Rendell's Budget Shortchanges Needy," *Philadelphia Inquirer*, February 15, 2010.

32. http://www.nj.com/news/index.ssf/2010/12/nj_workers_to_face_reductions.html.

33. David Abel, "Budget Cuts Will Imperil State's Poor," *Boston Globe*, November 17, 2009, p. B1.

34. Patricia Wen, "Part 1: A Legacy of Unintended Side Effects," *Boston Globe*, December 12, 2010; "Part 2: A Coveted Benefit, a Failure to Follow Up," *Boston Globe*, December 13, 2010; "Part 3: A Cruel Dilemma for Those on the Cusp of Adult Life," *Boston Globe*, December 14, 2010.

35. Ibid., Part 2.

36. Ibid.

37. Ibid., Part 1.

38. Yvonne Abraham, "Murky Path to SSI's Fixes," *Boston Globe*, December 16, 2010, p. B1; "Youth Disability System Is Fraught with Abuse," *Boston Globe*, February 4, 2011, p. A12; "SSI Program Needs Close Look, but Provides Critical Support," *Boston Globe*, June 7, 2011. See also, Sally Pederson, "Let's Not Act Precipitously on SSI Allegations," *Des Moines Register,* June 1, 2001.

39. "Aid Sought for Vulnerable Families," *Boston Globe*, December 23, 2010, p. A14.

40. Jonathan M. Stein, "Program Is Critical for Low-Income Disabled Youth," *Boston Globe*, January 29, 2011, p. A10.

41. Joan Vennochi, "Blame It on the Sixties, Man," *Boston Globe*, May 29, 2011.

CONCLUSION

1. "The SSI Program at the Millennium," *Social Security Administration Report*, November 2000, SSA History Archives.

2. A provision enacted in October 2010 with a sunset date of 2015 is still active, as is a provision enacted in December 2010 that is due to expire in January 2013.

Index

f = figure